"The wittiest, most searching sports writing since A. J. Liebling, *Sunday Money* is a brilliant stream-of-consciousness documentary of America's whirl into the twenty-first century, dragging its fierce love affair with internal combustion into the realm of a metaphysical circus. This is a book that anyone in pursuit of the American nation's secret resources, spiritual and automotive, must read."

—Robert Stone

"One part comic travelogue, one part cultural history, and three parts kick-ass sportswriting, *Sunday Money* is an exhilarating ride from pole to checkered flag. Jeff MacGregor is a witty, sharp-eyed observer; you couldn't ask for a better guide to the mysteries and unexpected pleasures of NASCAR."

—Tom Perrotta

"Jeff MacGregor shows a discerning affection toward the folks and the folk customs which inhabit this squirrely piece of Americana. He's heard clearly over the din, seen through the smoke and the haze, and gotten it all down perfectly."

—Frank Deford

"Even if NASCAR isn't your speed, MacGregor's colorful, original language and knack for finding the perfect detail will keep you riveted. . . . Entertaining and lively, packed with examples and anecdotes and written by a sharp mind with a gentle hand."

—MSNBC

"*Sunday Money* is MacGregor's attempt to grab the torch from [Tom] Wolfe. . . . In that regard, he triumphs. [It] is, for my money, the first (and maybe only) book that nonfans or casual fans or just the mildly curious should crack in order to understand the 'noise and speed and glory and death that is NASCAR.'"

—*New York Times Book Review*

"[*Sunday Money*] is hard to put down, even if you don't have the faintest idea who Jeff Gordon is."

—*Chicago Tribune*

"*Sunday Money* is filled with passages readers will want to share with friends. Anybody who finds his or her way vicariously into one of the loud and unapologetically soused and sentimental neighborhoods of motor homes and pickups parked at the track or at the Wal-Mart down the interstate will come away from the immersion with a favorite character."

—*Boston Globe*

SUNDAY MONEY

SPEED! LUST! MADNESS! DEATH!

A Hot Lap Around America
with NASCAR

JEFF MACGREGOR
PHOTOGRAPHS BY OLYA EVANITSKY

HARPER PERENNIAL

NEW YORK • LONDON • TORONTO • SYDNEY

HARPER ● PERENNIAL

Portions of this book have appeared, in slightly different form, in the *New York Times* and *Sports Illustrated*.

A hardcover edition of this book was published in 2005 by HarperCollins Publishers.

P.S.™ is a trademark of HarperCollins Publishers.

FIRST HARPER PERENNIAL EDITION PUBLISHED 2006.

Designed by Elliott Beard

Library of Congress Cataloging-in-Publication Data is available upon request.

ISBN 0-06-009471-0
ISBN-10: 0-06-009472-9 (pbk.)
ISBN-13: 978-0-06-009472-0 (pbk.)

06 07 08 09 10 ❖/RRD 10 9 8 7 6 5 4 3 2 1

For Olya, without whom none of this would have been possible;
and to Polly, without whom none of this would have been necessary

Welcome back, my friends, to the show that never ends . . .

—EMERSON, LAKE AND PALMER

BEGINNING

Might be he was dead. There was no way to tell from the grandstands. It happened too far away and everyone up there was too tired or too drunk to squint away the glare from that thin indifferent sun. Even on television, the Numinous Absolute, where everything is known and everything is seen and everything spoken and shown and everything is by God under control, they didn't know. They didn't know what to say or how to say it, so they just kept talking.

The whole thing happened too fast, too slow, and after that day you'd watch the replays again and again, for months, not believing. Even in real time it still played out lazy and deliberate, the car yawing slow left, then correcting, swerving slow motion right, up the banking, tires feathering smoke, into the wall, then the impact, a sharp sound inside a dull one, and you thought—maybe—it wasn't bad, he wasn't going very fast, he didn't hit very hard. Maybe you thought, okay, it happens every year, every weekend, over and over, they crash but they all just walk away. Don't they all? To this day, years gone and the whole world spun another billion miles through the void, you don't believe it. But when the car finally slid to rest the netting never came down and the first man up to the window seemed frantic, waving like mad for the others to get there, C'mon! Sweet Christ! C'mon! and for a long time after that every gesture was panicked, emphatic, and then they pulled him out of the car and all at once the adrenaline was gone and it didn't seem urgent anymore, and even if you couldn't see it you could feel it somehow, that absence, that stillness, and the twilight quiet descended across the ridiculous immensity of that place, and it was like something being pulled out of you, too, and the celebration in Victory Lane was small and fretful and wrong in the foreground, and way out there below the loneliest reach of the far turn, so steep

you can barely walk it, that black car sat empty and if you were still in your
seat that's when you knew. You just knew.

The rest of it—the ambulance, the lights and the sirens and the hurry, the
hospital—was wishful ceremony. A prayer.

By the time they got back to their hotels or made it to the airport, most of
the others knew too, the scores of thousands who'd headed for the gates to
beat the traffic. They heard it on the radio or their cell phones or saw it up on
the screen behind the concourse bar. In every airport from Miami back to Jack-
sonville and out to Orlando men and women stood crying, and in hotel rooms
and motel rooms and in the endless stream of cars moving up or down the
great vein of the I-95 people sat abject and sobbing, and the news flew out
from Daytona in fast concentric circles, across the country, swift rings of
grief, until everything in America sat within the blast radius of that elaborate
sadness, because Dale Earnhardt was dead. That was February 18th, 2001.

America dreams driving. In these dreams you are alone. Flying low
and loud and fast down a long, straightrazor stretch of Nebraska interstate, perhaps in late autumn, headed west, sharp cold just coming
on, the desolate geometry of those golden stubble fields strobing past
you, the sun wobbling low and weak on the horizon, your windshield
embroidered with the glare of it, and in your rearview mirror the sky
behind you as blue and deep as a bruise. You are cupped in the heated
seat. The earth spins beneath you. All the shining instrumentality of
uncomplicated power falls easily to hand. Your body dissolves into the
machine until you are no more and no less than acceleration itself.
The brute music of the engine rises up through the floorboards and
the soles of your feet and into your blood until your heart pounds
with it, the world blurs and the vast web of human complication dissolves somewhere far behind you and there is no past and no future
and nothing bad can ever catch you. Nothing can touch you. *That's*
the American dream. *That's* freedom.

Junior got him sideways then T-boned him coming out of the first
turn, that awkward radius where the track doubles back on you and

you're in there pedaling like E. Power Biggs at his Mighty Wurlitzer, both feet pumping away, feathering the brakes and the gas with your right foot and double-clutching that mother with your left and fanning the gears like mad trying to downshift, trying to find a gear, any gear, to get the power down to the pavement without sliding the rear end around or squandering all that speed you bought coming down the front straight and you're penned in on three sides at what, 150, 160, while all the others are fanning and clutching and pumping and braking, too, and then you're pouring on the coal coming out of the turn, back in the throttle, and everybody's trying to exit that two-wide bottleneck at the same instant, field still bunched in two tight lines, freight trains on parallel tracks, sweeping left out of the first turn at Pocono, where there's no bailout, no room, no margin if anybody fucks up this early in the race because the whole field's hard on the gas and trying to straighten up for that odd, too-short backstretch, and some of the cars are loose this early and some are tight and if you could see it through the blur and chatter of your windshield reinforcements you'd see it's not a freight train at all, it's three dozen cars at 150 miles an hour pointed every which way for a fraction of a second, nearly weightless, up on their toes and ready to bolt, ready to head for the wall, and that's why when Steve Park fucks up and misses a shift and slows down in front of Dale Earnhardt Jr., Junior's got no place to run but right into him.

Junior's red DEI Chevy smacks the rear of Park's yellow DEI Chevy, so Park slews, loses it, and clocks around to the left, broadside to the red car, and Junior can't get off the gas or get on the brakes or steer out of the way. It's too late to do much of anything but hang on and let 'er buck. The nose of Junior's red #8 hits the yellow #1 right in the driver's door, T-bone perfect. Junior could probably see Park's face, his expression, his eyes, except for the helmet and the visor and the fact that they're locked up now at 150 and about to hit the infield grass sideways.

The grass is wet, of course, jungle Pocono, it's been wet the whole season here, the track pouring water like a cataract first go-round, humid and miserable the entire summer, so when the cars hit the grass they don't slow down any, none, 200, 300, 400 feet they slide in the same perfect T, like Junior's car has got its teeth sunk in Park's and won't let go, and they slide that way across the grass at 150 miles an hour for what seems like a very long time but isn't.

When the yellow car's right-side tires finally dig into the turf, the left side of the car lifts just enough to get the red car's nose underneath it. What Junior sees through the gouts of water and mud and the chunks of sod flying up in front of him is Park's cockpit, then Park's car number. Park's yellow car is balanced on the hood of the red car for the part of a second it takes to reach the infield catch fence. Then it's gone, launching itself onto its nose, while Junior slides away underneath it.

Junior goes flat sideways along the infield catch fence, spinning, then spinning again, the front of his car throwing off torn sheet metal and broken frame bracing every time it hits the steel Armco.

Behind him, Park's #1 pirouettes along the top of the fence, tearing it out of the ground as it goes, almost tumbling into the infield and the fans and the motorhomes, riding the top of that fence and shedding bodywork and debris until it catches a seam in the steel and slingshots up into a tight barrel roll, the car throwing water and mud and parts in a hard, perfect arc, the sheet metal blowing off it in billows, the hardened cage with Park inside still tumbling and rolling down the catch fence until what's left of it comes down hard, steaming and smoking and crushed.

By the time Park's car stops moving, Junior's got himself unharnessed and out of his car and is running through the mud back to Park. The ambulances are rolling and the yellow comes out and the grandstands are quiet and in the pits the crews don't know whether to watch the television to see what happened or get ready in case the crew chief calls their car in. They shuffle around getting ready but keep turning to get a look at the monitor. It was bad and everybody here knows it.

When the emergency crews arrive, Junior's already wrestling Park out of what's left of the #1 car. When Park finally stands, every team on pit road stands too, and the fans, and the officials. Everyone applauds. It was bad. The red flag to weld up the torn fence lasts over an hour.

Park goes to the medical center. He's no worse off for the crash. They haul Park's car back to the garage. There isn't enough of it left to fill a 4–gallon bucket. Junior's crew swaps out the front end of the battered red car and pulls chunks of turf out of the air cleaner, and Junior runs the rest of the day with a car held together by duct tape. Thirty-three laps down, he finishes thirty-seventh.

Asked later what it was like to career through that accident; to see Park's car tumbling behind him in the rearview; to run to the wreckage to see if Park was hurt or helpless or dead; to get back in the car and run the rest of that long, humid day with all that dissipated adrenaline gone sour and toxic in his system, what could Dale Earnhardt Jr. possibly say to anyone anywhere who didn't get it? Or to anyone who did? If you understood what it meant to be a racer, if you got it, no explanation was necessary. If you didn't, no explanation was possible.

"I don't know, man, he's my teammate. I just wanted to make sure he was okay. We fixed the car, so I got back in the car. Besides, we needed the points."

Walk into the Cup garage at 7 A.M., quiet and solemn before the first impact wrench turns, before the grab-ass starts up, the sun hidden behind the grandstands and the dew thick on the tents and the grass, fans still sleeping, and look at the checklist. The big-money crews, all dialed-in mechanical intelligence and 80-gig hard-drive organization, work from checklists taped to their cars. Nothing is missed. Everybody knows what they're responsible for.

There's a list on the quarter panel, on the hood, the rear deck lid, the fender. Lists on clipboards, lists on the toolboxes. A list for everyone on the crew. Twenty, twenty-five items each for the engine tuner, shock specialist, car chief, all the others. Lists for practice, for qualifying, for race day.

_____ Grease Center Link Bearings
_____ Center Link Bearing Adjustment
_____ Record Skirt Heights
_____ Duct Tape Crush Panel Seams
_____ Crush Panels Secure and Sealed
_____ Jack Post Clearance

Complete an item, initial the checklist, move on. Account for everything. In this small world, where what you don't know or didn't think of or forgot to do can kill somebody, where there are as many ways to die as there are parts on the car, the checklist is the ritual inventory of mysteries, the systematic application of information and effort and hope against the unknown. Do everything, do nothing, the world turns.

I've seen crews run a 200-item checklist four times in 12 hours, fussing it like a rosary, a daylong act of pure gearhead devotion, trying to get the car right, or at least keep it from going wrong. "Live and die by your lists," a tuner told me once, sweat pouring off his chin onto the rocker arms of an engine that was doomed to fly apart in the late summer heat 68 laps short of the finish. "Try to prepare for everything, 'cause you miss the least little fucking thing and you don't know which kind of hell it can lead to. And even then . . ."

SUNDAY MONEY

ONE

This is a book about our year on the road, my wife and me, chasing NASCAR. In a motorhome.

No matter which quiet corner of America you inhabit, you've heard of NASCAR by now, and of its meteoric rise to sporting and economic prominence; hottest show on the continent, The Great Inescapable, the 200-mile-an-hour platinum-plated V-8-powered Stars and Stripes hero machine. The National Association for Stock Car Auto Racing: a multi-billion-dollar crossover sports entertainment empire set suddenly and squarely at the confluence of popular culture and politics and commerce and mythology.

For longtime fans of stock-car racing this wild success comes as no surprise. It was only a matter of time before everybody caught on to how sensational this whole million-horsepower traveling tent and revival deal really is, a boom sport in a bad time. And once television got hold of it, well, its coast-to-coast and border-to-border and top-to-bottom-line triumph became almost inevitable.

The casual fan, though, the nonfan, the anti-fan, thinks: How did this happen? It's the dullest thing I've ever seen! Cars driving in a circle! For *four hours*! It's barely a *sport*! The drivers aren't even *athletes*!

So you go to bed one night confident in your convictions and certain that everything's as it's always been in this stick-and-ball world. Next morning you wake up and while you're blowing the hot off that first cup of coffee, some statistician, some sportscaster, some condescending pop-cult socioanthropology stooge is online or on the air or on the front page telling you that NASCAR now has 75 million fans; ardent, ravenous fans, a quarter of our entire national population, more fans than Turkey has Turks or Great Britain Brits, and that no sport anywhere in the entire unhappy history of the world has ever grown so far so fast and that if there's a higher per-event attendance figure anywhere in the sports universe he/she hasn't found it yet, and that this year alone Americans are going to spend something close to $2 billion-with-a-B dollars on NASCAR-licensed gear like hats and jackets and souvenir shot glasses that read "Drive it like you stole it!"

A circle! Four hours! On top of which, NASCAR Dad gets to elect the president.

While you were sleeping, stock-car racing became America's national pastime and baseball crawled up under the house to die.

No matter where in America you try to hide from it, there it is, NASCAR, spooling out its story, making its case, thumping its tub, selling itself 24/7/365 on every flat surface in America.

Athletes or not, there are the drivers, the clear-eyed heroes, Rushmore-jawed and implacable, giving you the gunfighter squint from the magazine rack at the checkout stand. They glare down from those billboards out on the bypass, stare out from the weekly four-color insert in your local paper, smile back at you from a thousand boxes of three-for-a-buck mac-and-cheese on aisle 7. From the 10-foot 12-pack sudsweiser pyramid at the Pump 'n Run to the PS2 on your JVC to the bestseller stacks of your big-box bookstore, they are everywhere.

The cars, too, all that sleek Dee-troit iron, sculpted and sexy and not so vaguely threatening, tattooing your candy bars and your condiments, your waterproof grout and your frozen waffles.

And every one of us, from Maine to Mission Beach, is in on it, whether we chose to be or not. You can't opt out, even if you want to, even if you're stuck in neutral, even if you're among that handful of benighted citizens not yet in receipt of the glorious message of NASCAR's commercial and cultural revelations, even if you're one of those people who by God think it's all just noxious monotony and hillbilly cliché and hayseed blood sport. Fine by me, brother, but you're still a paying customer. Go to your kitchen cabinets right now, your refrigerator, your medicine chest, your nightstand, your garage, your cluttered hall closet and find a dozen dozen products proudly branded and cross-pollinated with that NASCAR stamp. Your batteries and your beer, your cookies and your corn flakes are probably running the low groove in this week's race. Your last oil change or pack of smokes or dip of chew paid for some racer's shocks or valve springs or cylinder head. You bought someone an illegal magnesium intake manifold last week when you signed up for broadband. That last 'scrip the urologist scribbled for your, um, "erectile dysfunction" meds paid a portion of Mark Martin's qualifying run at New Hampshire or Richmond or Vegas. How'd Mark Martin do this weekend? How'd *you* do? You're part of a hard-charging All-American NASCAR race team now, mister! Or at least a part of that hard-charging All-American hard-on ad budget.

So this is a book about NASCAR. Stories about cars and heroes and money and fame. Stories about racing, of course, and about brilliant machines and solid men and splendid women and noise and speed and glory and death. Stories about how the sport died that day with Dale Earnhardt and was born again in the very same instant. This is the story of a hundred stories, long and short, comic and tragic, sacred and profane.

It is the story of what my wife, the Beep (the B. P., the Brilliant, Beautiful Partner), and I saw and heard on a hot lap of America, the year we crossed the breadth of the country 10 times in 10 months, shuttled up and down the East Coast for entire calendar pages and drew smooth arcs and sawteeth across every battered roadmap we had—47,649 miles by the time we got back. More than three hundred nights on the road. Nearly a hundred auto races big and small. Thirty-five states. Hundreds of towns. Millions of people. In the fall of 2001 America felt lost. We set out to find it.

Winter

Some nights, chasing all those famous racers and their truckloads of hardware on the long clock to the next track, going west or east or north or south into your nineteenth or twentieth hour, straight and numb down the interstate, no lights but your own on the highway, too tired to think, you could feel the whole wasted nation exhale, breathing out something sour and exhausted all around you. Everything and everyone was restless everywhere, aching with what seemed like fever, twisting and sleepless in the sheets. Run too long, make too many miles after midnight, and you were overwhelmed by it. The blank fields and the lightless houses harbored every kind of evil and the stars poured down only sadness. You'd drive until your eyes burned, until your hands slipped from the wheel, until your mind failed and those ghosts rose up wavering from the pavement. If you made it another mile, if you made it to the next exit, if you didn't hook a wheel off the blacktop and go flying up into the trees or down into the mist along the river, you'd pull off anywhere you could and try to sleep, your head still sizzling with wind noise and grief and fatigue.

Next morning maybe you'd see one of the hauler drivers pulled up at a truck stop, or tucked in behind an off-ramp donut shop, his rig idling garish and incongruous in those empty, woeful places, and you'd know that he'd felt some of it, too. "Lord, what a misery that was," he'd say, stirring three creamers into his coffee and squinting back at that highway as if it had wronged him somehow, and you'd wait for him to finish the sentence. But he already had.

Other days, on the same stretch of highway, you'd see everything bright with life and purpose, green fields waving in the yellow sun and people happy everywhere, the miles unspooling easy beneath you, engine spinning, and the jackpot promise of a new horizon not very far ahead.

Neither America was real, and both were real, and you had to keep driving no matter which America you chose, spooks clattering in the boneyards or the heart of everything pumping joy, because the big American speed circus doesn't slow down for anyone.

Why go? Why not? What are you chasing? What's chasing you? In 2001 everything changed and then everything changed again, and by the time the 2002 season began there were ghosts everywhere. No place was safe. So you run your checklist. Inventory the mysteries. And try to prepare for everything.

February: Daytona, Rockingham. March: Las Vegas, Atlanta, Darlington, Bristol. April: Texas, Martinsville, Talladega, California. May: Richmond, Charlotte. June: Dover, Pocono, Michigan, Sears Point. July: Daytona, Chicago, New Hampshire, Pocono. August: Indianapolis, Watkins Glen, Michigan, Bristol. September: Darlington, Richmond, New Hampshire, Dover, Kansas. October: Talladega, Charlotte, Martinsville, Atlanta. November: Rockingham, Phoenix, Miami.

Someplace to be every week for nearly 40 weeks. Holding the NASCAR schedule in my hand, printed wallet-sized so it fit a pocket, was a mistake. It looked plausible that way, an index of discrete place names. They should print the thing on a bedsheet or a spinnaker, a circus tent, to give you some idea what you're in for. Print it out on foolscap cut to fit the continent and maybe you'd get the sense of what you'd bitten off.

We bought a motorhome, and loaded it until it groaned on the springs with books and clothes and food and office supplies, with board games and hockey skates, boomerangs and folding chairs, tool kits and business cards and frying pans and tennis racquets, a set of Guess-the-President laminated placemats, CDs and DVDs, binoculars and cameras and computers, guides to every campground in America, quart after quart after quart of the powerful chemical toilet deodorizer we'd been warned was of paramount importance to the enjoyment of one's footloose, if not entirely stink-free, RV lifestyle, and all the many maps and items of travel tackle our friends and relatives had given us to send us safely on our way. Of these last things we cherished two above all: $100 worth of McDonald's gift certificates tied up in a white satin ribbon, and an "I ♥ NY" bumper sticker. Armored thus with sentiment, if not sense, and a month's worth of Happy Meals, we set sail south from New York, Orlando and Daytona-bound.

Inching from the driveway and out onto the street, I checked the mirrors; there behind us were my in-laws, waving in the snow, promising to forward mail, blowing kisses, growing smaller, receding into the distance and the past, along with everything else of comfort and sanity we had ever known.

The drive south, especially in a motorhome, from New York to Florida on the I-95, the East Coast's main peristaltic organ for the ingestion, digestion, and evacuation of manufactured goods and retirees, chokes the last few notions of romance and freedom on the American highway right out of you—mile after mile of corroded chain-link fence streaming by as you blink in and out of the fretwork of shadows thrown down by rusting cranes and collapsing derricks, abandoned refineries and derelict water towers.

Wheel to wheel and bumper to bumper and running five wide sounds mighty exciting when you're talking about the backstretch at Talladega, but when you're trying to thread your brand-new honeymoon cottage through knots of angry commuters in the never-ending rush of south Jersey traffic, it's more like shock than excitement. A recurring series of shocks, like being clamped to a broken defibrillator.

It is here, caught between hell and Philadelphia, that my education in driving our house truly begins. In the churn and lurch of high-density urban traffic, we are helpless. Cars recklessly porpoise in front of us, cutting us off, taunting us with their dexterity, their speed, their agile, fundamental, not-a-motorhomeness. We could be flying along at Mach 4, the aluminum skin of the mother ship glowing red hot from the laminar flow of the atmosphere across its wide bulk, and some co-ed from Swarthmore in a clapped-out '89 Cabriolet with an

Amnesty sticker on the window would still find a way to veer in front of us.

We'd gotten a taste of the immensity and absurdity of what lay before us on our December 2001 trip to pick up the motorhome in California.

Why go all the way to California for a motorhome? Because there are only two kinds of motorhomes in New York City—the ones used as mobile dressing rooms for movie productions, and the ones wedged beneath the Jerome Avenue underpass, driven there by panicked retired couples from Wisconsin who lose their mud on the Cross Bronx Expressway and pull blindly off the highway when teenagers start shouting at them in Spanish from passing cars.

We did our research over the Internet. Like convertibles or sports cars, motorhomes are an embedded subset of the American car culture. All you have to do is watch TV, see the $70,000 Bavarian sedans sliding sideways across the alkali flats outside Twentynine Palms in the commercials, to know that all cars everywhere have at one time or another been marketed as the truest expression and instrument of personal liberty, the mechanical means to transcend time and place. For auto makers, advertisers, and brand strategists, anything with wheels is a getaway car.

Use the correct search engines, visit the right chat rooms, and you'll find that the Internet allows RV owners the chance to express their delight at the footloose, freewheeling lives they've chosen for themselves.

> Tex225: I was the last twenty feet of the assembly line I'll tell you, and if I'd had to get down and root that damn fridge drain line out one more time I don't know who I'd have shot. I've worked long enough. T——is no good.
> PokieD: That's the truth.
> WebSter8: Does anyone in here know the stock number for the

replacement fuel filter cartidgidges on the new 4K W——sideoiling built-ins??? We're stuck with no lights.

SleekPup: If you take the hub down an eighth with a grinder, then radius the sleeves, you'll get a better vacuum in the 6500 to 6780 rpm range. They set them wrong at the F—— factory and by doing this you'll get a 1.9% improvement across most of the powerband. Just don't take off too much material, because you can actually LOSE torque at altitudes above 7,300 feet, unless you reset all the throttle body software, too. Whole project takes about 22 man-hours, but I was able to do it right at our campsite. Good luck.

PokieD: It just chaps my butt that you pay 200 thousands and it's fiddle with everything to make right what should of been done when it came off the showroom. Beautiful unit the S—— but hasn't had day one without me on my knees and a wrench. Better than the last one though.

Knkkrs4: Any women inside here? Any big brests?

Even under the weight of all those complaints, a couple of names bobbed up again and again as reliable manufacturers of high-quality RVs. In fact, in forums and chat rooms where people vented their serial and colorful disenchantments with RVs of every kind, they wrote of these things as though they were as rare and desirable as Duesenbergs or holy relics, true shards from the rood. "Dependable, beautiful unit," they'd write, "wish I could lay hands on one. Never even seen one on the road. Hear they're the tops." We called around and got some further recommendations from motorhome magazine writers, a professional courtesy. All this led back to the same small, quirky outfit in Montclair, California. Lazy Daze.

So sought-after are these things, it turned out, that there was a six-month waiting list to get one. You can't buy them from a dealership. You custom-order everything you want in it or on it or upholstering it, and they build it to order. By hand. They deliver one a day at the factory gate.

I picked up the phone. I called the factory. I explained what we were about to do to one of the brothers who founded the company. He had a voice like a flat file, but treated me kindly. He sounded like Tom Joad grown old.

"It takes six months to get one right now. We build 'em all custom."

"I've heard they're very well made. Everyone thinks very highly of the, um, Lazy Daze."

"Well, thank you. We think they're the best they is."

"Do you ever have any used models come through?"

"Don't do used, just new here at the factory."

"Does anyone ever not take delivery of one they've ordered?"

"Sometimes, but that's real rare."

Having seen all that desperation expressed on the Web, I had become desperate myself. I needed something we could count on. I cajoled, I wheedled, I soft-soaped. I paid compliments gleaned from the compliments of others and ladled on concern for my wife's comfort and safety behind the wheel, and for the fate of our unborn children, should the Beep and I ever discuss actually having any.

"I'll call you back," he said.

Ten minutes later he did.

"We might have a man sick," he said, "or something. Not sure, but in any case, the sales manager says the man might not take delivery on a twenty-six-and-a-half-foot rear kitchen unit. You familiar with it?"

"I saw it in the brochure," I said.

"Have to take it the way he ordered it, 'course, accessories and extrys and so forth, but you'd get to choose the exterior paint. We haven't got it to the paint booth yet. It's got the teal interior."

"Teal?"

"Blue."

"Okay. My wife and I'll need some time to think about it. Discuss it. Check our family finances and so forth, inquire about the loan process, interest rates. It's a huge investment after all, and it's going to take every dollar we have, and we, well, we try to make important decisions like these together. Can I call you back next week?" It was Friday morning.

"Well, sir, that might be a problem. Seems they's a gentleman out here, already called on it, willing to pay cash. Wouldn't even take out a loan. So I'd have to hear from you real—"

"I'll take it."

"Say again?"

"I'll take it," I said again, firmly, hearing myself as if from very far away. There was silence on the line, then ol' Tom Joad cleared his throat of all that dust and hard Oklahoma mileage.

"Hrrrwk. Well, now, if you're sure . . ."

"I'll take it." Having said it, I couldn't stop saying it.

"Sight unseen?"

"Why not? I mean, okay! Sure! Yes!" I sounded like a lock-down patient at Bellevue who'd gotten an outside line on his doctor's phone.

"We'll need a deposit, 'course, and then the down and the paper-work on the loan and so forth. We can help you with all that."

"Okay. Sure. Yes. Teal, you say?"

"Yep."

I sent the first check an hour later.

A few weeks after that we climbed onto a plane for California. It was a bad time to fly, the worst in history, and every passenger sat rigid and white-knuckled and flew the six hours west facing straight ahead with their eyes wide. We spent the night in a motel near the little factory and arrived there early the next morning.

Our new RV, our motorhome, our *unit*, was parked next to the gate. It was white, with the contrasting panels of silver and charcoal-gray metallic we'd chosen. It looked almost stately, like a catering truck in a tuxedo. It was an aesthetic understatement, especially compared to others we'd seen, done up as most of them are in mad, Kandinsky brushstrokes of candy-apple red or blue or green.

"There it is," said the Beep, with chipper dread. Sight unseen! Our life savings! The phrase "I'll take it" rang in my ears.

"It" seemed at once too big and too small. Too big to drive and too small to imagine living in. Modest by motorhome standards, from the outside it still looked gigantic to the two of us. Walking around it seemed to take quite a while. It was beautifully painted and stylishly designed and looked as sleek, as aerodynamic, as something with the drag coefficient of a refrigerated boxcar could.

From tip to tail it was the specified 26.5 feet. From top to bottom, satellite dish (!) to Firestone tires, was roughly 10 feet; and the width, sideview mirror to sideview mirror, another 10 feet. There was a ladder to the roof at the rear, windows everywhere large and small, a built-in roller awning along one side, a series of storage compartments built low into the body, and a baffling array of small access panels and doors and connectors and fittings and louvers set variously around the exterior. All of them were explained to us. Numb, though, with fear, I took none of it in and thought only about how huge the broad stern seemed. I kept staring at that monstrous rear end; its ass was bigger than a garage door. I imagined backing into many things, backing over many things, hitting things, crushing things—curbs, cars, parking meters, pets, children. I could hear their piercing screams. I wouldn't be seeing America so much as laying waste to it.

Happily, though, it looked big from the inside, too. In a sweet compensatory paradox, the motorhome wasn't much smaller than the average $1,000-a-month Manhattan studio apartment, one of which we had already lived in. The kitchen was exactly the same size as the one we'd be leaving. There was a sleeping loft above the cab, and two facing sofas amidships that could be pulled together to make one big bed. Aft of that were the two mirrored wardrobes, one on either side, and the short hallway back to the kitchen and dinette. The dinette, too, made into a bed, in case we had unexpected, tiny weekend guests. And there were plenty of cabinets, of medium oak finish and ingeniously situated, like those on a well-designed boat, for storage. In the hall space, the refrigerator door faced the door to the bathroom, which was modest, but which had a shower and a toilet and a vanity and had the additional aesthetic benefit of housing the only set of interior surfaces, horizontal or vertical, not covered somehow in teal fabric.

They showed us how everything worked, and reminded us to read our owners' manuals, the size of small-town phone books. We filled out the paperwork and they gave us the keys. We said goodbye to everyone. Packed our bags in the unit. Took our seats. Turned the key. And sat there.

It struck us, hard, what we were about to do. The scale of it, the epic, crackpot foolishness of it, the hubris and sheer coast-to-coast dopiness of it. There was no going back, though. We owned our first house. And now we had to learn to drive it.

"I just need you to promise me one thing," the Beep said, putting a hand to my arm and looking at me with the same earnest expression on her face that I'd seen when we exchanged our wedding vows.

"What is it, honey?" I said quietly.

"Slipcovers."

Slowly, very, very slowly, we pulled away.

You eventually get used to driving something this big, I guess, although we never did. Terrible parody of the Freedom Dream! Even on the wide-open interstates, ribbons of nothing but asphalt and winter sky, our spatial paranoia radiates out from us for hundreds of yards in every direction. What's that over there? Are we far enough away from it? How fast is it moving? How fast are we moving? Slow down! Speed up! More to the right! More to the left! Where's that honking coming from? I can't see anything! The animal panic I'd seen in the eyes of every RVer I'd ever honked at and flipped off and passed made sense all of a sudden. I burned with shame and empathy. Every other vehicle in America was now a threat. Stay away from us! Every penny we have is tied up in this thing! We're trying to maneuver a Pullman car made of Tiffany glass here! Get back, you bastards! We're recreating, God damn it!

We made no attempts to "camp." We'd drive until we were utterly depleted by anxiety and then pull off at a lonely rest area or hard-shadowed truck stop and shudder into a thin, nervous sleep, limbs twitching and eyelids flickering, waiting to be mocked, vandalized, robbed, raped, kidnapped, murdered. The highway and everything along it felt suddenly lawless and unconnected, anonymous, malign.

When the wan light came up a few hours later, the long-haul diesel rigs barking and farting and throttling up around us, we'd turn the key and start again. This is the retirement your parents are saving toward. Tell them that the leaden dawning of the day across the snot gray asphalt of the Petro travel plaza just west of Joplin, Missouri, is rarely pictured in the RV sales brochures.

We awoke Christmas morning in a rest area on the Ohio Turnpike. Somehow made it up to New York State that night, exhausted, incoherent, where we huddled around our folks' glowing tree, staring into the middle distance and mumbling into our eggnog. How high is that bridge? How low is that underpass? Are those kids yelling at us in *Spanish*?

Having fled Trenton and pinballed past Philly, we cross the Delaware, then Delaware itself, then descend into Maryland. To your right the charming, crumbling city of Baltimore; to your left the grand, antique mirror of the Chesapeake Bay.

Maryland and aggressive driving bring us, briefly, to the history of NASCAR.

I say briefly because the genesis of the nation's most successful auto-racing sanctioning body is already well known to faithful stock-car fans. It's part of the big-block catechism. Whole bookshelves are lined with its histories and devotionals and hymnals wherever orthodox motorheads gather. Anti-fans are unlikely to be moved no matter how detailed or broad the telling, like land-grant college students in a required course made to memorize the dusty plats of Babylon or the genealogy of Romulus. It all seems so long ago and far away. Still, origin stories are the foundation of every culture, so here we go.

•   •   •

In 1934 a young man drove south out of Maryland with his wife and son. He was headed for the bright shores of Florida, trying to guide his family out from under the hardscrabble bondage of the Depression. His name was Bill France.

He was 25 years old and stood 6-foot-5. He was heavy without being fat, "imposing" as the sportswriters say, round-faced and smart and ambitious. Next to him in that rattling car were his wife, Annie, and his year-old son, Bill Jr.

As the car ticked and pottered along the narrow concrete ribbon of U.S. Highway 1 bearing south, France was leaving behind him what is referred to in the sacred scrolls as "a service station along the Potomac" and squinting through the windscreen into a future he could not possibly imagine.

To finance their flight to better prospects, France, a mechanic, had emptied his savings account in its entirety, $75, of which he immediately spent $50 on tools. These he would use to repair automobiles broken down along their route in exchange for the cash he needed to make it to Miami.

This he did, but the little family stopped 250 miles short. Upon arrival in Daytona Beach, warm and sunny, France liked what he saw of those famous Atlantic sands, and the wetlands just west of them covered with palmetto and cypress and slash pine. That his mechanical skill and charming persistence won him a job at a local automobile dealership in that bleak economic year was evidence enough that this was indeed a promising, if not the Promised, land.

"At least in Florida I could work on cars out of the cold and the snow and the rain," spake France to the scriveners half a century later.

By the time the France family wheeled into town the packed sands of Daytona were already long famous. Since the turn of the twentieth century the flat, hard, wide-open beach had been a global destination for hot-shoe speed demons and internal combustion record setters of every kind. Even Barney Oldfield, the hurtling Oldfield, most recognized name in the booming early business of going fast, first man to drive a mile a minute, had run those sands to glass beneath his lightning wheels.

They came from everywhere on every kind of brutal contraption to claim the world land-speed record. X-body streamliners and shade-tree hot rods and modified sedans ran that empty strand from Ormond to Daytona on a long, straight-line course chasing the title of Earth's fastest. The year that France arrived, Malcolm Campbell, the Brit, was routinely making passes at near 250 miles per hour in his experimental supercars, built wide and sleek and long as hell's own low-rider.

This suited Bill France fine. He was a car man in a car town and he was a racer too, of course, a man who had wrung out a canvas-bodied hot rod Model T on the boggy short tracks back home around D.C. To hear those record-seeking engines fire and whine at sunrise above the lapping of the waves must have seemed the very song of dawn to him.

But the beach course started going quiet in 1935, when Malcolm Campbell went to Utah. He was chasing 300 by then, and had gone west to the tractless salt flats out at Bonneville. He needed more room, more miles to run than the ocean beach could give him. On those blinding, primordial wastes he ran 300 miles per hour, the fastest ever, which brought all the others west as well, the fastest of the fast, now quick to abandon that too-short stretch of Daytona's famous shore.

By 1936 the city fathers were contriving new attractions to bring the motor tourists and their dollars back to the beach. Among these they promoted a closed-course race on an oval track laid out, in part, along those hardpack sands. Race up the beach, scattering the gulls and flinging spray, turn left into the banking of bulldozed sand, slide wildly, rooster-tailing, bump hard up onto the asphalt of Highway A1A, run fast south along the blacktop, bump down hard onto the sand, turn left in to the banking, slide wildly back onto the beach, scattering the gulls. Repeat. Hope the tide stays out.

The race and its $5,000 purse pulled in entries from all over, leather-helmet roundy-rounders and ridge runners of every style and stripe; even a former champ from the Indy 500. Most drove lightly modified sedans—the precursor to stock cars. Despite a crowd estimated at 20,000, though, the race day was a bust—cars buried axle deep in the dunes and no clear winner, to this day, declared. Somehow, Daytona Beach lost money. Mythologically at least, Bill France is said to have run fifth in that first 250-miler. (But not knowing who won, how to know who finished fifth? The ancient texts, to say nothing of the NASCAR media guide, thwart scholarship with riddle and contradiction. Faith alone is what's needed here.)

However many cars Bill France may have seen in front of him that day when the checkered flag at last fell, one thing he certainly saw out beyond the salt-rimmed hood of his car was new opportunity. Over the next few years France himself—ambitious, smart, civic-minded— began helping to promote these races on the strand. By 1941 he and his partners and the city fathers were organizing, sanctioning, and advertising four races a year. And turning a tidy profit.

World War II intervened; attentions and efforts were turned elsewhere, and racing did not resume in earnest on Daytona Beach until 1946. Bill France did his bit for victory and went to work for a local shipyard. And though it is worthwhile to note for the purposes of this story, this condensed history, that the war unleashed a torrent of global horror unlike anything imaginable in the minds of good people anywhere, it is also worth mentioning the benefits of it to at least some good people somewhere when it was over.

In postwar America, money was back—money in places and quantities never before seen. The Depression was washed away in a money flood, victory bringing not just peace but industrial and individual prosperity and jobs and opportunity for anyone with the savvy, the grit, and the energy to reach out and grab them up. That energy, so long sapped by economic struggle, so long pent-up in service of the war effort, exploded in places and ways never before imagined, arcing and crackling the length and breadth of America.

G.I. Joe was now home and safe with a pocketful of folding money and the whole luscious country lying back on its elbow for him like a lover: a job if he wanted one, or a house, or an education, newsreel America spinning with a new dynamism, a new sense of unbuckled freedom, the middle class thrown wide open for what seemed like everyone. All these energized young men were set suddenly loose everywhere to pursue whatever American Dream they might want for themselves. What many of them wanted first, had always wanted, was a car.

On the rising tide of leisure time and all that new money and all that new freedom and all that newly loosed juice, auto racing really took off. And—keeping in mind that this is just a book about NASCAR and therefore we're skipping over vast amounts of semirelevant stuff, like the sudden boom-fluidity of a now-permeable class system, or the generation of women who gave up their wartime jobs so Joe'd have a place to work when he came home, or all that dizzy postwar voltage coursing through the arts, sparking some of the most original work in American music and painting and writing in history, bop and beat and Pollock—this is how we get back to Bill France, a car man in a car town at a car time.

He hadn't stopped thinking about racing. In '46 and '47 he was back promoting those beach races, more popular than ever, and saw all around him those young men back from the war, felt the tingle of all that postwar voltage, heard the crisp snap of all that new money being counted out, and he had an idea. Idea or epiphany, it was a genius thing. Racing needed change, thought Bill France, and he was going to change it.

To most racers back then, "change" was a stiffer set of springs or a new exhaust manifold. But big-picture Bill France didn't want a new cylinder head or a new carburetor. What Bill France wanted was organization.

Understand that racing had been popular, as Richard Petty famously said, from the day they built the second car, and that it had been popular everywhere in this country. There wasn't a county fairground anywhere in America that hadn't been the site of a short track race or two, usually to the chagrin of the local decency committee. There were racing circuits from Long Island to Long Beach going all the way back to the nineteen-aughts, all with different organizers and rules and stars, and after the war there were probably, per capita, as many hot-rodded prewar Fords and Chevys rattling the maple buckets up in Rutland County, Vermont, as there were shaking the stills down in Wilkes County, North Carolina.

The barnstorming promoters who organized these races were often unscrupulous wide-lapel types, pomaded snuff dippers who smelled of the shot glass and last night's lilac perfume. That these men so often blew town with the gate receipts stuffed in a battered Gladstone bag as soon as the race got under way and never paid out any prize money was the heartbreak of local racers everywhere.

Racers and their fans were hard to discourage, though, and there was plenty of evidence that well-run races paid hard money and civic dividends. The Indianapolis 500, for example, had been a national in- stitution on the order of the Kentucky Derby or the World Series almost since its first running in 1911. Whoever won it was considered the national champion racer of the year. Indy ran a tight ship, and flourished, but it was singular, an open-wheel supercar annual. Motor sports across the rest of the country were a patchwork, a crazy quilt of fly-by-night operators and flyblown small-town dirt tracks, conflicting rules and competing schedules, a maddening variety of car types, and uncrowned regional "champions" peppering every inch of the map.

In the most reverent of stock-car racing's illuminated manuscripts, what happened then is sometimes referred to as a "vision." That he stood so tall (his nickname *was* "Big Bill," after all) may have been what allowed him to see what others could not, the worst of these suggest: a conspiracy of bad poetry and bad theology.

In any case, the scrolls report, one day the skies open and the thun- der cracks and the vision thing is glimpsed! And the dazzling sight that comes to Bill France is an organization, a sanctioning body, that would oversee the staging and promotion of all these smaller races, paying out the purses, standardizing the rules and enforcing them, making regulations for the preparation of the cars, creating a points system to crown a series champion, and eventually perhaps, a true national champion. The fiery wheel in the sunrise sky and the burning palmetto bush say organize! But the genius of it was that he imagined all this for stock cars.

Height-assisted or not, what made France's idea unique was its understanding of what people wanted to do and what people wanted to see. He had a hunch that folks in this newly revved-up postwar culture would want to see the cars they themselves drove (and in many cases built in all those booming factories) being raced hell-for-leather around a decent racetrack. And he knew from his own experience that what the racers wanted was a chance to run hard on the up-and-up, to blast around those little tracks on a Saturday night or a Sunday afternoon with at least a sporting chance to make back what they'd paid out on gas and tires and time.

But how to make it work? Even in that postwar rollick the squares and elders of the shareholding bourgeoisie didn't want much to do with stock-car racing. In those tidy precincts, in those manicured minds, it was still thought of as some sort of outlaw foreplay, a prelude to utter debasement. Tut-tut, they'd say, tut-tut. Not that I don't enjoy something like that myself now and then. I was young once, too. But, er, hrrrrrmph, that sort of excitement is, well, it's fine out on the edge of town, occasionally, I suppose—a working man's entitled to his entertainments, his, er, animal diversions, hrrrrrmph, his battered cars and his paper cup of beer—but it attracts the wrong crowd, doesn't it? The wrong element. Tut-tut. All that noise and smell and, er, *sensation* and so forth.

Which is approximately the answer Bill France received when he took the idea to the triple A, the American Automobile Association. In those days the AAA was more than towing and maps and fix-the-flat on Granny's Kaiser; it was a leading motor sports body, too. It was, in fact, an "august" body, per the moldering scrolls. And to the AAA, perhaps Indy was one thing, with its stylized, ultraexpensive, open-wheel cars and its grand traditions, but stock cars? Those are just jalopies, after all, mere hot rods! They have backseats, for goodness sake! And, hrrrrrmph, we all know what goes on in backseats!

The AAA wanted nothing to do with rollicking stock cars or energized young men or all that coursing proletariat juice.

France tried, and failed, to sell his idea to the racing establishment. He also tried and failed to float programs on his own: a National Championship Circuit and the appallingly acronymed Stock-Car Auto Racing Society among them. Undaunted by failure (and it's a poor origin story that has no triumph over failure in it), he did what organizers do. He called a meeting.

On December 14, 1947, France met with 35 other men at the Streamline Hotel in Daytona Beach to fashion the very thing he had seen in his mind's bright eye. According to those holy scrolls, three days and nights these red-meat racers met atop the streamlined Streamline, in the Ebony Bar, a room forever smoke-filled in the telling (the burning bush, perhaps), and there they stitched out of gossamer Bill France's vision thing.

They would organize themselves into an organization, and that was good, and there would be races with rules and regulations, proper purses and disbursements, a real champion, and that was good, and it would be called NASCAR, the National Association for Stock Car Auto Racing, and that too was good, and Bill France would be its first president, and, as soon as the tab was settled up, he would carry down from the Ebony Bar atop the Streamline Hotel and into the world not the chiseled tablets of the Decalogue, for that would be silliness and sacrilege, but the charter for NASCAR, which would prove to be more flexible, more fun, and just about as profitable in the long run, and that was very good, indeed.

NASCAR ran its first race two months later and was formally incorporated one week after that, with Bill France, driver and mechanic, husband and father, oracle and prophet, as president, grand pooh-bah, and majority stockholder.

The Beep and I are riding a ghost road south. Stretches of the I-95 and I-85 and I-20 interstate corridors were laid down right on top of the old meandering Highway 1, the same route Bill France traveled nearly 70 years before. I don't think he'd recognize much. When they buried that old road they buried most of that old America, too, the narrow-gauge America of small-bore entrepreneurship, of idiosyncratic road-side services and small amusements, of tidy motorcourts and white-lightning jukejoints, of hitchhiking bindlestiffs and chauffeur-driven Packards, of itinerant mechanics driving toward their fortune, earning their way as they went.

It happened that way all over the continent; interstates laid down to cover parts of the ancient two-lanes like the epic 66 or the serpen-tine 40, the old toll roads and post roads interred; all of which them-selves had been poured out over the thin ribbon of original macadam, over the older corduroy, over the first dirt roads and the long-gone wagon ruts. All the archaeology of American restlessness abiding just beneath your tires.

What wasn't buried was marginalized, made quaint, left to die. Where the original roads run parallel to the interstate they are often lifeless, forlorn, alt. routes used only by the locals. Get off the inter-state and America is just mailboxes.

The businesses are years abandoned, overwhelmed by standing waves of kudzu and muscadine, doors banging in the frames and the windows clouded and blind, all of it powdered with the dust that progress threw up as it passed. If you look, you can see that old road from the highway, and along it the broken three-wire fences and the petrified one-pump filling stations, the swayback six-stool diners, the mothballed stucco cabin courts.

How different it all must have been once. In those Hopper-dark days before air-conditioning and satellite radio and sport-tuned, air-assisted, computer-leveled suspension, driving was still a sensory experience, an effortful physical sensation of heat and cold and noise and strain and muscle fatigue, an actual engagement with the elements, the ride in some of those old flivvers as punishing as a day behind the reins of a buckboard. You earned your way south in more ways than one.

Now the interstate south (or north or east or west) is largely another hermetic American experience, the miles and hours between the bottleneck cities streaming by unmarked by effort or event, families vacuum-sealed in their mobile entertainment capsules as they download their GPS coordinates from outer space and upload their DVD of SpongeBob SquarePants. Outside, the franchises blur past, zipless and endless, the American habits of reassuring identicality and relentless architectural gigantism flowing together to compose our seamless national cyclorama of colorful, comforting uniformity. When you finally have to stop and step out of the car, you could be anywhere. One spends little and earns nothing for having made one's way.

The genial landscape of Interstate America is exactly what it purports and aspires to be: antiseptic, interchangeable, frictionless. Safe.

I guess that's a real letdown if you're out on the road for a week in a rental car every two or three years to research your next book. Where's the adventure, after all? Where's the local color? The mom-and-pop diner (the American sociologist's cultural touchstone!) with the really great chili and the fine apple pie? They've been driven out of business by heartless, corporate monoculture!

Trouble is, way back when, Pop's chili might have begun its career as a late scratch in a stakes race and Mom's crabapple pie may have been more laxative than luscious.

This is the part the popcult sociologists forget or ignore. If they'd ever actually had to walk into one of those old roadhouses they're forever elegizing, they'd have likely gotten their ass handed to them. "Mister, in these parts we don't much cotton to *cross-cultural survey*." And Mom and Pop? They had their appeal, certainly, and their place in history, but most of the people who actually live and work out here and travel frequently along the interstate would rather take their chances on corporate cleanliness and homogenization. Most of us are willing to trade a certain "charm" to hedge our bets against a certain "salmonella." Modern franchises may not be any good, but they are, on average, perhaps a little less bad. And as a nation we all agreed a long time ago to institutionalize mediocrity, didn't we? I mean, if we really wanted something better or different, America would be a different, better place. Wouldn't it?

Enough. The Beep is reading aloud, which I always enjoy very much. Tonight, as we roll down through the Carolinas, it's Edmund Morris's biography of Teddy Roosevelt. Yes, clearly, we are dorks. But as dorky as reading to one another may seem to some of you, it beats listening to the radio. As comforting as they are, how many times can you hear "Dream On" or "Stairway to Heaven"? Another triumph of corporate conformity! Want a different playlist? Dream on! In any case, while the Beep and I revisit the geopolitical infighting that accompanied the construction of the Panama Canal, you can begin the second installment of NASCAR's familiar history.

I say familiar, because the sport's early greats and its most important moments are cited again and again during the four-hour yeshiva of the weekly race broadcasts. How else to fill all that time? So on we go, peeling away the windings from those mummified scrolls.

In 1949, NASCAR ran its first all stock-car field at a June race in Charlotte, North Carolina. Set aside were the modified prewar hot rods used by most of the drivers in the inaugural 1948 season. Bill France was insistent that his premier racers run only unmodified, or "Strictly Stock" cars, like those found on any dealership showroom floor. (The vision thing.)

That race was momentous not just as the vision writ plain, or as the Jurassic ancestor of the Cup racing we know today, but also because it demonstrated France's absolute authority over the drivers, the cars, the races, the Show. *His* drivers, *his* cars, *his* races. *His Show.*

As the story reads in the NASCAR Torah, the first car across the line that dusty June day in Charlotte was a '47 Ford. It was discovered, postrace, perhaps by Bill France himself, that the car had an illegally modified suspension setup. France disqualified it and assigned the victory to the runnerup. When the owner of the disqualified Ford took the matter to court, the law sided with France the lawgiver, thereby chiseling his powers in stone. Cheating (as fundamental to the sport as fire, air, water, and earth) was not to be permitted (except when it was). The iron fist now wore an iron glove.

Thus clad, France's guiding hand was a heavy one indeed and success came steadily both for the man and his plan. What only a few years earlier had been a rabble of races and racers was becoming a caravan of willing gypsies, running a regular schedule of events.

And while the history of NASCAR seems largely a southern phenomenon on first look, it should be pointed out that in the cradle days of the infant sport it toddled far and wide. NASCAR ran on tracks from Pennsylvania and New York out to the West Coast as early as the late 1940s. Stock-car racing certainly caught on in those places, but it truly caught fire in the South.

The fact that France himself was based just to the south of the South, as was NASCAR, accounts for some of this, simply as a practical matter. It was easier to husband and promote nearby tracks and races than those far away.

More to the point than administrative efficiency, though, was a felicitous collision of disparate factors unique to the South in those years, among which, in no particular order, were boredom, bravery, moonshine, money, lust, heat, humidity, poverty, honor, ingenuity, revelry, Rebel-ry, Baptist-ry, and the love of felicitous collision.

The general post–World War II boom was a particular boon to much of the American Southeast, where economic depression had seemed a near-constant condition, not just since the Crash of '29, but back through several other wars and national catastrophes, dating to the fiery Jubilee days of Sherman's March to the Sea. The Civil War, and the corruption and failure of the Reconstruction, had left the rural southern economy crippled, and crippled it remained for the better part of four generations. So when new businesses and new industries and all that money started rolling in after 1945, the South wasn't expanding its middle class so much as it was creating one.

Cars were an integral part of that process. What good is a new job at a new factory 30 miles distant if you have no way to get there? What good is the G.I. Bill if you can't get to a school? In addition to the jacked-up existential joyride a car represented elsewhere in America, in the South it was a vital lifeline to, and a reflection of, the new prosperity. As Detroit's skyrocketing regional sales figures proved after the war, the South needed and wanted cars.

What better way to ease that stifling heat, that humid, airless southern summer funk, than a long night drive with all the windows down, world going by in a blur and the limpid dark and the honeysuckle air pouring over you? And God forbid if you had a big convertible, you'd have the kids and the neighbors and the neighbor's kids packed in behind you as you nudged it up to 50 on the county road trying to cool yourself down enough to go home and sag back onto those damp sheets for a few hours' restless sleep.

When all you have is land, what sounder antidote to the colorless oppression of rural boredom than to get behind the wheel of something, anything, and move fast across that land? What smarter answer to the question, "Man, waddawe gonna do d'night?" than "I dunno, let's drive into town"? What finer way to let everyone know who you really are than to make the car a clean canvas for your artist's soul, painting it with chrome and Continental Kits, foxtails and spinners and sun visors and fog lights? What greater privacy for you and your lover and the urgent tangle of your arms and legs and need than the tuck-and-roll heaven of that Hudson's big backseat? What faster way to haul that load of untaxed homemade whiskey into Winston-Salem or Greenville or Atlanta?

Cars completely transformed life in the South. They could make any man, everyman, into Calder or Caligula, into a boulevardier, a swashbuckler, a capitalist. Good old boys unchained! With a car any man, everyman, could thwart nature itself, escape his workaday fate. Or at least outrun the law.

Now, at last, to the central pillar of NASCAR mythology, moonshine.

In the shadow economy of the illegal corn likker business, cars had been the backbone of the distribution system since the age of the Model T. Men had been making whiskey in the mountains and the foothills of the South long before that, of course, back to the time of the first push west out of the colonial capitals, but the automobile, while a recent arrival to this ancient process, quickly became integral to it.

Corn whiskey is good business. Set aside legality or sobriety for a moment and pick up that bushel of corn. What's it worth when you take it to market? A dollar? Two? And you're out the cost of the seed plus the price of the land and the labor to grow it? Build a still, cook that corn into mash, and distill that mash into whiskey, minus the cost of the additional labor, and what's that bushel worth now? $20, $50, $100? That's value-added manufacture, same as they teach at Wharton.

The trouble starts if Uncle Sam's not getting his cut. Upwards of 50 percent of the purchase price on every drop of liquor you drink goes to taxes, and has for a very long time. In fact, the first internal revenue law this country ever saw was a tax on whiskey, circa 1791. And the first internal revenue tax rebellion this country ever saw was the Whiskey Rebellion, circa 1791.

Moonshiners, in most cases men trying to earn a living by nothing more sinister than adhering to the backwoods principles of supply and demand, paid no taxes on the whiskey they made and sold, and that set them, centuries ago, at odds with the law.

So south from Washington, D of C, came the tax agents, the T-men, the revenuers, hunting for stills and distillers, trudging up and down those bony hills, cussing and crashing through the thickets and the breaks and the briars, hoping to dissuade folks from trafficking in illicit, untaxed whiskey by sending them off to jail.

For years, all along the Whiskey Belt, the Appalachian hill country running like a bent spine from Pennsylvania down to north Georgia and Alabama, this went on in a quiet way, without much violence or excitement on either side. It was understood that this was all just business and not something worth getting busted up or cut up or shot over. Relations between stoic government T-man and taciturn Scots-Irish moonshiner were never cordial, mind, but each could at least respect the other's devotion to his career. It was all pretty unspectacular, to tell the truth, city men stumbling through the huckleberries looking for country men tending their mash fires or leading their mule down out of the piedmont with a load of Mason jars in the buckboard. The feds bitched and suffered their time in the woods, the 'shiners kept their mouths shut and suffered their federal incarceration as a cost of doing business. If it hadn't been for the cars, you might never have heard about any of it.

Cars made the whole thing fun.

By the 1930s, bootleggers were routinely running loads out of the hills and into town using whatever old cars and trucks they'd traded their mules for, and of course the police had cars by then, too, so the whole thing got faster, mechanized and competitive and, to professional storytellers at least, colorful.

It is a common misconception these days that the moonshine drivers of the 1930s and '40s and '50s were all fireballin' Li'l Abner types, all balls-out full-time Rebel yellers and a hunnert miles per through every narrow mountain pass. Sure the haulers were fast runners, when they had to be, or when they were just kickin' up some dust for fun, but it was a stealth business, too, and the smarter among them made a point of driving cars that looked as much like stock as they could make them, but could go like hell when they had to. So, shade-tree ingenuity being what it is, the key to success was building yourself a nondescript car with a whole lot of go, one that wouldn't sag at the rear under the weight of a full load of whiskey, that being a dead tip-off to the T-man or the local sheriff. A stock automobile, in other words, with heavy-duty suspension and a giant engine. Hmmm.

The ridgerunners built faster and faster cars and the cops built faster and faster cars, and pretty soon the woody piedmont was full of hot-rodded brown-bag sedans and V-8 engine noise and young men and coursing juice and money and corn likker, and you can bet it didn't take too long before somebody gouged a little red-dirt track out of a field somewhere with a bulldozer, where a man might go of a Sunday to see whose car was really fastest and maybe wager a dollar or two on his friends or against his enemies. As long as you didn't skip too much church to do it.

By the time NASCAR came along, '47, '48, '49, whiskey runners and moonshine haulers were well established factually and mythologically as being among the fastest men with some of the fastest cars. And obviously they made up a substantial part of that early stock-car racing population. But there was at least an equal number of racers who had nothing to do with moonshine. Trouble with them was their stories weren't as good.

In the best of the moonshine stories modest, God-fearing men like Junior Johnson are forever throttling their 4-barrel chariots hard and handsome along those lonesome roads, outrunning and outfoxing the law—the hillbilly Apollo laughing and flinging bolts of white lightning back at an invariably fat and hapless sheriff.

Tales like that grew like kudzu down south, of course, where the oral tradition and the necessary exaggerations of storytelling were well understood and the need for heroes was great indeed. And those stories were immensely important, because for white folks about the only thing left unscorched or unsullied or unstolen or unfucked with in the South after the Civil War were stories and ideas. Mythological stories, mostly, about ideas like Honor or Bravery or Independence. Those being the holy ideals, of course, behind which the South thought it fought the Civil War. So fast cars + young men + physical courage + moonshine + the honored roll of Rebel dead = early NASCAR.

That France the Lawgiver had organized a racing circuit made up of actual and aspirant outlaws isn't so much paradoxical as it is perfect, and it lies at the heart of NASCAR's popularity even today. It's how Bill France turned Sherman's march back on itself and brought the Jubilee north.

The Beep reading sweetly, musically on, we glide smoothly down through Georgia, where General Sherman won his terrifying fame. Having laid waste to so much here, he is not well thought of in these precincts, where the past is always present and 137 years is no more than the pause required for a storyteller to draw another breath. Legends and heroes and villains and history all abound in the piney woods hereabouts, and southern ghosts are the liveliest we have. How else to explain all the Confederate flags flying by on bumpers and aerials and rear-quarter windows? Haunted flag of a whole ghost nation!

Past Savannah on the east, south past all those placid coastal sea islands, down across the red-clay low country and flat out past the Okefenokee, bound for Florida, strange American outpost, fantasyland beyond the South.

Bill France cut a wide, hot swath through the South, too, but built as he barnstormed and brought boon to every corner of his early empire. He and his hot rod outriders charged across the country from track to track to track, racing everywhere and anywhere, laying waste only to boredom and quiet in the small-time short-course small towns. In those red-clay days most of the racing was done in the dirt, on fractional tracks of one-quarter or three-eighths or half of a mile. The circuit was nearly agrarian in its commitment to the fertile earth, and it was a rare thing for a racer's wheels to roll across a proper blacktop. Daytona still ran its race on the beach layout, half sand, half asphalt, and NASCAR could sometimes leverage the use of a local airfield to run a race on concrete, but mostly the tour plowed long furrows in its native soil.

The first Great Leap Forward occurred in 1950, after an ambitious peanut farmer built an asphalt racetrack on a little trapezoid of fallow land up at Darlington, South Carolina. Inspired by a trip to Indianapolis to see the 500, and looking to bring the happy anarchy of a NASCAR date home, nut wrangler Harold Brasington laid out the 1.366-mile high-banked track that became stock-car racing's original citadel. It was and remains the Mother of All Superspeedways.

Racing opened there on September 4, 1950. The event was called the Southern 500, and reports of the day put the starting field at more than 70 cars. It was a hit the moment it opened. To accommodate a neighbor's pond, the peanut farmer had built the track as an oval, but pinched narrow at one end, like an egg. It was steep in the turns, banked nearly 25 degrees, and was as fast a place as anyone had ever seen a stock car run. The odd shape and the high speeds and the racing traffic and the rough paving had a decided tendency to fling cars up into the wall, too. People loved it. The winner that day was a young man named Johnny Mantz.

And if you're wondering where Bill France is in this chapter of the origin story, one need only haul out the magnifying glass to consult the agate type of the hotshoe Pentateuch. On that first day of racing's new age, Bill France was present and accounted for, not just as sanctioning-body commander-in-chief or race steward, but as part owner of the winning car. Just as he would become part owner of the track itself in later years.

This was the year that NASCAR changed the name of its premier series, too, abandoning the blunt, blue-collar literal alliterative Strictly Stock for the higher-flying title of Grand National, a tea biscuit mouthful of ambitious pretension that France borrowed from British horse racing.

The beginning of that new half-century saw the early stars emerging as well, drivers like Lee Petty and Fireball Roberts and Herb

Thomas and the Flock Brothers and Bill Rexford. These were the public faces of celestial creator Bill France as he raced his way across the land. And Darlington, "The Track Too Tough to Tame," was France's first mighty fortress in the battle to win the nation's hearts and minds.

To this day the track remains an eccentric old dame, also nicknamed by her fans "The Lady in Black" for her habit of breaking the hearts, to say nothing of the bones, of the young men who fail in their haste to seduce her. And to a fast-vanishing generation of southern originals, it will always be the truest home of what they still remember as "racin' strickly stawk."

Sufficient history for one trip, I think. The Panama Canal is built, NASCAR is well launched, and, window down to the warm, jungle air, the Beep is at this very moment tracing the late-night neon skyline of Orlando with her slender finger as we pass. We have arrived in Florida.

Right now we're rolling in to Disney World, the biggest, most bodacious roadside attraction in human history. We'll "camp" here tonight, at one of the Magic Kingdom's many fine RV facilities. Fort Wilderness. So named, apparently, because cable television is an additional $5. Cruel frontier! There's no time tonight for television in any case. I need my sleep.

I have an important appointment in the morning. A kind of physics class.

TWO

The first time I drive the car it feels like rage.

Apocalypse in every cylinder, pistons hammering hot and remorseless as hell's forge, the manifold ravenous, roaring for air and explosives, belts shrieking, crankshaft screaming threats, spinning off shavings like a lathe, the oil tortured and useless, a black ruin of subatomic corruption boiling in the spattered bowel, the rods, the valves, the lifters, the springs flying apart, colliding and crashing back, the relentless cycling of a hundred kinds of shrapnel a hundred times a second, metal on metal, sickle on scythe, hairline fractures everywhere, cracked scalpel edges clattering in the dark, anxious to fail, to escape, blazing, on razor wings, scissoring through sheet metal, sunlight, flesh, mechanical anarchy biding its time, waiting, waiting, patient, waiting, and the exhaust down there thundering fire and stench and the mourning blast of Armageddon—

"Don't blow it up."

all of it held together by nothing more than an idea, by the faded ink on an engineer's blueprint, by the dead tension of mechanical habit—

"Don't blow it up!"

and like everything else in the universe, the inevitability of its own spectacular end was sown in the first moment of its creation, a big racing V-8 is all intricacy and vanity and the outrageous noise of self-love on the way to self-destruction, after all, it's only a matter of time—everything in this engine is beating itself to pieces—Jesus, this isn't a car, it's entropy, a fast unraveling of thermodynamics, it's the cosmic triumph of chaos, it's *war!*—

"I SAID DON'T BLOW THE GODDAMN THING UP!"

Oh.

This time I can hear him. I ease off the gas. Leaning in my window while the car idles on the pit road, he's got his face about an inch from mine. I've been revving the engine. Perhaps more than is strictly necessary. He's so close to me his nose is out of focus. He's in his late thirties maybe, very tan and just at the end of handsome, with a slender face, sharp crow's feet framing bloodshot blue eyes, and big pink gumfuls of tiny white teeth. He has the kind of fine platinum blond hair that looks stunning on a 10-year-old girl, but makes a grown man seem insubstantial somehow, tricky, and about seven-eighths untrustworthy. Not surfer blond. Not starlet blond. Swindler blond. Alcoholic-philanderer-embezzler-who-cries-when-he-gets-caught blond. It makes him look like the kind of guy who'd drive a Chrysler convertible with one hand on the wheel and wear a monogrammed blue blazer without irony and call you "Sport" when you showed up to repossess his car. The kind of guy who might have moved a folding card table, two folding chairs, and his shaving kit into a dingy junior studio in an apartment complex out by the airport after his second divorce. View of the interstate off-ramp and the exhaust fans at Hardee's. The kind of formerly modern, two-story suburban cell block that has a phony mansard roofline and cedar shakes gone flat, silverfish gray. Name like Terrace Oaks or Oak Terrace. Two stunted Japanese maples dying by the front door. It would be built around a swimming pool too small to do anything with but glare at in frustration. Biannually he and his neighbors would stand self-consciously on the cracked concrete pool deck to eat barbecued ham cubes and canned pineapple chunks served on charred bamboo skewers. Luau Night at the Oaks. Tiki torches flickering and smoking, pool flashing blue, they'd drink too many Bacardi-and-RCs while they talked about bin Laden and sports and pending deadbeat dad legislation. Boz Scaggs would be laboring away inside somebody's boombox. No. Jimmy Buffett. Around 9:30 Blondie here'd start hitting on the hard-boiled but still vulnerable, divorced flight attendant from down the hall. She'd go upstairs alone at 10. He'd drink himself from wistful to loud to angry to combative to sad and then pass out on a damp couch in the multipurpose lanai/party room that smells like mildewed carpet glue.

That's the kind of hair this guy has. Luau Night at the Oaks blond.

"REMEMBER YOUR EXTINGUISHER! 'COURSE IF THERE'S FIRE, I SAY FUCK IT! DROP THE NET AND GET OUT FAST! HAVE FUN!"

With that he pulls his face back from mine, yanks my harnesses even tighter, shoots me a smile that never makes it to his eyes, and eases his shoulders back out of the driver's side window. I didn't get his name. He's one of the ten or twelve employees here at the morning session of the Richard Petty Driving Experience. He tugs my window net up into place and levers it tight in the frame. The net's there to keep your left arm from flying out the window when the car starts tumbling down the track at 165 mph, like Petty himself at Darlington in 1970, when the 43 car got turned sideways and took air and barrel-rolled seven or eight times with Mr. Petty's slender left arm flopping out the driver's window like the off-arm of a bull rider or saddle-bronc cowboy, fully extended, circling wildly, while the car bucked and spun beneath him, shedding metal and rubber and churning up the asphalt, until you figured him for dead before the debris even stopped falling. Amazingly, he wasn't much hurt.

That experience, however integral to Petty mythology, isn't pictured in the brochure. We are here, instead, to scare ourselves a little, to show off, to pretend for eight laps that we're racers, to do a dangerous thing without really doing it. In America this is possible. For $349, Visa or MasterCard. There are 20 of us.

This is Orlando, Florida, in the first week of February 2002. Walt Disney World Speedway. Fantasy inside fantasy inside fantasy.

The day starts at 8 A.M. in an infield classroom. Turn in your liability waivers and medical forms. Just in case. Half an hour or so of whiteboard instruction on safety, strategy, technique. Gas on/gas off. Half-attentive, we fidget in our seats. How hard can it be? We want to get in the cars and *go*. No camaraderie, just staring at the back of one another's heads. An inventory of male-pattern baldness. We are all of a kind here this morning, white guys on the crumbling brink of middle age; retail managers, orthodontists, salesmen, master plumbers. One writer poised on a brink of his own.

Then a couple of fast laps on the tri-oval track in passenger vans with one of the instructors driving, six or seven of us piled in and hanging on like grim death behind him as he shouts tips about angles of entry and apexes. There are orange highway cones at the entrance and exit to every turn—70, 80 miles an hour wallowing and squealing around the banking in what amounts to a senior-center ambulette on the worst ride ever to the respiratory therapy center. "All you need to remember are the cones," he says, as we stagger out, weaving like we've been at sea. "The cones remind you when to let off and when to pour on the steam. 'Kay?"

We gather beneath a trackside tent. We are given helmets and sanitary helmet liners, little white cotton yarmulkes, to absorb the Brylcreem, presumably, and coveralls in Petty's famous medium blue. We look like fat, excited children wearing medieval skullcaps and novelty pajamas. The cars, the reason we came, are just on the other side of the low pit wall.

The cars. Used to be that racers were simply hot-rodded cars off the showroom floor, but that hasn't been the case with stock cars for a generation. The cars are loosely based on American sedans—Ford Taurus, Chevy Monte Carlo, Pontiac Grand Prix—but they share nothing more with them than the model name.

They are done up in the same corporate circus wagon paint schemes as the cars on TV. Low, wide, heavy, and fast, these are de-tuned versions of the Cup racers and make only about 600 horsepower, but when the instructors fire them up, the noise is an assault.

One by one, we're going to get in the cars and drive them as fast as we can, following an instructor in another car around the track. "Git tucked in right behind him, now. Stay on him like a tick." First, though, the driver introductions.

Mimicking the canned heat that precedes every big-league stock-car race, we are each introduced over the PA system. Every balding manchild in his officially licensed fireproof PJs gets his turn at stardom as his name is shouted out over an obbligato of prehistoric arena rock. Unlike drivers up in the Big Show, however, we are not humbled by the ovation of a quarter million ardent fans, nor are we driven around the track in the back of a camo National Guard Humvee. We blush, rather, at the bland applause of 19 indifferent strangers and a few of their sunburned wives and children while we walk the 12 feet from one side of the tent to the other. The infrequency with which their own children bring their hands together for Dear Old Maximum Dad, to say nothing of the nearly audible rolling of their little Oliver Twist eyes, would indicate that in some degree their applause is to be taken ironically.

Helmets cinched tight, jowls bulging, the first two drivers are led to their cars. They struggle to squeeze themselves in through the driver's window. They fiddle with the harnesses. Then they're gone.

Two instructor-student pairs are sent out half a lap apart so there are always four cars on the track. Those still waiting watch from beneath the tent. We have been divided into four teams of five men each, on the theory that we will pull together to post the fastest aggregate team time of the morning, thereby earning brag and swagger rights and a complimentary 4-by-6-inch color photo in a decorative cardboard sleeve. The Petty folks want us to have a rooting interest in our teammates' performance. We do not.

We will remain strangers until the day we die. I don't remember being introduced to the other four, even during our group photo. In fact, team member or not, we mock and kibitz the others as they orbit the track.

"He's too far behind the instructor. He's not gettin' the draft. Slow-poke."

"Yeah, that's some chickenshit bullshit all right, you gotta tuck right up in there."

"Christ, he even *sounds* slow."

The one thing no one wants to do is drop the clutch and stall the car as they're trying to pull away. Weakling! Candy-ass! Of course, some do.

"Weakling!"

"Candy-ass!"

"Oh, you gutless fuck!"

So much for team-building. That's for sniveling middle-management lickspittles on corporate outings anyway, not for Rebel heroes and Yankee hotshoes and tough-guy dentists who stare down gingivitis every goddamn day.

After eight laps, each one run at increasing speeds, the cars roll back onto the pit road. The drivers are helped out of their harnesses and hauled out through the small windows and walked back to the tent while the next pair of students jog to the cars. Flushed with what they've just done, the returning heroes are red-faced and engine-deaf and loud with excitement.

"Man, that was just unbelievable!"

"Incredible! Just incredible!"

"WHAT?"

"I said it was UNBELIEVABLE!"

"OH, YEAH! INCREDIBLE!"

Then, invariably, overwrought with recreational adrenaline and caught up in the moment, Maximum Dad hugs the wife and tries to high-five one of his kids. And while the wives are tolerant enough ("I'm just happy to see him happy," I heard one say to another later, "especially for three hundred and forty-nine GD dollars"), the kids want very little to do with that big sweaty palm. The younger ones are stuck, certainly, and suffer Daddy's new enthusiasm with a flaccid, noncommittal hand, but the adolescents, knowing the rudiments of public cool, blush with shame. One, a girl about 13, refuses entirely. Her father comes at her with that high five raised like he's won the Super Bowl and she just stares back at him like he's exposing himself at the junior high sock hop. I have never seen a man look sadder than he did in that instant, high five hanging there unreturned and the future all at once upon him.

This is the moment when the instructors announce that another eight laps can be had for only $199 American, and lots of the dads start digging for their wallets, anxious to get back in the car, where there is only speed and freedom, and time, paradoxically, stands still.

Not long after, my number comes up and I am beckoned to the pit wall by an instructor. With the helmet on, all I can hear is the rumble and buzz of the cars and the quickening pulse of the blood pumping in my ears. Lubdub. Lubdub. He points me to a car.

It is small. On television the cars seem huge, monstrous. In part I think because of all those low-slung onboard camera shots, the wide-angle lens in the rear roll pan of one car looking back at 200 miles an hour to another car nosing up behind it so that it fills the entire frame and blocks out the very sky. But everything you've ever seen on television looks bigger and grander than it really is—let's face it, that's what television's for. Any video engineer will tell you that it's a function of the aspect ratio of the screen, that things appear proportionately wider than they really are, and farther apart (Matt and Katie and Al are practically sitting on top of each other every morning!), but that misses the point. Mythology, not technology, is what makes these cars big.

The real thing, though, is small. Lower and sexier than what you'd see in the showroom, wide at the front and rear, slender and sculpted at the waist, it's still based on a midsized Detroit sedan, and when you stand next to it your first reaction might be disappointment. Mine was, mingled with a bright excitement and the dark fear that I'd screw the pooch in front of that dentist.

Long ago, when the cars were hot-rodded on the cheap from showroom models, the racers would tie their doors shut with a length of rope or a belt or, like Ellie Mae Clampett, the rope they used as a belt, so they wouldn't fly open during a race. Eventually they started welding them shut. Now the cars are built without doors at all, so Maximum Dad's first challenge, and mine, is to climb into the car through the driver's side window.

Watching the men who precede me, there seem to be two ways to do this. One: Lift the right leg up as high as you can. Higher. Higher. Okay, now right foot into cockpit. Right foot onto car seat. Two hands on roof. Lift left leg. Crush testicles on windowsill. Pause. Breathe. Left leg up. Higher. Higher. Fold left leg. Bend into cockpit. Unfold. Crush testicles on steering wheel. Pause. Breathe. Slither down onto seat. Or, Two: Lift right leg. Right foot into cockpit. Two hands on windowsill. Bend forward at the waist. Farther. Farther. Now lever torso into cockpit. Reel in left leg. Smack face on steering wheel. Fall across roll cage cross-member and crush testicles on fire extinguisher bottle. Pause. Breathe. There.

Eventually it dawns on some of us to wait for the instructors to remove the steering wheels before we try getting in. That's why the steering wheels are removable.

Compounding the entry problem is the horse collar they hand me to wear right before I climb in. Another safety device, it works just like a neck brace to limit the range of motion between your head, neck, and shoulders. This will be helpful in a crash, but in the meantime it also limits the range of your vision when you're trying to hoist your testicles over the windowsill of the car, which may explain the strangled screams of my classmates.

The cockpit of a stock car is small, too, of course, nearly claustrophobic. Tucked tight in the seat, you're surrounded by the thick tubing of the roll cage. The seat itself is designed to hold you almost immobile, so you don't go sliding all over the place when you're running at speed on the track and the G's are pulling you out toward the wall. The seat also restricts your range of motion in a crash, so you don't go ragdolling all over the inside of the car. The seat grips you from the back of your head all the way down to your calves. It's like falling over backwards into a giant pile of modeling clay. Idling on pit road it's a restrictive feeling, but on the track at a buck and a half the driver's seat feels natural and necessary. Cup drivers, like astronauts, all have seats custom-molded to fit them.

The tubular steel roll cage runs vertically and horizontally and diagonally around the entire interior of the car. It's there to prevent the cockpit, and the driver, from being crushed in an accident. It also makes it impossible to see out of the car through anything but the windshield or the rearview mirror, which is fine since you can't move your head in any case.

Like an amusement park funhouse, everything in the cockpit of a stock car is comically and incorrectly scaled. The steering wheel is the size of a manhole cover. The gearshift lever comes up out of the transmission hump like a sight gag, the thing as long as your arm. The tachometer, a gauge the size of a pie pan for reading your engine speed, is, in this car, centered above the steering wheel. Strung along the dashboard are seven or eight other gauges so small as to be useless, even if I knew what they were for.

The entire interior is sheet metal painted with a couple of coats of what looks like gray semigloss primer. Worn down to bare steel in places, the interior of this car shows a lot of use. Cup cars always look brand-new when they roll off the hauler, because they always are. Even if it's a car a team has been using for more than a season, it gets a fresh touch-up every time it goes out the shop door.

Down near the firewall, just a few inches behind the engine, the pedals are tiny and very far away. My right foot knows why it's here, though, and immediately begins tickling the accelerator. The throttle return springs on racing cars are stout, like the springs on the screen door of a west Texas bunkhouse, and it takes more than tentative pressure from a nervous foot to make any real noise. Flexing your foot forward from the ankle, the way you do it in your econo-lozenge at home, your Maximum Dad minivan, isn't going to get it. You need to put your leg into it.

Once you do, the results are very satisfying.

The whole car resonates as the engine spins faster. You come up out of that mud-lumpy vibration you get at idle with a big racing V-8, the exhaust thumping so arrhythmically that you can't focus your eyes, and you begin to get that urgent, perfect frequency of everything spinning and oscillating and pounding in harmony. Your vision clears and the exhaust rumble tightens into a growl into a whine into a scream. These cars really bark when you put a foot to them. The sound of a race engine is the biggest part of its appeal, I think, even more than the power it might actually deliver. There's excitement in that noise, of course, and brutality and the promise of bad fun, and for those who love cars and racing and speed, the sound of it is what grabs you first and it grabs you low in the belly and shakes you hard. A big V-8 sounds like America.

The bottom of the ridiculous steering wheel actually rests in your lap, angled nearly straight up and down like a ship's wheel and almost brushing the top of your thighs. I am trying to figure out how to overcome this, and relentlessly revving the engine, and musing absently on the nature of chaos and internal combustion when the blond man sticks himself in the window and then buckles my five-point harness. Shoulders, hips, and peevish man-tackle all have their own heavy, webbed belts to secure them. The belts meet at a quick-release locking mechanism just below my navel, and when Blondie cinches them down he's not kidding. I can barely breathe. He's also not kidding when he yells that reminder not to blow the car sky-high before I ever get going. And, last of all,

"REMEMBER YOUR EXTINGUISHER! 'COURSE IF THERE'S FIRE, I SAY FUCK IT! DROP THE NET AND GET OUT FAST! HAVE FUN!"

And while I'm wondering if anyone's ever died doing this—if any Maximum Sansabelt Dad from Pleasant Valley, USA has ever come here for a morning's fun and instead gotten loose at speed and lost the rear end and gone hard into the wall fully locked in a hopeless slide, the wheel useless in his hands, bracing his feet against the firewall and watching the infield and the wall and the infield and the wall spinning past him, the tires screaming and sending up billows of yellowed white smoke, the G's twisting him in the seat until the moment of absolute deceleration, instantaneous, 50 G's in the opposite direction, and in the same second hearing the terrible noise of the impact and the utter quiet that follows it and people running and the car rolling slow and broken down the banking of the track—the instructor in front of me pulls away. Don't think and drive. I'm already behind.

Left foot hard to the floor, slam the shifter all the way left and forward, whatever you do don't stall in front of the dentist, don't stall, don't stall, right foot hard to the floor, left foot up, drop the clutch, light the tires, up through the gears out of the pits, I'm *thrown* back in the seat, lubdublubdublubdub, lift that right foot a quarter of an inch, left foot hard to the firewall on a clutch sprung like a squat rack, the shifter throw laughably, impossibly long, like a farm implement of poor manufacture, a Bulgarian combine, a North Korean forklift, slam it a yard and a half back into second, right leg locked again, foot back to the floor, power shifting, the acceleration almost yanking my hands off the wheel, the noise is fantastic, the carb gaping wide open and gulping fuel and air up front and the exhaust thundering unmuffled out of the headers down by my left hip, wind ripping through the netting now, out of the pits and onto the track apron, steering hard left with both hands, the car wants to go right, up the track into the wall, steer hard left with both hands, lubdublubdub, hard left foot for the clutch, feather the throttle, right hand off the wheel, yikes! grab the shifter, throw it right and up to the dash, slam it into third, back hard on the gas, stay on the gas, coming out of the second turn now, down off the banking, the car bouncing on the shocks and drifting right, floating out toward the wall, right foot to the floor, halfway up the backstretch and running at redline and grab the shifter and pull all the way back and right and at last I'm in fourth gear and by the time I'm into the bottom of the third turn I'm running 90 miles an hour.

I've also caught the instructor. This would be a good time to lift my right foot, so I do, barely feathering the pedal so I don't rear-end him. You're supposed to stay close, but ramming your instructor is discouraged. You're not even supposed to pass him, much less bump him up the track out of your way and then slip under him for the win, Rusty Wallace–style.

My instructor's name is Chad, I think. He was presented to us in the classroom earlier in the day and I recall him vaguely as young and slender and completely wrong for the part. Chad. I wish him well; a lot of the guys working for the Petty school are racers on their way up looking to earn some extra cash until they get their big break, but "Chad" is not a driver's name. "Chad" is for underwear models or graduate TAs in the Anthropology of Cinema sequence at Cal State Northridge. "Ernie" is a driver's name, or "Joe" or "Fireball."

Running down out of the fourth turn I'm tucked up right behind him. A single car length off his rear end. I'm not scared, but I'm very busy. Stuck somewhere between sensory deprivation and input overload. I don't have to worry about shifting anymore, but the steering wheel has every bit of my attention now. The *principles* of driving a stock car on an oval track really are as simple as you know they're going to be. Gas on/gas off and turn left. The physics of it, though, and the sensation of it, the stress and effort of it, the very things that make it so challenging, are also the things for which you're utterly unprepared.

Howling down the frontstretch now, for example, I'm trying to inventory what I can actually *see*. It isn't much. Outside, I can see the hood of my car, sort of, the short blur of track between my car and the one in front of me, the rear window of Chad's car, and the back of Chad's car seat. I can just see the top of his helmet. I have a general idea that somewhere in front of him is more racetrack, and the horizon, but I don't feel like I'm actually seeing it so much as I'm remembering that it's out there. There's a flag stand halfway down the front straight on the right side with a flagman standing in it, and across from that on the left is the tent with other drivers and their families. But I can't register any of the detail of those things, they're gone as soon as I recognize them, and since I know they're supposed to be there, I'm filling in broad strokes of the picture from memory. My eyes have got their hands full. The faster you run the more your field of vision narrows and the shorter it becomes, until everything in the world telescopes down to the 40 or 50 feet in front of your car in an arc about 10 feet wide. That the shatterproof windshield is etched with scratches and smeared with oil and explodes with glare every time the sun hits it doesn't make the driving any easier.

Seeing things inside the car is even harder. Everything is vibrating like mad and your head's vibrating like mad, and banging from side to side as the car bobs along, and the centrifugal force is pulling you and all your soft tissue up, up, up to the right at a couple of times the force of gravity, and where the dashboard and the gauges used to be is only a colorful impressionist painting of a set of instruments. By tightening my jaw muscles and stiffening my neck and concentrating on the immense tachometer, I can just make out the orange needle pointing to about the nine o'clock position. In the time it takes me to see it, though, I've run 100 yards down the track at well over 100 miles per hour with no idea what was in front of me. I could be picking shards of instructor out of my grill. So. No more looking at the gauges. Forget the rearview mirror—we'll all die. To my right, peripherally, out the open passenger window the wall cascades past, a rushing, deafening brightness without detail.

I can hear the exhaust noise and that's all. The pitch changes a little when I move my right foot. I can feel the lubdubbing in my ears but I can't actually hear it. As we come up on the end of my first lap, I'm lubdubbing like Krupa drumming the first eight bars of "Sing, Sing, Sing."

The front straight of a tri-oval track isn't strictly straight, but in fact has what amounts to another, very gentle turn in it. At the apex of that turn, at least here at the Disney track, is the start/finish line. You don't turn hard through this additional corner, but you do aim your car for the inside of the track so as to make the shortest route possible from the exit of turn 4 back to the first turn. By the time Chad and I run across that line nose-to-tail, we're up to speed and probably running 110 mph or so. There's no speedometer, of course, and I couldn't read one if there were, so I won't have any idea how fast I've gone until I pull back into the pits.

Going hard into the first turn now I catch a glimpse of the orange cone set at the base of the wall. Chad's car slows slightly in front of me. I lift my right foot a quarter of an inch. Gas off. Sort of. My hands and arms are cranked full left on the wheel to make the turn. Oops.

Still going straight. Lubdub. Heading for the wall. Lubdub. If I don't hit Chad first. Lubdub. I take my foot off the gas altogether and the car dives left, back to the bottom of the turn, but I've lost some momentum so I stomp the pedal back to the floor to make up the ground I'm losing. By now I'm halfway through the second turn. This is where the rear end of my car starts to ease loose. Lubdublubdublubdub. "Gas on/gas off" is more complicated than it first appears.

Having gone into the turn too hot, and stabbing the gas to catch Chad while my arms and hands are still locked over to the left, means that I'm now powering the rear end of my car out from under myself. I can feel it in the seat of my pants and in my stomach, and down there it feels just like the first time I ever spun my dad's VW Squareback in a snowy parking lot, or dropped a motorcycle on a rain-slick sidestreet, sick and exhilarating. The parallel ends there. This time I'm crossing up at 100 mph with 3,400 pounds of car sliding around under me.

I correct by spinning the wheel back right, steering into the imminent skid, and pulling my idiot foot off the throttle. Now I'm headed for the wall. I wrestle back left into *that* impending slide. Where any of this is coming from I have no idea. Kinesthetic instinct roused by panic, perhaps. Latent genius. Dumb luck. But it's just like the driver's ed film! Except for the part where I hammer the gas again as hard as I can as soon as the car straightens up. By the time we're down the backstretch I've reeled Chad in and started breathing again. That Chad is being paid to let me reel him in seems unimportant.

Into turn 3. Smooth this time. Gas off. Muscle the wheel left. Halfway through the bottom of the turn, the car starts to straighten up and I pound my right foot down. That's it. Chad and I roll down out of the fourth turn a car length apart. Hard down the straightaway. Into turn 1. Gas off. Steer. Gas on. Fast. Smooth.

Smooth is a relative term. For a stock car, "smooth" can mean simply that you weren't knocked unconscious by the headrest as you pounded around the track. The car seesaws and wallows and pogos in

all three attitudes at once, yawing, pitching, and rolling simultaneously, violently. A racetrack may look flat, especially on TV, but none
of them are, and every surface imperfection is transmitted directly up
through that stiff, stiff suspension into your ass and your hands and
your brain. A racecar doesn't feel right until it's running at speed, and
then the ride is purposeful and brutal. Even with power steering,
sawing the wheel back and forth to keep the car on the right line is
mentally and physically exhausting. After a couple of laps there's the
heat to deal with, too.

By the time I've made my fourth lap of the 1-mile-plus track, I'm
pouring sweat. It's in the mid-70s outside, but in here it's closer to 100
degrees, even with the side windows missing. Down by my feet, next
to the firewall, it's more like 125 degrees. I'm spent and I've been on
the track a little less than four minutes.

But the sensation of this kind of speed is electrifying, and by the
time we circle the track for the fifth time Chad has upped our speed to
130 or so on the straights, down to perhaps 100, 105 in the turns. If the
Cup racers ran this track they'd be a third again as fast. I'm running on
adrenaline now, and cocky from having kept death at bay for four endless minutes, and start edging my car up so close to Chad's that he
waves me off. He raises his hand in front of his rearview and moves it
back and forth, lazy and slow, the signal to stop tailgating, and it
occurs to me that while I'm back here struggling to keep up with him,
strangling the wheel and yanking it side to side in effortful spasms,
kicking at the gas pedal like I'm trying to kill a snake, gasping for
breath, heart drumming away, he's up there in front of me going into
the turn, the death turn, with one hand on the wheel. He's probably
whistling.

In these last few laps, gathering speed and something like confidence, I try to make my exits and my entries, conveniently marked by
the giant orange cones, gas on/gas off, with something like grace.
This is called "hitting your marks" by those who actually know what
they're talking about. Once the initial shock wears off, the sensory

overload that has you driving that first handful of laps with nothing but your inner ear, your bowels, and the reptile core of your brain stem, there's even time to think.

This car is a pig. That's what I'm thinking. This isn't some nimble, responsive little sports car you can flick back and forth with surgical precision on different lines through the turns. It isn't some effete, high-revving, hypertech European blitz-sled built for schussing the Autobahn at 200 kph, or for cornering nimbly up and down the narrow hill roads of the Amalfi coast. It isn't some luxo Japanese ultracar, either, silent and slippery and fast, all silicon-chip efficiency and Tom Swift gadgetry and motherboard performance, polite as an appliance.

This thing is a grunting thug, as dim-witted and overmuscled and clumsy as they come. Even with the power steering it's a workout to keep the beast running straight, the wheel cycling vaguely in your hands while the nose of the car wanders and hunts and sniffs down the track. There's an arc of about 30 degrees at dead center where the steering wheel can be wrestled back and forth with no discernible effect on your trajectory. The whole steering assembly has more slop in it than a Tobacco Road hog operation.

Granted, this is a rental unit, the stock-car equivalent of a theme park ride, and after a couple of months of hard use in the wet, clenched hands of overeager money-market managers and data-entry specialists and cops and bakers and dentists there's bound to be some play in the linkage, but the fact is, these racecars are brutish and primitive and imprecise from the moment they're built.

Stock cars are living history. A pushrod V-8 engine with a carburetor, mounted in a box-section ladder frame, driving the rear wheels through a manual four-speed transmission and a solid rear end is a trip to the local showroom circa 1955. Dig that swingin' new two-tone DeSoto FireDome! Maximum Dad's embarrassing WindStar or anonymous late-model Camry is more technologically sophisticated than a Cup racer by several degrees of magnitude.

To say nothing of the designs in other popular racing series, like Formula One, or the CART or IRL championship cars. Those racers are built out at the very limits of contemporary chassis and engine design, using materials and construction from the cutting edge of composite science. A Cup racer is old-school shop class, simple as a brick.

That engine hammering away up in front of me is powerful, certainly, but then it has to be to drag the backbreaking weight of all this antique cast iron around the track. And once it gets all that bulk pointed in a particular direction, it's damned stubborn about changing its mind. The brakes, for example, seem largely decorative, and simply turning left starts an argument with the car you can't really win.

This despite the fact that the cars are engineered to ensure they can't do anything *but* turn left. They even sit cockeyed on the frame. The right side of the car rides higher on the springs than the left side, and the rear rides higher than the front. Seen from behind, at rest on pit road, the cars all sit tilted from the high right rear to the low left front, rakish as Sinatra's hat brim. At speed, then, with centrifugal force at work on them, they should want to dive smoothly into a left turn and then ride level all the way around its banked radius. No one seems to have explained this to the car itself, though.

Hard as I try to let the car have its head, it isn't very interested in carving neatly into the turns. Depending on my speed, it either plunges for the infield, yikes! or spits the bit and bolts for the wall, lubdub. You're really steering the car with the throttle. The car's comic book geometry makes it incredibly sensitive to speed, but horsing that laughable wheel around only seems to make it angry. The constant corrections required to track through the turns are hardest on your arms, your shoulders, and your patience. The only thing harder to drive is a motorhome.

That I have any unassigned higher brain RAM left to even consider the efficiency with which the car handles comes as something of a surprise to me. On the sixth lap, coming down the backstretch at 140 or so, I notice something else. It doesn't feel like I'm going very fast. This is at least in part because I'm getting used to it. But it also has to do with being 15 feet away from another car going exactly the same speed, a kind of visual relativity. If I were out here alone at 140 or 145 I'd be screaming as if I'd been scalded, but tucked in behind Chad like this, my eyes focused on the back of his car, the speed feels apt, proportional, manageable; no worse than going 60 in moderate traffic on the interstate. Only by stealing a peripheral look at the palm trees stuttering past do I have any real sense of how fast we're going.

I have no sensation of turning individual laps, either, no sense of a discrete 1-2-3-ness. Rather, it feels like we're running along a continuous infinite surface, an immense, hypnotic Möbius strip, along which at intervals recur the same flagman and palm trees and tents and buildings. It's hard to describe, but it feels like one long, seamless process rather than a series of divisible events. And it feels good.

This is the feeling I paid for when I signed up for the class. The Maximum Dads, too. This is the feeling you're trying for when you mash the accelerator at a suburban stoplight, or when you're running two dozen clicks past legal on the interstate. This is the feeling they're selling you in those car commercials and in all those video games. It is the feeling of disembodied, concentrated velocity, velocity without consequence, the swift disconnect, speed freedom, you with your foot to the floor outrunning whatever it is that's after you. You are pure sensation, heart in your throat, internal gyro spinning at the base of your spine, deafened by speed and nearly blinded by it, your vision tunneling down to nothing, the world flooding by unseen and harmless, your immediate future rushing at you very clearly for a change, as if seen out of the long hard dark of a shotgun barrel. You are empty—happily, peacefully empty—of everything but the present moment.

Thus, way out past that initial panic, and past the breathless effort of working the car, and way out past the novelty and specificity of driving this car on this lap at this track on this day in this year, lies a few seconds' worth of near-transcendence.

Not that you've shucked self-awareness exactly, or overcome your own piddling and loathsome consciousness. The banal monologue always running in your American head about your next chicken dinner or the erratic pendulum of your self-esteem or why in the world is Oprah reading *Anna Karenina*? is still there, still whispering, but it's drowned out by the engine noise and the pounding in your ears. Wrestle that snarling motherfucker around the track long enough and you'll drive yourself, if only briefly, to Walden Pond.

It is a version of the experience described ad nauseam on television by adrenaline junkies and extreme-sport thrill-seekers—sky divers, BASE jumpers, free climbers, contestants on *Fear Factor*—in which your squalid little life is briefly reduced to its most primitive psychomotor essentials, and your struggle for personal understanding and human dignity is at last made meaningful by endeavoring to soil your fire suit without actually killing yourself. The ennobling effects of recreational terror. An entire industry within our mighty national entertainment complex has been built around it. Extreme sports, extreme theme parks, extreme cruises, extreme fabrics for your extreme technical outerwear, extreme soft drinks. When did they start building climbing walls at the mall?

Only by tugging hard on the trouser cuffs of the infinite can we truly be said to live, the squids and grinders and big-wave surfers tell us; the rest of life is just an unhealthy accretion of errand running, wage earning, and summers at band camp. The proximity of calamity is what scrubs that callus off your spirit; danger exfoliates your soul. The quality of your life can only really be measured against the imminence of your death. A philosophy, I'd guess, at which most combat soldiers can only snicker. Before they punch you out.

And while it's certainly true that we might all invigorate ourselves through the rare scrape with death ("I've never felt more *alive!*" is the line they teach at Hollywood Boulevard Screenwriters Polytechnic to delineate such moments), history more often teaches that prolonged exposure to mortal risk does one of two things. It either desensitizes you to the experience or it drives you insane.

In other words, transcendence out here on the track is possible, perhaps even inevitable, but it is fleeting and it is singular. And maybe that's enough in our new Sensation Nation.

It is pleasant to get out of my own head, though, as you might imagine, however briefly, and drive a hired car much too fast. As proof of same, I spend laps 7 and 8 with the nose of my car tucked pretty much under the rear roll pan of Chad's car. I'm hoping he'll pick up the pace a little, because, desensitized to the life-threatening nature of what I'm doing as per the above, I believe we should be going a whole lot faster. They warned us about this, of course, and insisted that closing in on the instructor would not result in higher speeds. "DO NOT run down the instructor," I believe the emphatic phrase was. "He's going to go as fast as HE thinks you can go, not as fast as YOU think you can go." Still, I'm hoping Chad will make an exception for me, having seen in his rearview mirror my manifest talent for all this.

Sadly he does not. No matter how far up under him I drive now, no matter how elegant a line I follow around the track, no matter how nonchalant I now seem as I wrench the big wheel to and fro, Chad does not quicken our pace. In fact, he spends our final two laps waving me off with all the indifferent languor of an embarking French sailor leaving his wife and children behind on a Marseilles dock. His wave says, "I see you, bébé, but I do not care." We go no faster.

After the eighth lap I follow Chad back onto pit road, coasting, as instructed, in neutral, using only the car's brakes to slow down. Overweight as the car and I are, the brakes do nothing. The car doesn't really decelerate, it just loses interest. Brake pedal to the floor, I nearly tap Chad on the turn back into the pits, then come close to mowing down the Luau blond as he waves me into my parking spot on the grid. Eventually the car succumbs to its own weight and rolls to a stop. He shoots me another vampire smile and takes down the window net. "How was it?" he shouts.

"INCREDIBLE!" I hear myself screaming. "UNBELIEVABLE!"

·   ·   ·

Unhitched from the harnesses I struggle out of the car so the next guy can take my place. I resist the impulse to throw him a high five as he jogs past. Swapping students in and out of these cars all morning before the seats can even cool would seem to indicate a healthy appetite for speed here in America and an equally robust revenue stream for Richard Petty and his employees. There's a group session booked for this afternoon, too, the sort of corporate-bonding nonsense that'll have the tasseled-loafer types from some human resources department in and out of the cars, and their catering tent, until it's too dark to see, and high-fiving each other like Little Leaguers. And this is only one day out of the year, at one track out of many. No wonder Richard Petty always seems to be smiling.

Back in the tent I give the Beep the mandatory post-Experience hug, which, adrenaline-assisted, comes off more like a chiropractic adjustment.

"Oooof. Easy there, Slugger. How was it?"

"INCREDIBLE! HOW'D I LOOK?"

"Like a man driving a car. How did it feel?"

"UNBELIEVABLE!"

Another few students make their laps as the morning winds down. Having stripped off my jumpsuit and yarmulke I no longer feel like part of the day, and I wander off to make some notes.

Sitting on some bleachers by the Porta Potties, I wonder for a while about the nature of chaos and speed and risk-taking, about the bone-deep need that Americans (and most other postindustrial humans) have for driving too fast. I wonder whether professional racers feel the same way I did when I took the wheel of that car—at once powerful and panicked. Have they had the excitement conditioned out of them? Or is every race a 500-mile freefall into darkness? What about the enlightenment? Do they experience the same sense of high-speed satori, however brief, however bogus, that I did? Or is it just another afternoon struggling for a buck to them, every bit as stuck in their own heads, in the unrelenting Q & A of human consciousness, as I am?

When the last Dad unfolds himself from his car, we gather again very briefly for the closing ceremonies. They are understated. As the families chatter and mill around the tent, one of the instructors thanks us all for coming and points us to the photo trailer on the way out, in case we want to buy souvenir albums of our day at the races. A moment later yet another Petty employee approaches me. She presses into my hand a small photograph in a decorative cardboard sleeve. I open it. There in front of a racecar I stand with four strangers. We are all smiling and looking straight into the lens. Embossed below the photo in tiny letters it reads, "The Winning Team."

My fastest lap, according to the accompanying printout, was run at an average speed of 124.60 miles per hour. In my ringing head I am convinced that I am the fastest man in that tent. They do not announce anyone else's speed, though, probably to prevent fistfights among the wives and children, so I'll never know for sure. But I know I could have gone faster, so much faster. I will have to satisfy myself instead with being part of the Winning Team. Which sucks compared to individual glory. I brag to my wife, and briefly swagger, but I buy no additional photos.

Our last responsibility before we scatter and return to our separate lives is to fill out a customer response sheet. I grade the whole day very highly and promise to recommend the place to my friends if I ever get home. In the space for suggestions at the bottom of the page I write two things:

"Scariest part of the experience was the Porta Pottie."

and

"Chad needs to drive faster. So much faster."

But there's something else, too. A small realization. I do not comment on it, because I get the sense suddenly that it's a common enough phenomenon out here. In fact, I suspect that almost every driver who comes here walks away feeling something similar—by their expressions I can tell that a couple of them have caught the same thought and that it excited and then confused them.

Driving a racecar? Driving it really fast? Driving it way out past whatever limits the law sets for you on the streets, or way out past whatever limits you've drawn for yourself in your own head?

It just didn't seem that hard.

Don't misunderstand, I'm not saying that it's not dangerous, or that doing it week in and week out professionally doesn't require a set of specific, original gifts and long training, or that any Tom, Dick, or dentist can just pick up a helmet and run in the lead pack at Talladega. I'm only saying that there's a moment after you've gotten out of the car when the voice in your head whispers, "*I could do this.*" And for a second or two this is incredibly exhilarating. But in the next instant, the fall back to Earth: "Well, shit, if *I* can do it, how hard can it be?" For a peek at your dream, you've squandered your innocence.

The Petty Experience is only a simulation, of course, mechanical role play, but our daily familiarity with driving a car breeds not only that initial heroic delusion ("I can drive!"), but also leads immediately to the contempt that follows ("Who can't?"). Still, I think it's that very intimacy, our collective love affair with the car, that accounts, at least in part, for NASCAR's popularity. Most Americans can relate more directly to driving than to almost anything else in sports. It's hard to imagine yourself tomahawking some stank down on Shaq's head, or shooting a 59 at Medina, or turning on a Clemens fastball thrown in on your hands. But driving too fast? You did that last night on your way home from work. And you'll do it again tomorrow.

As we lumber away in the motorhome, headed for Daytona and the first race, the biggest race, of the NASCAR Winston Cup season, the Beep has two suggestions for me.

"Stop yelling," she says,

and

"Slow down."

THREE

We arrive at Daytona late the same afternoon, fantasy and swagger and $349 worth of high-speed near-transcendence giving way to bottleneck and stop-and-go and the soothing monoculture of off-ramp America.

The Daytona International Speedway looms up out of the sawgrass and slash pine not far from the I-95. You're not ready for the speedway when you pull off the interstate. You need some time to prepare yourself for it, to reset the sense of scale in your head, but you don't get the chance, there it is, first thing, immense, bigger than any stadium or refinery or factory you think you've ever seen, far bigger than the little racetrack we just came from, gray as a battleship in the fading Florida sun, impossibly long, grandstands that seem to stretch to the sky, millions of girders crosshatched beneath them, a geometry of hard shadows and sunlight and steel and emptiness. Banners are draped from top to bottom along its great length—NASCAR, Winston, NASCAR Winston Cup, Daytona USA—and there are flags everywhere and banners hanging across the width of the boulevard on the pedestrian bridge, and there are signs for parking here and camping there and signs for the businesses along the strip and in every parking lot there are tents, white or blue or red or green, hospitality tents, attraction tents, catering tents, tents striped like circus sideshows, motorhead carnivale, people walking and wandering everywhere, and these small things, these things on a human scale, make the speedway bigger still, a dark vision, the nightmare thing from which there's no escape in your dreams, and the traffic signals pulse green and yellow and red and the traffic stretches, accordions, stops, and as slow as you're going it's still too fast to take everything in.

It is nine days until race day and already this sclerotic artery is clotted with cars and motorhomes and motorcycles and trucks of every size and style and description.

Driving a motorhome 10 feet high and 10 feet wide is murderous in festival traffic like this. By the time I register a few hallucinatory first impressions, we're past the track.

Weeks before, over the phone, I'd made reservations at a campground adjacent to the speedway. "It's right next to the track," the woman on the phone assured me. Now, dazed by my morning in a racecar, drugged with a speedball of fatigue and anxiety, hyperactively inattentive to anything I'm not about to ram with the motorhome, I can't find it. I can't find the campground. They never sent us the street address—a vacant lot. I don't have a phone number, either. Under normal circumstances this would be something we could solve pretty easily. Not today.

We decide to orbit the perimeter of the track complex to see if anything looks familiar. Never having been here before, this is of course unlikely. But maybe the name of the place, the logo on the sign, will jog something up out of our heads. It does not.

This is a long trip, too, the track itself being 2.5 miles around—probably 4 or 5 miles to circumnavigate, the way we're squaring it off on these bordering streets. And the traffic isn't thinning. Turning east, coming around the track we see the huge earthworks of the north turns, the white concrete wall of the speedway above them, the whole radius strung high with steel catchfence. The entire earthen assembly like the dry side of a dam. Below it a sprawling midway complex of giant tents and outdoor stages and attractions, a fair for the fans. Motorhomes parked all around, at every angle, filling every inch of space in the lots across the street. Tiny campsite signs when there are signs at all. I think the logo for the place is a checkered flag. The logo for everything in Daytona Beach is a checkered flag. Nothing we recognize anywhere. As we turn south we drive down the length of the backstretch and the backstretch grandstands, directly across the road from the Daytona airport. To our right hundreds more motorhomes.

Turning right again, west, we see a thousand more motorhomes parked in the flat fields adjacent to the southwest end of the track.

Back right onto International Speedway Boulevard, we see the Home Depot for the second time. Then the greyhound track nestled at the foot of the speedway grandstands. They're running 10-minute $25 helicopter rides out of the parking lot. There's a Barnes & Noble in the mall across the street from the track, and a Kia dealership. Across the street from the self-styled World Center of Racing? And am I the only one bothered by that sad sequence of letters? There's a Circuit City and an Old Navy and a Bed, Bath and Beyond, too, another name that's always confounded me. Beyond *what*? The bed? The bath? The continental shelf? Why not just say "kitchen"? Or is it meant to be metaphysical? Like the *Great* Beyond? Is it an ectoplasmic trance-state spirit journey into the infinite and unknown parallel planes of human consciousness? Or is it just waffle irons and aromatherapy candles?

There's every kind of off-ramp America restaurant, too, Cracker Barrel and Bob Evans and TGI Friday's, Fazoli's and Friendly's and Hooters, Olive Garden and Red Lobster and Outback, IHOP, a score of others, anonymous and interchangeable and so much a part of the landscape like soil-tree-sky that the sight of them rubs your retinas flat, they're nearly invisible until you're inside them; and there's fast-food, of course, and smoothie booths, and sub shacks and pizza places and chili-dog stands, but the only identifiable smell is from the thick ropes of barbecue smoke rising from the Speedweeks catering tents in the parking lots.

Crazy as Ahab, I make three more laps of the track. Nothing. Fourth time around the Beep, calm, strong, smart, exhausted, suggests the campground on the southwest end, outside turns 1 and 2. Even with a thousand others already pulled in, there are acres of space left for our small motorhome. "We can stay here a couple of days, call the other place, sort out the deposit we sent, and then we can move or stay." We're parked 20 minutes later: $120 for the rest of this week, no hookups; $120 more next week, through race day, if we stay. We find a spot. We park. We level the motorhome so the presidential placemats don't slide off the dinette table. We eat. The day still roaring in our ears, at 8:30 we sleep.

Daytona Sketchbook

Here's the motorhome protocol for flag display as per this morning's unscientific survey of our campground neighbors. The flagpole, 15 to 20 feet, fiberglass (think pole vault), is mounted vertically to a fitting on the rear bumper. The poles fly the following flags, in descending order (both in their arrangement and their rate of occurrence): United States of America, Dale Earnhardt #3 (white numeral, red drop-shadow on black field), Confederate States of America, Dale Earnhardt Jr. #8 (white numeral, black drop-shadow on red field). In lesser numbers the other team colors follow, including: Mark Martin, Jeff Gordon, Rusty Wallace, Dale Jarrett, Tony Stewart, Bobby Labonte, et al. (The ratio of Dale Earnhardt Sr. to all other racers combined is 25 to 1.) Below that are the checkered flags, the NASCAR/Winston Cup generic pennants, and the generic product pennants (beer, cigarette, laundry detergent, home improvement). Also seen, flags of Brazil, Australia, skull and crossbones, Union Jack.

Variation: CSA flag appears on top, USA just below, rate of occurrence, plus or minus 10 percent. CSA flown alone, plus or minus 10 percent.

Got our official credentials at the track office. Long lines and throngs of people. The Beep, like all photographers, is required to get new credentials every race. We don't know why, and the time-consuming weekly mystery is never explained. Large, colorful tickets, cryptically coded (A, P, G, R, etc.), some embossed with gold foil, are to be placed in a clear plastic sleeve and dangled around her neck. They must be dangled visibly at all times, to accommodate heightened security concerns. The Beep dangles hers with grace.

My credential is a laminated ID the size of a business card. Good for the entire season, I'm told, all-access. Called by cognoscenti a "hard card." I have a DMV-style photo taken for obverse of same. In the result I look like a human thumb with eyes. Dangle—undistinguished.

This is a good time, and it's only fair, I think, to (thumbnail) sketch the two of us.

The Beep is tall (near 6 feet) and strong (former college rower) and smart (master's degree, English lit., summa). She has shoulder-length brunette hair shading to auburn once the sun gets it. Big hazel eyes and pale skin. She is long-legged and a tireless walker. She is a singer of songs and a knower of poems. She carries three camera bodies, five lenses, and a fannypack with film, flash, batteries, notebooks, water bottles. She is uncomplaining. She is cheerful, an optimist, and a very hard worker. She has a great laugh (contralto whoop). Ditto her sense of humor. She is a shy woman with no known affinity for the racing of cars. She wears mostly jeans, T-shirts, and sneakers. The sunglasses balanced on top of her head double as a stylish hair holder. She is 30 years old as I write this.

Me? 45 years old. (Cad!) I met the Beep in grad school. I am 6 feet even, 195 pounds, rapidly softening. My eyes are blue, set against a freckled, moderate complexion. I favor jeans, work boots, and button-down shirts with the sleeves rolled up. Thus clad, I look poised for activity, and yet am rarely active. I spent a long career as a professional sarcast. I am very proud now to make a living writing. I often write about sports.

The truth, though, is that I'm less interested in sports for their own sake than as a compact theater of human experience. It is the perfect postmodern laboratory of the human comedy, a hothouse for everything noble or squalid in our character. I'm fascinated by the nature of our recreational struggles, by our persistence in the face of recurrent failure, and by our uncolored joy on the occasion of rare triumph. I pay attention to what people do, not what they say. Especially professional athletes.

I can neither sing nor retrieve long-form poetry from storage. I enjoy hockey, meatloaf, and classical music. To my credit, I quit smoking not long ago. To my shame, I am still chewing the horrible, horrible gum.

A moment of full disclosure: A long time ago I used to love auto racing very much. Then I went through puberty. I didn't think often of racing thereafter.

The schedule for the next week includes practices at the track, qualifying, the Twin 125s (whatever those might be), a Busch race, a truck race, further, other races the nature of which remain a mystery to me (info forthcoming), and then, on Sunday, the 500. Question: If it's the signature event of the year, why hold it first? The entire season is a footnote to Daytona. It's like playing the Super Bowl and then working your way back to training camp.

The good news is that our parking spot in the campground is excellent. The bad news is that it's perhaps a mile, a mile and a half from our workplace at the infield Media Center. It's a long, hot trudge on foot with the laptop and our other gear. Note: The racetrack looks mighty small in your officially licensed NASCAR atlas. In point of fact, it is not.

We walked into the track for the first time this morning. About twenty minutes, moho to tunnel mouth—time enough to break a healthy sweat. The security's tight. A gate attendant looks at your picture, looks at your face, looks at your picture, looks at your face. Repeats. Then the cursory bag check. Then you're waved on.

Enter through the tunnel under turn 4. It is low-ceilinged down there, cool and dark and damp as a root cellar.

You exit the tunnel into the impossible dazzle of the Florida sun and that dramatic vault of untroubled sky. Shock. Awe. Where even to look? The track banking is mountainous above you. The whole distended bowl is a study in perspective and passive-solar heat retention. No cars on the track, but you can hear a few howling high and hard in the garages you can't yet see. A year ago, a few hundred yards from here, just there, to the left, Dale Earnhardt was killed.

A handful of early fan motorhomes are parked in the infield. The racers' motorhomes, of course, are already here, their homes away from home, parked in their gated, manicured compound near the garages. These are the $1 million-plus Featherlite conversions, 50-footers, Prevosts with 20 coats of candy-apple lacquer and matching trailers and toads (towed cars—I overheard that this morning). There aren't many fans out yet. The concession stands are just opening. Turkey legs, burgers, the usual state fair stuff. There are golf carts whizzing every-where, and electric urban X-vehicles, scooters, minibikes, and electro-moto-skateboards. All of which are driven or ridden very brusquely by officious types with two-way radios and monstrously complex credential sets. Their subliminal message: Walking is for suckers. Point taken.

Made it to the Media Center. Two more checkpoints. Face. Pic-ture. Bag check. Face. Picture. Bag check. Everyone very pleasant. "Have a great day," etc.

The main Media Center is brand-new, a gleaming bunker in the low Bauhaus/high Formica style. TV monitors hung everywhere.

Oops. I was just told my seat assignment's in the little rabbit hutch across the way. (Beat reporters get the seats in Mission Control. The Beep and I are late entries, here to gather "literary color." Literary color sits across the street.) The security guard is pleasant, but firm. "Have a nice day." Just don't have it here.

The smaller building is the original press center. Tiny, it now holds the "overflow," which is us, all the website reporters, all the other pho-tographers, and the foreign press—so far represented in its entirety by a young, pretty, terrified woman from Japan. The room is low-slung, loud, crowded. There are cigarette burns on every horizontal surface; a reminder of the golden, Viking mead-hall days of motor sports writ-ing. Breathtakingly expensive pro photo gear is piled everywhere. The help desk is run by helpful Kate and Betty and Bill. I set up camp in a corner and immediately take several elbows and telephoto lenses to the head. I receive pleasant, hurried apologies in our cramped new quarters. Suddenly despondent, I walk to the desk and ask Kate (or maybe Betty; both are sweet, grandmotherly) when the fans will start arriving in earnest for next Sunday's race. "Today, probably," she laughs, "and tomorrow for sure. They'll be rolling in twenty-four hours a day the whole week." She shows me on a map how to get up to the press box on top of the grandstand. She smiles. This makes me feel better. It looks like she knows her way around an apple pie, too.

I wander up to the press box atop the grandstands, the race-day vantage for a lot of reporters. It's a long trip uphill. Twenty minutes. I break another healthy sweat, but the payoff is an incredible view. It's a great perch for the biggest race on the calendar, with nifty workstations at which to write lyrical, masterly race reports. Or at least figure out who's driving what for whom. Curious, the guard rechecks my credential. No assigned seat in here, either. "Have a nice day." I descend to the garage to take more notes.

Before the real crowds, the locust crowds, of fans arrive, the garage area is strictly Triumph of the Machines.

Titanic haulers parked like they've been laid out with a T square and a laser level all around the perimeter of the garages. The haulers are the semi trucks that bring the cars and the team equipment to the racetrack. Seventy-six feet tip to tailgate, the immense 53-foot trailer box holds two complete cars (primary and backup), three spare engines, a dozen spare transmissions and rear-end gears, shock absorbers, springs, thousands of spare parts of every kind, a car's worth of replacement body panels, tools, tool kits, toolboxes, pit boxes, generators, compressors, computers, radios, satellite dishes, uniforms, kitchen equipment, food, luggage and a hundred other sundries. The cars ride in the overhead loft. The hallway below runs between the hundreds of cabinets necessary for the squared-away storage of the aforementioned gear. Sliding glass doors to enter. The jackscrew lift gate at the rear doubles as car elevator and cabana-style roof. The lounge in the front of the trailer, a 10-foot by 8-foot multipurpose workstation cum meeting space, is usually fitted with a desk, a black pleather sectional sofa, some charcoal industrial carpet and a mirrored wall—in the manner of a chiropractor's waiting area at a Milwaukee shopping mall. Or the set of an '80s porn film.

The paint jobs on the haulers are nearly identical to those on the racecars. They're like the calliope in a circus parade, colorful, cheerful, immense, irresistible. They're also indescribably clean. Spotless. Literally. Someone must polish them with Windex or Pledge. Then buff, buff, buff with a cloth diaper.

Charmed, I watch one hauler driver running an upright vacuum over the Astrocarpet beneath the patio roof/lift gate at the entrance to his trailer. It is a scene of perfect domestic tranquility. Above his head, the racecar.

Racecar. Say it fast, one word, racecar, a grade-school palindrome swollen with a hundred epic meanings and ringing with the sound of money and glory and fame. One word running the high line, living the high life, tolling death by fire, by impact, by misadventure.

Racecar.

Roaring, screaming, snarling id, howling nightmare thrill-killer, holy lifetime love machine, lumbering golem, hungering junkie. Backbreaker, ballbreaker, recordbreaker. Death sled as fragile and bright as a butterfly wing.

The cars are just cars. Always referred to by literalist crews, drivers, owners simply as "racecar" or "the car" or "car." No diminutives, nicknames or terms of endearment. Car. Racecar.

"We had a real fine racecar today."

No simile, no metaphor, no affection, no embellishment. Until the car fucks up, overheats, breaks, spins, crashes, loses. Then: "That car wasn't nothin' but a damn hot rod."

Racecar. Purpose-built and handmade, they are in no way stock. They are based, in theory and in language, on practical, anti-sexy sedans popular with the diehard buy-American American public.

Taurus, Monte Carlo, Intrepid, Grand Prix. The sheet metal panels for the hood, the roof, the rear deck (trunk lid) must match the dimensions and specifications of the stock model. Engineering research, and the engine block, come from the affiliated manufacturer. That's it. Those are the vestigial remnants of the "strictly stock" concept.

Ford, Chevy, Dodge, Pontiac. 3,400 pounds maximum; 200.7 inches long, 72.5 inches wide, 51 inches high. Wheelbase 110 inches; 358 cubic inch, single-carb, cast-iron Methuselah V-8 making plus or minus 775 horsepower at 9,000 rpm. 550 ft/lbs of torque. Ladder frame made of box-section tubing, with built-in roll cage.

Suspension, chassis, engine all infinitely, endlessly, infuriatingly adjustable.

Runs on 110-octane gasoline, but the car is truly fueled by money.

Cost of new chassis: plus or minus $150,000.

Cost of new engine: plus or minus $50,000.

The big-money teams have stables of cars for each driver. They have an arsenal of primary and backup cars specially built and dialed in for the superduperspeedways or the short tracks or the road courses or the mile-and-a-half ovals. As many as 15 or 16 cars per driver.

The mid-money teams might top out below a dozen cars, doubling up their short-track and road-course cars, or trying to run their mile-and-a-half cars at the superspeedways.

The no-money, shoestring teams try to find a soft-touch, one-shot sponsor, then buy a single, hard-used racecar from a more successful team. They have no backup car. They try extra hard not to crash in practice.

Paint schemes vary from car to car, sponsor to sponsor, but the basecoat palette is usually black or red or midnight blue, hunter green or bumblebee yellow, hi-ho silver or refrigerator white. The trim and number colors run to black, white, or wild; emergency orange, hazard green, neon red, second-degree pink, threat-level amber. The interiors are most often high-gloss gunmetal, eggshell, or cream.

All the cars are covered in corporate signage, but every car would look better without it. Slicker, racier. Whatever happened to racing stripes? Another big clean canvas squandered on product placement, and another lost opportunity for American art. Still, somebody's got to pay for all this mech, all this tech. The hood, roof, and rear quarter panels are generally reserved for the signage of the primary sponsor. The associate sponsor usually gets the rear deck, the rear spoiler, the rear roll pan, or the front air dam. Little stickers for the million and one contingency awards swarm the fenders and the roof pillars.

Cost of primary sponsorship per season: $5 million to $15 million and up.

Cost of associate sponsorship per season: $1 million to $5 million and up.

Contingency stickers usually ride in trade for equipment used, but pay out a bonus if the driver finishes in the money. E.g., the piston manufacturer pays a $5,000 bonus to the winning racer for using its pistons and running its sticker.

The cars are lined up in the garage stalls like thoroughbreds. Instead of a feedbag, the car noses into a walk-in toolbox.

Walking back and forth and back and forth from the hauler to the car, from the car to the hauler, are the crews. The crews are responsible for the care and feeding, prep and tuning, of the car while at the track. They handle the pit stops during the race, of course. The crew is to the car as the worker bee is to the helpless queen, or the personal assistant is to the Hollywood studio head.

Most crew members are also employed at the team headquarters shop during the week, fabricating or assembling or painting the cars.

Diversity check: The eyeball ratio of men to women on Cup crews is about 25 to 1. The unscientific eyeball ratio of white to Black/Latin/Asian/all others, 100 to 1. And don't expect to see "NASCAR Eye for the Openly Queer Guy" anytime soon.

Crew sizes vary—a function, like everything in this world, of money. Big-money teams may have 25 highly trained race veterans flown into the track on a private jet to service one car. The mid-money teams, flying commercial, 15. Field-fillers, back-markers, and the hardscrabblers, maybe 5, all arriving in the hauler, including the driver's best friend and his well-meaning but mechanically inept cousin—and perhaps the useless, sullen teenage son of the low-rent (udder unguent, bingo parlor) one-shot sponsor.

Crews are clad in corporate colors, usually a short-sleeved cotton-poly logo shirt with black pants. No glam, they could be the day shift at the local brake-and-muffler franchise. On race day, though, the pit crews wear iridescent, fire-retardant one-piece suits. Fantastically sexy on the right body type, per passing female fans ("Look at *that!*") but not so much on fat guys (*"Look* at that.").

Pit crews aren't necessarily the same as car crews. Specialists everywhere now. Over-the-wall crew—front-tire carrier, jackman, gas overflow catch-can guy, et al—are most often engine builders back at the shop, or hauler drivers, or sheet metal fabricators during the week. Others might be a personal trainer at the local gym, or a junior high athletic coach, or a catch-can-gifted food-and-beverage manager.

Crews are on the road a minimum of 36 weeks a year, with a 50-hour workweek at the shop and a 40-hour workweek at the track. Plus travel time. Big-money crew members can earn over $100,000 a year. Mid-money crews, $30,000 to $100,000. Shoestring crew reimbursed in expired unguent and bingo markers.

Quick hierarchical breakdown: The team owner (sometimes "car owner") is financially and organizationally responsible for the operation of the racing team. Employs driver, crew, crew chief, car chief, et al. The owner solicits the sponsorship to cover the costs of operations, but owns the car (natch) and runs the day-to-day racing effort. E.g., the "Budweiser car" is not owned or operated by Budweiser. The sponsor simply pays the fee and then realizes the advertising benefits of a weekly appearance on the race broadcast, the affiliation with an exciting proto-American sport, and the marketing opportunities associated with the heroic/charismatic/telegenic driver.

Sponsorship fees and operating costs are usually a break-even proposition. A top-tier, competitive Cup car will burn through $15 million a season. Top dollar from primary sponsorship, plus or minus $15 million a season. A wash. Additional revenue from associate sponsorships is plowed back into making the car *more* competitive. It is a paradoxical double-bind—you can't run fast without the money pump of a big sponsorship and you can't get a big-money sponsorship without priming the pump by running fast.

Successful big-money team owners generally rely on a secondary revenue stream to supplement their racing operations. A chain of auto dealerships, an automotive engineering business, etc. Run right, the whole shebang might even show a profit come year's end. Mid-money teams are a dollar or two on either side of breaking even. No-money teams become owe-money teams every time they turn a wheel.

The prize money is some consolation. The biggest purses are well in excess of $10 million dollars, disbursed across the 43-car field. Owners split with drivers. The driver cut varies, from 0 percent (not uncommon—the driver takes a flat salary) to 40 percent (rare) of prize money. Owners, drivers, and crews also share in the huge points fund money distributed at the end of the season.

For the purposes of the season championship, the racers (and the owners) accumulate points across the entire year based on their finishing position in each race.

First place = 175 points

down to

Forty-third place = 34 points

Bonus points are awarded for leading laps and for leading the most laps. The team with the most points at the end of the season wins the championship. Simple. The points fund, anted up by the series' sponsors, is immense. Winning the season championship is currently good for a giant novelty check in an amount over $4,000,000.

Time to find the Beep and make the long walk back. We are cooking, as opposed to unboxing and reheating, our first real meal in the motorhome tonight. Rice and beans. Olé!

Here at Daytona, and for most of the rest of the year, we'll be dry camping. Unhooked, unplugged. Off the grid. We have 55 gallons of fresh water on board in a tank below our portside sofa. Two holding tanks of roughly 30 gallons each for the storage of same once it's been used. One is for "gray water", i.e., shower runoff, dishwater, etc. The other, the waste tank for the toilet flushings, betraying both the sense and spirit of the old Doobie Brothers tune, is for "Black Water."

We have solar panels on the roof and great big onboard batteries and a gasoline-powered generator for electricity. We have propane to fuel the furnace and the water heater and the stove and the refrigerator. We have a satellite dish and a standard TV antenna and a TV and a VCR. There are elaborate control panels in our kitchen and in our living room for the management of all these systems. We are as self-sufficient as cosmonauts.

Our thousand-plus neighbors in all those other motorhomes and campers and schoolbus conversions have variants of these same systems, some more complex, some less so. A few of the million-dollar 50-footers (just like the ones the drivers use) could last for months without resupply; some families in their tiny mesh-and-canvas pop-up tent campers are going to have to haul water every day and perform their morning *toilette* at the closest Portosan. According to my calculations (based entirely on conjecture and a close reading of *Mutiny on the Bounty*), we'll have not quite enough water to get us through our time here even if we conserve.

We're all camping out here on what appears to be the racetrack drainage plain, a flat grass field crisscrossed with flood-control ditches. We were lucky we arrived when we did—we were able to score a view lot next to one of these canals. The arroyos are dry for the moment, but if a hard tropical rain comes, we might be in trouble. It's worth the risk, though, because the space we grabbed, the NASCAR equivalent of a cliffside lot on the Kona coast, allows no one to park on either side or behind us. Picturesque real estate this good is a rare thing out here from what I can see, where the mohos are sardined in at about an awning's width apart, 5 or 6 feet, row upon row upon row, as far as the eye can see.

This kind of camping is the antithesis of the high-concept private parkland back in that quiet Fort Wilderness–themed fantasy glade. This is a city made of fiberglass, a two-week good-time boomtown dense with sprawl and loud with living. By some estimates, come race day, inside the track and out, there will be more than 10,000 motorhomes here. The generators and the boomboxes start when the sun comes up and don't get dialed down again until long after midnight. Mardi Gras, NASCAR style. Party Gras. There is something extraordinary about tailgating two weeks before the actual target event that puts even the lunatic, 40-degrees-below-zero, bratwurst-and-kielbasa diehards at Lambeau Field, the platinum standard for such things, to shame. "We've been out here since last night," they'll shout on a Sunday morning in December, the words billowing steam, their voices thick with PBR and Leinenkugel's. Here they'll shout at you over the noise of their 4-stroke, 10-horsepower margarita makers, "We've been out here since January!"

At all hours there are people walking the narrow lanes between the motorhomes, or riding scooters, or driving the cars they towed down here behind them. There's a refreshing egalitarianism to the place, too, the 24-karat Daddy Warbucks coaches looming up next to the meanest Okie truckbed Pop-Tents, the juxtaposition of the one and the other like a photo layout for "Lifestyles of the Grapes of Wrath," everybody in this thing together, whatever this thing is.

That'll take some time to figure out. But we're here.

Scrambled eggs for dinner. Excellent. I even had enough energy to make some notes in the dinette when we were done cleaning up.

The Daytona track opened in 1959. It's a two-and-a-half-mile tri-oval, banked 31 degrees in the turns, and it is incredibly fast. It was built by Bill France Sr. to succeed the site of the ancient beach race. It is the first "jewel in the crown" (quoting from media guide) of the International Speedway Corporation, the publicly held, France-run companion company to privately held NASCAR. ISC owns or co-owns 12 racetracks. The gross receipts last year for ISC were in the (no doubt gated) neighborhood of $500 million. For NASCAR? Those numbers are unknown to anyone but the accounting gods and the France family, but they may be well north of $1 billion. The France family also controls Americrown, the trackside concessions and services arm of ISC, and radio's MRN, the Motor Racing Network. A crowning achievement in vertical integration, perhaps?

10 P.M. And so, to bed.

10:05 P.M. Nearest neighbor begins Lynyrd Skynyrd marathon.

1:30 A.M. Last replay of "Free Bird" (studio version). Sleep.

We took a cab out past Pasha's Middle East Food and the Bikers Depot and Tobacco Exotica and Bethune-Cookman College to the famous beach today. The fine, light, hard-pack sands streaked with quartzite gray and mica black shimmer in the sun. It's a beautiful day. There's a short parade of cars on the beach, slow cruising; up and down the strand are families on blankets, couples walking, kids tossing Frisbees. And people standing in the churn of the surf yelling into their cell phones, "I'm standing in the ocean!"

From the T-shirts and the beach towels it looks like a 50-50 split between NASCAR fans and generic winter vacationers. The fans are almost always identifiable by the souvenir gear they wear. Honest question: When fans choose to wear the cap or jacket or shirt of a certain Cup driver or team, are the fans trying to say something about the driver? Or something about themselves?

There's an amusement pier with a restaurant and a tourist chair lift and an immobile space-needle ride. Up on the boardwalk are more restaurants and bars, and temporary fan attractions set up by Ford, Dodge, et al, with a couple of live bands hacking away at classic covers in the empty beer gardens and on the desolate patios. The big Speedweeks crowds won't wash ashore until evening. Still, you can hear the misfiring drum solos half a mile away. Planes fly past the beach just offshore, towing banner adverts for AOL, for shrimp dinners, for Gallagher. The Spring Break sensibility overwhelms any resonance of record-seeking leather-helmet speed demons long gone.

The Beep, clad in her sturdy but beguiling swimsuit, stands under one of the public beach showers. For quite some time. Our H_2O conservation strategy this hot week has, I think, been tough, but evenhanded. Perhaps not. "Ready to go, Captain Bligh?" she asks with a smile as she towels her hair.

We wander into town, over to the Daytona 2000 store. Store names with built-in historic dates represent only an opportunity for regret, it seems to me.

The place is filled from floor to ceiling with NASCAR-licensed souvenir merchandise and is abustle with the buying of same. Partial inventory: hats, caps, sunglasses, shot glasses, drinking glasses, postcards, flags, banners, pennants, placemats, plates, license plates, license plate frames, picture frames, lawn ornaments, porcelains, T-shirts, sports shirts, dress shirts, sweatshirts, sweat socks, Christmas stockings, twill jackets, leather jackets, satin jackets, ponchos, seat cushions, beer cozies, umbrella stands, umbrellas, swizzle sticks, pocketknives, money clips, hair clips, neckties, lunch boxes, key rings, refrigerator magnets, belt buckles, CD wallets, and 1/4-scale renderings of your favorite drivers' racecar hood ("for wall or tabletop"). Every item available in a range of colors and numbers representing the most popular teams and drivers.

There are elaborate glass cabinets packed with diecast collectible cars, in all the popular sizes (1/18-, 1/24-, 1/64-scale) and every conceivable paint scheme ever run by any team at any track on any date in the entire history of racing. In showroom version, or race-run version. At the moment they're selling decidedly better than crack-batter hotcakes, even at $99.99 a pop.

Back on the street we make our way up to 140 Atlantic Avenue, where the second Sinai rises into the world of man in the form of the

Streamline Hotel. Here it was that those tabs and tablets were handed down so long ago.

The Streamline's best days are behind it, certainly, but for $89 a night you can check yourself in and listen to all that history, with its whiskey-and-cigar breath whispering down the halls. The art moderne, four-porthole front it shows the street is done in rose and aqua and cream, but the colors have all wilted in the sun and the heat, and the place has an air of tropical exhaustion about it. Still, it is a stately old boat and deserves a marker, if not in the National Register of Historic Places, at least in the hearts of the fans.

It's late in the day. Clad as we are in our casual Capri wear, and depleted from last night's Free Ride, we decide not to go in, but resolve to return and explore the noble wreck properly when we come back here for the second Daytona date, in July.

From the cab back to track, it's plain that race week is now fully engaged. NASCAR "show" cars (retired racecars) are parked in all the major commercial parking lots in town, the Winn-Dixie, the IHOP and Best Western and Volusia Mall, etc. Huge Pepsi promo trucks are parked for deafening merchandise giveaways nearby. The traffic lock from beach to speedway is bumper to bumper to bumper, ad infinitum.

The long trip affords a rare opportunity to check out a street-legal replicar. These are not to be confused with show cars, which are used by companies involved in racing to advertise their goods and services. Rather, these are family sedans painted to *look* like racecars, which are then driven by private citizens to advertise their obsessions and fixations. Spent a few minutes idling next to a Pontiac Grand Prix painted up to look exactly like Bobby Labonte's #18 Interstate Battery racecar.

The #18 paint scheme is chromatically alarming even by NASCAR standards, so it attracted plenty of attention. But when people honked or yelled or waved at the Munster-green replica, the driver didn't wave or smile or return a thumbs-up. He just sat.

But he didn't shrink down in the seat, either, or shrug with a grin when people whistled or hollered ("Go, Bobby!"). In fact you got the feeling that this was the car he drove every day, and that he was on his way home from work like anyone else.

I'm not sure why, or even if, this bothers me. A 1/64-scale replica seems to me one thing, though, and 1 to 1 entirely another.

Are there more like him out there? How many? Do they bang fenders on the way to church, try to take the air off one another on that run to the dry cleaner's?

But he's a fan and he's entitled to his self-expression, whatever form it takes. And I understand what it means to be a fan. I love hockey. No more or less eccentric in its way than Cup racing, certainly. I play, I watch, I go to as many games a year as I can afford. I have favorite teams and players, and I own a couple of souvenir hats and jerseys. Go Leafs!

Still, I wouldn't drive the goddamned Zamboni to work.

The line snakes around the building, folding back again and again on itself. A labyrinth traced by sagging lengths of yellow police tape winds through the spears of palmetto and twists across the white-hot decorative gravel, then threads back between some leafless, blasted saplings before wandering all the way out past the molten parking lot until it turns again, back up the alley, hundreds of feet, into the last little rectangle of lifesaving shade left anywhere in Daytona, Florida, where it loops the Dumpster twice and finally meanders, unmercifully, back out into that terrifying supertropical sunshine and then along the malarial drainage ditch that parallels International Speedway Boulevard. There are hundreds of people in the line. The line does not move. The line only gets longer.

At the racetrack across the street practice is still running wide open and the whole blinding afternoon buzzes like a hive. Over there, the line moves at 185 mph. From the pedestrian footbridge, fans leaving the track notice the sunstruck crowd surrounding the Barnes & Noble.

"Looks like Disneyland from up here, don't it?"

"Those people look baked."

"Those poor folks look like they been *clubbed*."

"What time's he comin'?"

"I don't know what time he starts, but I know he's gonna have a writer's cramp by the time he's done."

And at nearly that moment Dale Earnhardt Jr. ducks out of a bone-stock, slate-gray SUV and into the side door of the bookstore. He has come here to sign books. Many, many books.

It is 51 weeks to the day, almost to the hour, since his father was killed, not quite half a mile from here, in the last turn on the last lap of last year's Daytona 500.

It is a long time gone and he is mended now and it is safe for him to be here; or it is an excruciation, an aching, heartbreaking effort. No one who is allowed, at last, to walk up for his swooping lasso of a signature can tell which. The weight of that name, the noise in his head, the surge and ebb in his chest are none of their business. He is unfailingly pleasant and polite with everyone.

He wears a red polo shirt and baggy khaki shorts and a red B (as in Budweiser) baseball cap clocked around aft in the trademark manner. A lefty, he is pale and slender with sharp features and a quick, thin smile that seems to flicker out the moment he isn't paying attention to it. "Good to see you," he says quietly to each of them as they arrive at his table. "GOOD TO SEE YOU!" they shout or shriek or sob in return, unable to modulate themselves a moment longer.

The first fan in line, Charles Long, 27, of Winter Springs, Florida, has been here since 4 A.M. because, he says, "Junior is a regular guy. Just like me. Who drinks beer. Just like me." He hoots and whoops and pumps his fists and jumps up and down when his two copies of *Driver #8* are signed. He is then overrun and subdued for comment by a squad of beautifully groomed local television reporters.

For hours the others will shuffle forward, the mother-and-daughter teams in from Ohio, the glowering bachelors out of Tennessee, entire tomato-red families down from Jersey. Silent 60-year-old shirtless fat men in straw hats and coveralls, quivering 14-year-old girls blow-molded into their black spandex crop tops, husbands and wives in matching pictographic Dale Jr. T-shirts—everyone has a copy of the book, two copies, three, nine, to be signed. "No other merchandise," shout the book people, "will be signed!" Cameras flash, teenage girls flirt or stare or tremble in their weeping, cops roll their eyes, the line inches forward, people scale the Art & Architecture shelves for a better look.

"Junior!" they shout, "Hey, Junior!" until one no-longer-young woman climbs up the wedding planners display to croon, "Hel-looooooooooooo, Sexy!" and everybody breaks up. The thin smile flickers. This is how the book about #8—the son of #3—made it to #4 on the *New York Times* bestseller list.

A mother guides her son toward the table. He is a little boy, maybe 9, 10 years old. "Hey, buddy," says Dale Jr. softly. The boy doesn't say anything, nor does he have a book, and he freezes for a second, unsure what to do. His mother nudges him gently from behind. "Go ahead," she says. Expressionless, the boy hands Dale Jr. a picture he's drawn. It is a smudged pencil rendering of Earnhardt's #8 Budweiser car, complete with cartoon speed lines trailing off the roof and rear spoiler. It is neither precociously good nor unimaginably bad. Earnhardt accepts it and says, "Thank you, buddy." Someone turns the boy around and his mother says "Smile," but he doesn't and then the flash explodes blue and white and impossibly cold and the two of them, man and boy, are frozen together for an instant.

Next to the dais at which he sits is a small wicker basket into which the many gifts brought here by his fans will be placed. He takes the gifts graciously and thanks each fan and then hands the gifts to his publicist, who puts them in the basket. In it with the boy's drawing there are Teddy bears and greeting cards and rabbits' feet and jars of homemade jam.

I'm not sure I understand our impulse to give gifts to the stars we admire, but it's a gesture I've seen many times across many fields. Our stars and mediated heroes are richer by far than we are, and more powerful and better looking, and they seem to inhabit a faraway world of unimaginable privilege and ease. What do they need with our little bits of paper and string?

A cynic might look and see the sad obeisances of celebrity worship or a line of supplicants waiting to tithe their kings. At its simplest, though, it's probably no more than a way of saying thank you, a polite bread-and-butter gift for having brought some joy or laughter or awe into our lives. Or to further personalize ourselves and our admiration. Or maybe it's a way to say "I like you, and here's a reason for liking me back."

I like to think, especially with athletes, that by giving them these small tokens we're giving them a part of ourselves to take back to their rarefied world of what we hope is honorable competition and clear-cut outcomes. Carry us with you, we're saying, and do us proud. Remember us. Make us better.

Professional racers often refer to Cup racing as "The Show." "If he doesn't get his foot in it, he won't make The Show" is a common construction you'll hear during qualifying. The Show means the big Sunday race, the big noise, the big money, the big crowd. The big leagues.

While clearly a borrow from baseball, where the phrase originated generations ago to describe the major leagues, such openly theatrical shorthand better suits Cup's rumbling, tumbling tent circus. For decades, long before and after Bill France Sr. turned the key to start NASCAR, minor-league baseball players were a southern export crop on the order of tobacco, cotton, and rice.

NASCAR runs something like 2,200 races a year at 135 tracks across the United States. There's still lots of small-town action out there in America, and the Cup series remains the brass ring. The Busch series and the Truck series represent the AAA and AA minors, respectively. That young southern ballplayers and young southern racers shared the language of ambition makes perfect sense. "Man, I *gotta* make The Show."

And The Show must go on—and on and on and on. The second

Speedweek is a blur of qualifying and practice and more practice and further practice and bonus practice and extra qualifying. Cup cars on the track, Busch series cars on the track, Craftsman Truck Series trucks on the track. Endless. After a few days you almost stop noticing the noise. What you notice is the instantaneous silence when somebody crashes. It's like flipping a switch.

Practice looks like a race, but isn't. When the cars practice, they're running laps at race speeds to check the settings and adjustments on the car. The drivers are out there to get a feel for the best suspension setup, to trial-and-error the most efficient gear sets, to get a sense of how the car handles in traffic and how it changes from lap to lap to lap. The cars and their infinite settings are all dynamic, and the handling degrades or improves as the tires wear and the fuel burns away.

The fans don't take much notice of practice, the stands are nearly empty most days, the roar of the cars echoing off the seats, but I watch the speed parade with great fascination, trying to find meaning in it.

Smoking the tires, famous names and familiar logos accelerate hard out of the pits to join the rehearsal. Earnhardt, Gordon, Stewart; Bud, DuPont, Home Depot; 8, 24, 20. Names and numbers and paint schemes and trademarks. A faceless sport, happily inhuman. Out on the track, strung out like junkies, 40 more cars hurtle past in a blur. Five minutes later Gordon returns. In six minutes, it's Stewart. Then Earnhardt, his red car ranting and fulminating, sweeps across the garage apron, seven minutes out and back.

All the cars in the field are on and off the track during a practice session, and in and out of the garages constantly so the crews can make minor adjustments and perform further diabolical experiments. The coming and going feels incredibly chaotic, but out on the track the drivers are on their best behavior. They lap in large packs or all alone, trying to sort out their cars and each other, but doing their best to tiptoe around one another and not race, or worse yet, crash. At 200 miles an hour, even careful practice has a sense of urgency about it, and that line of cars still cracks like a whip coming out of every turn.

The last practice every week is called, not unironically, "Happy Hour."

Qualifying is the process whereby they set the field for the race, in which cars and drivers take to the track one by one to post their best lap times. The driver with the best time (often called "first quick" by announcers) is assigned to the pole position, at the front of the field on the inside. The rest of the qualifiers work their way back accordingly, in two rows, until the field is filled. Some of the positions at the tail of the grid are reserved for "provisional" qualifiers, the strange calculus whereby cars are entered in the race based on the number of points they've earned over the season. This allows drivers to chunk a lap or two and still make the race. It also helps ensure a full field.

For the rest of the season qualifying will be a pretty straightforward proposition, a couple of hours on a single afternoon, but here at Daytona they complicate things up just a little to get some midweek fannies in the $100 seats. Hence the Twin 125s.

From what I was able to follow this week, which wasn't much, only the top two qualifiers from actual qualifying qualify for the front row of the 500. Okay. Subsequent positions are set by relative performance in the pair of 125-mile races held Thursday called the Twin 125s. Okay. Referred to by a NASCAR apparatchik in one press briefing as "the biggest midweek sporting event in, well, I guess, sports." Okay.

Standing behind the haulers, I heard a lovely little phrase as it skittered along the wind. "Sunday money." Out here it means race winnings, prize money. In my mind those words seem to glow like gold.

Been hearing the word "racer" all week, too. Thought at first, as you might, that it simply meant "driver." Turns out to be a small word with an astonishing weight.

Racer means more than driver. Racer means the old-school truth. Racer means run what you brung. Racer means engine hoist on the low branch of a live oak. Racer means supper three hours cold on the table. Racer means Not Sufficient Funds to Pay. Racer means never strokin' it. Racer means lead with your chin. Racer means you don't go to funerals, especially your own. Racer means midnight radio out of Memphis, you and Jerry Lee on the long haul home.

It has nothing to do with money or fame. Nothing to do with talent. Nor with personality or popularity or modesty. Not even success or courage. When I hear it being used it seems to have everything to do with whatever constitutes the character at the deepest core of a person in this life, the life at the track. Grit, maybe, clarity of purpose, single-mindedness, willingness to sacrifice, simplicity of motive, stubbornness, strength, guile, sense. Maybe some of those, maybe none. In any case, to be called a racer here, a real racer, is perhaps the highest compliment possible.

A racer can be a driver or an owner, a crew member, a wife, a mother, a daughter, a son. A fan. A journalist. An entire family. Anyone in whom racing resides not as a thing done, but as a way of breathing.

But very few drivers are racers these days, to hear the press box lifers and the backstretch duffers up in the chickenbone seats tell it. A deplorable absence of grit. All Hollywood and soda pop, these kids.

"Mind my French, but shee-it, ain't but one or two boys left out here you couldn't knock down with a hard look. Not many *real* racers left alive anywhere."

FOUR

Daytona Sketchbook Part 2

The Cup garages at Daytona midweek: cars and men and women smelling of fuel and sweat, Old Spice and hot rubber, White Shoulders and solvent and deep fat. Stand here long enough you'll see everything and everybody—the whole fantastic cast of The Show.

Richard Petty is a set of teeth coming at you. Big white teeth. Under big black hat. Ten-gallon big-block bull-rider model in midnight 100X beaver, with a feather fan hatband. Tail-feather plume so large at the crown Sally Rand could've danced behind it. Peacock? Eagle? Dodo?

Sunglasses, black as bandit's mask, nasty, wrapping back past eyes, nose, crow's feet, temporal ligaments, Dentyne-masticating jaw hinges, whirring, clicking brain lobes. Never without sunglasses. *Never*. Incongruous cowboy combo: Level Cross, North Carolina, by way of the OK Corral, Caesars Palace, and the West Boca Cataract Clinic. Polite Methodist mustache, nonthreatening, promising neither Old West saloon bloodbath (Earnhardt/gunfighter mustache) nor lively, sweat-slick bathhouse scrum (Freddie Mercury/stadium rock/gay icon mustache).

Always real skinny-like, he's a stick figure now, whittled thin as a picket. Jeans pressed to a decent Main Street crease. Tall. Cattle baron c'boy boots out of ostrich, python, 'gator, croc, yak leather, mastodon hide, tanned vestal virgin pelts—who knows? Belt buckle on him like Commodore Vanderbilt's best brass platter. Gargantuan fighter-pilot wristwatch, compound/complex nine-dial tachymeter chronograph, milled from a flawless brick of cold-rolled surgical steel, accurate to the nanosecond over every billion years.

White-cream-blue button-up/button-down shirt with logo. Team jacket usually, sponsor, garish: Honey Nut Cheerios or Sprint or absurd one-shot Garfield the Cat; simple Petty Enterprises in red, white, and powder Petty blue.

He has a long, oval face gone jowly and a little hangdog. Except when he smiles—then it's spotlight night at the Steinway showroom. The face is tanned, the skin etched and tooled by the sun. Forearms dark, too, where he's rolled up his shirtsleeves. You conjecture the rest of him pale as skim milk, helpless on the beach, tender as an orchid.

He is the angular figure you see walking the garage apron or the pit road trailing a wake of older fans, nodding, shuffling supplicants; or he stands alone, propped up, lean and neat as a broom, against a toolbox next to one of his cars.

The King.

Everybody calls him The King. And I mean everybody and I mean all the time. The King. Or just King. His employees call him The King. His fans call him The King. His children and his grandchildren call him The King. Presidents and pressmen and the panjandrums down at the local Rotary, part-time axle waxers and junior nut buffers clad in Petty Enterprises coveralls—all call him The King.

"It is always a pleasure to shake hands with a King."

"How they runnin', King?"

"Mr. King? I mean, er, King, I mean, um, Mr. Petty? Could you sign some of these T-shirts for our next silent auction? It's all for the kids? Down in Vidalia?"

"The King come by and told me . . ."

"And then King kindly said to . . ." And so forth.

Nothing like him in any other sport—any other field at all. Not just by dint of his achievements, his records (likely to remain unbroken forever), but because he's *here*. Day in, day out. Still. Maybe the greatest who ever lived and he's perched on a workbench in the garage, chewin' it with the crews. Like having Casals backstage at Carnegie Hall every Friday night on his knees shooting craps with the stagehands; or Nicklaus down at the caddy shack, cleaning sticks with the loopers on tournament weekends. Aaron and Ruth stroking fungoes at practice.

If you don't know anything about anything, you've still heard the name Richard Petty. Biggest name in the sport. The Pettys *are* the sport. Richard, born 1937, won 200 races over 35 seasons, '58 to '92. Next best man, lifetime, has 105. Won seven championships. Racer.

His father, Lee Petty, was the first driver to win three championships, racing from 1949 to 1964. Won 54 races. Lee Petty ran his first NASCAR event at that Charlotte race in '49. Raced in the family car that day. Rolled it. Whole family had to hitch a ride home. Won the first Daytona 500 in '59.

Kyle Petty, Richard's son, Lee's grandson, is the CEO of Petty Enterprises. Runs the whole shebang. He's a racer, too, been driving Cup since 1979, winning eight times.

Adam Petty, Kyle's son, Richard's grandson, Lee's great-grandson, won races from the moment he took a wheel in his hands. Slender and exuberant, gifted with the family knack, with a smooth, open face and his family's wide smile, he was killed in a crash at the track in New Hampshire on May 12, 2000, while testing a car. He was 19.

Lee Petty had died a month earlier, 86 years old, and the bookends to four generations of racers were gone in a single spring, and now in the winter of 2002, nearly two years later, there persists a melancholy around Richard, around Kyle, around their families and their most loyal fans, a halftone of sadness and stillness, solemnity, even when they smile, even in the midst of all this color and noise and absurdity.

Kyle wears his long black hair gathered in a neat ponytail. Goatee. Out of his firesuit, he wears crisp black slacks, dress shoes, and a Petty Enterprises button-down shirt. He has a purposeful walk, and often as not, he talks into a cell phone as he strides past the garages. Modest wristwatch. Looks studious if not scholarly in a pair of wire-rimmed eyeglasses.

When he's worried, standing over the engine bay of a car running dog slow in practice, say, he'll fiddle with the small black scrunchie he uses to hold back his hair. Or he'll twist long hair around his fingers while the tuners grunt and swear under the hood.

Lee Petty drove car #42. Richard drove #43. Kyle drove #44. The car waiting for Adam when he made it to Cup, when he came up to The Show, was to be #45. Kyle drives it now, and has about him in unguarded, off-camera moments the haunted look of a man forced into bankruptcy by the debts of his ancestors. I try to imagine the strength of character, or the weight of tradition, or the devotion to family, that gets him into that car. I try to imagine how crippling and bitter your own history can become.

The second time I saw Dale Earnhardt Jr. I couldn't see him at all. Like certain dark stars he is sometimes detectable only by the incredible gravitational force he exerts on other bodies. He was walking from the team hauler out to his car on pit road. He was surrounded by fans. I caught just a glimpse of that sharp face, that signature goatee, vulpine, and then he was swamped by the crowd. He moved fast and the crowd moved with him, swirling and orbiting, tighter and tighter, and the crowd grew as it jogged across the asphalt, 20 becoming 40 becoming 60 as Junior hustled past the garages. I wasn't even sure it was him until I heard shouts of "Go, Junior!" as the crowd surged by. People were running, flat out sprinting, trying to catch up to that rolling boil of celebrity, trying to aim their cameras as they ran, fans and professional photographers tottering backwards, ricocheting off one another, holding their cameras high over their heads trying to shoot down into the dense center of all that celestial adulation, the red-hot nucleus of all that superatomic love.

Junior is unquestionably the hottest commodity on tour. He's not the best driver yet, or even the best-looking driver, but in a sport full of overheated, undercooked sex symbols, he's the genuine article. In 1999, when he was 25 years old, he drove his first Cup race and the fans have been swooning ever since. When his father was killed, a lot of the fevered devotion and love that had been the elder Earnhardt's was set loose. Some of it was fixed forever in the mourning rituals and eternal passion of the death cult, certainly, in the maintenance and worship of the glorious immortal, but a great deal more of it was simply left to float sizzling in the ether like background radiation until it could be brought to bear on a worthy successor. Junior is the most likely candidate for that, of course, but the fans are demanding of their heroes and want more than just grief-stricken matinee idols. They demand results. It's not enough to be the son of a famous dead racer. Junior's got to prove to them that he's a racer too, a winner, and worthy of their suffocating love.

His win in 2001 at Second Daytona, the July race, first race back at that track since his father had been killed there, was as stirring and cathartic as anything scripted by Sophocles or Spielberg. It was the most satisfying kind of mythological victory, the son rising to avenge the father's death. Trouble was it may have been too perfect, this sunny climax at once too predictable and too unlikely, and it struck some cynical fans and veteran sports reporters that this particular story of vengeance and redemption was being a little too well told. For months thereafter, even when Junior won at Delaware, the first race held after September 11, there were mutterings and grumblings that favoritism may have played a hand in things—that NASCAR was so intent on brightening Junior's star power they allowed his car to slip through inspection without the close scrutiny other drivers might get. "Mechanical advantage" was the phrase. Don't misunderstand, there was never a hint that the fix was in, never an intimation that other drivers were tanking for the sake of the greater good of the sport. What was suggested, in the grandstands and garages and press box alike, was that Dale Earnhardt Jr., unwittingly and without volition, was being allowed to drive a marginally hotter car than anyone else. The community was in mourning, and maybe a tech inspector, only human after all, and wanting so much to help heal all that hurt, might look away at a crucial moment. What Junior might be able do with incrementally better equipment was solely up to him.

So even at the moment he swept past me, inundated by the love of strangers and inciting the kind of fissionable passions rarely seen outside the holiest shrines at Mecca or Jerusalem or Grauman's Chinese Theater, the true measure of his full inheritance was still in doubt.

Nevertheless, the fans pour hope and lust and sugar all over him everywhere he goes. Drives the iconic #8 Budweiser car.

Fans pass in every shape and size and style, batter themselves against the garages and the cars and the drivers and the crews like moths. Officials, dressed in red-and-white Winston Cup uniforms, try to wave them away, keep them back along a safe perimeter around the garage apron, away from the cars.

Large groups of marketing specialists or regional distributors or area franchisees in matching cotton sport shirts follow tour guides bearing signs with corporate logos: Kodak, Lowe's, DuPont. A lot of corporate favors being repaid here, client grease, payback for rising widget sales or that third-quarter uptick in the share price. The guides wear radio transmitters and microphones, and everyone in the group wears a radio scanner and headphones tuned to that same frequency, and as they walk from place to place amid the din, the guide gives a walking audio tour of the madness.

"That's Jeff Gordon's hauler," the guide will say, pointing, as they gather 10 feet away from the thing. And 50 people in corporate polo shirts will smile and nod in unison. Every one of them clutching a slippery plastic bag full of freebies from the corporate hospitality tent.

She'll turn to the right, point another 10 feet. "And that's Tony Stewart's hauler." Half a hundred heads bob up and down.

Struggling to make their way past the tour groups are the friends and families of participants. People with somewhere specific to be, sort of, who look at least half like they know what they're doing or where they're going—or at least walk like they do. They are identifiable by the unusual absence of driver-themed T-shirts, hats, and jackets.

They've been to races before. They're wearing Sunday clothes. A jack-man's mom and his brothers, down from Beloit, a publicist's husband and her sister-in-law in from Atlanta, a driver's mom and dad from Virginia. They'll take a seat at the hauler tailgate once they get where they're headed, mop their faces with a kerchief, sip a Diet Dr Pepper and stare back wide-eyed at the wandering throngs.

Wandering, the dead tip-off of the unaffiliated fan—the fan who got a pass from a friend of a friend of a friend. Wears the gear of her favorite driver: Hat. Check. T-shirt. Check. Jacket. Check. Smiles like a lottery winner whenever asked to present credentials to security guards or gate attendants. Holds plastic sleeve containing passes up at eye level, beaming proudly, behold the mystical ducats.

These are genuine fans, fans here only because they longed to be and somehow found a way to make it happen. No company leverage, no family ties, just the desire to see it all up close and a guy somewhere who knows a guy. They carry binoculars and cameras, souvenir bags, earplugs in pink and orange and blue, portable radio scanners with giant Princess Leia headphones, water bottles, autograph books, marking pens—the whole Daytona 2000 floor inventory, anything their hero might sign. If they see him. If they can get his attention. If they can catch him. So they wander. Looking.

They'll orbit the garages again and again and again. They'll stake out his garage space. If he's not in there, they'll wander back to his hauler. If there's a big crowd there, they may stay, thinking that all those other people must know that he's coming out soon. They'll ask, "Is he coming out soon?" and someone dressed in the same hat and T-shirt and jacket will turn to them and say, "I don't know. I just got here." So they'll wait. Eventually he'll come out. Or at least his publicist or his engine chief or his suspension specialist will come out and shake his head and say, "He's not here." The group will slowly disperse, wander away again, take pictures of other drivers, other cars, each other, return later. They'll be back here every half hour all day.

The sun riveting the heat right down through those hats, they'll wander and return, dehydrated and pale, as long as there's even the slightest chance they'll see their driver.

These are genuine fans, certainly, core fans, but not *hard*-core fans. Not the truest of the true believers. The diehards, the maniacs, the desperate pilgrims are the ones who can't get into the garage area. They don't know anybody, have no juice, no contacts, no help. No credentials.

They can buy an infield ticket, though, and hope. They gather early, 7 or 8 A.M., and wait outside the garage fence by the gate. Maybe they can catch their driver on the way in or the way out. They'll stay here all day. 100? 200? 300? of them depending on the hour. They joke with the guards. They sit on folding stools. They ask you to take pieces of paper in with you when you walk past for their favorite driver to sign, but they aren't disappointed when you say no. They kid about knocking you down and stealing your credentials. They pull sweating cans of Mountain Dew out of tiny cooler bags and wait.

They are a gauntlet. They line both sides of a driver's approach to that gate, and the drivers know that to stop for one is to stop for them all. Their publicists know it too, and will walk in front of the driver, fast, holding up their hands, saying, "Not right now, folks, he's gotta get in the car for practice. Maybe later this afternoon. Thanks!" and the guards will hold up their hands now, too, and say, "Move it back, please, folks, move it back," and inch the crowd back and politely cordon off a path between all those reaching arms, and the publicist and the driver and perhaps his wife or girlfriend will struggle past.

Every day, though, a few drivers stop to sign, and when they do the crowd surges forward and the gauntlet collapses. All those people reaching and leaning, the driver all alone in a forest of arms and faces and hands. "Please!" they shout, "Here, please, sign for me!" and "We love you!" and the arms and the hands reach up, beseeching, over other arms and hands, waving papers and pillowcases and pieces of wrecked cars from bygone seasons.

"Hey, watch it, man! That thing's sharp!"

People elbowing each other aside, unthinking, not rough, but this may be their only chance, children tangled in all those legs, bending to pick up the pens that clatter to the pavement, "Oops! Thanks, sonny!" and the laughter and the jostling and trying to stay polite and not deck somebody, and the crowd packs itself tighter and tighter, and the first ones begin to turn around now and struggle back out of that dense circle of faces, give someone else a chance, they squeeze their way out and walk a few steps, stop, catch some air, look down at that signature and beam, show it to their friends, "Dude! Damn! You got it! Cool!" and then the guards finally start to move the crowd back, "C'mon, folks, back it up now, back it up," and as the crowd splits into two ragged halves again, you can just see the driver jogging away into the garage on the other side of the gate.

People return to their original positions to wait for the next driver. Some of the faces are sullen, some are smiling. "Did you see that?" they'll say to one another. "Did you see that? Wasn't he nice?" they'll say as they rearrange themselves on their stools or smooth their posters, "Is anyone else coming? Do you see anybody else?"

One of them, a man in his early thirties, tall and thin, the length of him strung from tendon and sinew, with a dark face as sharp and hard as a hand ax, will lean down to talk to his wife. She is pregnant. As round and pretty as a new copper teakettle. She is holding a little boy's hand. He is blond, tired, three or four years old. All three are wearing bile-green T-shirts trimmed with black and red. The Interstate Battery color scheme. More Bobby Labonte fans.

"Next time by," he says, smiling, "next time by, hold up the kid. They always sign for kids."

At most big sporting events I can identify other members of the working press simply by what they're wearing. Not the clothes so much (jeans, T-shirts, sneakers; khakis, dress shirts, loafers), or even the perpetual expression of bemused resignation, but the gear: complicated two-way radios, expensive cameras, XXXL photo vests with Velcro epaulets and multiple grenade loops, tape recorders and notebooks, elaborate necklaces of multicolored credentials. Trouble is, everybody out here is loaded down with the same stuff. Many of the fans look like most of the press look like all the off-duty cops look like some of the publicists. Everybody looks like they're on long-term assignment from the *Daily Planet*.

How is that a problem? Access. To NASCAR officials and track security guards, all hard cards look alike. So as you try to ease your way into the garage, hoping to get a good look at what the crews are up to, crib some interesting details of the tuning process (not that you're strictly sure that the gesture in question is interesting or even part of the tuning process, but that's why you have to get in there, to ask those questions), you get shooed away with all the fans.

If you make it past the officials, you've got to deal with the clannishness of the crews and their technical paranoia. Notions of regional hospitality aside, they don't *want* you to see what they're doing.

Teams guard their technical setups closely. Fanatically. Dodge doesn't want Ford to know what it's doing; Roush teams don't want Penske teams to know what they're doing. The way a team makes horsepower or traction is proprietary voodoo out here, and you don't reveal your madstones and incantations to just anyone. So of course everyone's trying to reverse-engineer everyone else's most potent juju. What lifters/rockers/springs are those guys running? How do they set up their front/rear end to gain all that mechanical grip? Where's all that power/mileage/speed coming from? Everyone wants everyone else's magic.

The corollary to all this is that all the teams are running black ops on each other all the time in an effort to police cheating. Or to at least curb cheating. Or to at least steal the best cheats from each other.

I've been told it's not uncommon for teams to send one of their anonymous operatives out in plainclothes to wander the garages with a disposable camera or a notepad, looking for all the world like any other fan, to nose around the other teams and perhaps try to sketch or photograph their supersecret hocus-pocus.

Even espionage has its etiquette, after all, and it wouldn't do to get caught peeping under the skirts of another man's car. So crews pretend not to look at their competitors' bespoke components, and the competitors mostly pretend not to catch them doing so.

All this furtive byplay means that a Cup garage is shot through with sensitivities and intrigues. Strangers are viewed with preemptive suspicion. Never walk to the front of a Cup car unannounced, for example, especially if the hood is up, its tenderest, most intimate parts exposed, and begin staring. Certainly not if you're a stranger—making notes in a notebook.

Crew chief: "Who the hell are you?"

Me: "I'm a repor—"

Crew chief: "Get the hell away from that car!"

Welcome to The Show!

I am unlikely to learn the dark arts of tuning and timing the big steel this go-round. Once everyone gets to know me, they'll warm up, I'm sure. Until then, here are the other stars and supporting players, in no particular order, upon The Show's great stage.

Mike Helton, president of NASCAR. Big man, tall and broad and heavy. Imposing as hell. Moves with a light tread, though, almost graceful, lithe as Gleason back in the day. Big black push-broom mustache, black hair combed straight back off his high forehead. Looks fierce, serious, rarely smiles. Sees everything. *Everything*. Slacks, dress shirt, black leather jacket.

Can't walk 10 feet before someone—crew chief, owner, official, driver, publicist, reporter—stops him to ask a question. Listens intently to everything he's asked. Glowers. Answers. Moves on, nimble and huge.

The publicists. Look for the affable men and women yelling into their cell phones and tip-tapping their Blackberries and shooing away the Make-a-Wish kids simultaneously. Every team has a publicist.

NASCAR has publicists. R. J. Reynolds has publicists. Goodyear has publicists. The car manufacturers each have publicists. The networks have publicists.

NASCAR's Cup racing business model: Let nothing we do or say here today go unpublicized.

The biggest marquee teams—Roush, Penske, DEI, and such—might have three for each *car*: one for the sponsor, one for the driver, one for the team itself. Most teams get by with one or two. Even the no-money teams have somebody's sister working the phones and the angles, trying to get their enterprise noticed.

Demographic split, 50-50 male-female. Most under 40 years old. On call 24/7 to start/quell rumors about their clients. High stress. High psychic flameout rate. Thanks to tiny cell phone headsets, often appear to be responding nonsensically to evil voices in their heads. Often are.

Publicists' koan: "If a tree falls in the forest, and no one is there to hear it—it means my assistant forgot to issue the fucking press release."

The owners. There are 23 listed in the Cup media guide, perhaps half of whom have a legitimate chance at fielding a race winner this year. (Only half that number, a championship.) Their stature/power/influence/bankroll is second only to NASCAR's own on race weekends. Most own multiple cars in other series, as well. The remaining half represent the shade-tree strugglers and low-tech holdovers from the days when it was still possible to fashion a team out of baling wire, tobacco juice, and force of character. Those days will end shortly.

The elite team owners are elusive. I watch them pass, walking quickly, followed by trains of reporters and petitioners. Busy at all times, they are especially so here at the Great American Race. There are all the material and mechanical and strategic worries of the competition side you might expect at the opening of a new season, compounded by the time-consuming backslapping and power-lunching and cocktail hour smoke-blowing required to service their major sponsors, all of whom descend on Daytona in large numbers, anxious to see the heart-stopping, 200-mile-per-hour wheel-to-wheel battle between 43 cross-promotional marketing platforms.

The rainmakers:

Jack Roush, owner, Roush Racing. Looks to field four separate teams this year. Primary sponsorships: DeWalt tools, Viagra, Rubbermaid products, and Citgo lubricants. In any other context those brands might only appear in sequence during a customs search of a Bangkok-bound sex tourist. Here they circle the track as the #17 Ford, the #6, the #97, and the #99.

Highly respected, Roush is compact, 60 years of age, a former community college instructor of math and physics. Sterling record in sports-car racing. Came to Cup in 1988. Fifty victories overall, no championships yet; several heartbreaking misses. Smart. Tough. Still tunes the carburetors on his own racecars. Aviator. Also CEO of Roush Industries, a large automotive engineering company. Omnipresent, distinctive slouch hat provides easy fallback for lazy headline writers: The Cat in the Hat.

Richard Childress. Red-faced, bull-chested proto-owner. Age 57. First made his bones as a driver, but won everlasting fame as the owner of the black #3 Chevrolet. As Dale Earnhardt's car owner and perhaps closest friend, Childress won six Cup championships. In the wake of Earnhardt's death, the #3 was mourned and set aside, but not formally retired. Instead the familiar Mr. Goodwrench car became the #29. Richard Childress Racing will also send out the #30 and the #31 cars, AOL and Cingular wireless, respectively. Childress is a sportsman and a hunter.

Roger Penske. Dapper former racecar driver, now monolithic name in racing and business. Pulls the strings for the #12 Alltel Ford and its stablemate, the #2 Miller Lite car. White-haired, Windsorknotted, and immaculately tailored, Penske looks like the U.S. ambassador to Cary Grant. He made his name in open-wheel cars, both as a driver and an owner. In the latter role, he's an 11-time winner of the CART championship, and an 11-time winner of the Indianapolis 500.

At 65, he now owns interests in everything from trucking to manufacturing. He's even partnered with International Speedway Corp. in the ownership of several racetracks, including Michigan and the 2-mile oval at Fontana, California. With 41 victories, he has yet to win a Cup championship.

Joe Gibbs, Washington Redskins coach. A three-time Super Bowl winner with one Cup championship and 32 wins as the 2002 season opens. Been winning since he showed up in the garage 10 years ago. He fields the #20 Home Depot and #18 Interstate Batteries Pontiacs. Even without his whistle, at 61, he still looks like the fittest man in the room.

Robert Yates. A preacher's kid who builds hellacious engines, Yates is famous for his powerplants. Runs two cars in Cup, for Texaco and UPS, the #28 and the #88 Fords. He's 58 years old, won his championship in 1999, and has 50 wins overall. Yates is an old-school tuner succeeding in NASCAR's age of wretched excess.

A. J. Foyt. I include Foyt on this list not because his single-car team, the #14 Conseco Pontiac, is likely to do well this year, or because he's a powerful owner with many diverse interests who is likely to influence events in pressrooms or boardrooms around the circuit. He's not. What he is, is a bandy-legged, barrel-bellied throwback from the firewater days of American racing. Foyt's mere presence is a punch in the face, an inoculation against milquetoast corporatism. There wasn't a car anywhere anyhow anytime that Foyt wouldn't put the boot to, and there hasn't been the race devised he couldn't win. Neck and neck in the minds of motor sports writers with Mario Andretti for best all-around American driver in history, Foyt hasn't mellowed any with age. Nearly 70, he still has the legendary temper and the mallet fists and the hand-lasted Texas kicks. Don't let him catch you eyeballin' him.

I just saw Foyt's entry go hurtling past on its way to a twelfth-place finish in the second 125 of the day. Unspectacular, but good enough to qualify for a midpack start in this Sunday's big show.

I've been down here on pit road trying to watch this afternoon's qualifying races, but not having much luck. From ground level on a track this size, stuck behind the immense rolling tool kits the crews use, your vantage is restricted. I couldn't see a thing, in other words, except what I could glimpse between the toolboxes as the cars flowed past or on the television monitors the crews have built in to the toolboxes.

Daytona's a "restrictor-plate" track, which means NASCAR insists that every car be equipped with a plate between the carburetor and the intake to strangle some of the fuel and air mixture out of the engine. This limits horsepower and slows the cars down a little —to keep them from getting airborne and flying into the grandstands during a crash, thereby saving countless human lives. The drivers hate it.

Because it also has the unintended effect of leveling the field. The cars wind up more nearly equal with the plates installed, so no one really has the horses to pass anyone else. This effect, combined with the fluid dynamics of drafting, where you tuck your car right in behind the one in front of you to benefit from the hole it's punching through all that heavy air, means that the cars at restrictor-plate tracks tend to orbit the course in long freight trains, one car behind the other behind the other. Pull out to pass and you're hung out to dry—no slipstream and no horsepower. You'll drop 15 places if you figure your move wrong. Or, because the cars are all bunched so tightly, start a terrifying chain reaction accident referred to as the "Big One."

Depending on whether your seat is in the stands or behind the wheel, the Big One is either the most exciting moment in sports or the most terrifying. Or maybe it's both. A mistake measured in inches can send two dozen cars slamming into one another—instantly sideways at 200 mph, a Force-5 cyclone of flayed sheet metal spinning inside angry thunderheads of tire smoke, some cars thrown blind into the wall to explode, some tumbling and taking flight, trailing graceful tails of lethal debris, a few others left to limp off in the sudden quiet of the aftermath and die alone.

So the drivers go around and around and around, fretting the Big One and waiting for the last lap or two to try their move to the front, when maybe they can slingshot past the man ahead of them. Or not.

The whole thing can be fiery carnage. Or it can be quite a yawn, the latter being the case today. Jeff Gordon won the first race pretty much wire-to-wire, towing behind him a tidy laundry line of 26 other cars. Michael Waltrip won the second session, almost as anesthetic as the first, in nearly the same fashion. Waltrip won the main event here in 2001. That he did so as Dale Earnhardt, his car owner, was crashing behind him was perhaps the most poignant moment in the history of this unsentimental sport.

Dale Earnhardt Incorporated will run three cars in The Show again this year, the #1, the #8, and Waltrip's #15. Pennzoil, Bud, and NAPA Auto Parts. When Earnhardt Sr., the Intimidator, was killed last winter, the responsibility for running the company fell to his widow, Teresa. And while she had helped found and operate DEI with her late husband, there are still questions about how the three teams will perform in this, the first full season since his death.

Gordon drives for Rick Hendrick, who won the fifth of his Cup championships last year. Hendrick signs the work orders for the #24 DuPont car, the #5 Kellogg's car, the #48 Lowe's car, and the #25 UAW car, all Chevrolets. He was the technical adviser on *Days of Thunder*. Alternative revenue streams include a national network of automobile dealerships. A former pro baseball prospect, Hendrick also wrung out dragsters and drag boats for laughs when he was young. Risk taker. In fact, took a risk so big in the mid-1990s that he had to plead guilty to a federal charge of mail fraud—for making illegal payments to Honda executives to keep his dealerships furnished with new cars when sales boomed and national supplies dwindled. He received a presidential pardon for having done so in December 2000.

In his early fifties now, Hendrick has paid his dues and his debts twice over. He is gray-haired and pleasant and successful and seems at first glance, perhaps, to have only a dull competitive edge. He does not. He beat leukemia in the late 1990s. He can probably beat you, too.

Details on other owners when we encounter them.

•   •   •

Oh, and the überowner is around here, too, somewhere, but like the Father himself, remains unseen—Bill France Jr., chairman, CEO, and hereditary ringmaster of everything the eye can see.

Pairs of young women, and not-so-young women, women 15 to 50, undulate from hauler to hauler, from garage door to garage door. Almost always pairs, rarely alone, rarely in threes or fours. Uniformly: tan, tight clothes, cleavage, savage heels. Some pretty, some not. Full makeup and lots of hair. Blonde, brunette, the rare redhead. Complicated sunglasses and great white teeth. Pit pass hanging into plunging neckline of 80/20 rayon/silk semi-see-through blouse with slit balloon sleeves and ribbon trim from L'Express, $49.99 on sale last week at nearby Galleria. Paris, France ÷ Paris Hilton = Paris, Texas.

Always looking for something, someone, sweeping their heads from side to side and staring out to the near horizon just beyond your shoulder as they pass. Whatever or whoever it is they're looking for, it isn't you. One always assigned to carry clear plastic bag of trackside souvenirs, and glossy promo card for drivers to sign. Other carries stylish little knockoff purse, tiny gold-tone digital camera, and 1-liter domestic water bottle in sports-club mesh bag designed for same. Both wear clamshell cell phones clipped to waistband of cream linen pants.

Often stop to consult security guards, who smile, nod, then point. The women's sunglasses follow the finger, they smile in return, thank him without looking at him, walk off in that direction. His eyes follow those cream linen pants.

They never seem to have earplugs or headphones. Instead they clap manicured hands to their ears—bracelets, purses, cameras, and bags dangling and swinging from their wrists like Christmas ornaments, as they make sour pouty faces against the explosive noise of the cars running in and out.

Often as not they have to scatter, running on stiletto heels, delicate and prim as shore birds, when the cars come thundering off the track during practice on the way to the garage. They are always halfway to someplace and right in the path of the cars. Officials screaming and blowing their whistles and waving frantically at them seem to have no effect. The women run and jiggle and shrug, and when they reach safety, they make that sour pouty face.

They will make that face again and hang the big glossy lip if Mike Helton sees that they are wearing open-toed shoes or sleeveless shirts. He will ask them, politely but firmly, to leave the garage area, where they should not have been allowed in the first place with unsafe open-toed shoes or sleeveless shirts. He dials down the glower, but he brooks no argument. They stand chastened in his shadow. He does not stare at their pants as they walk toward the gate.

These women, thousands of pairs of them, young or young-seeming, swim through the crowds. They cruise two by two through the pits. They stop only long enough to chat with a crew member or, more rarely, a driver. Otherwise they keep moving. Patrolling. In the taxonomy of NASCAR, they are referred to, at least by the worried wives and mothers of churchgoing male crew members, as Pit Lizards.

Stunning as some of them are, they are not to be confused with starlets or Playboy bunnies or Internet lingerie models, although there are hundreds of those, too. The models and starlets and bunnies are always escorted or accompanied or supervised by some sort of starlet or bunny wrangler. Usually a man in his fifties, graying, stylish, tasseled-loafer type with a vibe halfway between distinguished and dissolute. Agent? Flack? Daddy? He walks with one hand in the small of her back and makes damned sure she isn't wearing any open-toed shoes or jiggling where she shouldn't. In his other hand he holds an envelope of her naked 8-by-10s, or a copy of the latest issue of the magazine or catalog or calendar. These are not Pit Lizards. These are professionals. They are networking.

The Beep and I had to haul water today. The 55 gallons we started with sounds like plenty, but for two biggish people living in a metal box on an equatorial savannah, it's not going to last long. Even showering in the manner prescribed by the strictest navies of the world—

brief rinse, turn water off, lather, brief rinse, turn water off—we didn't make it quite an entire week.

Took a 5-gallon jug over to the nearest community faucet on the other side of the campground to fill and haul back, hoping it would be enough to make it all the way through the race weekend. Long trip.

On the way back to our unit, walking between the rows of motorhomes, we took turns carrying the unwieldy 40-pound jug. I had just heaved the thing over onto the Beep's mighty shoulder when we turned a corner and came upon a five-top of jovial old snappers sitting around their collapsible picnic table. Walking toward them, I could see what was coming 20 feet away.

"Hand it back," I whispered.

"What, honey?" she said.

"Hand the jug back, please," I implored more loudly.

"No, that's okay, I've got it."

"*Please*?" We were just about to pass in front of them.

"Honey, it's heavy, and you already . . ."

Too late. Here it comes.

"You bet it's heavy, man! Good thing you brought the little lady to lend a hand!"

"Brother, you got it *good*! Haw!"

"Man, that's the life, huh?"

"Whyn't help her out there, buddy?"

"That's a man who knows what he's doing."

And we were past them. Neither of us said anything for a few more steps. "Have some fun with that, did you?" I asked.

"Kind of," said the Beep, smiling. "Just remember, brother, you got it *good*."

The first time I see Jeff Gordon in person he is pretending to eat a piece of cake. That he is pretending to eat a piece of cake with an actress and an astronaut should come as no surprise, given the setting.

A press release went around early in the morning notifying the press that at noon, in front of the media center, Jeff Gordon would help the DuPont Corporation, primary sponsor of his famous #24 car, celebrate its 200th anniversary. There will be a cake. And an actress. And an astronaut. It is a photo opportunity.

The astronaut is Al Worden, from *Apollo* 15. It says so on the patch of his NASA flight jacket. He is fit and square-jawed, but if you didn't know he had gone to the moon, you'd think he was the evening manager at an upscale pool and patio furniture store. The actress is Drena De Niro. Of whom you have never heard at all, except by association, perhaps. She is Robert De Niro's daughter. I only know who she is because I read the press release. In it, her name was misspelled "Dinero." Typographical accident or acid bilingual wisecrack on a life of presumed privilege, I do not know. She is in her late twenties, tall and slim with short dark hair and a fine smile. She is wearing what appears to be an emergency-orange prom dress. The spike heels of her matching shoes keep sinking into the little square of turf in front of the media center where all this is taking place.

The three celebrities are standing behind a table on which rests the anniversary cake itself. It is a sheet cake 2 feet by 3 feet, frosted with pastel buttercream that is running and puddling in the punishing sun.

Gordon is of course a very big star in this world and is the only one of these three who looks like he belongs out here. He is compact, solid, handsome. He is perhaps 5 feet 6 inches and weighs about 150 pounds. He is wearing his driver's firesuit. It matches the cake. Gordon, only 30, has won 58 races, 4 Cup championships, and over $45 million in prize money. The greatest racer of his generation, he stands under that brutal sun with a pleasant expression of exquisite neutrality.

One of the flacks from DuPont has a microphone for the little public-address system they've set up, but the engine noise Dopplering in off the track is enough to drown out whatever she's saying. When the cars explode past, Ms. De Niro's expression is that of a child being vaccinated with a dull needle. Messrs. Gordon and Worden, on the other hand, react not at all.

There are 15 or so still photographers, a couple of television crews, and a handful of newspaper and radio reporters. The radio reporters are furiously murmuring descriptions of the cake into their microphones.

Gordon is presented with a cake cutter. With the cutter poised above the cake, the astronaut and the actress are told to put their hands on his. This they do. The three of them holding the cutter above the cake detonates another round of shutters and flashes and motors. They hold the pose, strange newlyweds, until one of the shooters yells, "Thank you!" The cutter is brought down into the soft body of the cake. Shutters, flashes, motors. "Thank you!" At which time Jeff Gordon cuts an actual piece of cake and brings it to his face. He opens his mouth as if to take a bite. Shutters and flashes and motor buzz. He does not eat. The other two celebrities pretend to eat the same piece of cake in turn but never do. Stunt slice.

By now everyone involved is glistening with sweat, stars and media drones alike. The flacks begin cutting the cake and setting pieces around on paper plates. Gordon heads back to the garages, trailing behind him most of the photographers. Ms. De Niro is interviewed by local television. She describes in a lively way the chemical composition of her dress. Al Worden stands quietly forgotten behind the cake. It was no lonelier on the moon.

Fifteen minutes later in the same spot they do the photo op for the Raybestos Rookie of the Year program. Raybestos makes brake pads, presumably out of some inorganic material ending in "bestos," and sponsors the prize given at the end of the season to the Rookie of the Year.

They are going to introduce this year's rookie class. The four of them, three men and a young woman, are to be posed in chairs. They will be looking at veteran driver Jeff Burton, who will be standing at an easel with a pointer. The layout will mimic, if such a thing is possible in the concrete courtyard of the Daytona International Speedway Media Center at high noon under a withering sun, a classroom.

Burton is one of the names you recognize out here, a pretty consistent Top 10 runner with 17 wins in nine seasons. His older brother, Ward, is a driver, too. They're from Virginia. Terrific haircuts, both of them—modified fighter jock flattops.

The rookies are seated. Ryan Newman, Jimmie Johnson, Carl Long, and Shawna Robinson. They sit up very straight in their chairs, and a flack from Raybestos hands each of them a steering wheel. Photos are taken. The sun is hotter than a Baptist church furnace, but they are smiling and playing along.

The flack runs to a nearby cardboard box and gathers up four mortarboards. The rookies are told to put them on. The drivers struggle to situate the mortarboards on their sweaty heads.

Once the grad hats are crookedly on and the tassels deployed, each rookie grabs their steering wheel and sits up again. They smile in exactly the manner you would expect of a nervous person on a hot day in a silly hat holding a steering wheel with no car attached. Burton gestures at an easel with the traditional tool of the academy, a paint stirrer. The slender paddle reads "Raybestos."

For the next 45 seconds 20 photographers, some newly arrived, some left over from the DuPont shoot (buttercream chins), yell, "Look this way!" at the rookies.

I'm still trying to figure this out. They're rookies, right? Just starting. So they're in class. To learn. From Burton. But they're wearing mortarboards. Aren't you supposed to get the mortarboard on your last day? Having learned? Having graduated?

And they're in a courtyard outdoors. Holding steering wheels. Smiling glumly at a man with a flat stick.

"Thank you!"

By the end of the week, this photo will run in actual newspapers, always above the same caption, "Rookie Class." In each case, the word "Raybestos" will be clearly visible on that little paint paddle.

Rusty Wallace. Rusty? Given name? Nickname? For hair color? Freckles? For scrappy Little Rascals upbringing? Who out here knows that real first name anymore? Or cares to? Born 1956, former champion, 54 wins through this year. Racer. Two racing brothers, as well, Mike and Kenny. Missouri boys.

Rusty Wallace in a shimmering dark blue driver's suit, Miller Lite, walking fast through a crowd of fans, signing hats, shirts, notebooks, pads, scraps, hands, then offering them back without looking. Pens coming in over his shoulders, held up to his face, ignored—he's already got a pen, the drivers always do, and if they don't, their publicist does—a seamless procession of walking and signing and fan chatter from the back of the hauler to the garage door of the #2 car, 50 feet in 10 or 15 seconds, then he puts up his hand, he's done, thanks folks, and he's into the garage where they aren't allowed to follow. Smooth.

Still boyish, sandy-haired, and handsome, Wallace wears a grin (rueful? devilish? knowing?) at almost all times, and when he moves through an adoring crowd he looks the way your favorite uncle would look if your favorite uncle were a rock star.

Real name, disappointingly, Russell.

Tony Stewart has a face as soft and pale as unbaked dough. But he's a sex symbol, too, in his way. Where Earnhardt Jr. or Gordon or Ricky Rudd are thought to be conventionally handsome by the arbiters of such things, angular and symmetrical through the face, lean and hard in their firesuits, Stewart has the rounded features and thick trunk of a young Telly Savalas. Were Stewart to shave his head, he'd look exactly like him. Perhaps that's why he's so popular with a certain portion of the audience out here. Or it may simply be that they see in him the intensity of a true racer, all competitive fire and iron determination and all-or-nothing single-mindedness. Those are attributes about which fans love to read and sportswriters love to write, but in actual fact those very qualities often make athletes (and others, of course) a pain in the ass to be around. Stewart looks like one of those to me, a brooding tough-guy, shooting angry looks at the fans and the press and the rest of humanity out from under those dark brows like a challenge. He makes a point of it, in fact—the meanest kid in shop class, daring you to fuck with him. That he somehow manages every day to look like he's three days past his last shave only heightens that effect.

I may have it wrong, though, confusing Stewart the human with Stewart the brand strategy. They sell him as a Bad Boy. He is pictured in almost all his corporate advertising layouts wearing a nasty glare or a sulky pout, the sullen expression marketing executives and art directors somehow mistake for heroic and sexy. In Stewart's defense, that's how all the drivers are portrayed, really; it's the NASCAR aesthetic in everything from print ads for deodorant to promos for TNT to the pictures on the grandstand tickets. Bright, raptorial eyes gazing out on a distant horizon, jaw tight and shoulders squared for whatever might come, blah, blah, blah. A visual cliché unloved in the rest of American culture since about 1970, with the exception of Vin Diesel movie posters. In most cases it's just funny (Kurt Busch, Dale Jarrett), but in some others it almost forces you to dislike the person before you've ever actually met them. Such is the case with me and Tony Stewart.

Almost the only place you can see pictures of the drivers smiling is in the media guide, where they all wear the same goofy face you brought to school the day they shot your class picture. Those portraits are used all year long as graphics on the television broadcasts, too, and it softens my opinion of Stewart when I finally get a look at his. He has a big cockeyed smile, the left side of his mouth drawn slightly higher than the right, and he looks altogether an engaging goofball. Somewhere under the weight of all those contrived images lies the truth about Tony Stewart. Maybe he's a really tough, competitive goofball.

Born in 1971, he is from Indiana, drives the pumpkin orange #20 Home Depot car, and the word is he can race the wheels off anything he sits in.

If Stewart et al. are oversold as mythic heroes, all slow-motion swagger and glycerin glisten (question to production company makeup artists: Why are the drivers always sweating like crack addicts in the commercials and print ads? I know the cockpits are hot, but doesn't anybody out here have a hand towel?), rookies like Ryan Newman are largely ignored by the media and the mythmakers and the ad agencies until they prove themselves, if not worthy, at least marketable.

Unlike other pro sports, where even untested high schools kids can snag huge endorsement deals on the promise of what they *might* do in the bigs, Cup stardom is based largely, charmingly and anachronistically, on actual results.

So Newman is introduced to the world through events like the laughable "Rookie Class" photo op. Thereafter he is entirely and conscientiously ignored by the stock-car community. Whatever he's done to get himself here is forgotten. He will become whatever he can make of himself.

He is another Hoosier, from South Bend, and has a recent BS in vehicle structural engineering from Purdue. He's listed in the media guide at 5 feet 11 inches and 207 pounds and that seems about right. He is solidly built and walks with the bearing of a second-team blocking back, agile but densely made, and wears an expression of complete placidity on his face at all times. He will drive the #12 Alltel car for the Penske team. Where it might take him no one can say.

Another rookie from Raybestos Brake Pad University, Class of 12:47, is Jimmie Johnson. He is a Californian, out of El Cajon, a former champion in off-road truck racing. Chosen one of *People* magazine's "20 Sexiest Men in the Fast Lane" in the year 2000, he is alarmingly good-looking. Two strikes against him right there—at least with the core fans and the old guard of the press corps, all of whom seem to like their household gods a little less pretty and a lot less from California. This in concert with the fact that he's Jeff Gordon's protégé and employee (Gordon owns a half-interest in Johnson's #48 Lowe's Home Improvement car, along with Gordon's *own* owner, Rick Hendrick) means Johnson could be in for the same cascade of invective that greets Gordon wherever he goes.

The love-hate split on Gordon is fascinating to watch, thrilling really, even this early in the season, because so rarely does America come down so vigorously on one side or the other of anything anymore. With the exception of a few tyrants and terrorists, nobody cultivates much demonstrable hatred for public figures these days; it is politically incorrect. And that hatred is almost never played out in public. It's not that we're more enlightened or better informed or less polarized or more polite. We're not, certainly. It has more to do, I think, with wallowing in the great national data stream every day, and the cultural fatigue that comes with it.

Hardwired to that Numinous Absolute, and confronted by tens of thousands of images and individuals, real and imaginary, who among us has the moral or physical energy to really focus their feelings on something/someone/somewhere they don't like? Nobody. You don't hate Britney Spears, necessarily; you're just exhausted by her. You don't hate George Bush; he just wears you out, so you dial him down, turn him off, slide in a DVD. It is a rare thing in America to see genuine, energetic hatred expressed publicly, except in the usual television news productions of the KKK parade or the neo-Nazi rally, the screaming protest against gay marriage or the stock footage from the parking lot of the suburban abortion clinic. Hate played out as theater, a 15-second rip-and-read with some B-roll behind it. We seem content otherwise to keep our loathings private, and thus generally reserve our biased tirades for our families and the drunken holiday dinner table, as is the American tradition.

Jeff Gordon, refreshingly, inspires the kind of lurid, operatic public hatred one might better expect to be directed at murderous despots, megalomaniacal evildoers, or Jane Fonda. I can't recall, for example, even once since September 11, having seen Osama bin Laden hanging in effigy anywhere in America. I'm sure he has, in a sports bar somewhere, or in the employee locker of a sawmill or the parking lot of a long-haul freight company. Maybe I missed Brokaw that night or logged onto CNN.com after they'd already taken down the jpg, but I never saw it. Gordon, though, at least at Daytona, is being lynched around the clock.

Doll Gordons, puppet Gordons, scarecrow Gordons, store-bought or handmade, twisting slowly in the tropical heat, swing from little gibbets and gallows of every description. Cabbage Patch Gordons hang from motorhome awnings and telephone poles, Thumbelina Gordons choke their last from car bumpers and aerials and rearview mirrors. And, no, you can't mistake the display of Effigy Gordon Being Hanged with Beloved Hero Tiny Gordon on Proud Display: the noose is your first clue. The X-ed out eyes your second.

Whenever he's introduced over the track PA, his name is met with a 50-50 roar from the crowd, half ovation, half wet and thunderous raspberry. He is booed not just ecstatically, but spectacularly, by fans of every class and clan and way of life. (He is loved with equal ardor by an equal number, but more about that later.)

Makes you wonder if young Jimmie Johnson will suffer the same fate.

Shawna Robinson, the woman in that group of rookies, is a sharp-featured, pretty blonde in her late thirties. She is the divorced mother of two and a racecar driver, and in 2001 she was the first woman to start a Cup race since 1989. On that same day, she became the first woman to finish a Cup race since 1980. That she is an interesting story in a sport so long dominated by men goes without saying. That it gets little real play during Speedweeks, except as a kind of comic sidebar (waterskiing squirrel, horse counting to 10, woman driving racecar), also needn't be mentioned. Sitting silent in the heat beneath her mortarboard she is a threat to convention, conviction, and history. The press and the public know what they think of the Pit Lizards and the trackside skanks and bunnies and calendar girls, and they know how they feel about the crew members' mothers and the drivers' wives. They have a good understanding of the responsibilities of the pert, kissable and spectacularly pneumatic Miss Winston. Shawna Robinson, racecar driver, seems to have everyone stumped.

And while the number of women working here behind the scenes, as reporters, team publicists, photographers, etc., seems semirepresentative of society at large, not since the barnstorming NASCAR of the early 1950s, when women like Louise Smith raced the men on equal terms, have women been anything much on the track other than ornamental, occasional, or ceremonial.

NB: That Robinson drives for BAM racing is, at least onomatopoeically, not a good omen.

Bill Elliott, the matter-antimatter opposite of Jeff Gordon, has been voted by fans and pressmen the Most Popular Driver in NASCAR something like 15 times. In fact, when he retires, the National Motorsports Press Association is going to name the trophy after him. He's plenty popular with the fans this morning, bending to sign autographs at the tailgate of his hauler. As of this A.M., he's won 41 races. First Cup start in 1976. Born in Georgia in 1955, he's known to the fans and the press as "Awesome Bill from Dawsonville," perhaps the longest, hardest-working, most lyrically ambitious but least poetically successful nickname in professional sports. Drives the red #9 Dodge. Looks, at least in his media guide photo, uncannily like Nosferatu.

Kurt Busch, on the other hand, looks like a choir boy. Apple cheeks buffed to a high, rosy glow, he is tall and slender and seems in his apparent beardless innocence completely out of place. He is not, of course. In fact his reputation is one of channeled aggression and a willingness to do whatever it takes to root slowpokes out of the low groove. Picture a choir boy licking the blood from a bayonet, perhaps. At 23 he is a sophomore out of Las Vegas, where legend has it that he earned a living, briefly, digging ditches for the water company. He now drives the #97 Rubbermaid car for the Jack Roush team. Buzz is that big things are expected of him.

Kevin Harvick is another second-year racer of whom great things are anticipated. Recognized smartass. Nickname, "Happy." Took over the Goodwrench Service Chevrolet, now #29, after the death of Dale Earnhardt. Won two races that season. Must have driven every mile of every race with that holy ghost whispering and screaming in his ear.

· · ·

"He was cold as ice, but a helluva driver." That from a fan standing at the base of the statue of Dale Earnhardt in front of the Daytona track. A year after his death Earnhardt is still the biggest star out here by a factor of magnitude and by any measure—admiration, adulation, tears, merchandise sales—and his absence looms over everything. I expect it will the entire season.

If Petty is the NASCAR alpha, then Earnhardt is its omega. Beginning and end. Millions of words have already been spent on Earnhardt's career and life and legend and final sacrifice, and I won't add much to the word count here, not yet, because to understand the depth and intensity of the feelings for him here, in the garages and in the grandstands, doesn't take many.

I was talking to the service manager at the local motorhome center up north before we'd even left town. He's a man in his forties, Jack Phillips, and he was helping us prep for the trip and we got to talking about what the Beep and I were about to do. He envied us the lap of America, he said, because he loves Cup and tries to get to as many races as he can. Takes the family—in a moho, of course—and makes three or four race dates a year. Always Watkins Glen, sometimes Michigan or Bristol or Pocono. I asked him who his favorite driver is. Everybody has a favorite.

"It'd still have to be Earnhardt, I guess."

So I asked him why. He thought very carefully and then spoke a perfect summary of all the public grief and all the hard mourning that had run through the sport and the country since Earnhardt was killed.

"He drove the way I feel."

I finally made it out to the fan midway in front of the track this afternoon. Heartbreaking. What looks from a distance as festive and fun as a county fair is actually a corporate reeducation camp. No Ferris wheel, no Tilt-a-Whirl, only brand strategies. The sponsor tents and their sideshow barkers promise entertaining info on smoking, beer, erections, cars, motorcycles, candy, cereal, tools, tires, telephones.

Hands-on fans can wait in a very long line for the Dodge 3-D racecar simulator; or they can assault a Rubbermaid storage unit with a baseball bat in front of a chanting crowd; or they can join the chanting crowd next door in front of the immense Pepsi stage for a deafening, thought-erasing, Peron-style product rally ("Pep-si! Pep-si! Pep-si!", etc.), with a slim chance at winning a T-shirt fired randomly into the crowd by a Pamela Anderson look-alike wielding a Buck Rogers compressed-air T-shirt shotgun.

Fans circulate or wait in line holding 16-ounce beers at $4 apiece. Clutched in the other hand is the clear plastic bag of big-business giveaways: souvenir photos, key rings, brochures, cigarettes (ubiquitous, although the fan must be over 21), T-shirts (rare).

What they don't give you, you can, and apparently must, buy. The merchandise haulers and trailers form a long lane leading to the fan festival area. Every marquee team has one, every marquee driver. The Dale Earnhardt "Forever the Man" trailer is six-deep in buyers. Hats, jackets, T-shirts flying from the hooks and hangers, world without end.

Overwhelmed by sour thoughts of hardworking fans spending money they probably don't have on things they probably don't need, I return to the motorhome, semidepressed. Where's the Prozac tent when you need it?

Dark thoughts soon crowded out of head. "Pep-si! Pep-si! Pep-si!"

That's better.

The Beep delivers a disturbing update. "Show us your tits!" is now the official greeting of the crowded turn 3 infield. Mardi Gras beads are being offered in exchange for same. Accompanying homemade signage: "Dale jr. sez let the puppies BREATHE."

Welcome to The Show!

Another non sequitur, in the form of a wildlife interlude. Saw a small hawk today. It was perched on a telephone line running across an unused swath of the infield, way out beyond the buildings and the people and the commotion. On race day that empty patch of grass will be parked solid with cars, but today it belongs to this small hunter. Except to swivel its head, very slowly, watchfully, it never moved. Huge hooded eyes blinking at the glare, it was about 8 inches high, flat brown and flat gray, and it stood perfectly upright, a little Egyptian statue of a bird.

There are gulls over Lake Lloyd today, too, the long expanse of flat water that parallels the backstretch here. There are fish in the lake and there are occasional famous-racer fishing tournaments here. They used to race hydroplanes on it, too. Just empty water today, bright with sunshine. The gulls circle and flare and dive, flutter and land, and you see them arguing and squawking and scavenging from the trash cans. With cars on the track, you can't hear them, though, and without those raucous, comic voices they seem somehow more beautiful than usual.

I mention this only because racetracks seem such utterly unnatural and lifeless places.

Saw Dale Jarrett today, too, tall and gray-haired, walking long-armed past the haulers. He drives the #88 car, sponsored by UPS. He is the son of Ned Jarrett, "Gentleman Ned," one of the greats of racing, a two-time champion in the 1960s, and a longtime broadcaster and ambassador for the sport. DJ won his first championship back in 1999.

Racing is a sport with long family lines stretching back across generations. Jarretts, Earnhardts, Pettys, Bakers, Allisons; all fathers and sons with storied histories in the sport. There are plenty of others, and lots of brother acts, as well. As a practical matter, it's an expensive sport, and once somebody in a family gets into it, the whole bunch sort of falls in and sticks with it. It's more than that, of course—it's a trade, a profession, that some families practice across the years with great pride and pass along to their kids. Makes you wonder if there's a driving gene, though, a go-fast chromosome.

Ricky Craven drives what many consider the coolest paint scheme on the circuit, the orange and yellow and white #32 Tide detergent car. A marketing icon, if not always a front-runner lately, the Tide car has been a fan favorite for years. It is the perfect postmodern conflation of subject and object. Looks just like a box of soap. In a sport where more than 80 percent of self-styled "core fans" faithfully make retail purchases based on their brand loyalty to NASCAR sponsorships ("Sure, we use Tide," a man says to me in front of Craven's garage. "It's a great car."), strong return on investment is as important as high MPH.

Mr. Craven himself is a veteran racer, pale and blond and animated, hailing from Maine. From what I hear, he's welcomed as the king of all New England when the tour travels to the pine-scented track at New Hampshire.

Robby Gordon is another racing Californian, but seems to stir no passions pro or con among the crowds. In fact, he's walked past me several times this afternoon in street clothes, and the fans idling around the garages don't even recognize him. Whereas Junior or the other Gordon (unrelated) seem to be easily detectable, even in disguise. Or from great distances. Like, say, outer space.

Robby Gordon, an eight-season veteran with the face of a prank-prone 10-year-old, has raced everything from off-road trucks to GTS-class sports cars to open-wheel championship cars at Indy. Now drives the #31 Chevrolet.

Caught just a glimpse of Matt Kenseth today, too, not because he was swarmed by fans but because, like Robby Gordon, he walked past me, alone and virtually unnoticed, before I had the chance to match the face to his media guide photo. He is a pleasant-looking young man. (I honestly can't think of another way to say it. He really looks pleasant—not serious, but not *not* serious, either; he looks like an ambitious young H & R Block branch assistant on his way out of his boss's office after a really good annual performance review.)

He drives the #17 DeWalt Tools car for the Jack Roush team and the bright yellow suit looks incongruous on him, loud and showy, and you suspect, even from 20 feet away, that there's only barely enough money in the whole world to get him to wear it in front of other people.

With all due respect to him, Jeff Green, like a lot of other drivers out here, doesn't look much like what most of us think of when we think "racer." Which is to say that he looks too much like the rest of us, too round, too soft, too vulnerable. Dark-haired and barrel-chested at 5 feet, 8 inches, he seems implausible to me. Completely believable as father, son, husband; butcher, baker, candlestick maker. In his royal blue firesuit, though, he looks like another urologist waiting to struggle into the car at the Petty Experience. He drives the #30 car this year, the AOL machine, which I, as a longtime dial-up customer, suspect will run only slowly when it runs at all.

In fact a lot of the men out here, the drivers, look like I do, or you do, which is to say ordinary. This is, of course, a shock and a disappointment to many of us, those folks who arrive at the track assuming all the drivers are going to be 11 feet tall and look like Clark Gable or Steve McQueen or Tom Cruise, whichever matinee idol blueprint your generation drew for its racetrack heroes. Spend an afternoon watching the fans watching the drivers, reacting to their favorites, and you're deep in the dynamics of human attraction.

Handsome is as handsome does, and everybody loves an Ordinary Joe when they succeed, but looks count heavily in a star system like this one. Fan reaction isn't just a function of a driver's won/lost after all, it's a response to chemistry, pheromones, passion, mojo, funk. The "it" factor.

The best example of this phenomenon might be Michael Waltrip, driver of that #15 car, who, until he won the 500 last year, had gone something like 462 starts without a victory. At 6 feet 5 inches, dark and camera-handsome, he's Darrell Waltrip's younger brother and a near doppelganger for John Wayne's son, Patrick (for those of you with the DVD of the original *The Alamo*). With one win in 16 seasons, a record that surely would have bounced less popular drivers not just out of the car but out of the sport entirely, Michael still makes the fans squeal wherever he goes. In other words, it doesn't hurt to be good-looking in racing—much like anywhere else on the planet.

Of the other drivers who look the part, and based solely on how the fans respond to them (more weight in this unscientific test is given to female fan squealing than to male fan hollering), I would include the following: Sterling Marlin, blondish driver of the #40 car; the Labonte brothers, Terry and Bobby, both former champions, drivers of the #5 and #18 cars, respectively, and favorites of the female 25–49 demographic; Ricky Rudd, driver of the #28 car; Elliott Sadler, driver of the #21 car; Mark Martin, driver of the #6 Viagra car (the hubba-hubba factor of which may or may not skew these findings); and Hut Stricklin, driver of the #23 car, a son of Alabama and your first choice in the role of Conrad Birdie if you're ever casting a community theater production of *Bye-Bye Birdie*. Great name, too.

For Cup drivers with talent and a good work ethic but a low mojo quotient ("deficient fuckability," per Hollywood), there is applause but no hysteria, some hollering but little squealing, approbation but not much passion. Sometimes fans don't even know who it is walking past them.

"Is that really him?" is a question I overhear, many times, as the drivers pass the fans on the way to and from the cars. "Are you *sure*?" comes the inevitable follow-up, a question founded not on factual uncertainty, but on a sense of affectionate letdown. "*Really*? That's him?"

Men like Johnny Benson, 6-year Cup veteran out of Grand Rapids; Ken Schrader, two decades behind the wheel of a Cup car; Mike Skinner, yeoman driver nearly 20 years on and off the tour; John Andretti, member of one of America's great racing dynasties, driving stock cars for another, the Pettys; Dave Blaney, flat tracker from Ohio, driving the yellow Jasper Engines car; Bobby Hamilton, 13 years a stocker who got his start in the seat of a stunt car on the *Days of Thunder* shoot; Stacy Compton, Virginian, made his first ride 6 years ago when he mortgaged his house to finance a racecar; the Bodine brothers, Todd and Brett and Geoffrey, successful veteran runners from apple country in upstate New York; Jeremy Mayfield, young, buzz-cut ham-

and-egger in the #19 Dodge; Jimmy Spencer, Target car, "Mr. Excitement," a holdover from the precorporate Bronze Age and a stout, loudmouth fan favorite; Joe Nemechek, workhorse 10-year Cup veteran, former Busch champion; Buckshot Jones, tiny 5-year vet, best nickname on tour, could fit in a thimble, driving for the Petty team.

These solid drivers, the men who form the backbone of the Cup series this year, like Jeff Green, look only human.

Understand that these men are still highly valued as drivers; each man has the chops to win any race he's in, given good-enough equipment, but these guys don't generate the ardent animal panic among fans that a handful of the others do.

The superstars out here are the handsome swashbucklers and the slick villains. Old Hands and Young Guns. Black hats and white hats, Galahads and Mordreds. They are, in other words, clearly identifiable characters ready to be plugged in to those collective grandstand fantasies. So the journeymen are just that, hardworking dress extras in somebody else's fairy tale.

Why even mention it? Because my sense today, making these notes as the cars hammer around the track practicing, watching the fans wade through the heat, is that Cup racing stands at a singular intersection of sports and theater. All sports are theater of a kind, but the intensity of the fans' passions out here—"We love you, Junior!"— is profound, different, and runs much hotter and deeper than anything I've seen in other big-league sports. It has to do with the life-and-death stakes, I think, and with the haunted history of the South and its cult of personality and our yearning for simplicity and our insatiable craving for celebrity and our ache for fable and our need to live vicariously in the glamour and accomplishment of others and our persistent American itch to create heroes.

And only willful ignorance or fear or blindness could deny the obvious: that whether by design or apathy or a simple circumstance of history, in an age of hugely successful, high-visibility African American athletes, it's the last professional sport in this country that's overwhelmingly white and male.

•　　　•　　　•

The combustibility of emotion out here also has a lot to do with the relatively tiny number of Cup drivers compared to the number of players in other sports. How many players in the NFL—1,400 or so? What about major-league baseball—600, plus or minus? Even the NBA spreads a fan's passion thin with over 300 players to root for.

Out here there are 43 drivers.

Just 43 drivers to bear all the ardor of that huge fan base. Just 43 people to shoulder all those ambitions and affections and devotions; to satisfy all that want and longing and need, to feed those ceaseless appetites; to quicken all those dreams, enliven all those fantasies, inspire all those feelings. Just 43 drivers to win or lose, live or die in service of all that coast-to-coast heat and love and hope. These are the principal cast members of the Big Show. Of that number, only half a dozen name-above-the-title stars.

Any one of whom might be killed before I close this notebook today.

They ran the race this afternoon. At last. You think you know what to expect. From TV. From everything you've seen and heard. You do not.

Coming down out of that fourth turn at Daytona hard on the gas to the green flag, 43 cars are bunched two by two and nose to tail and door to door and the sound they make is the horn blast you'll hear at sunrise on the dawning of the Last Day. Underneath it, behind it, above it, barely heard, the tidal roar of 200,000 people screaming. Seventy-three tons of cars pounding out apocalypse in every cylinder and pouring color and money onto the frontstretch, 34,000 horsepower from $2 million worth of engines wrapped in $7 million worth of sheet metal thundering fire and stink under Florida's grinning, idiot sun, every car gleaming and bearing forward, before more than $15 million worth of paid attendance, the urgent messages bought by half a billion dollars' worth of corporate sponsorship. The cars are irresistible, as useless and beautiful as jewels.

The drivers are handsome, courageous, omniscient.

Up and down pit road more men and women stand; 500, 600, 700 of them, sweating in iridescent firesuits and wicked visored helmets, officials and crew members, everyone shimmering in that sea of heat rising up from the pavement, hyperadrenal, anxiety and elation running just ahead of nervous collapse, everyone jumpy, pumped, ready to be ready; close to a thousand men and women wired together across a hundred radio frequencies, voices crackling static in and out of every helmet, a dense web of chatter and lunatic crosstalk, with 10 times 10,000 tools at hand for what's to come, weapons against chaos and bad chance, more millions spent to keep those wheels turning no matter how far wrong things go in the next four hours, and those teams and those tools and all that maniac energy flare and glint under that broiling motherfucker of a sun.

Staring at them all, the deep ocean eye of the television camera. On the rooftops, on the track walls, on the dashboards and the roll pans and the air dams and the toolboxes, carried on the shoulders of young men and women dizzy with the heat, there are cameras everywhere. Everything is seen, everything is shown. Nothing is missed. Hundreds of millions of images are captured and compressed and beamed and bounced and sent streaming into 20 million American homes. Millions more worldwide. In those homes they see the cars and the drivers and the fans and the men and the women shimmering in the heat. They hear the noise. In your living room it is just another thing on television. For us it was different.

No matter how many more races the Beep and I may ever attend, we will both, I suspect, experience our first Daytona again and again—likely as a series of vivid, unbidden flashbacks. It was our first bite of the apple, or in this case turkey leg, and marked our fall from innocence and ignorance. Along with the fragmentary memories and the 64X fast-forward pictures and the echoing explosions, will come perhaps a brief period of night sweats, a few posttraumatic tics. Not entirely sure. A year or two, probably, spent poised to flinch, no more. Knowledge has its price.

The scale. The sensation. The concentration and compression of all that ambition and emotion and showmanship. Its daylong detonation. The Super Bowl is an afternoon spent on a morphine drip by comparison.

I remember standing there inside it, overwhelmed. From the moment the gates opened and 200,000 people boiled up into the seats, I rattled and wandered from one flash frame to the next, from one part of the track to another. Noon heat, blue sky, blinding light, driver meeting, chapel, parade, speeches, introductions, invocations, benedictions, pomp, music, ceremony, honor guard, anthem, flyover, fireworks—

"Gentlemen, start your engines."

and the cataclysmic eruption, then the pace laps and finally hard on the gas and the hornet-swarm sound of 43 cars on the track at last, and swooning, mesmerized by it, standing at the start/finish as the colors pour by, I imagine the cars spinning out enough power to roll the very earth beneath them, the whole happy planet turning and spun through space by these 43 cars. Cars orbiting the track, Earth orbiting the sun, wheels inside wheels inside wheels.

Racing in circles chasing a buck, our national analogy. Raging, trapped in the fast lane, the free-market allegory of the citizen consumer, the Great American Race.

Those are my thoughts, scattering like birds, as the green flag flies and the earth shudders beneath my feet and the air tightens around me, dense with that murderous noise and pressurized by expectation, the crowd on its feet, mouths wide to scream, mass hysteria, the moment blown so full of anticipation and sensation that it's hard to catch my breath, impossible to think, every sense firing at maximum, my brain at the short end of a funnel too small to ever carry what the first five seconds of the Daytona 500 pour into it.

Confused and stupefied I watched at least half the race on television, in the holding cell/media annex. You can't see anything from the pits, just that short crescent of track right in front of you and the jitterbug blur of the cars every 50 seconds or so. You see them briefly flying high along the wall of the turns in the distance, but the continuity of the race is lost to you. Even the pit crews watch the race on TV, standing in their firesuits. I spent the first five or ten laps trying to watch the race over their shoulders. By then Tony Stewart's crew was already packing up to leave—he'd blown an engine on the second lap. "His motor laid down," I heard one fan on the walkway ahead of me shout to another, tearing the radio headset off his head, upset, "Mother-fucker laid down *already*."

I stood for a few more laps in Stewart's empty pit stall. More fans threw more radio headsets when Junior blew a tire a few laps later, effectively ending his shot at winning. Eventually I walked back to the little press room. All the photographers, including the Beep, were out working the race, but I was surprised to find all the reporters still there, writing their race coverage from the television broadcast. Across the garage apron, in the main media bunker, most of the national deadline press were in their seats, too, watching the monitors; it makes sense—you can't cover what you can't see. The rest were up in the press box.

As the cars fail or spin or crash, they're brought back into the garage. Occasionally the print reporters stir and run out to the garage to check the extent of the damage or grab a quote from an angry or disappointed driver. Mostly, though, they remain where they are, watching TV and taking notes. Even inside, here in the vault, you can hear the cars buzz-saw past on the track.

My notes for the race itself offer little insight into who was leading when or why or for how long. The cars circled the track in those long, uneventful trains or clumped together in tight, tentative squadrons three abreast. The lead was taken or lost without much fuss, 10 different drivers pulling ahead for a lap or two or twenty, then relinquishing the spot to the next car in line. Dave Marcis blew an engine on lap 79. Kyle Petty blew another 60 laps later. Pit stops for fuel and tires came and went, reshuffling the field, then came and went again, reshuffling it further.

At the halfway point of the race, 100 laps, I'd left the press center to meet up with the Beep for our inaugural racetrack turkey leg at the stand in the middle of the track, an attempt to experience the race the way a fan might. She and I both must have looked blasted, sunburned, parched, and untethered from the day, the way everyone around us looked. We shared a grilled turkey leg without much enthusiasm or conversation.

Just as we finished, we heard the distant crunching of sheet metal and the crowd gasping, and then the track went quiet, the cars and the fans all at once off the throttle. A pall of yellow tire smoke hung over turn 2. The Big One! I looked up at the scoring pylon and made a note of the lap number. 140. We dropped the legbone into the trash for the gulls and hustled off for the garages.

Eighteen cars were gathered up. Track workers were hauling the wreckage in on flatbeds and the crews were already hammering and pounding and laying tape on the earliest arrivals, trying to get them back into the race. Torn metal, fluids hemorrhaging across the floor, fans and reporters gathering, crewmen running and grunting and swearing.

"Pull the housing, pull the housing!"

"It won't let off!"

"Pull the goddamn lines first, then pull the housing! Jesus!"

Some were salvageable, some weren't. In a few cases the crews tried to straighten out hoods or deck lids with baseball bats and sledge-hammers. Faces streaked with grease and sweat, contorted with effort, it looked like they were punishing the cars for what they'd done.

Crews with terminal damage simply stood and stared at their cars, suddenly exhausted, then turned and started packing up the tools. Their drivers were already long gone.

By the time I got back to the press center, they'd stopped showing the replays, so I never saw the accident, only the consequence. The race settled back into its rhythm for another few minutes. Then, with just a handful of laps left, another pileup. Jeff Gordon gets knocked sideways and takes part of the field with him. One of the reporters calls out low, "Oh, no," and grabs his notebook and runs for the door.

There's so much debris on the track that they red-flag the race, stop the cars completely for the 20 minutes it's going to take to shovel up the wreckage. The cars sit on the backstretch, silent, baking in the sun. You can see the shot on the monitor and feel the eerie stillness. Some reporters run out; some run back in. No announcement about any injuries yet. They show the replays, somebody getting into the back of Gordon's car, he gets loose sideways, and the pack running behind him atomizes, comes apart, and then there's so much smoke you can't see what happens. I stand up, but I'm not sure what to do—stay inside and take notes or run outside and get comments? Paralyzed, I stand there, halfway to the door, doing neither.

On the monitor there's a shot of Sterling Marlin climbing out of his car on the track. He was leading when the field was stopped. Now he's trying to pull some bent sheet metal free of his right front tire—but you can't work on the car under red, so the track marshals shoo him back into his cockpit. Penalized for the infraction, he'll get moved to the back of the pack on the restart.

They restart. Two laps to the finish. One. After a race that took nearly four hours to run, Ward Burton beats Elliott Sadler by 0.193 seconds. Burton wins $1.4 million for having done so. Sterling Marlin finishes eighth. Getting out of the car to yank on that fender may have cost him the win—it probably cost him the $1.2 million differential in prize money, too. No reported injuries.

I run to Victory Lane but can't get close enough to see Ward Burton, much less interview him. I run back to the garage. Woozy. Dehydrated. Nearly mowed down by a Cingular pit box as a crewman hurries to roll it back to the hauler. Lightheaded. See Michael Waltrip doing a network television interview in the doorway of the garage men's room. I take further illegible notes. I find the Beep at the rabbit hutch press room. Spent, we stagger home.

Twenty-four hours of brushing, flossing, and gargling cannot ameliorate the taste and consequence of our first and last NASCAR turkey leg. We roll off the blocks filled with regret. And Pepto.

On to Rockingham, back north to get to the South.

FIVE

"Does that *ever* work?"

It is the Beep with a question as we hurry up the interstate.

"Does what ever work?"

"Yelling 'Show us your tits'?"

Her Speedweeks experience in the Turn 3 infield has left the Beep curious, if not a little shaken. "I mean, what woman responds to that?"

The Turn 3 tent city has a reputation as the bachelor party precinct at Daytona, a kind of plywood and framing-lumber Bourbon Street. Not as many well-scrubbed motorhomes out there, but lots of pickups and box vans with handbuilt viewing scaffolds as ingenious and elaborate as medieval siege engines. From which parapets and balconies men shout down their instructions and incentive programs. Let the puppies take a tumble in the sun, they say, in exchange for free drinks, free mammograms, and/or a string of colorful Mardi Gras wampum.

Every track has at least one famously debauched district from which innocents, newcomers, or those of delicate constitution are warned away. To earn that special distinction must take some doing, too, because from what we saw, the entire fan encampment is pretty well hammered and partially clad the whole two weeks. Still, Daytona may be an exception, first race of the season, all that pent-up fan juice, etc. From what we've been told, the Darlington infield used to be the liveliest place on tour long, long ago. These days the infields at Talladega and Michigan are the most renowned for their bumptious fun and drunken carnality.

"And it wasn't just *one* guy," the Beep continues, "and it wasn't just *young* guys. I couldn't walk ten feet without hearing it. 'Show us your tits!' From guys my dad's age. And it's not like I'm walking around in a bikini top carrying a beer mug, I've got a long-sleeved shirt on and long pants and all the credentials and equipment on top of that. 'Show us your tits!' And then they'd *grab* themselves, too."

We pass a quiet moment to allow the picture to fade.

"It's way worse than what you get from construction workers in New York," she went on. "They just make those weird sucking sounds. It's street noise. And okay, I saw a few girls wearing Mardi Gras beads, but, really, how often do you get any kind of positive response when you stand there with your hairy beer belly hanging out and your hand on your crotch shouting 'Show us your tits!'?"

Honesty is the preferred policy in our family, and the honest answer to my wife's question lies in a man's DNA, and in the persistent male arithmetic of horny optimism. Still, one mustn't generalize. "Honey, I think I can speak for middle-aged shirtless sunburned drunken fat men in tiny orange nylon shorts and novelty suspenders the world over when I say, it only has to work once."

I doubt you'd have heard the phrase "Show us your tits!" used aloud 50 years ago at a racetrack infield, it being perhaps a more circumspect time; but I suspect that the thought was just as much on men's minds, and the desire to see it fulfilled just as strong. Not many opportunities to try it out certainly, as women weren't often in evidence among the fans at the track in the early days. (Although it is worth mentioning, perhaps at this moment more than any other, that exactly as many women, seven, competed in NASCAR Grand National racing in the decade of the 1950s as have competed in it in all the years since.) Thus we rejoin history where we last left Bill France Sr. and his rollicking tent-and-revival show.

Between 1950, when that track at Darlington was built, and 1959, when Daytona opened, stock-car racing continued to flourish. It spread itself farther across the country (first NASCAR race west of the Mississippi, 1952, in California), running more dates (up from just 6 in

1949 to nearly 50 in 1958), creating more stars (Petty, Flock, Johnson, Roberts, Baker, et al.), and growing steadily more prosperous under the powerful green thumb of France the nurturer.

That decade's big breakthrough, though, came in 1955, courtesy of a man named Carl Kiekhaefer. Careful students of NASCAR's illuminated manuscript will find his name cited a handful of times therein, usually preceded by the modifiers "brilliant," "wealthy," "eccentric," "angry," or "crazy."

A cigar-chomping prophet at once mad enough and powerful enough to envision the future and then create it, Kiekhaefer's forever gift to roundy-rounder fireballin' was this: major sponsorship.

Mr. K. was the man behind Mercury Marine boat motors, founder and owner as it's told, and he was, as stipulated, wealthy and eccentric. And he was looking, as the wealthy and eccentric often do, for new ways to become a little more of both. He fancied stock-car racing and he had boat motors to advertise, and in a cigar-smoke halo of inspiration decided to do the one by doing the other. He and his idea arrived fully formed for the opening of the 1955 season with new Chrysler cars, new personnel, and new trailers in tow; each of them painted up to read "Mercury Outboards."

Before Carl the K arrived, sponsorship had been a hit-or-miss deal. Owners scrambled for operating cash and necessary services among their friends and business associates. To make good on those contributions, a car might hit the track with a small, hand-lettered shout-out to the local gas station to acknowledge the loan of a service bay or thank a parts supplier who'd kicked in some leaf springs. Mostly, though, the cars rolled onto the grid naked but for their scrawled numbers, and returning little but whatever prize money they might win for anything invested.

Teams, too, were more informal affairs in those days, made up mostly of part-timers and friends and friends of friends. You drove them in the crumpled racecar to the track, let them out, crumpled it some more, and then drove them home. The organizational flowchart ran only from Mom to Pop.

Kiekhaefer changed all that. Steady money cascaded from his Mercury Marine business into his racing business, and his racecars, sometimes as many as five in a single race, returned the favor when they took the track as mobile sandwich boards, wearing those Mercury Outboard colors. The scheme was both prim and primitive by today's standards, the cars igloo white with some modest lettering running along the fenders, but it was the first time a racecar earned back some of its costs by drilling a brand name into the heads of the folks in the grandstands.

And they earned prize money, too. Spectacularly. In the 1955 season, Carl Kiekhaefer's teams entered a total of 40 Grand National events. They won 22 of them. One of his drivers, Tim Flock, won 18 races himself that year and took the championship. The year before, the 1954 champion Lee Petty, had won 7.

But the sudden, outrageous success of those Kiekhaefer Chrysler 300s wasn't just about great, horse-choking rolls of cash; it was about the careful application of great, horse-choking rolls of cash. Like France, Kiekhaefer was an iron-bound organizer. And he organized his teams, his cars and personnel, for maximum output. His cars were expensive, beyond the reach of other teams, and fast. His people wore uniforms, they carried *clipboards*. They brought the pristine racecars to the track on pristine trailers. They were disciplined and efficient. Professionals. In other words, he ran it like a real business. Consequently, Mom and Pop took their lumps.

In 1956, same deal. Driving another Mercury Outboards Chrysler, Buck Baker grabbed the championship with 14 wins. A Grand National dynasty begins. And here you would expect to see the name Kiekhaefer chiseled all the way down the page into history as the dominant stock-car owner of the 1950s.

And yet, you do not. In fact, unless you're an officially licensed NASCAR scholar, this may be the first you've heard of him.

Because not long after changing the business model of the sport forever, winning everything in sight, attracting the actual manufacturers of the cars into the sport, and predicting a NASCAR future that wouldn't fully take hold for another 40 years, Kiekhaefer took his cars and his clipboards and his cigars and went home.

NASCAR rewrote some technical rules before the 1957 season, it seems, specifically to curb Kiekhaefer's free-spending multicar dominance and return parity to the sport. In short, they drove him out of racing at the end of a sharp pencil. Given Big Bill France's iron grip on his company, and Carl Kiekhaefer's iron grip on *his* (his biography is actually called *Iron Fist*), there was bound to be some ponderous arm-wrestling between the two.

Out-fisted, Kiekhaefer abandoned the circuit. At this moment, having won 54 races in just two seasons, he remains among the Top 10 all-time in owner wins in the Cup media guide. Soon enough the long, slow descent. But he left behind him two ideas that enliven NASCAR even today. The first is simple: If you have a roll of money big enough to choke a horse, you need to buy a bigger horse.

The second, his truest legacy, is the concept of major sponsorships, with which NASCAR fans are now so happily familiar. In fact, just there, up ahead, in the window of that Rockingham grocery store is a sign that reads: "Food Lion, where NASCAR shops for groceries." So shall we.

The Rockingham track, a.k.a. "The Rock," is a gravel pit of a place up in the pine hills southwest of Fort Bragg. It's an hour's drive east of Charlotte and an hour's drive north of Darlington. If you come up from the south, it's woods and pine duff all the way in. Come in from the southwest off Highway 1 and you'll see Alonzo's Restaurant and Mark's Funeral Home and the spindly tin woodsman of the Rockingham water tower. After the immense sunny Woodstock of the 500, the Rock, rock gray in every regard, suffers some by comparison.

But it is the real deal, too, an old temple of the true V-8 faith standing right in the shag club and bird dog fanbelt of NASCAR country, and worthy of a certain respect. The seats along the frontstretch are steeply raked to follow the contours of the hill of banked earth against which they lean, and the concession stands and the press box and the VIP boxes above them are built atop the hill itself. It gives the track the look of an ancient amphitheater, an age-old hippodrome, grown up out of hard ground.

Got the Beep credentialed and found our campsite, out on the steeps behind the backstretch grandstand. A hillside lot; close to the gate, great view, but a mother to level, two bubbles off plumb, a three-board stack of scrap lumber under each rear wheel.

First night in, we wander the track to get our bearings and watch the painters lay down the logos on the infield grass for the weekend's race. The Cup race is called the Subway 400, which seems reasonable to me, and to the painters, but the signage for the Busch race on Saturday has everyone rolling their eyes. It's the 1-866-RBCTerm.com 200, quite a bucketful, and an early front-runner in the best/worst race name of the season sweepstakes. Would it be any worse to call it "The insurance company you've never heard of whose slogan is 'Great Rates for Smokers!' 200"? That a small army of perky Winston employees will be handing out free cigarettes and lighters all weekend long at the track might best be described in a business school textbook as "synergy."

The track's an honest oval a little over a mile around. Built 1965. Garages small, battered. Rough track surface famous for wearing out tires. Its formal name is the North Carolina Speedway. No one calls it that, though; it's just Rockingham.

Out here on tour, tracks and events and the calendar are referred to sequentially and geographically by the roustabouts and riggers: hence, "first Charlotte" for the first event of the season there, "second Charlotte" for the later go-round, etc. No one pays much attention to track names (invariably it's the something-something speedway or the something-something international speedway), and they pay none at all to the event names, as per the above, which change frequently and are pretty cryptic in any case. No one asks, "How'd Rusty do in the UAW-GM Quality 500 last season?" It's "How'd Rusty do at second Charlotte last season?"

Other entries in the language notebook:

"Awesome." All-purpose adjective, adverb. Replaces old-fashioned, more modest modifiers, "good" or "great." Never inappropriate. Used mostly by drivers during interviews, press conferences, to describe car/sponsor/team. "We had an awesome racecar in practice today," or "Car ran awesome all day, least 'til the motor let go." Sometimes used to describe off-track activities. "Being a judge for the Miss U.S.A. Pageant was an awesome personal experience." First extensive use in '70s stoner/surf culture long forgotten. Now cross-cultural convention, staple of Christian rock. Consequence: one less word available to describe Everest, sunrise, actual Voice of God, etc.

Corollary: skyrocketing modifier inflation means "good" now equals "bad." Thirty-seventh-place finisher: "Had a good car out there today. Track just never came to us, was the deal."

"Deal." Noun, global. Indeterminate, infinite catchall. No longer limited to the idea of transaction or binding contract; can now mean anything: state of mind, process, occurrence, rules change, thing, place, person. E.g., new NASCAR rule is "an engine deal," getting caught up in someone else's wreck is "just one of those racing deals." Being wrecked intentionally, however, is "a bad deal." When describing the guy who wrecked you: "I do not know what his deal is."

"Run/ran." Noun, verb. Long, uninterrupted series of laps is a "run." Some tense confusion over verb form. "We run good today" heard as often as "We ran good today." Never heard: "We ran well today."

"We." Imperial first-person plural characterizes driver, owner, car, crew, crew chief, sponsor, family, et al., ad inf. Most often occurs when discussing race performance. Generous use by driver helps make point that racing is a team sport, with many people contributing to ultimate success. Overuse can lead to occasional verbal dissonance.

"How are you feeling after last week's accident?"

"Well, we're a little swollen and sore, but we're fine."

•   •   •

The Beep, refreshed and renewed post-Daytona, sets out for photo ops. I wander the infield complex, watching. I hover, trying to get the crews used to seeing me around. They are skittish as elk. I use the same strategy with the drivers and my press colleagues. I mostly wind up lost in the shuffle. The first lesson from Daytona: Pace yourself— it's a long season.

That seems to be the lesson for everyone here. The engine noise is the same, a constant, but the tempo of all the human movement is slower, the crowds and the stakes are much smaller, the crews are all closer to home, and it feels for the first time like the beginning of something rather than the end.

An item from the local newspaper this A.M., a free insert for posting on your car window, your RV window, your living room window. It reads, "Sterling! Stay in your car!" By eleven o'clock they're everywhere.

We met Ernie Irvan's brother today out by the motorhome. Or not. It's impossible to know.

Ernie Irvan was a very popular Cup driver in the 1990s. A series of accidents eventually cut short his career, but he was and remains a real fan favorite. Nickname, Swervin' Irvan.

Returning to the motorhome, trundling the laptop and the usual work kit, almost at our door, I hear from behind me:

"Hey, Big Daddy!"

So of course I turn, although just why I'm not sure, no one has ever called me Big Daddy before, certainly no man has ever called me Big Daddy before, but it sounds half-flip and half-respectful, just the way it sounds in *Cat on a Hot Tin Roof*, and there's nobody else around, so I turn.

"Heyyy, Big Daddy," says a man I've never seen before. It's pretty clear, even from a distance, that he's baked. He has a red plastic party cup in his hand and he's gesturing as he walks, toasting me with the red cup, which slops a little brown liquor over the rim and down his fingers. He's walking like he's trying to stay on a bongo board. He's in his mid-forties, I guess, dark-haired and thick-featured with wide round cheeks and a strong chin. He is neatly dressed in dark slacks and a white dress shirt under a bright red sweater. Medium height, powerful build on the way to slack. His eyes, dark brown but shot with red, are so glazed they look like they've been tattooed on his face.

"Heyyyy, Big Daddy, how you doin'?"

"Real well. How 'bout you?" I'm at the door.

"Doin' great. Where you from, Big Daddy, you don't sound from around here."

He has a nonspecific drawl, the kind of neutral uptown syrup the airline pilots pour. Before I can answer, he says, "You know I'm Ernie Irvan's brother, right, Big Daddy?"

"No, I guess I didn't." I'm not sure whether to open the door, say goodbye, and climb inside or play this with a smile out here. At that moment the Beep opens the door from inside and says, "Hi, honey, I heard your voice so I came to . . ." She looks down at us both.

"Heyyyy, missus, I was just tellin' Big Daddy here I'm Ernie Irvan's brother."

She raises her eyebrows.

"Honey, why don't you take my computer back inside. I'll only be a minute or two." And she does and I sit down on the steps, thereby undoing, I hope, any notions Ernie Irvan's brother may have of being invited in. I shouldn't have feared it. All he wants to do is make his case.

"You know Ernie Irvan, right, Big Daddy? You know who he is and know about him winnin' the 500 in '91 and so forth I 'spect and the crash in '94 and about the comeback in '95 and about how much people take to him and about all those times at Richmond and North Wilkesboro . . ."

. . . and he went on like this for three or four minutes, specifying the victories and the reversals and the triumphs over injury, the failures and the adversity, the talent and the persistence and the personality and the love, the ardent love, of and for the fans, and the swervy style and the balls-out, go-for-broke heroic life story. That it was someone else's didn't seem to matter. When he lost focus again and wound down, he said, "I just wanted you to know that you met Ernie Irvan's brother today, okay? Stay safe now, Big Daddy." And, never having mentioned his own name, he tips himself back down the hill, the way he'd been heading when he called out to me, and reels off. I unfold myself and go inside.

"What was that all about?" the Beep asks.

"I'm not sure." And we start dinner.

I hunted up a picture of Ernie Irvan a couple of days later. For whatever it's worth, this guy looked a little like him.

I did get a kick out of being called Big Daddy, though. All that magnolia and Spanish moss and moral rot. Highlight of the trip so far. Sadly, I do not expect to be called Big Daddy ever again.

Grandstands mostly empty for practice this week. Half-full for Saturday Busch race. Most of those who show up know to sit in turn 2, where the track surface and the angle of the turn contribute to excellent racing action when the drivers get back on the gas.

Vocabulary add: "action" generally synonymous with "crash."

Saturday night at the Rock is quiet, or at least quiet-seeming, after the fleshpot blowout at Daytona. Fewer people, and their music seems to soften in the trees. Stand on the camera platform of the track roof and look out over the camps and the forest and see the faraway people and the campfires flickering in the woods and smell the pine smoke and it feels like a battlefield Christmas.

Started the Sunday Cup race down in the infield, right on the exit of turn 2, but walked back and forth through the narrow tunnel a couple of times to see the race from the front straight stands.

Turn 2 fulfills its action/crash promise. There's a great view on the down-low from the infield wall as the cars get rammed there and crossed up and slide straight toward you. Bang! Boom! Yeehaw!

While I've got my head hung out over the wall to watch the cars powering out of the turn, a nearby track EMT shouts some good advice, "Watch for flying debris! Always look upstream! Keep your eyes open! Might just keep your goddamn head on that way!" Oh.

With an average race speed around 115 mph, racing at the Rock seems more meditative in comparison to Daytona, but is more fun to watch. It's easier to follow the tactical skirmishes as the logos and trademarks succeed each other. Slipping and slithering around the slick track, the Tide car leads the first third of the way. Thereafter, the lead cycles from AOL to DeWalt to Coors Light every 30 laps or so.

There are 10 caution flags during the race. Bang! Boom! DeWalt, Matt Kenseth, eventually win under yellow. Sterling Marlin stays strapped in his Coors Light car long enough to finish second, making him the current championship points leader.

There was a kid down along the frontstretch fence at the foot of the main grandstand. He was in his late teens and wore a red Budweiser T-shirt and blue jeans and a dishwater-blond mullet with the number 8 neatly shaved into the fade on either side of his slender head.

He was a skinny, snow-white kid in a big red shirt, with a seat right in the front row nearest the fence, and it was easy to see him. Every time the field raced by, he would spring out of his seat, stand for a second, bend his knees, aim his slender arms at the passing cars, and elaborately flip the double bird. The twinned fingers would follow the cars down the track for a moment, then he'd retract them and sit down again. It only takes about 30 seconds for the field to make a lap at Rockingham, so he was up and down like a piston.

I watched him for a long time. It took 10 or 15 laps just to figure out if this was a blanket indictment of the entire deal (minus #8 Junior, of course), or a grudge held against an individual. It finally seemed to me that he was singling out Jeff Green in the #30 AOL car. Perhaps the kid was a Time Warner stockholder.

The day wore on and the young man never flagged. In fact, he became more theatrical as the afternoon passed, a maestro of digital insult. Once the spidery fingers went up, he would bounce from the knees or swivel his hips or pump his arms like he was dancing the Monkey. He would cross his hands, then recross them; cross them again and again, one above the other, so fast that it looked like he was waving off a carrier landing. He fired the fingers like pistols and blew smoke from the tips. He threw lightning bolts and stink bombs. He was a jackhammer, a steam engine. He shook and he shuddered. No matter how he moved or what he did, he was a Zen master transcendent; nothing remained of him but the gesture.

I came and went all day, down to the track, up to the press box roof, back down to the track. He never stopped. As far as I know he flipped those fingers the whole afternoon, every time the cars went by, all 393 laps. Nobody in the crowd seemed to take any notice. It was the purest kind of artistry. Like Coltrane in the studio or van Gogh in the wheat fields of Auvers, that young man never turned around, even once, to see if anyone was watching him.

Early Monday morning, dawn mist and wood smoke still thick in the forest, we bounce down off the blocks and leave for Las Vegas. We'll run over through Charlotte, get the I-77 north, grab the I-40 west, and ride it all the way to the desert—2,400 miles. Three days. Anywhere from 12 to 16 hours or more in the seat (at roughly legal speeds), staring down at the lane markers as you gobble them up. Same route and rate as the race teams.

We come out of North Carolina rolling along on the momentum of hope and inexperience, the whole happy country coiling beneath us like a wave.

Carrying everything and connected to nothing, our plan is to hopscotch from one free layover to the next. No campgrounds, no fees, no time wasted hooking up or hunkering down. Run as long as we can all day and into the night, with only quick pit stops for gas, then pull over at either one of two free oases to sleep: the Flying J truck stop or the Wal-Mart.

We had discovered the Flying J just a few weeks earlier, right before we rolled into Daytona. A well-run, tidy chain of 150 or so immense truck and travel plazas, the J suited our needs right down to the roadbed. Special, wide-lane islands at the RV fuel pumps for the steering-impaired, propane sold in bulk for our stove/heater/fridge, free potable water to refill our tank, showers and restaurants and a launderette inside, game rooms and TV lounges and barbershops and computer connections and little variety stores. It was a clean, well-lighted place on a sometimes dark landscape, and we welcomed it.

That the J's gas prices were generally a penny or two less than everyone else's was another powerful incentive to fetch up there.

Open around the clock, there was almost always an elongated parking lot set aside for units like ours, where we could drop anchor for the night, loud and bright though it was, bathed in the reassuring security of that mercury-vapor glow.

On nights when the J didn't rise up on the horizon, we'd have to hunt up a Wal-Mart. There has been an informal, but widely acknowledged, arrangement between RVers and Wal-Mart for years. It is considered acceptable practice to overnight a motorhome in one of their store parking lots, having first obtained the permission of the local management. To those who don't know anything about motorhomes and don't much care to learn, this may at least explain why you pull into your local Wal-Mart first thing in the morning and see so many RVs. So common a thing is it, in fact, that the snowbirds refer to it as Wally World.

The benefit to Wal-Mart, historically, has been the diehard loyalty of the Wander-Lodge crowd and the reasonable assurance that upon waking, a well-rested overnighter would walk immediately into the store and spend some American money.

The return to the weary traveler is obvious, too—a nationwide network of brightly illuminated parking lots in which to knit the raveled sleeve of care, some even patrolled by orbiting security guards. Three thousand points of light. One finds them, of course, by buying a Wal-Mart atlas. At the Wal-Mart.

Sam Walton cut the ribbon to open the first Wal-Mart store in 1962. His biography is a story for someone else to tell, but Bill France Sr. was ribbon-cutting in the 1960s too, and while the Beep drives and sings us sweetly down the road, why not make quick sense of two parallel successes, both so ubiquitous here in Fortress America?

By 1960 NASCAR was runnin', well, *good*. New blacktop tracks opened that year in Charlotte and Atlanta; the first live broadcast of a NASCAR event was carried on CBS; the Detroit manufacturers were pouring engineering and money and support and northern industrial ambition all over the sport to make sure that fans got the message that Ford or Chevy or Chrysler or Plymouth was the baddest, fastest mother out there. "Win on Sunday, sell on Monday" was the sampler stitched and hung on the walls of every executive mansion in Grosse Pointe, at least until the moment a car got loose and flew off the track and killed somebody; or the horsepower race got too contentious or expensive; or *they*, audible gasp, started losing. Samplers were then stashed in the breakfront drawer. Fickle manufacturer teams came and went erratically as pot-metal clockwork in those days, hypersensitive to every whisper on the marketing breeze. Racing went on with or without their official help, of course, guided as it was by the unflappable and breeze-proof Mr. France.

That Messrs. France and Walton must have shared some quality of stubborn grit seems obvious to me, but whether they were alike in other ways is harder to say. I would venture a guess that the burning bush of their original vision flamed brightly in them both, long before the billions started rolling in, and long after, too. How else to explain such excessive success? They must have had the common touch in common, as well, at least insofar as they could sense what it was folks really wanted. And rarer still, the savvy and the leverage and the energy to give it to them. Or, more truly, sell it to them. Both were showmen, that much I know, and understood the need to catch a customer's eye, to tickle their guarded fancies, to lift them up out of the furrows of the rural ordinary, if only momentarily.

Certainly both responded and adapted to the changing tastes of their times and clientele; a retailer had to, whether he was selling Sunday shows or sewing notions. Through the upending '60s, then, both not only kept their feet, but flourished.

Like Wal-Mart, NASCAR was still a regional success story in those tumultuous times. For truly national glory it would have to wait patiently a while, to be discovered, then rediscovered, then discovered yet again, by television. Still, the gate was good and steady and The Show ran up to 60 dates a year; everywhere from the asphalt palace at Daytona to the red-dirt fairgrounds back in Raleigh. The stars changed some, but the newest seemed even brighter than the old. Gentleman Ned Jarrett now, and Joe Weatherly and David Pearson were the names that every trackrat knew. But the biggest of them all was Richard Petty, whose first of those seven championships came in 1964. And it was on Petty's slender shoulders that the sport would be publicly borne forward in the years and decades ahead.

In the 1960s, though, NASCAR's home in the Solid South seemed exactly that when viewed from way up north—a solid, all one thing and indivisible. Opaque, impenetrable, indistinguishable from one part to the next, a monolith of cracker cult and culture. And all those firehoses and attack dogs on the news didn't help any when it came to growing NASCAR's brand. Stock-car racing got filed in the brain pans of all those Madison Avenue television programmers and taste- and style- makers right along with all the other grace notes of Faulkner and Carson McCullers—race hatred, casual sadism, intractable poverty, religious zealotry, small-mindedness, drunken revelry, and every other gothic cliché of violent southern horror. Now whether these things were true or not was not the point, per ABC or NBC or Y & R. Perception, per se, was the problem. The American South was nothing but hot buttons to media mavens, a lose-lose all the way down the line. (The only other TV South you ever saw was pickin' and grinnin' played for laughs—à la Andy Griffith and Jed Clampett.) As television sports themselves came of age, NASCAR was thought of as not much more than a novelty act, an occasional eight-minute filler on *Wide World of Sports*, like barrel-jumping from Lake Placid. In any case, northern prejudice regarding southern prejudice kept NASCAR's national growth in check at about the line of Mason and Dixon.

It still grew up a money tree in home ground, though, and more tracks got paved and opened, including the monster ring at Talladega, Alabama, the superest, duperest superspeedway of them all, in 1969.

So fast was the 2.66-mile track that the marquee drivers balked at running there. They presented, in a group, their objections to their boss, Bill France. It was too fast and the surface wasn't right and the cars would get airborne and come down who knows where and a man could get himself killed there just trying to earn a paycheck. They weren't cowards, but they weren't dumb either, so they got together and said they wouldn't run it.

Paradoxically (or not), France the Master Organizer was no fan of unfamiliar organizations. Like ad hoc drivers' associations, say, one of which this appeared to be. His reply to the drivers, per the scabrous scrolls, was to call up minor-leaguers and let them run the Sunday Show. A few years earlier he had put down another such putsch, on similar blunt terms. Bill France was not a union man. Which makes some sense in its time and place, because there was precious little southern love for Union or for unions.

Which brings us back, neatly if not swiftly, to Sam Walton of Bentonville, Arkansas, another organization man with no taste for organizations other than his own. Another parallel uncovered! Few unions ever signed a charter under either man's visionary gaze or loving thumb.

So two more iron fists shake hands across the arc of our small story.

NASCAR ran its final race on native dirt in 1970, the same year one of its cars first topped 200 mph, taking us deftly into the next decade when we reopen our pocket history somewhere down the road.

Back on the wide-open interstate our confidence has been partially restored. It's much easier to drive a motorhome when there's nothing around you to hit but north Texas, so the trip's been a good one, fast and loose all the way—with the exception of Arkansas itself, where Interstate 40 runs the breadth of the state as rough as a cob at every inch. Oklahoma, though, is smooth satin.

Saw the Tallest Cross in the Hemisphere a few hundred miles back, just outside Groom, Texas. Saw it for what seemed like a long time, too, coming upon it mile after mile as it loomed up white and stark out of the low hills and the scrub and the puckerbush. No time to stop this go-round, but we'll be back again this way real soon. Near 200 hundred feet high from what I could judge as we passed. Which has raised a persistent question in my tired mind these last few hours, the expansion strips ticktock ticktock ticktocking away beneath our tires. Just how tall would this Texas Jesus be?

There's a theological question in the same vein that recurs out here in NASCAR country. Its answer is argued with passionate, if not always reasoned, debate. The question arose as a further, and infinitely more complex, adjunct to the headscratcher posed by those popular WWJD bracelets.

The letters stand for "What Would Jesus Do?" a handy, if somewhat monotonous, rhetorical reminder to consider the outcome when you're about to do something the moral consequences of which you're unsure. Like shoplift, for example. As you're about to palm that pack of Newports, or boost that pint of Old Harper, you see the bracelet swinging on your wrist. "What Would Jesus Do?" you ask yourself. Well, *Jesus wouldn't steal* comes the heavenly reply. Same thing as you're about to climb onto your neighbor's wife. Presuming you've even left the bracelet on, there it is, rattling away, asking you "WWJD" in a case like this? *Jesus wouldn't commit adultery.*

Honestly, in simple instances like this, the answer is always going to be Jesus *Wouldn't*. JW. Smaller bracelet. Less to remember. Any endeavor that requires you to pause long enough to even *ask* the question has already *answered* the question. Jesus *Wouldn't*. And if you enjoy spending your weekends thieving cheap liquor and riding married women like carousel ponies, you're not likely to be wearing the bracelet unless you've shoplifted it by mistake.

In trickier situations, frankly, the bracelet's of even less use. "What would Jesus do about getting those mocked-up wire-frames over to the software development guys by Friday?" Jesus isn't down in the mailroom, he's *Jesus*.

Paper or plastic? White or wheat? Lay up or play 3-wood? WWJD? You're better off with a Magic 8-Ball. Thus, in the last few years, some of the rhetorical utility and bracing moral impact of WWJD seem to have ebbed, leaving those letters and the nurturing spirit they represent to be found these days reduced to a peppy epigram engraved on marbleized-resin executive desk sets ordered through in-flight magazines.

"What do you mean they never got there? Jesus Christ! Connie! Get me Jesus Christ over in shipping! *Right now!*"

Gearheads, race fans, and the profitably waggish re-posed the original question on more meaningful terms. WWJD? has now become What Would Jesus Drive? A more potent form of dialectic by far for millennium America.

So far I've seen all kinds of answers, too, on hats and T-shirts and novelty can huggers (i.e., a Ford, Dodge, Pontiac, the usual lineup); heard the arguments raised and pursued. Daytona, Week 2: "C'mon, Jesus wouldn't drive a Firebird and you know it." I've considered the question quite a lot myself, especially on longer hauls like this one. As we near the track at Las Vegas, the Beep peacefully snoozing, I suggest to myself, an admitted reactionary, that there's one, and only one, answer to the question, "What Would Jesus Drive?"

A pickup. Chevy pickup. He's a carpenter.

There's a life lesson in here somewhere, I suspect, because here in America you are what you drive. The Beep and I, for example, are an infuriating impediment to progress and personal fulfillment. As powerful as our engine might be, all that horsepower, all that torque, is devoted to the painstaking long-term accrual of momentum, to simply overcoming the inertia of books and clothes and equipment, of bedroom, kitchen, bath. Sure, once we get up a head of steam, like a locomotive, there's no stopping us (literally), but a motorhome, it's become clear to me, is something, especially in close quarters, people instinctively, angrily pass.

No matter its speed or course or its position relative to your own, you must pass it, aggressively, smugly, closely. That was how I'd always treated them, certainly, as something to be swung around, briefly mocked, perhaps flipped off, then left behind.

Which makes practical sense, because you worry about being trapped in a motorhome's blind spot. (Note to drivers everywhere: From the cockpit of a motorhome, it's *all* blind spot.) So, honk, zip, flip, there you go.

At the level of thoughtful driver safety, then, passing a motorhome is an act of rationality.

Still, there is something like disrespect in the way people go zooming past us, something careless and mean. My wife and I are both pretty good people and pretty good drivers, and productive contributors to the national economy. But we are a rolling roadblock now, something to be got around. We are perceived as elderly, unsafe vacationers, oblivious double-dipping Social Security pensioners, unproductive back-markers in the Great American Race to Nowhere in Particular.

Struggling against the parry and thrust of our nation's traffic, I see this as an apt metaphor for growing old in America generally, for being passed up, for being swerved around, briefly mocked by cocky, indifferent youth, then left safely behind. Weirdly, I find these little insights liberating, almost soothing.

Because it means I can let go a little, throttle back a couple of clicks. Not so much literally as figuratively. Like every other American since the beginning of time, I buy a car as a reflection of my imagined character and then operate it in keeping with my fantasy self-image. For some of us that means the cowboy butch of the unnecessary pickup truck or the swinging dick swoop-and-zoom of the useless sports car. For others, it means the broad child-bearing hips of a minivan; the rock-jock bling-bling SUV; the 4-button, 4-door sedan with matching vest; the Kermit-green, Muppet-cute subcompact; and on and on and on, across every recombinant demographic of sex and age and race and class.

Pulling away from the curb, having donned those various identities, revved up on self-importance and a sense of indispensability and indestructibility, we engage in the mortal combat of the afternoon commute. Every one of us racing to the next pivotal moment in our lives, the next meal, the next Brazilian wax, the next exit; so much to do, so many places to go, so much aggression to vent. Honk! Honk! Get out of my way! Can't you see that I'm a hip/hungry/harried/hairy suburbanite of evident means and enviable ambitions and noteworthy taste with someplace important to be? Don't you watch television? Haven't you seen the commercials for my car? Get out of my way!

The mottled, raging face we show the world with our cars is part of our American entitlement.

For the rest of this year, happily, it's a war game I can't play. Since my highway identity is already fixed by the fact that I'm doddering along in a motorhome, I will be forced to learn patience and the principles of passive resistance. I will be made to turn the other cheek. I will be made to use the slowest wide-load toll booth, all the way to the right. Here, perched in my three-way-adjustable captain's chair, I will become Buddha, I will become Gandhi, I will drive as politely as Jesus. It's a feeling of ease and release, a setting down of grudges and swords.

SIX

Jackpot! Tits and tats everywhere! Easy money and showgirl sex for everyone!

The Las Vegas track complex is about 10 miles off the Strip, out past Nellis Air Force Base. Without a toad we're stuck at the track, so no gambling or Wayne Newton or $5.99 prime rib platters for us.

Great parking spot, however, our first time in an already-level infield. And there are pay-as-you-go showers, too, set up for the camping crowd in the back of a converted tractor-trailer rig—hydrotherapy and hygiene for high-mileage, exhausted us, two bucks a scrub.

The Las Vegas track is nearly new, built 1996, a 1.5-mile all-purpose oval, and the place has all the bells and whistles and fan attractors that the Rock lacks. Luxo skyboxes and lots of pearly bathrooms and a broad bazaar area out front for the fan midway, including thatched-roof margarita bars. Also a nifty infield press center. The claim for grandstand seating here is 126,000, twice what you'll find back at the little Rock. Up above the backstretch, a millionaire's row for motorhomes, flat pads for the Prevost high-rollers—near $1,000 for the weekend package, I'm told. Everything here as clean and sandblasted bland as can be. Generation Next for NASCAR.

The track's part of a racing park out on the sharp edge of the desert. A couple of short tracks and a drag strip and from the moment we roll in, not a second's quiet. Race engines winding hard at every hour. Beautiful view back down the mountain to the lights and enticements below, City of the Hard Six.

The southern California crowd is in attendance, it seems, more Rolex than Timex, lots of tailored slacks and $120 haircuts and faux alligator bags and weapons-grade sunglasses mixed in with the denim and the Vans and the home-perms. Long, lean suburban superwives knifing through the knots of slow-moving unattractive round people, hissing *"Excuse me,"* like an accusation.

Further proof that the Tide car has the bitchin'est paint scheme ever. Met a couple of guys up from SoCal with a moho parked in the infield. Mid-thirties, khaki board shorts, solid Gap Tees. Graphics designers/manufacturers of trade-show displays. Midmorning margarita blender set to frappé. At the top of their flagpole, an upended 300-wash jug of Tide. Tide banners snapping below. Inside moho, orange/white/navy accents from front to back. Dinette tabletop decaled up with perfect replica of life-size Tide car hood. "We just think it's really cool. We root the logo."

Kerry Earnhardt. Dale's other son. He looks uncannily like the Intimidator, right down to the mustache, though his braces lessen the intimidating effect somewhat. He's Dale Jr.'s half-brother. Kerry's a rookie driver this year in the Busch series. Drives the #12 SuperCuts car, co-owned by former Steelers quarterback, now Fox broadcaster Terry Bradshaw.

Saturday Busch race notes: As Kerry and his wife walk to the grid prerace, he signs a few autographs, a handful. Junior would have been overrun. He smiles a bashful smile, though, every time, and whenever fans thank him for signing, he thanks them back. Happy, clipped "thang-kyeeuw." More molasses in his drawl than Junior's. Pale skin, flushes red in the sun and the heat. He seems shy. Slim, he looks exactly like his dad one moment, when he tips his chin just right; then utterly unlike him the next—some quality of uncertainty in his eyes.

Bradshaw is on top of the pit box for the race. Wears his black Kangol cap backwards. When he lifts it, readjusts it, you see the glowing scalp, the perfect tonsure gone Harlow platinum.

Kerry runs as high as third late in the race, but with only 20 laps left he plummets back through the field on each successive lap. The car looks winded. I have him finishing nineteenth. He drives the car back to the foot of the SuperCuts hauler. Unhooks, unharnesses, un-helmets, pulls himself from the car with a wide smile, wipes the sweat pouring from his face with his sleeve, and walks into the truck to change. Behind him a woman turns to her friend. "It looks like his daddy just spit him out his mouth."

Outside the press center, I saw a woman with a disposable camera taking a picture of Dale Jarrett's picture on a Coke machine.

Stood with Kevin Harvick for a while watching him sign autographs as he sat behind the counter of the Mr. Goodwrench merchandise trailer. This is a regular chore for the drivers. Some aren't very good at it, from what I saw at Daytona—they sit there tight-lipped and tuckered out, heaving romance novel sighs when they think no one's looking. Harvick's a natural, though, full of sass. Easy with the fans. A hundred folks in line? Hundred and fifty? Harvick's from just over the mountains in Bakersfield, California. These are his people. They rib him and yell out as they wait,

"Kevin, man, you gotta run that late feature at Bakersfield! I'll take you over there myself!"

"Dude, I saw you in Chico!"

"North High sucks!" which gets a laugh from everybody.

"Kevin, you want a bologna sandwich?"

"Kevin, give us a smile!"

"Dude, you started using Viagra yet? Mark Martin's kickin' your ass!" which gets a boo from everybody. Harvick smiles.

A voice from back in the crowd pipes up, "Hey, Kevin, I'm a good friend of Jason Smalls!"

"I'm sorry to hear it," says Harvick and cracks everybody up.

He signs anything they hand him, including used race tires they heave up onto the counter (glitter-silver Sharpies are kept handy for doing so). These used skins are a popular commodity out here with the serious collectors. "Get a nice thick piece of tempered glass cut in a round, and it makes a decent coffee table."

He'll do this for another hour or so, the people arriving from the long line to his right, having their pictures taken with him, sliding their caps or photos or diecasts in front of him. He'll sign them with a black Sharpie, slide the item away to his left, the fan going with it, and say "Thanks."

"See?" the Viagra/Martin fan says to his friend as they walk away, Harvick's signature on a race program drying fast in the desert air, "I *told* you he wasn't an asshole."

I took my first official graft today. Some swag from Winston. I just wanted to see how it felt. The answer? Awkward.

Let's define our terms. Swag is the free stuff given away to print reporters and members of the electrified press by various institutions and organizations for no apparent reason other than goodwill. Also known as boodle or loot. Promotional "gifts."

It can be absolutely innocent; or it might imply a devilish reciprocity between giver and taker. Those implications and the consequences vary, of course, from individual to individual and setting to setting. On a hard news beat (statehouse, city government, etc.) taking almost anything from almost anyone is frowned upon; not that you're ever offered much. On the entertainment desk, the gifts pour down like manna, in the form of elaborate press kits for movies and TV shows that contain lots of swell Hollywood stuff. At the Style section it's fragrances and cosmetics and clothes. Most of it goes in the trash or to charity.

In the Venn diagram of journalism, sports is that awkward overlapping figure between news and entertainment.

Especially vexing to the press box fussbudget is this NASCAR deal. Huge sponsor corporations have millions of dollars literally riding on these Cup race weekends, trying to hammer those names and logos down into the heads of the fans, and it's certainly in their direct interest to have the press on their side in doing so.

Unlike football or baseball or hockey, where I'm only ever going to write "Giants," "Astros," "Blackhawks," out here I have to make a decision between using "the blue #15 car" in a story or "the blue #15 NAPA Auto Parts car." They might or might not take it out when the editor sees it back on the sports desk, but you can see why it's to the sponsors' advantage to keep their name, their brand, rattling around in the desiccated noggins of all us writers and broadcasters.

So I was sitting up in the press box when the lead Winston PR guy, to whom I've been introduced exactly once, came up behind me and put a hand on my shoulder. Real soft he said, "Go on downstairs." I wasn't sure what he meant and my expression evidently made that clear, because then he added, "Go on downstairs. We've got a little something for everybody. Right behind the staircase."

Behind the stairs was a small office, in which one of the other publicists was handing out nylon jackets promoting Winston's season-long "No Bull 5" program, a complex, recurring driver-participation sweepstakes in which fans can win $1 million. The fan could actually *earn* a million faster than I can explain how it works here.

"Here you go," was all he said to me. The jacket was nothing special, navy nylon with the logo and the promotion name stitched in. It was wrapped in plastic and I took it and said, "Thank you," and walked back out of the little room. I tossed the jacket into a cabinet when I got back to the motorhome, resolving to give it or throw it or send it away later. And sat for a while, thinking.

I didn't feel like I owed anyone anything. But still I felt complicit. Roped in. The jacket's a goad to memory. Like any advertisement, its function is to help me remember a product, a name, a relationship. What I'd sold for the price of a nylon jacket was one more little corner of ad space in my head, a few more synapses lost forever to commerce. When called upon to do so, my brain would now loyally spit out "Winston" or "No Bull Five" incrementally faster than it had before. And if that happened often enough, wouldn't the phrase, the product, the slogan be more likely one day to creep into the conversation, into the newspaper, the book, the magazine?

More dangerous yet is this: the grubby and unspoken premise that NASCAR and Winston and I are somehow all in this together. That we're friends. That we're all working the same smart side of the midway while we roll from town to town clippin' the straights. Welcome to the team! Man, you make that jacket look good! High five!

But we aren't in this together. Are we? At least we shouldn't be.

Go on downstairs, says the Devil, we've got a little something for everybody.

Walking around the infield before the Cup race I stopped and looked for a long time at Jeff Gordon's pit. It's a 20-by-15-foot space, tight and tidy as a hospital bed, marked off from the walkway behind it by lengths of lightweight plastic chain hanging between posts welded up to old automobile wheels. Like the velvet rope at a nightclub, the chain keeps out the unwelcome, in this case the locust swarms of fans. Not every team bothers—they don't have to. Nobody much trying to sneak into Hut Stricklin's pit to steal a lug nut (another item prized by fetishists). Everything in the #24 pit stall that's bigger than a hand tool and made of metal is painted in the DuPont sponsorship basecoat, deep metallic medium blue. Posts, chains, pit box, generator. Everything blue and dazzling, like it's sunk in the shallows of the Caribbean. The 11-gallon gas cans are the only exception; those are always red, no matter the team's colors.

Once Goodyear hands out the race tires to the teams, the teams lay them out flat in the pit stall. The number of sets of tires you get varies by event, by racetrack. Here at Las Vegas, there are six full sets laid out flat in the stall, ready for the race, and several more sets stacked against the fenceline behind the pits. Sometimes the crewmen have to struggle through a snag of fans behind their pit box to grab equipment. Mostly they're very polite about not knocking them down to do so.

The race rolled around this afternoon, almost an afterthought to a weekend's worth of lounge singers and sequins and roulette wheels. I still haven't figured out how to watch these races to best effect. If you're down on the track you can't see the grand, kaleidoscopic design. If you're up in the stands you can't see the hundred small skirmishes that make up any race. If you watch it on television, you're watching a four-hour television show. Maybe I need to start doing what the Beep and I see so many fans doing—looking out at the track while they sit on top of the coach or the scaffold watching television and listening to the race call on the radio, bathing in the sun and the catastrophe of noise and the oily mother funk and the Mermaid Parade of jiggling flesh. It's worth a try.

The Household Goddess and Queen Mum of All Pit Lizards Everywhere sat on Dale Jr.'s toolbox for as much of the race as she could stand today. Pamela Anderson and her retinue of show business underlizards cut a wide swath through the goggling human crowds as she made her way to the royal pit box. Grunts and groans and the low rhythmic wailing of male animals in distress were clearly audible, even above the hack and rumble of the cars. She is a tanned and tiny Barbie Doll, utterly unself-conscious and yet completely self-involved. She seems to move in a flawless bubble of perfectly tuned self-regard, knowing exactly, but not caring even a little, the effect she trails in her wake. She was wearing some sort of track-savvy, shoulder-modest T-shirt, too, instead of the black leather BarbWire bondage corset you might expect. No open-toed shoes, either.

The other celebrity sighting for the day was the famous professional wrestler Goldberg, wandering into the press box and asking permission to use the men's room. He had no bubble, flawless or otherwise, but looked only like a tall, broad man with an urgent need to urinate.

Sterling Marlin won what can best be described as a soothing afternoon of racing. The knock on these modern mile-and-a-half ovals is that, perhaps like Ms. Anderson or the city of Las Vegas, they promise nasty action but deliver mostly tepid letdown. In any case, the race was hypnotic in its 2 hours and 55 minutes of all those colors circling and circling and circling. Once roused from their torpor, the crews couldn't pack those haulers fast enough.

Sterling Marlin, son of beloved stocker Coo Coo Marlin and a Volunteer son of Tennessee, is still the points leader. He is on quite a roll.

The Beep and I convene a family meeting at which we briefly consider the many merits of skipping the next stop on the tour, Atlanta, 2,000 miles and three days away.

Instead, our flip-flops flapping with what sounds like resolve, we make our way back to the $2 washhouse to bank whatever cleanliness we can against a showerless, 72-hour leap to the east.

Scrubbed pink as newborns we light out into the rising sun. Flying from J to J to J, back through Kingman and Flagstaff and turquoise Albuquerque, past the Texas King Kong Jesus and those washboard flats of Arkansas, down through Memphis, Tupelo, and Birmingham, past. that scary fast track at Talladega, all the way to the city Sherman burned. We make good time.

The Atlanta track is not actually in Atlanta, but about 20 miles due south, just between Hampton and Inman, Georgia. Coming in off the highway you turn and turn again through the woods, passing lots of fine little white houses with green roofs set back in the trees, or tucked next to the fields, and then you turn a bend and without warning the track jumps out of the forest at you. There's a condominium complex built up behind the fourth turn, 10 or 12 stories it looks like as we pass, and it gives the isolated racetrack a sense of awkward disproportion from what surrounds it. And an ominous sense of being, well, lived at.

Parked and level outside the tunnel entrance by turn 1, we have a little time before lights-out tonight to devote another moment to the study of NASCAR. Not its history in this instance, but its arithmetic.

Bad Math 1

It is an article of faith out here that the NASCAR Cup Series is now the "number two sport in America." What that means exactly I have no idea, but it's a phrase the flacks and the glad-handers keep mumbling into their cell phones.

The idea that NASCAR has come so far so fast as to become the "number two" sport in the country has me vexed. Not *how* it became popular—that's pretty easy to see after a day at the track. It's a hell of a good time in about all the different ways a good time can be lawfully if not reasonably had, and its attractions for a broad audience (with noteworthy exclusions and exceptions) are easy to spot. And I take NASCAR's claim of 75 million total fans on faith, for now.

But "number two" in what way? Revenue? Ratings? The number of fans? The hearts of its countrymen? What's the method and what's the measure? If it's strictly an issue of television ratings, we'll return to the topic another time.

I did manage to download some numbers while we were in Las Vegas, though. They have to do with an assertion I see again and again in the press kits, which I then see repeated in various forms in the press. The gist, repeated in all its variations, is this: "NASCAR has the highest per-event attendance of any sport in America."

Bam! Take *that*, football! Take that, baseball! Take that, America! What do you think of us now!

While no doubt flattering to the sport's fans, it's also an impressive statement to share with potential investors like sponsors and advertisers, and it's clearly an in-house feel-good stat for NASCAR. It also floats unquestioned through a lot of newspaper and magazine and wire stories concerning the sport's astonishing growth.

Cup racing does have, by a wide margin, the highest per-event attendance figures of any major-league sport. On any given weekend across the 36-race season, NASCAR puts an average of 186,000 fans in the seats.

What do they pull for an NFL game in your hometown these days? Be honest—50K? 60? 70? The NFL, mighty gold standard for American sports business, pulls . . . not even *half* the NASCAR number—66,000 per event by their own accounting! Scrawny suckling-pigskin underattenders!

But there are 186,000 NASCAR fannies in the seats week in and week out. Major-league baseball? An embarrassment! Only 28,000 fannies through the turnstiles! The NBA, long-beloved business model of MBAs everywhere and '90s darling of Madison Avenue? A mere 17,000 fannies, including Jack Nicholson's. NHL hockey? A puny 16,500. Pathetic, eh?

So there it is: 186,000 NASCAR fans per event, 36 events, nearly 6.7 million devoted American fannies a year. Monster numbers.

This is where my vexations begin.

As true as all that is—and remember it's all absolutely, factually true based on the numbers I turned up from the various leagues—it also sounded terribly incomplete to me.

"NASCAR has the highest per-event attendance of any sport in America."

But aren't there an awful lot more events played across the seasons of those other sports? By an awful lot more teams? And aren't they playing in much smaller venues? There aren't many basketball courts the size of Daytona International Speedway.

If you add up the weekly averages of all the teams playing all the games to get the season totals, the gross numbers shake out like this:

Annual NFL attendance: 16 million
Annual NHL attendance: 20 million
Annual NBA attendance: 20 million
Annual MLB attendance: 67 million

In which case NASCAR's 6.7 million looks a little anemic. "We're number five of the five leagues in this statistical sample" doesn't have much lilt to it, either. Of course, there's no way to accurately project what might happen to the numbers if NASCAR ran a 162-race season; maybe they'd draw 200 million people a year. Just as there's no way to calculate what would happen if the NFL started playing a 36-game season and building football stadiums to seat 250,000 people.

But there's a warning inherent in sleep-inducing bedtime exercises like this. Beware of press-kit arithmetic.

So this is first Atlanta, the second weekend in March. We've made the trip back from Las Vegas, 2,002 miles by the official NASCAR road atlas, in three days. Last week, we drove to Vegas from Rockingham, North Carolina; 2,395 miles in three days. 4,400 miles over six days of driving.

On Saturday, worn out from the driving and sluggish from the frantic pace of the weekend work, we walked out past the big tunnel and all the way down the access road parallel to the backstretch and around to those chalet-style condos by the Richard Petty grandstands. As we were heading back up past the fan midway, it must have been around 6 in the evening, twilight just coming on, we saw a medevac helicopter landing next to the campground across from the frontstretch grandstand. It hovered for a few seconds, making the branches clatter in the trees, and then set down in a clearing about 100 yards away from us.

As soon as the skids hit the turf, an ambulance rolled out of the campground access road with its lights flashing. I jogged over to a Georgia state cop standing back in the trees to ask what had happened. I thought maybe I'd missed an accident on the track or something. For some reason I held up my NASCAR credential as I came toward him.

"Excuse me, officer, do you know what's happening?" I shouted.

He took my photo ID in his big thumb and forefinger and studied it for a second or two, comparing my face to the one on the small plastic card. It isn't a press pass, but it was the only thing I had with me that might differentiate me from any other morbidly curious passerby. Looking at him, with that squared-away campaign hat and those razor creases in his uniform, the crisp outline of his Kevlar vest beneath his uniform blouse, the patent leather Sam Browne rig creaking and jangling with hardware, you could see that he wasn't about to answer casual questions from the merely inquisitive. He was a large man, young and ham-faced, with a neck that went straight up to his ears.

"I'm a reporter," I yelled helpfully, as always. The thwack and rattle of the rotors was deafening.

"Had a man drunk," he yelled back, letting my credential fall.

Just then, behind him, the EMTs opened the rear doors of the ambulance. They tugged out the gurney. Lying on it was a man with his head swathed in bandages. The gurney was tilted up at a 45-degree angle and so was he. He was shirtless and bandaged like a mummy from his chest to the crown of his head, with only a small opening left in the wrappings for his eyes. What little skin you could see looked very, very red. We both watched for a second.

"Had a man drunk," the trooper said again, "and he fell."

I nodded. They were lifting the gurney very gently into the chopper. The bandaged man was held by restraints and was perfectly still.

"You know those backyard turkey fryers? So you can deep-fry your holiday turkey or whatever?"

I nodded again.

"Man was so drunk he fell into his, is what happened."

I don't think I nodded.

"Can you imagine? Too drunk to cook. He looked mighty bad, too, when we got to him. Went right in up to his arms I guess, like he dove into it headfirst. And he was in there for a while, too, 'cause there wasn't much skin left on him. But can you imagine?"

I could not.

Eventually the helicopter wound up and took off, the branches clattering again, and flew north to Atlanta and the hospital at Emory University, carrying the man I would forever after think of as "The Olde English 800 Patient."

I thanked the officer and left. When I ran back and told the Beep about it she was rightly horrified. As we talked about it, we were respectful of the man's terrible suffering. And we were sorry for the grief and pain it must have caused his family. Really. But I had the feeling that for the rest of the season, certain phrases were going to recur. Perhaps cracking us up. "Never drink and fry," maybe, or "Always fry responsibly."

"Friends don't let friends fry drunk," suggests the Beep.

In the spirit of self-improvement, I've been going back through the work of other, better racing writers when I can, to see if I can hone my race-reporting skills. I'm still not sure where to watch from, or what to watch for, but I'm not too proud to get tips from my colleagues or to follow the good example of others. I went back, in fact, a little further than I originally intended.

First written race report *ever*, from Book 23 of the *Iliad*, filed after the running of the chariots at Patroclus's funeral.

They then all mounted their chariots and cast lots—Achilles shook the helmet, and the lot of Antilochus son of Nestor fell out first; next came that of King Eumelus, and after his, those of Menelaus son of Atreus and of Meriones. The last place fell to the lot of Diomed son of Tydeus, who was the best man of them all. They took their places in line; Achilles showed them the doubling-post round which they were to turn, some way off upon the plain; here he stationed his father's follower Phoenix as umpire, to note the running, and report truly.

At the same instant they all of them lashed their horses, struck them with the reins, and shouted at them with all their might. They flew full speed over the plain away from the ships, the dust rose from under them as it were a cloud or whirlwind, and their manes were all flying in the wind. At one moment the chariots seemed to touch the ground, and then again they bounded into the air; the drivers stood erect, and their hearts beat fast and furious in their lust for victory. Each kept calling on his horses, and the horses scoured the plain amid the clouds of dust that they raised.

Homer goes on at quite some length, working under what must have been a generous deadline, and his descriptions of the event bear an uncanny similarity to what we've been seeing out here. Note, for example, the lottery for starting position. Exactly like the lottery for the Cup qualifying runs! Then there's the drivers' meeting and the eagle-eyed official taking up his position in the turn, and well, the parallels go on and on. That the drivers are all "fast and furious in their lust for victory" is a description so apt and timeless it could appear as a sports headline in any newspaper in the country tomorrow. It also contains about 129 plausible titles for your next screenplay.

Without reprinting Homer's entire lengthy dispatch (he was obviously being paid by the word), suffice to say that race day on the beach at Troy would have been utterly familiar to anyone who ever sat through an afternoon at the old track in North Wilkesboro. The crowd cheers. The drivers are introduced and commented upon. Their equipment and chances of success are analyzed. The prizes at stake are enumerated: cup, cauldron, woman, gold. The race begins and the action is described. We get the drivers' thoughts and hear them speak (just like listening in on the race radio), and we see them rubbin' and bangin' as they head for the far turn. Parts fail. Cheating occurs. Gods intervene. Race commentary from bystanders is overheard. Advice is shouted. The racers risk everything for glory on the homestretch. The winner gives a speech. The losers lodge a protest. Folks grumble about the outcome. Prizes are distributed and fines assessed. Drinks are served.

Only thing missing is the turkey leg.

Atlanta is a mile-and-a-half oval, high-banked and fast, and seems to reward the smooth application and maintenance of power and momentum rather than rubbin' and bangin'. Fast and furious in his lust for victory, Tony Stewart holds off Earnhardt Jr. by three-tenths of a second for the win after more than three hours and 500 miles of racing. Sterling Marlin is ninth and retains the points lead.

The race itself had a long-form, seamless feel to it, a streaming afternoon of color and engine rhythm, with only a couple of minor slides and spins and crackups to interrupt the flow and slow things down. Each race has a character of its own, I'm noticing, some of them brusque and halting and episodic-seeming, others nearly liquid over the length of an afternoon.

It depends which way you're looking. If you're looking down at the track on a day like today, the race flows past you easy and unbroken as a river. The only real tussle and grunt at first Atlanta came at the very end of things when Junior tried to get a run on Stewart in the last couple of laps but didn't have the horses, or more likely the tires, to catch him.

Down in the pits, though, the days come and go in spasms, the long wait between pit stops punctuated hard by the planned panic of the stops themselves.

Another phenomenon glimpsed today was the languor that sets in at about midrace. About an hour and a half into things folks start to lose their mojo. The fans are less attentive, the crowds in the pit lane start sitting down wherever they can, finding a little shade, wandering off to the concession stands. For about an hour, for everyone but the drivers and the crews and the officials, the day goes a little out of focus. I suspect that the car crews and the officials feel it too, even the drivers, but can't allow themselves to succumb to it. It's interesting to watch. The cars are hammering by and the blast of the track noise echoes up off the asphalt and everything's exactly as calamitous and explosive as it was five minutes before, but nobody cares. Nap time.

Everyone starts to stir again about half an hour before the finish. At the end, refreshed, they heave cheers and glory down on Tony Stewart's head. Prizes are distributed. Drinks are served. Rose-fingered twilight spreads her hand across the sky.

Monday sunup, we take our leave. Postrace, the Beep and I are off on a brief toot this week. A side trip to Savannah and Tybee Island, Georgia, before rolling up to mother Darlington for our first glimpse of the true old sod.

Savannah: statuary, cemeteries, stately homes, and Spanish moss. City Sherman didn't burn. We slept at the Wal-Mart. Midnight in the garden and patio department.

Out to Tybee Island. Sandy campground, empty beaches, lonely lighthouse, frozen custard. Altogether swell.

Visited Fort Pulaski, too, a national monument out in the grassland swamp mouth of the Savannah River. This stronghold of brick-and-earthworks, set to defend the city, saw hard use back and forth in the Civil War, violence and privation, and among the colonnades and arches and emplacements must linger many ghosts. Not many visitors, though—no more than a handful as the Beep and I walk the ramparts.

Down in the visitor center, a reminder of old joys even in hard times. The first known photo of a baseball game being played, circa 1862, right here.

We roll on to Darlington, South Carolina.

We're parked in the infield this go-round, on a little patch of grass reserved for employee parking and driver overflow. Convenient, yes, but loud during practice. Mighty loud. The infield nightlife is subdued, though, not the smoldering fleshpit of history we were warned of. No liquored-up naked people anywhere, in fact. Perhaps at the Labor Day date things will liven up.

From the roof of the press box here you can look away to the east and see the cottonseed mill rising up above the trees and look down at the odd asphalt oval and over at the minnow pond and out across the longline grandstands and back to the low, white track offices out along the S.C. 151/34, and the shape of these things to NASCAR fans is at once as familiar as home and as filled with unspeakable meaning as Angkor Wat or St. Peter's.

Right off, the Beep runs afoul of the Interstate Batteries crew in the garages. While trying to snap a picture of the car after practice, one of them shouts, "Get the fuck out of the garage!"

"What is *wrong* with people?" asks the Beep, with italicizable emphasis. "It was a picture of *the side of the car*."

I wonder what they're runnin' to make 'em so jittery?

Race day blows in with the threat of cold rain, and the crews put up tents and tarps in the pits just in case. A fan favorite is being reintroduced today, Steve Park, driver of the #1 Dale Earnhardt Inc. Pennzoil Chevrolet. Park was injured right here at Darlington last September in a Busch Series race and hasn't been back on a track since. Suffered what sounds to be a serious concussion—I heard him being interviewed on the radio and his speech is slurred and halting. Still, he assured the interviewer that no fewer than three doctors had cleared him to drive, so here he is. Gets a big hand when they announce him during driver introductions.

The honorary starter waves the green flag in weak circles, like he's trying to dust a ceiling fan, and we're off.

On lap 38 Park is gathered up in a nasty crash with Ricky Craven in turn 4 while leading the race. Huge roar as he walks to the ambulance. The stink from the tire smoke hangs in the damp air for a long time. Welcome back to The Show, Steve!

At Darlington they say you're racing the track as much as the other drivers. The cars are flung up those high bank turns and run the corners just an inch or two off the wall. Miss your mark and you've got a Darlington stripe, a scrape the length of the car's right side. Cars run upwards of 170 here, and a lap goes fast, a little over 30 seconds.

In the chill the crowd hunkers in blankets along the chain-link fence behind the pits. It looks like a refugee camp. Up in the grandstands the fans manage a cheer when Dale Jr. briefly grabs the lead, but remain impassive for all others. The midrace ennui takes hold early, and the crowd's not back in it until Mark Martin throws a shoe around lap 225 and backs into the wall. He runs the remaining 68 laps with a very short car.

Sterling Marlin wins and receives a moderate ovation for having done so.

After the race, Marlin idles over to Victory Lane. He is in his mid-forties, ash-blond and dashing, and a favorite of lizard and lady alike. Married, he politely reciprocates their appreciations by keeping the twinkle in his eye dialed up receptively at all times. His velvety drawl, nearly indecipherable even to Tennesseans without an official Shagbone Beauregard Pokeshank decoder ring, is compounded by his soft, rapid speech, and whole mumbled interviews come and go in which no one—bystanders, reporters, television viewers—has any idea what he's said. The only thing most casual auditors of a Marlin interview can understand is his smiling exit line, "Gotta go," which means it's time to fire up the car and get back to work. "Gotta go" has become an all-purpose punchline in the garages and press box these last few weeks, a perverse tribute to Marlin's sterling results, e.g.,

Editor, impatient: "How soon can you get that feature turned around for the Friday special section?"

Reporter, exiting: "WellnowwwwwwmmmmmmImalrdinnnnnna-bunchatrblwwwknwthasmbtchcommmafithreeohohhhmmmmm. Gotta go."

The real media stampede is for Junior, who came in fourth. As soon as he steps from his car, he is besieged by my pressmates. Nobody will say it yet, publicly, but it's apparent to me, an outsider, that Dale Earnhardt Jr. is, at this moment and into the foreseeable future, the most important man in stock-car racing. By far. In this new age, as Junior goes, so goes NASCAR.

No one took much notice of the holiday. It was March 17, after all, but St. Patrick wasn't in evidence at the track. Wrong crowd, I guess. NASCAR has few, if any, points of reference outside itself, out there in the world beyond the catchfence. Still, I saw at least one woman standing behind Dale Earnhardt Jr.'s pit stall who had noticed the calendar on her way out of the house.

She was in her early fifties, I think, and violently blonde. Her thin hair was teased up into a bright explosion of angelic platinum, a perfect halo, the radius of which was perhaps 12 or 14 inches from any point on her skull. To see the sunlight through it was to see the desert dawn rising beyond the antique ivory sheers of the late Liberace's Las Vegas master bedroom. Her eyebrows were black as anthracite.

She was wearing immense sunglasses, each lens the size and shape of a souvenir cast-iron frying pan. They must have weighed a great deal or been too dark, because she took them off every few seconds to look around and then, sighing, would replace them. She had pale skin lined just in keeping with her age, a small nose, enamel-blue eyes, and enamel-blue eyeshadow. She wore lipstick and nail polish one shade brighter than Signal Flare Cherry.

She was hammered and was suffering her variable center of gravity with as much grace as she could manage. She was completely aware of every move she made and she tried hard to move like Jayne Mansfield. She was wearing tight, complicated pants. They were black and they were trimmed at the low-rider waist and down the legs with silver conchos and they fastened across the front with a panel of big silver buttons, like the dress uniform pants of an admiral's cabin boy in the Gay Flamenco Navy. She wore black patent stiletto-heeled shoes. She was a short woman, but not when she wore these.

She was wearing a see-through crop-top peasant blouse of simple unbleached cotton. Seeing through it, one encountered a gigantic, maraschino-red brassiere. That she was a stout woman now, thick through the hams and hunkers and very large breasted is perhaps unnecessary to mention. That she had once been a bombshell was obvious.

She wore no rings or bracelets, but strung around her bare fish white waist was a fine gold belly chain as tight as piano wire. In honor of the day, hanging from the chain was a tiny green shamrock that jiggled whenever she did.

She was antsy. Maybe she was supposed to meet her date behind Jr.'s pit and he was late. Maybe she was bored. Whatever the case, she fiddled with her glasses or spun slow circles on one heel looking around or picked through her little quilted black patent purse while it hung from her wrist on a slender braided gold chain. Eventually she sighed again and dug out a cigarette.

Her cigarette was ultralong and ultrathin, and she smoked it with all the concentration and delicacy of an empress trying to suck the last buckwheat noodle off a single chopstick. She blew out the smoke like she was blowing kisses.

While she was thus engaged, a young man walked past her in a hurry on his way somewhere else. He was tall and lean and oblivious, a blur of blue jeans and black leather jacket, and as he passed the woman, he bumped her hard enough to knock the ash from her cigarette and spin her half a turn, and by the time she righted herself he was gone into the crowd. She looked after him, stood on her tiptoes, and craned her neck, but he was gone.

"That's just rude bein' rude," she shouted into all that engine noise and indifference. She collected herself. She had been a bombshell. She had been the 40-megaton belle of the Low Country, hotter than a two-dollar pistol in the phrase of her age, welcomed and wanted at every shag club from Pritchardville to Little River. She had been the Queen of All the South, and time does not, cannot, change that. She comforted herself in a voice like clouded honey. "That's just rude bein' rude," she said again, low, to no one, and went on waiting.

Off to Bristol. We take a quick spin through the resort town of Pigeon Forge, Tennessee, on the way up. Home to DollyWood, go-kart tracks, miniature golf, Lee ("Proud to be an American") Greenwood Theater, Mandrell sister theater (not Barbara. Lurlene? Irlene? Other?), many gift shops selling whitewashed butter churns and charmingly distressed farm apparatus, and candy stores to the near horizon selling taffy, candy apples, and every variety of fudge that the collective mind of all mankind might conceive.

It is early in the putt-putt/fudge/resort year, though, and we are nearly alone on the streets. I wrestle the unit through the gates of DollyWood, only to be told that it's not quite open for the season. The disappointment plain on the Beep's face melts the security guard's badge, if not his heart, so we get to park and walk around anyway. We visit the gift shop during inventory and are allowed to buy a souvenir refrigerator magnet. "Y'all were nice enough to come up to see us, I guess we can sell you one." The Beep beams.

Sometimes it feels so good to be out here.

Spring

Bristol is a tiny stadium track set in the hills of northeast Tennessee, a half-miler that seats 147,000 people. The drivers often compare racing here to flying a fighter plane in a toilet bowl.

We're camped on the drag strip that's been carved out of the hills and bare trees on an adjoining hillside. Great spot, but a long, long way down and up to get to the gate. As we walk out the first morning, though, a courtesy driver in a golf cart takes pity on us humping all our gear and gives us a lift. As we climb on, an older couple walks past, and I hear the husband say to his wife, "Thank God there's a Hooters car again."

The infield's so small here that there are no garages. The haulers are parked so close together you couldn't slide a dime between them. The crews work on the cars right out on the asphalt, and it gives the weekend the feel of a shade-tree race from 60 years before. It isn't, though. It's one of the hottest, best-attended stops on the schedule, with the bangin'est, crashin'est racing you can imagine. It's a favorite for the drivers and the fans.

Duly noted: Junior Johnson Pork Skins are $3 a bag at the infield concession stand. Reminder written on the #88 UPS team whiteboard for the day: "Keep a Kool head + a tight ass and let the left side drag." Sign towed overhead by light plane: "Erin will you marry me? Love, Stuart."

On Saturday I watched Kerry Earnhardt bounce around the track in the #12 car, clad for the Busch race in the bright metallic turquoise livery of the 10-10-220 sponsorship. As fast as the cars are going here, over 100 miles an hour on what amounts to a Roller Derby track, you turn to follow the last-place car go by, and before you can swivel your head back around, the first-place car has already past you. It's dizzying. Mesmerizing. Louder, by far, than any other track, too, because with the steep rake of all those seats, the sound has no place to go but straight into your brain. The fans, right on top of it all, can't get enough.

Midrace Kerry gets into the rear end of another car and crumples his front end, and by the time he makes it back to his pit, steam is boiling out from under the hood in magnificent plumes. The crew springs the hood with a pry bar and it's the noon show at Old Faithful. They swap out the radiator and the lines, at the expense of a great deal of burning and blistering and swearing, and get the car back on the track, but they're, what, 50 laps down?

The race is carnage: yellow flags every few laps, a demolition derby, every car on the track looks like a total-loss salvage from the

NYPD impound lot. In other words, best race of the season so far. Kerry Earnhardt finishes deep in the field, twenty-eighth, but wears that same wide smile when he climbs out of his battered car. Before the cars are even rolled back onto the haulers, workers are already out by the dozen, repainting the scarred walls of the track.

Sunday morning. Up in the press box, overheard: "This track'll give you as much speed as you want. Bring your space shuttle." Down on the track five people are riding around in a giant grocery cart firing T-shirts into the crowd with their T-shirt shooter. Cart must be 15, 20 feet high. Texas King Kong Jesus could use it if he went to Wal-Mart.

The cup race unfolds as hoped for by those in the stands and the press box and the giant grocery cart alike. Full-contact racing all the way around the track on every one of 500 laps. Cars into the wall throwing sparks, cars into each other by twos and threes, cars hit front and rear, cars spinning up the track and smoking the tires to spin around again and get back in it. It's a three-hour-plus chain-reaction accident. It's impossible to sort out, 14 lead changes and 14 yellow flags, and after an hour or so it's a continuous stream of cars all the way around and you have to check the scoreboard to see who's in front because whoever's leading is running neck and neck with cars a hundred laps down. Even the mandarins in the press box are excited, not talking or kibitzing as they normally might, but chain-smoking and eating Cheez-Its and staring down at the action like all the other fans.

Late in the race Elliott Sadler's engine blows up and oils the track and the whole field skates through the slick sideways. Coming out of the caution that results, Jimmy Spencer and Kurt Busch swap the lead back and forth, each running right up the back of the other trying to nudge their car out of the way. For the last 89 laps, the two pound back and forth like boxers. The preferred technique in these cases is known as the bump 'n run, wherein the trailing car gets the right side of its nose up under the left rear quarter panel of the leading car, gives it a little push coming out of the turn, thereby causing it to swerve and slow, at which point the trailing car speeds on by. The unspoken rules of engagement state that one ought not to put the target car in the wall, but these two have been drumming on each other all afternoon. With seven laps left Busch leads. Spencer bumps him up out of the way. With six laps left, Spencer leads. With five laps left Busch gets his nose up under Spencer's ample, dimpled roll pan and punts him near sideways coming out of turn 2. It's all Spencer can do to keep his car out of the wall and Busch steams on by for the win.

It's his first Cup victory and charmingly, he parks his car at the start/finish line, climbs out, stands on the windowsill, and waves like the king of the prom to 147,000 newly minted Kurt Busch fans.

On the way back into the pits, Dale Earnhardt Jr. and Robby Gordon bump and tussle to avenge some trouble out on the track. Gordon spins Junior out and throttles past. NASCAR officials glower and scribble notes.

Points leader? Still Sterling Marlin. Finished nineteenth.

Meanwhile, in the garage, over the sound of the celebratory confetti cannons, Spencer is muttering dark threats in the imperial first-person plural regarding young master Busch and his too-vigorous interpretation of the bump 'n run to the gathered media. "We never forget . . ." is the quote that runs everywhere the next day and the stage is set for a season-long feud between the two.

Or, as Homer put it, "Thus, while pressing on in quest of victory, they might both have come headlong to the ground. Menelaus then upbraided Antilochus and said, 'There is no greater trickster living than you are; go, and bad luck go with you; the Achaeans say that you have only poor understanding, and come what may, you shall not bear away the prize without sworn protest on my part.'"

Glory! Speeches! Grumbling! Protest! Prizes are distributed! Fines weighed! Drinks are served!

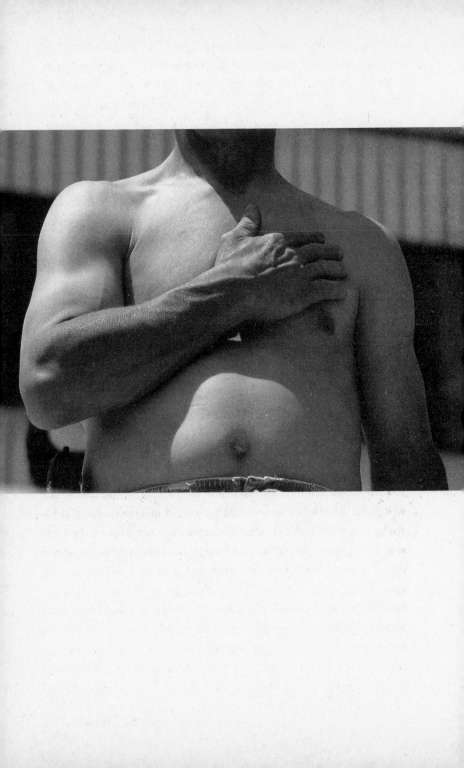

SEVEN

Suddenly we have no place to go. The Beep reminds me on Monday morning that the next stop on the tour, the Texas date, lies on the far side of the upcoming Easter weekend. This is one of the Cup schedule's rare down weeks. Mother's Day is another, and then another the last week in June. After which it's 20 straight races without a break. I'm so wound up and used to the quick ricochet from one track to the next to the next that I was halfway to Fort Worth in my racing mind before my head was even off the pillow. Without a race to race to, we are at a loss.

At breakfast, it is decided that we will pass the holy week in Mooresville, North Carolina, a northern exurb of Charlotte, just a couple of hours over the Smoky Mountains to the east from here. It is home to over 30 of these Cup teams, and most of the Busch and Truck teams, too. When we whizzed past it several weeks ago, it looked a likely place to cocoon for a few days.

We heave and roll through the morning hills and rumble out of the woods into Asheville, North Carolina. Then down the flume of the I-40 and the I-77 to Exit 36 and we are home. Not 200 yards off the highway the Mooresville Wal-Mart SuperCenter welcomes us, or so the sign promises. We'll set up housekeeping in the parking lot. All around us is spread the bounty of off-ramp America. Franchises and brand names and asphalt as far as the eye can see. Just over there is the AmStar 14 movie theater. Across the parking lot from it, the Atlanta Bread Company, a coffee shop and bakery, is the anchor store in a long one-story mall housing eight or ten little businesses. The Wal-Mart is ringed with other retailers and services, in fact; it's in a mall made up of other, smaller malls, 40 acres of clean fluorescence and customer satisfaction and free parking, and we can reasonably expect to find anything we might need during a short stay within walking distance.

The Exit 36 interchange is the new Mooresville. Here you'll find all these shiny new businesses humming away while construction crews frame up more new buildings across the street to bring in more shiny new businesses. The traffic runs thick at the traffic lights and the shopping centers, and there's a fancy new post office out by the fancy new water tower. The place bustles. On the water tower the sign reads "Race City, USA." Scattered beneath the compressed globe of the tower are many of the race operations for the Cup teams and the Busch teams. They're across the interstate from the Wal-Mart parking lot, 500 yards away, but coming out the door of the Atlanta Bread Company with your latte and your scone, you can still hear the engines being wrung out. Which doesn't seem to bother anyone, since most of the customers work in just such a race shop. "Timmy don't take no breaks, does he?" I hear a guy say into his muffin top as he walks past, head cocked to the noise on the breeze.

Mooresville's old town center is a couple of miles east of here, a short hop on Route 150, Plaza Drive, past a long succession of groceries and gas stations and lube 'n tunes and auto dealerships. The drive only takes five minutes, but you travel back 50 years.

At one end of the old business district lies the train station. It's a museum now. The tracks run double down the center of town, with Broad Street and Main Street running parallel on either side. At the other end of town stands the Bay State Flour Mill. Between them are the D. E. Turner and Company hardware store and several small branch banks and the town offices and Bob's Grill and the pawnshop and the racing-collectibles store and a bakery that does race cakes. Up past the flour mill are the pet shop and the Masonic Lodge. The Whataburger #11 is back by the train station. A few blocks farther on are the library and the Laundromat.

The buildings are mostly red brick and tired, and many are empty.

The Ford dealership moved out years ago, but on the side of the old building is the faded sign of an even longer gone tenant, W. W. Johnston and Sons Co., Inc. ICE and COAL. Might as well be a cave painting.

There isn't much traffic in town, wheeled or on foot, and the cop with the Snub Pollard mustache walks his afternoon beat smoking a pipe.

There are more race shops scattered across the industrial parks another mile or two beyond that flour mill. In the other direction, farther back into the fields and the woods, just past the last of the developments, 5 miles or so out the Coddle Creek Road, is DEI, Dale Earnhardt Incorporated.

Set out on rolling farmland, it's an immense two-story modernist cube with a three-story glass-sheathed cylinder fronting the road as an atrium and entrance. Against the hardwoods and the fields, it looks like it materialized there from a parallel dimension. The complex houses office space and fab shops and engine shops, all the work areas for the teams, the cars, and the haulers, as well as a gift store and some display areas. When shown the building after it first went up, Fox announcer and three-time Cup champion Darrell Waltrip reportedly dubbed it the Garage Mahal.

It is an easy building to mock, sitting out here in the middle of the alfalfa grid with its bland modular look and its blank walls and its gaudy reflective glass. But it's touching in a way, too; the building wears its ambitions right out where you can see them. A country boy who's outgrown the country. If you put the same building up in any office park in America, no one would look twice or call it anything at all.

This is where they came, for weeks in the winter of 2001, thousands at a time, to lay wreaths and candles and Teddy bears and elegies written on wide-rule notebook paper along the fence. The flowers were banked three feet deep. It is closed by the time we arrive.

We will return, certainly; Junior lives around here too, somewhere, and we'd be remiss if we didn't try to catch a glimpse of him in his natural habitat, Dirty Mo' he calls it, but the afternoon has made me mindful of all the tension at work around here between new and old.

That the two poles of Mooresville, stainless Exit 36 and ancient Main Street, share a town name in common and not much else is pretty obvious. It's happened that way all over the country. Life for a lot of us moved out to the nearest off-ramp a long time ago. That the DEI building looks vain and overeager set against a backdrop of second-growth hickory and beech is easy enough to see.

I have less evidence for my feeling that NASCAR itself is awkwardly caught between the old and the new. Despite its many recent successes, it seems hung somewhere between the city and the country, unsure how to shake its red-dirt past while grasping for its gold-lamé future. Is NASCAR Rockingham or is it Las Vegas? Can it be both?

It's more than a question of young gun drivers or new-generation skyboxes or $7 margarita huts. It's a sense that what happens on the track on Sundays is becoming a footnote to the *marketing* of what happens on the track on Sundays. The race itself is almost an afterthought, especially on television, where it's becoming a long-form infomercial, a delivery system for a syndicate of national sponsor brands.

I have a notion that somewhere behind all the sunny press releases there's a lopsided struggle under way between the runnin' and gunnin' fun-lovers at the sport's core, the holdouts and throwbacks—the *racers*—and the suits, for whom a slick, zipless corporate NASCAR makes perfect sense. It's a battle for what remains of the soul of the sport. Just a notion.

Not wanting to violate the unspoken motorhome covenant and live for an entire week in the Wal-Mart parking lot, we move to the Wildlife Woods campground in Sherrill's Ford on Tuesday. It's out on the shores of Lake Norman, about 15 minutes west of Mooresville, deep in Earnhardt country.

Lake Norman is the redneck riviera in these parts, a picturesque body of recreational water backed up into the valleys and hills when the Duke Power Company dammed the Catawba River. The rising water created a state park, and hundreds of miles of beautiful, buildable shoreline. Lots of Cup's biggest stars have elaborate homes along these pretty shores, with more moving in every year. Drive the winding lakeside roads and, behind the condos going up like game pieces and through the trees, you'll catch glimpses of gated estates that look like they were uncrated the night before last. French Normandy and Tudor and colonial and adobe styles all getting their chance, often as not on the same set of blueprints. Xanadu in a box. It's easy to spot the new developments out here. The fresh-turned earth is red as a pile of rubies.

Boaters dote on Lake Norman, of course, and when the weather warms, the bays and coves and cuts buzz with boats of every size and description. NASCAR fans know, too, that on any summer Monday, some of the larger boats—the long, sleek cabin cruisers— belong to their favorite drivers. Dale Earnhardt kept a boat here. A big one. The *Sunday Money.*

Our campground is a modest place, nearly empty of tourists this early in the season, but we've got a nice overlook of the small bay on which it sits. The lake level, regulated by the electricity-making needs of Duke Power, is low. There's a wide ring of cracked mudflat and marsh grass below the normal waterline, an extra 10 or 15 feet of beach, out beyond which the water looks tired and opaque. There's a shower house up the hill, and a pavilion, and the woman at the front desk tells us that Sterling Marlin's hauler driver lives here, too. Still, it's prettier than a parking lot, our new standard for such things, and much quieter.

In fact it is a quiet week generally, lots of thinking and walking, with only two events worth mentioning.

The first was a catastrophic midweek wastewater accident. It had nothing to do with Duke's nearby atomic reactor, but was infinitely worse. It requires an explanation.

Contrary to what your teenage son or daughter may unblushingly mean when they use the expression "hooking up," in the jargon of motorized camping it means plugging your unit into on-site services like water, electric, and sewer. What you're renting at a campground is a parking space with amenities. Some resorts, like Disney's Fort Wilderness, back there in central Florida's bear jamboree and encephalitis belt, offer cable television and telephone plug-ins as well.

At those windblown, hardscrabble campgrounds you see out in the howling middle of tumbleweed nowhere, looking like abandoned drive-in theaters with their electrical boxes and water faucets set cockeyed across an empty gravel pad, you might pay as little as $10 or $11 dollars a night. At a Disney resort, you'll pay $70. We're at the lower end of the scale here, and we get a break for booking the whole week. Most places offer discount rates for people who plan longer stays—or those who live in their tiny motorhomes year-round, as many do, going slowly, violently insane.

From one exterior onboard panel of your moho comes the thick umbilical line for electrical service, or "shore power" in moho lingo. Pull a sufficient length from the storage bay and plug it in at the service box. Now you can run your lights, microwave, air-conditioning, etc., on AC power. From the brass fitting a few feet farther forward on the port side, per what fragments I remember of our tutorial ("The white hose is for POTABLE WATER only! It is never to be confused with the something-something green hose! NEVER!"), you run the white hose from the motorhome to the outdoor tap ("DO NOT forget to install your inline PRESSURE REGULATOR! SOMETHING-SOMETHING!") and now you've got "city water" for showering, cooking, drinking, washing the dishes, and flushing the toilet.

There's also a big valve fitting at the lower left rear corner of our unit, to which one affixes a wide-gauge flexible hose for the drainage of any and all waters used or produced in conjunction with showering, cooking, drinking, dishwashing, and toilet flushing. One end connects to the holding tanks of the motorhome, the other to the on-site sewer fitting.

Here the problem begins.

Thumbs up. (*Dover International Speedway, September 2002*)

#6 crew. (*California Speedway, April 2002*)

Pre-race prayer. (*Darlington Raceway, March 2002*)

#18 crew. (*Talladega Superspeedway, October 2002*)

Fans on scaffold. (*Dover International Speedway, June 2002*)

Hot track. (*Martinsville Speedway, October 2002*)

In memoriam.
(*New Hampshire International Speedway, July 2002*)

Jeff Gordon signs autographs. (*DuPont Day, May 2002*)

Hero worship. (*Pocono Raceway, June 2002*)

Bangin' in the low groove. (*Martinsville Speedway, October 2002*)

Mission statement.
(*Watkins Glen
International,
August 2002*)

Junior in Victory Lane.
(*Talladega Superspeedway,
April 2002*)

Race prep. (*Indianapolis Motor Speedway, August 2002*)

Pit stop. (*Martinsville Speedway, October 2002*)

Race day. (*Michigan International Speedway, August 2002*)

Tony Stewart wins the Cup Championship.
(*Homestead-Miami Speedway, November 2002*)

Our steep hillside lot is situated in such a way that the sewer hose, once deployed to the site's sewer fitting, is stretched tight. Very tight.

Thanks to a pungent phenomenon known as the "outhouse effect," one doesn't simply leave the plumbing between the black-water tank and the sewer open during one's stay. Rather, the holding tank is emptied only as it becomes full. To do so, one walks, as I did one evening, out to the external valve at the rear of the unit and gives a stout yank on the valve handle. In 15 or 20 seconds, thanks to the power of gravity and hydrodynamics, the job is neatly done. The valve is then closed, and life goes on.

Unless the hose is stretched very, very tight.

At which point it is likely, given the force of the fluids moving through it, to unseat itself from the in-ground sewer fitting and begin spraying its contents, widely and wildly, like a fire hose.

I pull the handle and am instantly and comprehensively beshit.

Once again: *not mentioned in the brochures*.

Thus fouled, I rush to shut the valve and reseat the sewer hose. Pondering hard the true nature of metaphor, I walk around to the door of the motorhome. I do not go in.

"Honey, there's been an accident," I say through the screen. The Beep peers out. Slowly, she makes a very sour face indeed. "It isn't serious, but I need you to please throw some moist towelettes out here," I continue, "a lot of them. And set a towel and a washcloth and some soap on the steps, too. And shampoo. And a wire brush if we have one."

Stifling both comment and laughter, she complies. I spend the next half-hour hosing human waste off myself and the campsite grass. I do not use the white hose. I use the something-something green hose.

Half an hour after that, I return from the shower house, scrubbed raw. The Beep greets me. "At first I wasn't sure what was wrong—you sounded so calm when you said there'd been an 'accident.'"

Perhaps I should get a job in public relations over at the nuclear power plant.

The other big event, on Saturday, is the campground Easter Parade. It's not very long as parades go, but it's in the spirit of the holiday and the place. We stand at the edge of the lake to watch.

At around noon, four resident golf carts, including one painted up as an exact replicart of Jeff Gordon's #24 DuPont car, drive past us in procession. Each one is adorned with pastel crêpe paper and bears a couple of smiling kids and a smiling adult. They wave to us. We wave back. That's it.

Easter stirs some additional thoughts, of course, here in stock-car country. To arrive at them, though, requires a last brief swing through NASCAR's past.

By the early 1970s the organization Bill France founded had long since ceased to be an outlaw outrage or even a very speculative business enterprise. It was an established regional success, a profit-maker fixed in the public mind and on the chamber of commerce calendar, and was gaining some national visibility thanks to scattered television coverage and to the achievements of stars like Richard Petty and David Pearson.

But in 1971 the news of a NASCAR revolution wasn't to be found in the blistering on-track rivalry between these two drivers, nor was it really even a sports story. It was an item you'd have been more likely to find on the business page.

The R. J. Reynolds Company of Winston-Salem, North Carolina, handcuffed by new federal prohibitions against tobacco advertising on television and radio, was looking that year for alternative ways to market its cigarettes. It also needed someplace to spend the immense unspent portion of its leftover ad budget. Around that time a home-grown NASCAR fireballer named Junior Johnson walked through their door.

Johnson was hunting up money for his racing teams and had gone to RJR to ask some of its marketing guys for a couple hundred thousand dollars in sponsorship for the season ahead. RJR would be happy to write a check, they explained, but what RJR really needed was something more substantial into which it might put its idle ad dollars. Something big enough to make up for all that lost air time. Their roll of unspent cash could choke a horse, after all. To that end, could

Junior think of anything that might help in the dispersal of around, say, fifty million bucks?

That history records no conference room spit-take on his part further burnishes Johnson's reputation for unflappability. Johnson knew right then that what RJR really needed was a much bigger horse. So he gave them Bill France's phone number. By the end of 1971, following the trail blazed by Carl Kiekhaefer, Winston had become the title sponsor for the entire Grand National series. After which, the deluge.

Once Winston signed on, demonstrating the excellence of an investment in NASCAR, the rising tide of cash from other sponsors, especially the national breweries, lifted all boats. Pretty soon, every car on the track had a sponsor.

Having thus secured the sport's financial, if not respiratory, health with the RJR deal, Bill France stepped down, and in 1972 passed the orb and scepter of NASCAR's hereditary presidency and its daily operation to his son, Bill Jr.

That was also the year NASCAR shortened its season schedule, from 48 races down to 31. In the holy tablature, 1972 marks the beginning of NASCAR's Modern Era.

Petty and Pearson were the names on the marquee when modernity began, chased and sometimes beaten by costars Cale Yarborough and Bobby Allison and Bobby Isaac, and then-young guns like Benny Parsons and Darrell Waltrip.

But Petty dominated the 1970s, winning five of his seven championships while the decade bucked and spun from Hanoi to Watergate to the Bee Gees. In all that excitement it was easy to miss the Winston Cup debut of a young driver from Kannapolis, North Carolina, at the 1975 running of the World 600 in Charlotte. Starting thirty-third, he finished a respectable twenty-second. It was his only start in The Show that season. He got a ride here and there over the next couple of years, but passed largely unremarked in the documents of the time. In fact, it was easy to overlook Dale Earnhardt entirely until 1979, when, as a

28-year-old racer, he won Cup's Rookie of the Year award. The next year he won his first championship.

Earnhardt's legend, his mythology, so long ago overtook and outdistanced his actual biography in the minds of the NASCAR public that to catalog his statistics here would be as useless as tallying the trees planted by Johnny Appleseed or the bears done in by Davy Crockett. Arithmetic is no fit medium for a folk hero's portrait.

The numbers convey little but persistence and a knack for winning. First Winston Cup race, Charlotte, 1975. Seventy-six wins in 675 subsequent starts. First victory, Bristol, 1979. Seven Winston Cup championships. Final victory, Talladega, 10-15-00.

The fans know by heart the outlines of his worldly life. Dale Earnhardt was born in Kannapolis, a mill town, on April 29, 1951. He was the son of short-track racer Ralph Earnhardt, a star whose own nickname was Ironheart. Dale dropped out of school in the ninth grade, alienating his father, because he couldn't wait, he burned so hot to race. He struggled. He failed. He worked odd jobs as a mechanic, an insulation hanger, a welder. He reconciled with his father. They worked on cars together. Then his father died. Dale mourned and struggled. He failed. He borrowed money Fridays to pay for racing Sundays. He paid his debts, with prize money, on Mondays. He struggled. He failed. Until, at last, success, beyond anything he expected. Three times married, twice divorced, he had four children. Deceased 2-18-01.

In the arc of his early life the fans saw themselves and their own unending struggles. He *was* the fans. He failed the same failures and bore the same sorrows and suffered the same entanglements and hurts as do we all. His story was theirs, and anywhere you lived down south, you could see the world as he did: that textile mill dark above the treeline, looming immense and inevitable a few blocks away, the factory at the end of a too-short one-way street and the rest of your life a promise of nothing but hard work and making do. He was every fan who ever dreamed of better.

When better came, they believed he'd earned it. They took to heart the stories of Earnhardt in the middle of the night, under his car, working to make the dream come true, working after work, falling asleep with the wrench in his hand. They knew his grit and persistence as they knew their own, the stubbornness and the taciturnity. His passion and his focus and his talent were his alone.

To paint the legend full you had to see him on the track. "Establish your territory," his father'd told him, and that he surely did. A bruiser in the low groove, he won the nickname Ironhead early on, rooting out the short-track back markers and the weak sisters, banging his way to the front. He was tough as a hogjowl. He'd put the fender to anyone who got in his way. Eventually, just the threat of it, that glimpse of black in the rearview mirror, was enough to slow the others down. Even the toughest among them backed off the gas a little, backed down.

There was anger in the way he drove, and attitude and ambition. The car was a weapon against repression and he was the blue-collar backlash. The fans resonated to it. "He drove the way I feel." Before too long, he had become the Intimidator. He had established his territory. It was any track he ran.

But there was grace in it, too, and over the years a kind of mysticism grew up around him. On the superspeedways he was all fluidity and strategy, changing his racing line by inches to tuck into that fast vacuum, or to take the air off someone else's spoiler, get them loose, get them thinking, get them out of his way. Nobody had ever been better at it, and the fans would tell you that he could feel the pulse of a track quicken or slow as the sun dipped into the clouds, sense the fastest line with just his buzzing fingertips, see things others couldn't, do the impossible. Like a shaman, he could read the very air.

The last race he ever won, second Talladega in the year 2000, serves well enough to illustrate the nature of his genius. The opening few sentences of the story that ran in the *Charlotte Observer* the next morning are a shorthand for his entire career.

Nobody can do what Dale Earnhardt did to the Winston 500 at Talladega Superspeedway. Not even Earnhardt.

Forget what you saw. Forget what the official results show.

Nobody can be 18th with five laps to go and then have to spend the final lap worrying about being passed to have a win taken away. Nobody can run up the middle of a three-wide pack of screaming race cars and draft his way from oblivion to Victory Lane.

Nobody can do that. Not even Earnhardt.

And yet, it happened.

Season after season after season the legend swelled and grew, the numbers mounted and the wins and the trophies and the money piled up and at the end he was as big as any hero in any sport.

The man, Dale Earnhardt, had long since disappeared behind the legend of the racer. "Keep 'em guessing" was what he told his son Dale Jr., when fame turned up in his rearview mirror, too. "The less they know about your personal life, the better." And he practiced what he preached. What, after all, did the fans really know about him? The origin stories and what they saw on the track. By keeping himself to himself, he gave the fans room to fill in the picture of his fame in any way they chose. That he was a sportsman, a hunter, a fisherman was well known—you'd see him in the ads for deer stands and camo and buckshot in the magazines. The rest was guesswork and longing. He was kind and funny, he was hard and canny, he was generous and loving and a heartless brute. He was a doting father and a solid friend and a prankster and a churchgoing wildman and a warm son of the Old South. He was cold as ice. He was whatever his fans needed him to be.

"I think the thing that has made him so popular is that he really is a reincarnated Confederate soldier," Humpy Wheeler, president of the track at Charlotte, once said long ago. That daguerrotype mustache perhaps, and the look of the long campaign in his eyes. Ready for whatever might come at Chickamauga or Gettysburg or Shiloh. It was true, insofar as you chose to see it. Plenty of fans did. Dale Earnhardt was their surrogate in the unending War of Northern Aggression.

He died the same way Adam Petty had died a year earlier, and Kenny Irwin, too, blunt-force trauma and a ring fracture of the skull, a consequence of hitting the wall head-on, full-speed, with little but his own strength to absorb all that terrifying energy. Did his seatbelt fail? Did it matter? You can only make the cars so safe.

The memorial in Charlotte was attended by everyone in NASCAR, even the drivers, all of whom are famously unwilling to attend any funeral but their own. Three thousand fans listened to the service on loudspeakers while standing in the street. The funeral itself was private. The location of the gravesite kept secret.

Dale Earnhardt and Richard Petty are the yin and the yang of NASCAR, both planetary, both elemental, both bigger by far than the numbers they posted. In the years during which their careers overlapped, Earnhardt was the willing villain, the dour black hat to Petty's cheerful hero, and was booed as passionately as he was applauded. When Petty retired, Earnhardt was left alone at the summit.

Petty won far more races than Earnhardt, than anyone ever will again, but did so in the long ago Iron Age when Cup often raced more than 50 dates a year, when they raced on dirt, when they raced midweek against weak fields. And while Earnhardt and Petty share the same number of Cup championships, I suspect that in the years ahead, Earnhardt will be thought of as the greater man, the greater driver, the greater racer. He did the one thing Petty didn't do. He died behind the wheel of the car.

In doing so, Dale Earnhardt attained the final perfection of American heroism.

On the third lap of every race so far this season, the fans have risen from their seats and raised three fingers in tribute to him.

A couple of weeks ago I saw a motorhome at the track with a scene of inspirational art airbrushed on its side. It was a large painting, perhaps 5 feet by 5 feet, and in it the black #3 Goodwrench Service car was running the high line through the last turn at Daytona. The car was driverless. From the blue sky above it, out of the clouds, shone a single beam of light. The bright shaft tipped into the driver's window. He had been taken up.

It is Easter Sunday and out here on the holy ghost road Richard Petty may be The King, but he's not the King of Kings. In this part of the country, it would be sacrilege to suggest otherwise. The one true savior is Dale Earnhardt, and we are all of us redeemed and exalted by his last sacrifice.

Off the blocks this week to the Republic of Texas, an easy two-day drive. Roll down the I-40 to the I-30 all the way to Dallas–Fort Worth. Our only close call comes west of Texarkana, when we dodge a golf ball dropped out of the sky at us from a frontage road driving range. It hits about 20 feet in front of us and bounces away with an audible cart-path *click*. It's probably still bouncing, headed for Arkadelphia and all points east. 300,000 yards off the tee, but dead right. Welcome to Texas.

The Texas Motor Speedway opened in 1996, another mile-and-a-half cookie cutter, sparkling, sanitary, and charmless. But it's a fast track, with top speeds of 190-plus. Smooth power is the ticket here, just as it was at Atlanta, and I expect the cars and the colors to flow around the track like bright water.

Which they will, I'm sure, as soon as the water itself is gone. The weekend brings with it intermittent torrential rain. It takes three and a half minutes of steady rain here for the track to get too wet to run, and an hour and a half to dry it. They tow jet engines hitched up sideways on trailers around the track. Every time they finish, it rains again, so practice and qualifying for both the Busch Series and the Cup race have been postponed again and again. The one thing no one wants to hear over the radio from race control is "We lost the track."

The crews kill time in the garages pitching quarters up against the doors. They judge the results with a tape measure. Stay at it long enough and you can make some real money. Kerry's picked up a couple of bucks already in the Busch garage. "We used to do this all the time back at the dealership. I'm out of practice, but I used to be pretty good." Like Junior, Kerry was once a service writer and oil changer back at Dale Earnhardt Chevrolet. One week he brought home close to $90 in quarters.

On Saturday the Busch race starts four hours late and Kerry sinks like a stone through the field. The track is slick from the wash of all the rain and there are accidents every few laps. The sky lightens, then darkens. Michael Waltrip spins and flips his #99 car and catches fire. He bails out unhurt. Then it rains again. They dry the track. The lights come on. They run more laps, the cars spotlighted in the gathering dark, until it rains again. The stands are emptying. Any race can be called official after the halfway point, and mercifully they call this one without bothering to try drying the track. It's after 8 P.M. Running for the press room, I look up at the scoring pylon. Kerry finished seventeenth. I've learned a valuable lesson today. In fact I've heard the phrase several times. "The only thing worse than rain at a racetrack is rain at a racetrack with lights."

The Sunday Cup race is washed out completely. The Beep and I, parked in the infield, cook, play Scrabble, watch the Weather Channel for tornado warnings. They always come for the motorhomes first.

On Monday, a workday, everyone who held a ticket for the Sunday meet shows up. The grandstands are packed full.

The race goes off on time, after a Texas-sized B-52 flyover, the giant bombers a couple hundred feet above the crowd, pouring kerosene smoke and noise and martial pride down on everyone's head.

The race is loose and rhythmic, with an accident every 50 laps or so to keep the fans in it. When the race runs green for any length of time, the crowd loses interest, goes flat. When Junior backs into the wall at lap 184, the groan in the stands is audible, and waves of fans rush for the garage. When he rolls back onto the track in the battered car on lap 257, they stand and roar. Ryan Newman blows an engine, Ward Burton goes into the wall, the action doled out as if set on a timer.

Matt Kenseth begins to pull away from the pack late in the race and no one can catch him. The crowd comes to its feet as he takes the checkered flag.

Sterling Marlin remains the series points leader.

Best strange quote of the weekend comes from the winning owner, Jack Roush, to open the postrace press conference. Of having now won two races in a row: "These are the happy times, to quote the U-boat commanders of '39 and '40."

Now we bounce all the way back to the little track at Martinsville, Virginia, 1,100 miles away. The oldest course on the circuit, it opened in 1947, but wasn't paved until 1955. It is a perfect hatbox of a racetrack, only a half-mile in circumference. And just 90,000 seats.

Unlike the postmodern tracks built far out past the warehouses of urban-industrial areas like those at Vegas or D/FW, here at Martinsville modest houses run down the street right to the grandstands. It gives the place a vibe like Wrigley Field, something on a human scale set down in a real neighborhood.

The fans here are the genuine article, too, none of the effortful suburban flash or high fashion we saw last week in Nieman-Marcus country. Racer T-shirts and jeans.

The track's claim to worldwide fame appears to be its chili dogs. Once bitten, the dog bites back. The inner meat of the thing is an alarming shade of atomic pink. "This is what they give you right before a CAT scan," notes a colleague. The line at the concession stand is never less than half a dozen dogeaters deep.

Race day is NASCAR hot and the heat radiating up from all this cracked asphalt and concrete is absolutely going to cook these guys. F-15 flyover and an Air Force brass quartet and then they're off. The pace is slower here than at Bristol, the track's much flatter, so the cars only average 80 or 90 mph around the course. Last week it felt like the pace car ran that fast. But the view's good from every seat in the house, and the cars orbit in a state of entertaining and near-perpetual contact.

The drivers are hard on the brakes coming into the turns here, and hard on the gas coming out, so the race has an urgent pulse to it, on/off, on/off, on/off. Barreling out of the turns the cars even *sound* eager.

Down at ground level the whole thing's a hoot if you can sneak in close to the wall, or watch from the sheds on the backstretch. You're as close to it here as you're ever likely to get, and the sensation of risk, of the cars coming right at you as they slide and tussle coming out of the corner, is electrifying. Heads up for flying debris!

There's a yellow flag on lap 26 when Elliott Sadler's car blows up in a vicious cloud of steam and stink and smoke, the right rear all torn up and flames flickering beneath the bodywork. He probably detonated a brake disc. As at Bristol and Richmond, brakes here glow foundry red through every turn, so they have a tendency to fail spectacularly. It looks like a fire in a scrap yard as the car goes shuddering past.

The laps pass fast at short tracks, but there sure are a lot of them, 500 today, and with the race rumbling up to the fans through the seat of their pants, and the sun burning down, the fatigue sets in early. By lap 250, even as the cars squeal and slide and roll hard in and out of the pits, the audience looks exhausted.

Bobby Labonte outlasts the heat and the pounding delivered by his 42 colleagues to win today's punch-up. The fans reward him with their tired applause. It looks like his car's been gone over with a jackhammer. Every car here pulls off the track with comical amounts of body damage.

The bodies damaged most of all, though, seem to belong to the drivers. Four hours in a 90-mile-an-hour, 140-degree convection oven takes a real toll, and a lot of the drivers have to be lifted from the cockpit by their crewmen. Jeff Gordon looks like you could hang him over a towel rack. Labonte can barely lift his trophy. The rest are being packed in ice. Stacy Compton, a local stocker from just up the road in Grit, Virginia, has heat exhaustion and spent most of the race throwing up inside his helmet. "Our driver really gave it up today," his crew chief says. Wobbling next to the car, Compton's as pale as paste. The medics take him into his hauler to administer an IV.

Maybe this is harder than I thought.

Sterling Marlin still leads the points race.

•   •   •

A week later, down at Talladega, 600 miles closer to the equator, it's hotter; and here among the Alabama pines the air's like bath water. The crews labor and fume in the heat, and even with the big industrial fans blowing everywhere in the garage it's hard to catch a clean breath. The cars get the ice-bag treatment this go-round, too, with crewmen adding bag after 10-pound bag of picnic ice to the remote radiators the cars hook into when they're idling and stationary. Right after filling the reservoirs, the crewmen plunge their arms in up to the shoulder to steal some cool.

Late Friday afternoon comes word that Jack Roush has been seriously injured in a plane crash somewhere downstate. The information's bad, and comes through garbled. He was in his World War II P-51. No, he wasn't—but we don't know what it was. He's on life support, he's all right, he's critical.

There is a long, tragic history of fatal light plane crashes associated with NASCAR. Alan Kulwicki. Davey Allison. A dozen others. All that travel, and danger everywhere.

On Saturday morning there's a press conference. The media center is jammed, 50 or so reporters up front, the same number of photographers in back. Roush's drivers—Kenseth, Burton, Martin, Busch—stand on the podium while a company spokesman clarifies the stories.

At his birthday celebration at a friend's home down in Troy, Roush had flown a borrowed plane into some power lines. The plane was a small twin-engine rig designed for aerial photography. An air-cam he thinks it's called. The plane hung up in the lines and dropped straight down into a lake. Roush, certainly the luckiest unlucky man of that strange day, was fished out of the lake by a retired Navy rescue diver who lived 200 feet away. Currently in serious condition, Roush is on a respirator and has two broken legs.

The drivers shift and fidget, antsy and powerless. When Mark Martin bows his head for a prayer, you can hear half a hundred shutters firing from the back of the room.

On Saturday afternoon the Busch race produces a spectacular crash, 18 or 19 cars tumbling down the backstretch and flipping through the grass. There's only a fractional difference between the size and weight and speed of a Busch Series car and a Cup car, so this may be a harbinger of things to come tomorrow. A few reporters run to the infield medical center to see if anyone's been hurt, but by the time we get there, the drivers are all walking out under their own power. Most look dazed. One's still picking bits of turf out of his collar. "Sauter looks like he just came off a ride at the state fair," cracks one of the old hands.

Kerry got gathered up in the wreck as well, but was able to get the car back to the garage. The crews are pounding and hammering away. There are half a dozen others back there too, all in a rush to get back on the track. As the crews finish the repairs, the cars come tearing out onto the access road that leads to the track. One of them clips a spectator, knocking him down hard. He's lying on his back groaning while the EMTs cut off his shirt and load him on a backboard. Not long after they get him into the ambulance, Jason Keller wins the Busch race.

A few minutes later, back on the garage apron, driver Randy Lajoie is sitting propped up against the rear tire of his car. His face is mottled red and white and he is packed in bags of picnic ice from his toes to his waist. "Hoo, hoo!" he says, smiling weakly, to the crewmen gathered around him, "Ain't this *fun?*"

This first time around at Talladega, we went for a long walk through the infield campgrounds.

At the true superspeedways, Daytona and 'Dega, the infields are huge and there are thousands and thousands of people camped inside the track. Many more thousands outside, too, the motorhomes and campers and trailers and tents spread out in expanding rings and blocks and quadrants radiating from the track. Seen from the air, the wide-angle aerial shot in the movie of your imagination, they are like walled cities, each track a fortress at the center of all that boiling humanity. At night, with the bonfires everywhere, even in the heat, and the torches, and the shadows jumping, it is aboriginal, as primal a thing as you'll see anywhere on Earth.

Two weekends a year Talladega is a redneck Woodstock, the rowdiest party in NASCAR. It used to be that Darlington was the biggest blowout on the tour, as carnal and bumptious and drunken as Rio's carnival, but 'Dega is bigger and bawdier and louder and riskier by far and the whole place shakes and sweats in that Alabama heat for five days and five nights when the races arrive.

Through the center of the infield runs Talladega Boulevard, a straight stretch of asphalt and concrete a couple thousand feet long. On one side it's bordered by a chain- link fence, and on the other side of that fence, for the entire length of the infield, are parked hundreds of motorhomes. And to walk the length of that fence is as revelatory and creepy and satisfying and voyeuristic as walking down the alley behind your neighbors' houses.

It was early evening, coming on suppertime Friday, and on the other side of that fence there were kids everywhere running and riding their bikes and their skateboards, shouting, full of springtime vinegar, and lights were strung over and through and around everything, little strings of Christmas lights or garden lights, novelty lights shaped like stock cars, swinging from the awnings and the flagpoles and the windshield wipers, glowing white or red or green, warm and cheery in the blue dusk, twinkling on all that loud, insistent generator power, music on the breeze from every direction, too, "Sweet Home Alabama," of course, and jazz, punk, country, metal, rap, the whole place humming like a plucked string, and men and women sitting around the grill, the campfire, in lawn chairs, feet up, talking, laughing, drinking, happy, the light from the fires orange on their faces.

We were walking slow, half-drunk ourselves just on the colors and the noise and the vividness of everything we saw. It was like a midnight walk through Rome or Cairo, someplace ancient and alive, where the vitality and the history go on and on, past, present, and future seamless and without rest, life bewitched.

We were two-thirds of the way down that fenceline when a man called out to us, "Come ovah! You've just got to try some this.

Oooooo! You've nevah had betta. Come on ovah!" He was in his forties, a million-watt smile in a sunburned, sharp-nosed face. T-shirt, shorts, flip-flops. Tall and pot-bellied with lank brown hair, he spoke with an accent from the deepest reaches of the South, far deeper even than central Alabama. He was standing in what amounted to a small courtyard, the space made by three trailers parked in a horseshoe. There was a charcoal grill with several pots on it and a folding table with a blue-and-white-checked vinyl tablecloth and camp chairs and cans of beer sweating everywhere and the air was thick with the smell of pepper and ground sassafras. He was holding a steaming plate of shrimp out to us over that fence. "Oooooo, you love this!"

They were up from Gulfport, Mississippi, more than a dozen of them, men of several families and four generations, this the big annual outing to Talladega for the racing and the cooking and the eating. "C'mon, now, Cajun shrimp, try it, like to melt in you mouth. Or maybe just melt you mouth, 'f my son made 'em up too hot . . ." he said, laughing. "We got 'em just this morning down home and bring 'em up on ice. Try."

Thick as a steak, the tender flesh was red-hot and succulent, and before we could finish that first shrimp another plate was coming over the fence with more shrimp and hot sauce and Cajun potatoes now, too. "Thank you, Daddy," he said to an old man with the same smile, "Try these potato, too, oooo, but they hot and good!" It was as if we'd known them all our lives. Every one of them smiling like they'd just hit the numbers, grinning and singing to the zydeco being squeezed out of the boombox and dancing like Zorba, handing out plates. They were all drunk as lords and as happy as I've ever seen men anywhere.

There was no way to talk to them, much less interview them, they were dervishes, spinning from the table to the pot to the coolers, in and out of the light and the shadows, young men and old men coming to the fence for an instant with another plate, another cup, "Oh now drink this down with that shrimp, you!" and then dancing away, laughing, yelling to Grandpa, "Don't you boin them potatoes now, boy!" So we stood there eating, happy strangers, no questions, the only two people in the world on the other side of that fence. "Oooo, my son just shucked 'em," the tall man sang as he danced back to the fence with fresh oysters on another paper plate, "Use that hot sauce now!" and he watched us slide them down out of the shells, our heads tipped back, and a laugh rose full up out of him. "You like those, huh? We got four bushels iced that we hauled up this morning." And we stood there for a long time, eating whatever they handed us, watching them, trying to talk to them but not getting more than a sentence or two across the fence into all that happiness, listening to them talk and sing, until it got dark and we had to go. We said goodnight and thank you.

As we walked away, the tall man called out, "You come back now! I hate to brag, I do, but we live like kings!"

The grandstands at Talladega are so big that the cops patrol them on scooters. And on Sunday every seat is filled.

The race gets off cleanly, the packs of cars shuffling and reshuffling themselves, breaking into long fluid lines, as sinuous as the tail of a kite, Earnhardt Jr. and Jeff Gordon swapping the lead through the first hundred laps. Whenever Junior gets out front, the crowd rises to its feet.

The race is smooth and fast, seamless feeling until the very end, when Dale Jarrett gets sideways and takes the back half of the field with him. Twenty-four cars. In an instant there's so much smoke you can't see who made it through the crash, but a couple of seconds later cars start limping down the pit lane, sheet metal flapping and tires flat. Johnny Benson pulls in and his car's on fire and as soon as he falls out the window and climbs over the pit wall it's fully engulfed. They take him away on a stretcher. There's another stretcher in front of Mark Martin's #6 pit, and by the time I run to the medical center to find out that no one's been badly hurt, they've put out the fire in Benson's car and are actually trying to fix it. It looks like it was hit with a mortar round, so you have to admire the tenacity, if not the sanity, of his crew. It's Thunderdome out here. They red-flag the race with six laps to go so they can plow the debris off the track. When they restart, they'll run two caution laps, then there'll be a four-lap shootout to the finish.

The crowd is already spent. A day in this heat, basted in beer and barbecue, and they're reeling. I'm standing down along the pit walkway and behind me on the roof of a motorhome is a kid 9 or 10 standing next to his dad, shaking a can of beer as hard as he can. It's a can of Budweiser, so I'm guessing he's going to pop it for Junior if he can hold on for the win. The red flag lasts nearly 30 minutes. By the time they come around for the restart, that kid's can of beer is bulging like it's rotten with botulism.

Junior gets away clean off the line and cruises to a victory that has the entire grandstand on its feet. The kid detonates the can, but it doesn't spray like champagne—it just starts foaming slowly and won't stop. It's like he churned it into butterbeer. Even after Junior finishes turning donuts on the infield grass, the can's still up there, forgotten now, oozing foam down the side of Maximum Dad's camper.

An hour after the race Junior's still in Victory Lane getting his picture taken for next week's print ads, donning in sequence the twenty-seven hats of his twenty-seven odd sponsors. The Hat Dance.

Points leader? Sterling Marlin.

Going into our eleventh event, I've realized that the hauler drivers have earned my sympathy. The tour's stars and crews and moguls fly in and out, but, like the Beep and me, the transporter drivers make these transcontinental trips in days not hours, like Marley's ghost across the time zones, dragging their toolboxes and chains behind them.

Up and out from Alabama headed west. The 2-mile track at Fontana, California, is next on Cup's agenda; 2,100 miles to make by Thursday and no time to lose. The Beep and I read Harry Potter to one another to pass the miles. Past Birmingham and Memphis and Fort Smith. OKC again, J to J. The Texas King Kong Jesus comes and goes and we're into Amarillo. Then Albuquerque, Kingman, Barstow, up the Cajon Pass and down into sunny SoCal and the eastern reaches of L.A.

The California Speedway, added to the Cup rotation in 1997, is laid out adjacent to what looks to be an old steel mill. Acre after acre of rust and bankruptcy. But this track's the fanciest yet, on the sharpest part of the fan-friendly cutting edge, neat as a theme park and featuring its own stop on a special light-rail passenger line.

The crowd is a recapitulation of the one at Las Vegas, only more so. Tailored linen and leather, board shorts and Hawaiian shirts, daiquiris and frittatas. The surgically enhanced amateur lizards and hydraulically powered bikini-team professionals, of whom there are thousands in from Hollywood, seem to favor chardonnay over suds.

We are parked at one end of the drivers' lot here, a beautiful setup, griddle-flat and all the electricity we can eat. When I step outside to give myself a haircut, some of the soldiers working track security gather to offer helpful tips on how to keep things high and tight. "You have to blend it more at the top, sir, blend it. That's it."

The infield campground is like the set of *Leave It to Beaver*, polite kids everywhere on their bikes and blades, married couples walking, no one anywhere playing their music too loud. Surreal.

Walked over on Saturday to meet one of our weekend neighbors.

At 27, Dale Earnhardt Jr., "Little E," embodies NASCAR's radiant future.

He is the sport's first true crossover star, a full-bore billboard breakout MTV bad boy (That hat! Those glasses! Rage rock! Hip-hop! Lock up your daughters, America!), running wide-fucking-open down Madison Avenue, bringing beer and sass and sex into your shabby, joyless living room.

In the not-so-distant past the public model for the great motoring heroes was perhaps a little, um, straight-arrow. Washed out, colorless. The Other Other White Meat.

Commercial casting directors, on the other hand, thought there was a bit too much red, maybe, right around the neckbone. And those muttonchops and nylon windbreakers don't exactly peg the tach with the New Rochelle focus groups. Preaching only to the converted, these Bronze Age stars sold motor oil, brake rotors, and the promise of eternal salvation through clean living.

Earnhardt the Younger will change all that. Until the moment of his father's death, Junior, and to a lesser extent, his half-brother Kerry, had been held by the fans in only the kind of tentative, speculative affection that surrounds the son of any famous man. Sure, Little E'd won two championships in the Busch Series, but did he have the grit, the steel, the mud, to run in The Show? Plenty never make the leap. He could drive, sure, but the talk in the garages was that his balls-to-brains ratio was suspect, and when was he gonna step, as they say, UP? Lordy, even Frank Sinatra Jr. can carry a tune! The only question is, how far?

Flung far and fast into the naked limelight by that slow-motion crash up the mountainous reach of turn 4, Earnhardt Jr. might have become nothing more than a curiosity, another lounge act. Worse still, he might have believed all those newspapers trimmed in mourning black that presented him, generously but wrongly, as JFK Jr., the handsome, harmless attendant of the family's eternal flame, whose public life must be lived in the long cold shadow of a dead father, and whose accomplishments can only seem small in the wan reflected light that so infrequently falls on them.

So Dale Earnhardt Jr. goes out and does the only thing he knows to rewrite the terrible script that history's written for him. He races. He runs, as they say, good. Top 10. Top 5. He wins three times in 2001 and finishes eighth in points and earns $5,827,542 in winnings. On top of which he makes monster endorsement money. The fan's fevered affections, their rampant passions, unbound after his father's crash, are beginning now to bear down on him.

At Bristol, in the early-season cold of the Tennessee hills, he shows up in his pit thuggin' it, Eminem at Gstaad, with a knit cap pulled down to his nasty shades and a mustard ski jacket the size of a spinnaker. The crowd of 147,000 throws ovations down on him in that tiny, tidy bowl. The loudest of the day comes right after the race when he and Robby Gordon bang each other hard rolling back onto the pit road. It is intentional and juvenile and it will cost them both thousands of dollars in fines. But it is Friday-night, dirt-track, turf-war showmanship. The people roar for it, for him.

In the motoring press that week are the recriminatory gasbag editorials about sophomoric behavior and dark whispers about a missed promotional appearance at a local grocery store. As though those old rules still apply. Drowned out by the cheering, the gasbags go unheeded.

At Talladega, under that angry Alabama mother sun, they rose in the stands every time Dale Jr. ran his car out for practice. In the shade of the garage between sessions he would peel himself out of the top of his driver's suit, hitch his pants, and stand, flushed and frail-seeming, in front of the swamp cooler by the car. Yahooing cries of "Junior!" rang out during the prayer before the race, a 40-year-old echo of the days when Mr. Junior Johnson was the Last American Hero. When the race began, so did the roaring, from a grandstand nearly a mile long, louder even than the cars. Every time he ran out front the roar grew and people stood and people fainted in the heat and the roar swelled again and the roar became a living wall of noise for those last few laps and the people swooned in the light and the noise and the hot, heroic love of something they hoped was bigger than any one of them. And he won. At the moment he crossed the finish line, borne forward by the collective howl of 150,000 fans, scores of thousands of cameras flashed, impossibly cold and blue, that moment frozen.

This weekend a hundred thousand fans washed over Fontana, California, over the track and the stands and the garages, running and pooling everywhere, lapping gently against the fences and the walls and the cars and the drivers. On Saturday afternoon Dale Earnhardt Jr. can watch this tide flow quietly around him from the upholstered anonymity of his immense motorhome.

Even stretched to full length on the sofa watching the IROC race on TV with his buds, he seems restless and animated. He shifts his weight, sits up, reclines again, energetic but relaxed, ready for something. Tomorrow, maybe. Jeans, shirt, cap. Chin whiskers this week. He looks you straight in the eye when he listens and when he speaks. He can dial the North Carolina in his voice up or down, but it's nothing you could dip a biscuit in. He looks stronger, more substantial, away from the car. He is handsome, certainly, but he is not the billboard Apollo his advertisers contrive. He looks more like the service writer he used to be at Dale Earnhardt Chevrolet than the object of national obsession he's become. In the right light he looks like a guy who looks just like the guy on the billboard.

"Two years ago when I'd walk from my motorcoach to the car in practice there were less than half the people asking for autographs, so I see that there's a big change as far as the hard-core fans that we have now. It's changed quite a bit. There's a responsibility that goes with it now. A lot of the fans say, 'Man, we like you because you're yourself, stay yourself, always be yourself.' And that's true to a point, but I'm finding now more and more, now that we're under the microscope, that some of the things I would do in the past aren't accepted now—something that was just a prick on the rosebush before is a huge problem now." And he's right. His every remark is broadcast, typeset, satellited, sent resonating down that clacking NASCAR telegraph. Which bunny does he bounce? How many beers can he drink? What's his favorite food/movie/band? An encyclopedia of banalities. The better he drives, the worse it gets. And the fans?

"I don't want it to get to be where I can't go out and do what I want to do," he says, and seems to mean it. Too late.

On his way out the door for yet another interview he is confronted by thousands of reminders of his father—the portraits, the banners, the flags snapping in the breeze. And as his father embodied the sport to its last generation of fans, so will the son carry it into the next. "I used to miss him every minute," he says. "Now I've got it down to about every five minutes." Then he's gone.

On lap 228 of the Cup race on Sunday, Kevin Harvick cuts a tire coming through turn 4 and swerves dead left into the right rear quarter panel of the devil red #8. Betrayed by a sudden absence of traction and Sir Isaac Newton's buzz-killer logic on the subjects of orbital mass and force and momentum, Dale Earnhardt Jr. is launched uphill into the wall. Spinning, he hits, first front then rear, hard: hard enough to accordion the car down to about two-thirds of its original size; hard enough to bring an audible gasp from the frontstretch grandstand;

hard enough even to silence the TV announcers, if only briefly. The car slides down onto the grass, vomiting steam and smoke and oil, and sits ominously, heavily there for what seems like a long time. This is by far the worst hit of his career. In about 30 seconds the EMTs have him out of the car. Bent over, grimacing, he looks stunned, the wind knocked out of him.

Twenty minutes later he comes swinging out the doors of the infield medical center on crutches. He sprained an ankle when he braced his feet against the firewall. He's torqued a shoulder joint, too, and the russet bloom of his bruises is just beginning. Nothing serious. He is pissed off and joking, but mostly pissed off, and the one grumbled comment to his publicist, "I hit hard, God damn it, you know the rest," will no doubt have to be translated into uplifting, PG-rated sportsjabber for the morning papers.

Fans throng the fenceline as Earnhardt is driven away on a golf cart. They run three deep in places, men, women, and children, shifting from foot to foot, applauding, whistling, bellowing encouragement. One among them, though, remains still. He is a comical little handful of a man, maybe 40 or so, and he holds above the fence, at stubby arm's length, a mirror. It is 2 feet by 3 feet and is framed in rococo gilt. It's the kind of thing you'd see in a sports bar, or on the wall of an overdone rumpus room. Across its bright face in lurid Victorian gold-and-red stencil it reads, "Budweiser Congratulates Dale Earnhardt Jr."

He holds it as high as he can, dazzling in the sun, until Junior is gone. Before anyone can ask why he's brought it here he, too, slips away. Whatever did he expect Dale Earnhardt Jr., or any one of us, to see in it?

Jimmie Johnson wins the first Cup race of his career. And, as they're so fond of saying on the Motor Racing Network, "It's been a beautiful day for racing!" But not, with the exception of Junior's concussive moment in turn 4, a memorable one. By consensus up in the press box, it was one of the dullest races in history. Few lead changes, little battling for position. When Ricky Craven drops out at around the

100-lap mark, it is suggested that he was simply too bored to go on. Like a Dodgers game, most of the Los Angeles fans leave long before it's over.

Sterling Marlin leads in points.

We decide to play hooky, skip Richmond and the 2,500-mile rebound east. We will have a quick western vacation.

We visit friends in California and New Mexico and Colorado, walk the fossil beds and sand dunes and high desert. We breathe, eat vegetables, absorb some silence.

In a brief ceremony under the mountain stars we at last christen the motorhome, with a split of supermarket champagne. We call it/him/her "Homer." We veto a decorative nameplate stating same.

We watch the Richmond race from the Wal-Mart parking lot in Pueblo, Colorado. As the announcer says, it's a real wreckfest. Fourteen cautions and the cars slung and flung every whichaway on the slick little 3/4-miler. We wish we'd been there, but you certainly see a lot more on TV, the Argus that takes you everywhere at once. It's easier to keep account of who's where. And you can turn the sound down, which is nice. Without the smell, though, the rumble, it's not the same. Still, we sat through every minute and rooted the boys around the track and are now almost wary of how much fun we had watching. Race winner: Tony Stewart. And yes, Sterling Marlin is still the points leader.

When the state cop pulls me over outside Colorado Springs, he asks: "Are you tired, sir? You were weaving in your lane back there a-ways."

"No, officer, just fighting the crosswind is all. This thing's like a sail when it's breezy."

He eyeballs me and sniffs for liquor. "Well, just slow down a little and keep it under control, okay? Have a safe night, folks."

"Yes, sir. You too."

I should have told him, per Cup practice, that I was scrubbin' in the tires.

EIGHT

We live at the Wal-Mart. I do not mean by this that we spend a lot of time and money at the Wal-Mart. "We *live* at the Wal-Mart," you hear people say, moms mostly, a comic exaggeration, talking to one another in the checkout line, as they bend to unload a cart's worth of Moon Pies and octane booster, Huggies and Ultra Dove onto the endless belt, commiserating with each other beneath that dazzling aurora of fluorescence, smiling and rolling their eyes while they fish out their debit cards and stage-whisper gentle threats to their beautiful, malevolent children. "We *live* at the Wal-Mart." That means they're in here three or four times a week, doing the two "big shoppings" and then another couple of quick visits nights or weekends to buy the forgotten ingredient, the replacement bulb, the latest *People*. HubbaDaddy, too, in and out for a Keystone 12-pack, a 3/8ths drill bit, another midnight twinpack of Huggies. Everyone comes here. You can visit the optometrist, do your banking, plan your wedding here. Somewhere Stalin is beaming, his dreams at last made real—a nation has finally found the means and the courage to completely centralize the distribution of goods and services.

What people actually mean when they say "We *live* at the Wal-Mart" is "We might as well live at the Wal-Mart, because we're here so much."

That's not what I mean.

We live at the Wal-Mart. *Live* here. Covenant or no, we take our meals and our mail here now, we sleep and we shower here, we work and watch television and play Scrabble here. We are parked in the far southwestern corner of the Mooresville SuperCenter lot and have been dug in since the Mother's Day off-week and our return from the distant west.

In the morning we sit and talk about our plans for the day while the early shoppers head for the store. We watch them as we sit at the dinette table, unashamed, in our PJs. We walk a hundred feet to get our breakfast muffins and coffee, read the paper, then walk to the mailbox we rented a few storefronts over.

There are no sidewalks anywhere at this end of Race City (sucker!), so the Beep does her daily workouts in our parking lot, running a couple of laps around the perimeter of the place, getting her step-work in on the concrete lot dividers, doing her sit-ups on the little landscaped island of grass next to the motorhome. "People look at me like I'm in*sane*," she sighs. She's been trying to figure out how to incorporate the shopping carts, too, perhaps as resistance equipment.

In the afternoon or evening we walk the 200 feet to the movie theater. It doesn't much matter what's playing, we go in for the air-conditioning and the free matinee popcorn. We go to get out of our tiny box, to sit alone in a 200-seat midday theater, to slow the onset of RV fever.

Late on Saturday nights we listen to Mooresville's teenagers cruise past in their shrill, pristine econoracers. They park right next to us, talk, share cigarettes and furtive beers, make out.

"Man, don't be leanin' on that, you'll stove it all up."

"Where am I supposed to sit at, then?"

"I don't care s'long as it isn't the hood of my car."

"Then this is one cheap motherfucker, dude."

"You heard me."

"Japanese piece of shit's what it is . . ."

"Smoke *you* with it often enough."

"Shoulda got the Dodge, dude, shoulda got the Dodge."

Even at midnight the parking lot is well lighted and that rosy sodium-vapor glow must be a comfort to their spirits. There is no menace in the shadows here, only reassurance, starburst highlights coming off all that chrome, the hometown half-darkness easing the hard edges off everything.

We're in and out of the 24-hour store four or five times a day, browsing the magazine rack, shopping for dinner, using the bathroom, killing time, keeping an eye out for Junior or Rusty or Ricky. Everyone comes here.

Late at night, sleepless in the heat, we'll wander those heaven-bright, narcotic aisles while the swing crew restocks the shelves, the light and the quiet and the familiarity of all those products as soothing as a warm milk bath.

We *live* at the Wal-Mart.

We puttered down to the track at Charlotte for this weekend's All-Star event, the Winston. It's a fan favorite, a cannily contrived short-form street fight in which a select field of recent race winners runs balls-out for a huge paycheck. There are no championship points involved. The night race is usually 70 laps or less, run in three segments. Fan voting inverts the field for the last segment of the race, meaning whoever's been running strong all night starts the money run from the back of the pack. The whole deal's as complicated as an Aztec sacrifice calendar, and the rules change every year, but it's NASCAR showbiz at its best. It's the V-8 version of a slam-dunk contest or home run derby, a hoot for all concerned, and you can see what kind of dire goofiness is in store when former Promise Keeper Jeff Gordon ignites a firestorm of press attention by returning from his off-week vacation with a newly grown, indisputably Satanic, goatee.

Charlotte is another fast, high-banked mile-and-a-half track, with Cup cars running upwards of 200 miles an hour along the dogleg front straight and down the long smooth chute of the backstretch. For most of the teams and drivers, this is their hometown track, and the garages and stands are full of family and friends. The night has the feel of a big company picnic, at once impersonal and intimate, 100,000 people in the same place who all sort of know each other.

Fans love night racing. All those fantastic sensations seem heightened somehow—the noise, the stream of colors, the spotlights breaking hard on the immaculate paint and flaring across the windshields. And no killer sun beating you down, either. Others do not love these evening events. "Night racing cuts into my drinking time," grumbled one trembling photographer on the way out of the press center.

The night begins with the drivers and the crews introduced pageant-style to great fanfare and acclaim. There's a double flatbed parked at the start/finish line with a proscenium stage built on top, and as each team is introduced they jog out onto the runway high-fiving each other and everyone they can reach while applause rolls down out of the seats. On its own the new goatee would have received the loudest ovation. Attached as it is to Gordon, though, it also attracts the nastiest catcalls. "What a fucking dork!" "Pussy!" "Fag!" and so forth. Strangely, they can't get enough of Junior's stinger. The mob's a fickle beast. Palms pink and burning, the teams walk back to the starting grid just before the prerace benediction/anthem/fireworks show.

The grid was set much earlier, during a combined pit stop and qualifying lap. The Beep and I had a rare chance to stand about 75 feet directly behind the cars during the 15-second stops. Other members of the working press had been invited to do so as well, but declined. When that first lug nut came whistling back at us we understood why. As old tires are swapped for new, the discarded lugs fall to the ground, often directly in line with the rear tires, whereupon, when the car accelerates away, they are fired rearward by the spinning rubber with the muzzle velocity of a Browning gun. Exciting as it is to see the sparks flying and hear the lugs whizzing, they hurt like hell when they nick your shins.

In a stunt format like this one, the action is continuous, everyone in a rush to the front and damn the consequences. Marlin and Jarrett and Rusty Wallace all crash out in due course, as does Elliott Sadler, with an assist from the front bumper of Ryan Newman. Sadler climbs from his car, ignoring the track workers and EMTs, and walks to the foot of the track. As Newman idles by under yellow on the next lap, Sadler winds up and throws his helmet across two lanes of traffic and bounces it off Newman's windshield, a perfect strike. Yeehaw!

In the same spirit Kurt Busch intentionally hammers Robbie Gordon out of the way to bring out a yellow flag, which clumps up the field for a three-lap sprint to the finish. Earnhardt Jr. and Ryan Newman pull away hard on the restart and it will be their race to win or lose.

Newman is slightly faster, with Junior running hard a couple of feet off his tail for two and a half laps. Coming into the final two turns, though, Junior gets a run on Newman and has a decision to make. If he stays in the throttle he can tap Newman's bumper, spin him, and win. He's right there. For a full second, for two, three, Junior's car is poised half an inch from winning. Half an inch from Newman's bumper. Half an inch more on the gas pedal is all it would take.

Junior eases out of the gas and Newman wins.

By choosing not to recklessly punt Newman out of the way, Junior forfeits around $750,000 in prize money, but wins instead the manic affections of the motoring press, who will spend the next week spinning cliché into hundreds of 24-karat column inches of solid promotional gold on the topics of probity, maturity, sensibility, and sportsmanship. Junior's prize is a new and better reputation.

"Getting to him was easy," quoth Junior in the media center just before midnight. "Getting by him was something different."

Out in the parking lot, still choked solid at 1 A.M., the fans boom praise from car to car. "He made a helluva run," they shout, waiting for the gridlock to thin, "one helluva run!"

"His old man'd'a crashed 'im," the state cop replies, his arms windmilling, uselessly indicating the distant and unattainable exits.

It feels like I'm beginning to see the races with a better eye for the driving, and the small strategies are becoming more familiar. I don't see the artistry in it yet, if indeed there is any. Staying close to the front and out of trouble and making your move to the lead late in the race seems to be almost everyone's master plan. Lay waiting, then take the lead when it's too late for anyone else to take it back.

Some weekends a car might be strong enough to lead wire to wire, and a few do, but the unpredictability of crashes and yellow flags and the ensuing cycle of pit stops can doom even the strongest car to a twenty-eighth-place finish if joker fate intervenes at the wrong moment.

Junior's dilemma at the Winston makes a fit illustration. Strategically, he played the night smart, running just hard enough to keep the leaders in sight but not so hard that he got caught up in the accidents of the overeager. He succeeded in being right where he wanted to be on the last lap. But tactically, bumping Newman aside, crashing him, was the only way to win. At which point it became as much a moral decision as anything else.

At Martinsville or Bristol, sure, bump him up the track. Done right, it's not only within the rules, it's expected. At just 90 miles an hour he might hit the wall, but he probably won't get hurt. At Charlotte, though, at 190, where the risk of injury or worse multiplies exponentially, the question becomes, how much are you willing to hurt someone to win? Junior's decision to err on the gentlemanly side of things bought him a long line of credit with the press, and further differentiated his growing legend from his father's. Interestingly, the one thing not mentioned the following week is what the decision might say about his hunger to win. No one anywhere says he didn't want it enough. Rather, in this New Age of Earnhardt, his reluctance to boot Newman aside is evidence of a cool hand, a sound head, and a stout heart.

The idea, however, that individual drivers possess any definable driving style, other than I'm-willing-to-bang-you-out-of-the-way or I'm-unwilling-to-bang-you-out-of-the-way, still eludes me.

It is a commonplace, at least in Cup circles, to refer to Cup drivers as the best race drivers in the world. NASCAR certainly wants you to believe it, otherwise what are they selling? The corporate advertisers want you to believe it, too, because they've sunk millions into their annual sponsorships. They'll spend many millions more to remind you that these aren't just lead-foot rednecks with a talent for turning left and a pathological disregard for authority and personal safety, but rather the very best racecar drivers in the whole wide world. After all, who opens their wallet to a pitch by a third-class athlete in a second-rate sport?

More tellingly, though, the conviction that NASCAR drivers are the best damn wheels on the planet grows from the grass roots up. In the Letters to the Editor section of any NASCAR weekly or fanzine, you'll see the phrase laid down in defense of, or as an argument against, everything from restrictor plates to higher beer prices.

"I can't imagine why some fans complain about the cost of tickets," the letter writers write, "when they're paying to see the best drivers in the world," or

"Why NASCAR wants to limit speed at these tracks is beyond me. These are the best drivers in the world. Shouldn't they be allowed to race with the fastest equipment possible?"

The "world" according to most American sports fans can be a pretty small place. It includes perhaps half the contiguous 48 United States. It includes most cities with professional franchises in the National League and the American League and the National Football League. It includes most of the franchises in the NBA and a few stops on the PGA tour. It includes two cities in Canada, Toronto and Montreal. In Olympic years the world includes Russia and sometimes China.

As a tavern argument, the question is forever unresolvable, always apples and apple butter, a matter of patriotism more than proof. But any one of the 400 million worldwide television viewers of a Formula One grand-prix race would fling their Boddington's in your gob if you tried to assert that Rusty or Ricky was a better driver than Damon Hill or Nigel Mansell. Buckshot Jones versus Michael Schumacher? Not much of a contest there, I'm afraid, no matter how narrow your view of what makes up a "world."

Formula One racing uses cars with more horsepower, weighing half as much, on tracks that turn both left and right. They handle better, accelerate harder, stop faster. Empirically, it would seem that Formula One drivers *have* to be the more skilled. Racing writers around the world seem to agree, because their annual lists of the 10 or 25 or 50 best drivers rarely if ever include an American, much less a Cup driver.

While a handful of Cup drivers might give a good account of

themselves if set against the rest of the best, what's more to the point, and might make NASCAR fans more potent debaters on the issue, is that Cup racing is arguably the most *entertaining* racing on the planet. Formula One races tend to be orderly affairs lately, without much passing or passion, the sport in thrall to engineering and the electronic driver-assist gizmos that make the cars faster but the racing near-sterile. F1 is a study in driver refinement and the applied technology of money. Cup racing by comparison represents obsessive tinkering with laughably obsolete technology, but is an absolute hog wallow of event and sensation, as profligate and visceral and combative on the track as it is off. The difference between F1 and Cup is the difference between a hot lap and a hot lap dance.

With a week to idle away before the next race here in Charlotte, the Beep and I make the rounds of the race shops.

At the dawn of NASCAR, most of the racers were based out of Florida, as might be expected. Over time they moved north with the sport, settling eventually for the sake of convenience near the Charlotte airport and the speedway. Now they're spread across the outlying suburbs here, too, all the way to Mooresville and Statesville and beyond. And while there are still a few holdout shops up in Virginia, the vast majority of NASCAR team operations go on within a half-hour drive of downtown Charlotte.

A visitor's experience from shop to shop to shop, from Roush to Penske to Ganassi to Jasper, will not vary much. There's a lobby (fantastic or drab) with a car or two on display and a wall full of trophies. There is a gift shop. There is a viewing window through which you can watch the teams at work building the cars. The quality of your visit depends almost entirely upon how passionately you root for the team operation you're seeing. An hour watching them buff Jimmie Johnson's hood may seem but an instant to an ardent admirer, while 15 seconds watching someone do the same for Kevin Harvick could be purest torture.

We hit every shop from the modest Dodge/Ray Evernham operation next to the runways at the Statesville airport, back to the elaborate complex at DEI, and down to the Hendrick garages near the racetrack, the headquarters of which look like the Swiss embassy, if only the Swiss had some real money.

We lumber back to DEI. The lobby is about what you'd expect, well upholstered and Cup-luxurious and understated. Weirdly, though, because he drove for Richard Childress, there isn't that much race-run Dale Earnhardt memorabilia present. Those mourning black cars are all over at Childress's shop in Welcome. Still, there are plenty of Earnhardt widgets and whatnots in the gift shop.

What really remains of him here is a palpable sense of immediate absence, like walking into a room that someone's just left through another door. The fans move across the carpets whispering, quiet as pilgrims at the sepulcher.

His death left millions of fans feeling like the counterweight necessary to the smooth turning of the Earth had been taken from them. Who now to bear them forward? To make them better than they are? In fact, when we pull into the parking lot of the Sam Bass Gallery out by the racetrack, the first thing we see is a bright red late-model Monte Carlo with an Iowa license plate that reads "MISSN 3."

Sam Bass is the Thomas Kinkade of NASCAR, a hugely successful artist and painter whose work is as ardently adored by fans as it is fastidiously ignored by critics. His graphics and portraits and action scenes appear on everything from the cars to the tickets to the programs to the walls of the corporate offices. His painting of Dale Earnhardt walking out of the desert in front of his seven championship cars is the cover of this year's Mooresville phone book.

On the day we visit, the gallery is very crowded, very busy, with the salespeople patiently explaining to some customers that "The bathroom is broken for race week," and that "We only have two Rustys right now, they sell out pretty fast," to others.

The poster reprints of the original paintings sell for as little as $15 or $20 in some cases, but the originals themselves run well into the hundreds and low thousands. Even Bass's "Quick Sketches," pencil renderings that look to have been done very quickly indeed, sell for over $200.

The paintings can be categorized broadly into portraits, trackside action scenes, and fantasy set pieces. The portraits and racing scenes are reverent, literal renderings of famous drivers and famous cars and famous moments in the sport. They are lively and intensely colorful. I will not try to tell you whether the paintings are good or bad. I will say instead that the paintings are impossibly popular and sell by the truckload.

The fantasy set pieces are an interesting trip into the artistic mind, certainly, in which reality is rearranged, then heightened, then abandoned entirely to connect with a Cup fan's id. A stock car races across the plains in a midnight thunderstorm ahead of a stampede of wild horses, the sky cracked by lightning firing like ganglia across the blackness. Stock cars lift off vertically from the shuttle gantry at the Cape, roaring into space atop a billowing plume of smoke and steam, headed for a huge and distant moon. Stock cars outrun fire, tornadoes, lightning. In the paintings hanging next to them the cars *cause* tornadoes, fire, lightning.

The paintings reflect recurring themes in the coffee mug images and shirt art that surround NASCAR, in which the car is a force of nature, unbound and flattening everything in its path. No matter the driver, no matter the team, the car breaks away, breaks out, breaks free—and takes you with it.

Thus inspired, we spent the rest of the afternoon trying to break free by racing go-karts with some of the publicists. They book the indoor track near the speedway whenever they're all back in Charlotte, and we've been invited to join them. Karting is a recreational mainstay in the traveling circus, with many teams reserving track time as they move from town to town. More often than you'd think, their superstar drivers show up, too. Keep your eyes open the next time The Show comes to town.

Today, though, it's just the flacks and the hacks racing fast and furious in our lust for victory. Sanitary yarmulkes and helmets screwed down tight, a dozen of us fling ourselves around the little road course for the rest of the day until we're pale, dehydrated, and sick to our stomachs.

Which is exactly the same state Mark Martin finds himself in when his crew fishes him out of the #6 car a few nights later, after winning the Coca-Cola 600 at the big speedway up the street.

The 600 is the longest race on the schedule and it takes the starch out of everyone present, from the drivers to the crews to the fans. There were long moments midrace when the field was so strung out that cars were circling the track at precisely spaced intervals, a perfect parade of ennui, no leader apparent and no one rushing to the front, the crowd of 170,000 going flat quiet for 20 minutes at a time.

Jimmie Johnson leads most of the night, the few spins and crashes happening well behind him, and seems to have things wrapped up until late in the race when he gets tangled up on lap 359 with Hut Stricklin. Johnson's shuffled back to eighth on the restart and Mark Martin finds himself leading.

His Arkansas twang cutting hard through his Viagra commercials, Martin is mighty popular with the fans; he's a 32-time winner and consistent front-runner who has never won the season championship. Ever the bridesmaid, at 43 he's come agonizingly close to winning it all several times, only to watch helplessly as bitch destiny snatched that big, ugly Cup championship trophy from his hands. He's now known for his sad air of fated resignation. As one of the smart press boxers puts it, "If you gave him a solid gold lucky horseshoe, he'd tell you how worried he was about dropping it on his foot. Then he'd drop it on his foot."

Martin is a small man, wiry and fit, his face seamed with his disappointments. When he wins at Charlotte, the place erupts, his crew leaping over the pit wall and running out to the frontstretch, where Martin turns joyful donuts, filling the night air with foul, happy smoke. His win tonight has earned a million-dollar bonus for a fan (that tricky No Bull 5 promotion), and an armored car makes its way onto the track, too, fake bills spilling from its open doors.

A stage is rolled out to the start/finish line and Martin is pulled from the car. He's too spent to stand, so he sits on the edge of the platform. "I'd rather wreck it than give up," he twangs into a microphone, and the fans roar. "It doesn't get any better than this."

The millionaire fan is introduced, Janet Hogan of Sterling, Virginia. She is handed a check for a million dollars and a microphone but can make no sound. For a couple of seconds, before the confetti cannons and the fireworks and the rush to the exits, the great stadium is absolutely hushed, silent, and the only sound is the short, sharp breathing of a woman caught somewhere between laughter and tears.

We roll out of Charlotte at last and head to the concrete 1-miler at Dover, Delaware. The weekend is all cracked sun and dust and whirlwinds blowing cinder grit into your eyes from the harness-racing track inside the oval. There's a hotel-casino here, too, right along the back straight, where the quarter-slot zombies smoke gold-tipped Shermans and eat spongy shrimp cocktail around the clock.

Jack Roush, out of the hospital, returns to the tour on crutches and is welcomed all weekend by everyone he sees.

The race is a snooze, with Jimmie Johnson flatfootin' it for 400 laps to win. Ricky Rudd might have made a run at him but lost a loose wheel in the last few laps, the day's only excitement. By my count no fewer than three of my colleagues actually fell asleep in the airless press box over the long afternoon.

Still, Johnson himself is the hottest thing to hit American racetracks since funnel cakes or binge drinking. There's been no Gordon-style backlash at all.

Handsome, modest, and fast, he's on his way to becoming one of the sport's biggest stars. Even his name has a silvery ring to it—that heroic, alliterative comic book lilt. Jimmie Johnson! Racing Ace of the Motordrome! In an antique America he might have been the hardworking, square-dealing cover boy of an inspirational dime novel, the two-fisted milk drinker in a raccoon coat and celluloid collar with an appetite for moral uplift and sporting excellence. One foot on the running board of his yellow Stutz, a State U pennant in his hand, and his dark eyes turned to the faraway stars, he could have been "Jimmie Johnson: All-American!"

So Dink Stover wins at Dover. Sterling Marlin comes in with the points lead and leaves with it.

The Pocono track is tucked away in the vacation hills of eastern Pennsylvania. The Beep and I pass a couple of pleasant down days camping beside a mountain lake and visiting the SteamTown National Railroad Museum up in the Wilkes-Barre–Scranton corridor. In short, when you're visiting here, there is *nothing* to do. Be advised.

One of the few remaining facilities on the tour not owned by ISC or its only corporate counterbalance, Speedway Motorsports, Inc., the Pocono track is a family operation, and its eccentricities are at once endearing and infuriating. It is home, for example, to the "Long John," a single urinal hundreds of feet in length, so capacious as to be, perhaps, the largest of its kind in existence. The media center, done up in shiny panels of black and white, looks like the disco on a discount cruise ship. The garages are built to look like long white stables, and there's a chain-link fence nearby with ports cut in it through which fans can ask the drivers for autographs without having to overrun them. There's a viewing balcony for the fans above Victory Lane, too, which is great, but the sight lines from the grandstands are lousy, which is not.

The 2.5-mile track presents a lot of frustrating trouble for the drivers as well, because it is neither a true oval nor a road course, but rather combines the worst of both. Drivers actually have to downshift here several times, and the roughly triangular track is narrow and fast, so the opportunities to screw the pooch are many and varied.

Pooches remain unmolested both Friday or Saturday. The track's too wet to run, thanks to a spring bubbling up through the asphalt out in the far turn, a result of recent torrential rains. The Sunday race comes around when the water recedes, and Dale Jarrett takes the win when hard-luck Ricky Rudd flats a tire in the closing laps and drills his car right into the wall. Uninterestingly, Sterling Marlin maintains the points lead.

On Sunday, there were two fans up in the stands just above Victory Lane. These guys were big Dale Jarrett fans. Ardent. They were young men—late twenties, I suppose—and they were all done up in their Dale Jarrett and United Parcel Service gear. Dale Jarrett was about 10 yards away from them, standing down in Victory Lane. He had just won the June race. Dale Jarrett is a tall man, gray-haired, easy to spot in a crowd, and you could see him very clearly from where these guys were standing.

"Dale, we love you!" they yelled.

"Dale, we love you!" they yelled again.

Dale Jarrett didn't turn around or look. He was 10 yards away after all, covered in sweat and exhausted from running 500 loud, hard miles, and he was busy with all those other people, his crew and Miss Winston and the TV reporters and the photographers, and his crew was spraying champagne all over everything, and the music was playing and people were cheering and the track is a pretty loud place even when the cars aren't running, so maybe he hadn't heard them.

"Dale, you the man!" they yelled loudly in unison. Gathering breath they counted one, two, three and yelled it again. "You the MAN, Dale!" They waited for him to turn to them, but he didn't. They looked straight at him.

They were very loud, at least from where I was standing. But they needed to be louder.

"DALE, you the MAN!" They had really reached way down deep for one, and this time it boomed out across row after row of seats and out across the infield. They were sure he had heard it and they stared straight at him from 10 yards away and waited. They waited and waited, but he must not have heard them because he was still busy with all those other people down there in Victory Lane where so much was going on and didn't look up.

Undeterred, they tried once more. These two, serious Dale Jarrett fans, perhaps his biggest fans anywhere, would make themselves heard. They would get his attention. He would look up. He would take off his postrace sunglasses. He would wipe the sweat from his face with the little Gatorade towel. He would scan the huge crowd, but even in all the confusion he would spot them right away. Seeing them, seeing their passion and their dedication and their devotion to him, Dale Jarrett would surely walk over and climb right up to them. Maybe he'd even bring Miss Winston. He would sign two autographs, shake two hands, have a chat, compliment them on their persistence, and thank them each, warmly and personally, for being part of today's winning effort. Maybe he'd give them his helmet.

The two bowed as one and inhaled great barrelsful of air. Then, red-faced and straining, they stood upright, heads back, mouths wide, and sang out, shouting up to the sky, louder than they ever thought possible, all the way up to the place where wishes are granted for men whose hearts are true, "YOU THE MAN, DALE!"

And nothing.

One of the guys, skinny and handsome, dark, with greasy, shoulder-length hair and a sharp Mephistopheles goatee, stared at Dale Jarrett for a long time. Then he yelled out on his own, "We know you can hear us!"

The other, to his right, fat and blond, pig-eyed and small-mouthed, looked at his friend for a moment and then turned back. He leaned way out over the railing and yelled down, "Yeah! We know you can hear us!"

They looked tired and confused.

"Look up here!"

"Look up here!"

"We know you can hear us!"

"We know you can hear us!"

"Look at us!"

"Look at us!"

"Look at us, asshole!"

"Don't be an asshole, DJ!"

"Look at us, you asshole!"

Dale Jarrett didn't look up. The car was wet with champagne and beer and Powerade and Pepsi and Gatorade and Coke and the sour smell of that cheap champagne was everywhere and everything you touched down there was sticky and everybody was loud and happy and Dale Jarrett was having his picture taken again and again in different hats from different sponsors.

"We *made* you, you asshole!"

"Look *up* here, you asshole!"

"WE *MADE* YOU!"

"LOOK AT US YOU ASSHOLE!"

"LOOK AT US YOU FUCKING ASSHOLE!"

"LOOK AT US YOU FUCKING COCKSUCKER!"

"LOOK AT US YOU STUPID MOTHERFUCKER!"

Dale Jarrett never looked up. The whole thing took five minutes. Maybe they had come a long way to see him.

We make our way to the 2-mile oval at Brooklyn, Michigan. The infield here is raucous and loud without seeming fun. There's an edge to the voices and the music and the lights, something shrill and aggressive, the racket like bad impulses barely contained, and a long walk through it at dusk is like going out on patrol. You can feel the eyes on you and even the laughter sounds sharp and threatening. You move through it like you're walking on the lid of a pressure cooker.

The entire weekend carries violence around in its pocket, plenty of fast crashing and close calls. On Sunday, Matt Kenseth wins. It is Father's Day, and when asked about the victory and his son, Kenseth's dad refers to him proudly as "The Quiet Assassin."

Asked about the outstanding performances of all these young'uns, Rusty Wallace is equally avuncular. "They're outrunnin' the shit out of us." Sterling Marlin, dashing old goat, remains points leader.

•   •   •

Another long haul now, to northern California.

These nights on the road, parked at the track or on the distant fringe of some new town, or just as likely trapped out in the alien spaces between them, we watch a lot of television.

The nightly newscasts of the three networks, prophet and profit center of the Numinous Absolute, hadn't changed much in the months after September 11, 2001. Perhaps they gave the appearance of having changed. There were more ghostly flags waving in the semi-transparent graphics hovering behind Tom's or Dan's or Peter's head, and half a husky octave more gravitas in their line readings; even a few nights when one or the other cast his tired eyes down to his news desk in an unguarded moment of human exhaustion or heartbreak or shame. In a small box above his shoulder, the smoke poured from those disappeared buildings night after night after night.

But each broadcast still revealed more about America in its commercial sequences than anything you might find in the second-segment news hole. It was still a 30-minute journey through the spastic catacombs of America's overfed and overstressed gastrointestinal system: from its reflux-ravaged windpipe to its acid-lashed stomach to its aching, unassuageable bowels to its burning and inconsolable asshole.

America has diarrhea. America is constipated. America has indigestion with bloating and gas.

America's esophagus is as tattered as rotten lace. America can't get it up. America needs the little blue pill. America needs to know that side effects may include dry mouth, seizure, stroke. Ask your doctor.

America is tossing and turning. America needs its sleep. America needs the little yellow pill. Side effects may include dry mouth, fibrosis, liver failure. Ask your doctor.

The news was a half-hour catalog of our reeking winds and bubbling guts, our balky knees and stinking feet, our ringing skulls and our chalk-dry gonads, with a few 45-second stories of fear and fortitude, but mostly fear, thrown in.

Satellite and cable news had become a 24-hour streaming-media Ouija board, a confusion of signs and symbols and numbers and letters, fragments and mystic figments, which, arranged somehow into words and then interpreted, might tell us everything or nothing. The pointer only moves where it's pushed.

Still the Beep and I watched, awaiting instructions. Alert for warnings, harbingers, signs. Listening.

It was like sticking a fire hose in each ear.

The late local news as we moved from town to town was quaint by comparison: a brief sequence of accidents or assaults or acts of God, all visually rendered as squad cars parked in the murk with their lights turning, the video a study in pointillism, all leading up a 10-minute forecast of tomorrow's weather as determined by the sometimes accurate, but always promotable, WeatherCenter Radar 5000 or the AccuTrac Super-Ranging Doppler 10000 or the All-Powerful Sky Splitter of the Wizard Magnificent. Only the skylines changed behind the anchor desks. Everyone on camera neutral, transregional, attractive.

The Beep and I surfed and zapped and flipped with as much energy as we could muster, which wasn't much. As has been said, television is not about what's on, it's about what else is on. (And what else is on is *Law and Order*.)

The Beep and I sought and found our solace in home-improvement shows, in the ingenious reinvigoration of interior spaces, in the building of grape arbors or gazebos or barbecue pits, in a smooth run of bright copper pipe or decorative tile. The words alone were comfort: backsplash, cupola, bluestone, mortise, dovetail.

We never missed *Trading Spaces*, and would fall asleep imagining ourselves returning to the Homer after a day in the Darlington garage to find that our friends had snuck in and redone our interior in something, anything, but teal.

And we weren't the only carnies with an eye for home improvement. It was a conversational staple among the regulars on the tour, the willingly displaced, that when they got home they were going to redo the bedroom, the kitchen, the bath. That they never got home at all made it at once impossible and impossibly attractive to do so.

Home is a powerful idea when your mailing address is Aisle Seat on an Exit Row, U.S.A., and it makes sense that the Flying Dutchmen and -women of NASCAR would hunker down in their Dover motel rooms on a Friday night to see what a person might do to a lifeless living room with $1,000 worth of particle board and velveteen.

And where else would a detour past the intersection of television and home improvement lead us but back to NASCAR? The popular Home Depot and Lowe's cars are successful, high-profile runners in Cup this season, and those brands are familiar to fans of any minting; but the store names are perhaps more reassuringly recognizable to the new-generation stain-resistant Dockers Maximum Dad on whom NASCAR appears to be betting its future. Primary sponsorships from snuff, bird-shot, and lard are only going to hold you back when you're trying to cultivate a broader, more upscale audience for your national television broadcasts. And television is now the air that NASCAR breathes.

Cup racing's success as a television property has been incremental rather than overnight, but two events on the historical timeline are written and spoken of repeatedly as seminal.

"That race's one of the things that really accounts for all this," says Richard Petty, 23 years after the fact, gesturing toward the locust madness of the thronging Daytona crowds.

On February 18, 1979, CBS broadcast live flag-to-flag coverage of the Daytona 500. This was the first time a Cup race had been aired as it happened in its entirety. Prior to that, stock-car racing had been a hit-or-miss affair on the networks, stuck for nearly 20 years as a heavily edited 10- or 12-minute film or video highlight package on ABC's *Wide World of Sports*; or as a brief live insert on CBS's weekly *Sports Spectacular*. In the former case, a race might be two weeks over by the time you saw it. In the latter, you saw 15 minutes of a four-hour race.

The Indy 500 had been a live, marquee television event during most of that same period, but given its stature as perhaps the most famous automobile race in the world, the networks felt they could justify the trouble and expense of covering it. That CBS had acquired the TV rights to the '79 Daytona race for something like $25,000 made it more of a What the hell? proposition.

The race played out the way strategy always dictates—the leaders kept each other close, waiting for that last lap, that last turn, to make their slingshot move out of the draft to the front. Take the lead when they can't take it back. In 1979 it was Donnie Allison, of the famous Alabama Gang of stockers, and bulldog Cale Yarborough running wide open doorhandle to doorhandle coming down the landing strip backstretch into turn 3 on the final lap. Behind them, resigned to a third-place finish, was Richard Petty. Allison and Yarborough were so hard at it, so close to the limits of sense and adhesion, that they both got loose coming into the rising sweep of that final turn, got loose and squirrelly on those greasy old tires, and before anybody strictly knew what happened Allison was up the track into Yarborough, or Yarborough's down the track into Allison, and they're both sliding and wrecking down into the apex of the turn, while sly patient Petty gave 'er the gun and flew on by to take the checkered flag. On its own the moment might have been enough to make the race seem epochal. But as the rest of the field flickered across the line, the best part of the show was still unfolding.

By the time Yarborough and Allison had unbelted themselves and climbed from their cars, still steamed about what each thought the other had done, Allison's brother Bobby had circled the track on a cool-down lap and was pulling up to the wrecked racers to make sure that Donnie was all right.

As he rolled up, Donnie and Cale were engaged in philosophical colloquy regarding the nature of cause and effect.

"You dumb son of a bitch, you wrecked us both!"

"*You're* the dumb son of a bitch!"

And so forth.

Bobby's late arrival on the scene struck Mr. Yarborough as unnecessarily provocative, perhaps indicating that he was about to get Alabama ganged up on, so preemptively he took a poke at Bobby through the window of the car. Donnie came to his aid, Bobby was fast out of the car, and the fists and the feet and the helmets of all three were soon flying. On national television. Live. The drawlin' and brawlin' fun of Cup's hardest runners beaming out as it's happening from coast to coast to coast. And people were actually home to see it.

The fillip to the story, the kicker, the element of the elemental that makes the whole deal seem foreordained, was the substantial snowfall in the East that very weekend. It kept people inside, warming themselves by the sunny glow of the TV. More people saw that race than had ever seen any Cup race in the history of the sport. That one afternoon brought America into contact with something it might otherwise have never seen. NASCAR.

The other television watershed in NASCAR history isn't nearly as colorful, unless you're a tort lawyer, a media buyer, or a certified public accountant and the color in question is green.

In 1999, NASCAR announced that it was signing multiyear contracts with Fox, NBC, and Turner Sports to carry the entire NASCAR race calendar on a split schedule beginning in 2001. The contracts involved total $2.4 billion. When the contracts roll over in a few years, that number will be even higher, but in the meantime $2.4 billion is the figure they chant like a mantra out here to make plain that The Show has arrived in the big time and is no longer just a five-minute cutaway during another sporting event. Two point four billion dollars is also the club they use to beat people (reporters, I mean) over the head with how popular they've become. (The reporters then parrot the figure endlessly.) It's like having a neighbor who won't shut up about how much he paid for his car or his boat. Always unsure of itself in polite company, NASCAR can't stop bragging.

In any case the contracts are sufficient evidence that someone out there is watching the races on TV, and that someone's selling enough advertising to benefit from it. It's a substantial pie, and everybody's in line for a slice.

The teams get a cut of the television money as a percentage of the purse; the tracks get a cut and NASCAR gets a cut.

The networks get fed too, obviously. If they felt they could pay 2.4X, they're pretty confident they'll make back at least 3X over the life of the project, so the money pours a torrent through the whole system. Consider that during a four-hour race broadcast they'll be

able to sell at least an hour of total commercial time in 15-second increments and you can envision the returns. To say nothing of the
nearly invisible ancillary ads so common in sports television these
days, the Subway Leaderboard crawl or the McDonald's Pit Timer
graphic, or whatever that stuff is cluttering your screen. Somebody
paid something for every one of those little annoyances, too.

The advertisers and sponsors are seeing some healthy return on investment as well, with a recent study offering the example that during
the 2002 Daytona 500, the exposure value of the race coverage alone,
not including commercials, across more than 250 product and service
brands, was worth more than $225 million. In a single race. "Exposure
value" simply estimates what an advertiser would have had to pay in
order to get equivalent on-screen love by buying ad time. That phrases
like "exposure value" are crowding out phrases like "keep a tight ass"
in conversational NASCAR is telling, too.

It doesn't surprise me that the retailing of NASCAR's television origin
stories goes heavy on the cash, the crash, and the divine intervention
of Oz, the Omnipotent Snowmaker, but I'm not sure that the story
explains much in terms of the sport's current popularity. While the
two things dovetail beautifully as metaphor (it used to be about the
racin', now it's about the money), they seem to me a beginning and an
end, with the middle of the story missing. If that 1979 race was such a
seminal moment, after all, why weren't the networks queuing up back
then to offer juicy contracts to broadcast more just like it? And aren't
the current contracts a reflection not only of the *potential* popularity
of the sport but also of its preexisting hold on the public imagination?
I mean, do people love it because it gets such good exposure on TV, or
does it get such good exposure on TV because people love it?

I'm not sure there's an answer fine enough to differentiate chicken
and egg. For years between 1979 and 1999 NASCAR's television package was a patchwork of networks and cable, and it took a determined
fan to hunt up the coverage from weekend to weekend. Hunt some of
them did, certainly, but the sport didn't explode into broad (read: north-

ern) public consciousness until the last five years or so. It wasn't Dale Earnhardt's death, either, as huge and black a milestone as that was in terms of American awareness of the sport. The signing of the current network television contracts preceded by nearly two years that sad event.

At first I thought this might have as much to do with miniaturization as it did with expansion. The in-car camera is a staple of all the broadcasts now, with up to half the field carrying one or more tiny onboard cameras. The front-runners and matinee idols get multiple camera setups, top and bottom, front and rear, inside and out, while the back-markers may just get a single camera on the roofline or down on the airdam or in the cockpit to ensure that the television director has a shot from the back of the field when there's some "action" up ahead on the track. Maybe the swelling ratings were a reflection of these shrinking cameras and their ability to make every one one of us a Walter Mitty, runnin' the high line at The Track Too Tough to Tame, the wall roaring past just a few inches away, while we bump and grind for that extry inch with Jimmie or Johnny or Junior.

But onboard cameras have been in wide use for a decade now and there were early versions of the technology in Cup racing going all the way back to the mid-1980s. And in-car shots have helped CART and IRL not at all. The cameras have gotten substantially smaller, yes, but the refinements in placing them seem only to get sillier. Sure, I want to see those brake discs glowing cherry red at Bristol. But is it really any better to have the camera *inside* Michael Waltrip's helmet than it was to have it 2 inches away on the carbon-fiber headrest frame? What next, the sigmoidoscope?

"He looks to be tightening up nicely, Darrell."

"I'd like to check the PSA numbers on that prostate, though. Maybe next time he comes in for right-side tires."

As great a contribution as this sort of intimacy has made to the broadcasts, I'm not convinced it accounts for crazy new ardor among viewers.

Nor am I sold on the idea that the broadcasts themselves, more elaborately produced week to week—more cameras, more announcers, more sideline reporters, more meandering "behind-the-music" personality packages, more quick-cut, rock-inflected highlight reels—than those in any other sport, have brought new fans into the tent. A two-minute VTR exegesis of Kenny Wallace's home life isn't enough to keep anyone around for the four hours of racing that follows.

Is it the announcers, with their aw-shucks savvy and their cracker-barrel enthusiasm and their down-home expertise? You may love Darrell Waltrip or Benny Parsons, but are you willing to spend half a Sunday—a huge chunk of valuable disposable time—listening to them speculate about spring rubbers and tire wear?

And while I think that some of the new young stars have terrific crossover drawing power, e.g., Junior, I think that others of his generation remain mostly unknown beyond those people who already know and love the sport, e.g., Matt Kenseth. The audience for Rusty Wallace and Mark Martin and Bill Elliott et al. would seem to me a stable population over time, given to neither significant diminishment nor radical growth. The nubile, newbie bobby-soxers tend to swoon for the young'uns after all, not the graybeards. On the strength of Junior's global appeal alone, I'd have to say that having a new/old star name above the NASCAR title has brought at least some increase in fans at the track and at their televisions.

I honestly don't think, though, that even Junior, alpha male though he may be, can alone account for all this new accounting. Where did this new TV audience come from?

It doesn't help much to ask individual fans. They can point you in a direction, maybe even drop a few bread crumbs, but finally, their answers lead you in a circle.

"I don't know. The other sports seem pretty boring once you've seen it."

"The cars."

"I like the drivers' personalities. They seem to be real good people to me."

"We just like the racing."

•   •   •

The inventory of possible explanations is nearly endless, obviously, 75 million hearts beating their own rhythm for their own reasons. Reductively, maybe there's a short list:

- The sport's inherently exciting to watch: loud, colorful, fast, spectacular. Sensational.
- There's an element of fatal risk, so a great deal is at stake. Much more than is apparent in other sports.
- The drivers are in grave danger every time they get in the car. The drivers get in the cars anyway. The drivers are therefore brave. The drivers thus satisfy our ravenous appetite for heroes.
- It's catharsis. People love to watch the cars, the machines that so dominate their lives, get torn up. They don't necessarily (or at least consciously) want to see anyone get hurt, but seeing the cars destroyed one weekend, and then reappear brand-new the next, is very satisfying. The imminence of someone's death can't be ignored, though.
- It's as simple a sport as you want to make it. You can watch and be swept away by the spectacle without knowing a thing about it. It's binary. Win/lose. Most other sports require at least a baseline understanding of the rules. Cup racing can also be as arcane and complicated as string theory if one chooses to make it so.
- To embrace it, even on television, makes you feel like you're part of a large, stable (and homogenous) community. A rare thing these days.

Does this get us anywhere? Auto racing has always been all of the things just mentioned, but the new fanaticism for NASCAR is a very recent phenomenon. Maybe we need to account for other trends, other influences.

- *Triumph of the Machines*. The industrial revolution finally catches up with entertainment and sports. We're now willing and anxious to watch competitions between our inanimate surrogates.
- *Decline and Fall of the American Empire*. Just as the Romans whiled away the slow collapse of the republic at the Hippodrome or the

Circus Maximus, we are now embarking on our final descent into a long twilight of decadent blood sport and selfish, witless hedonism.

- *World's Loudest Soap Opera.* We have taken up with NASCAR because of the recurring and easy-to-grasp storylines: Black hat/white hat in noble struggle. Up from the dust to fame and fortune. Good man undone by fate. Good man tempted. Bad man made good. Bad man/good woman. Good man/bad woman. Good man/bad car. Everyone redeemed by hard work/sacrifice/grace.

- *Best of a Bad Bunch.* The TV numbers for baseball and basketball have been trending slowly downward for years. Hockey can't pull a number that would beat the National Math Bee. Gate attendance is off, or only holding steady, in every league. Has too much coverage exhausted our interest in "traditional" sports? As new sports rise, do the old pastimes fall? Does NASCAR suddenly look so good because everyone else looks so bad?

Who knows, maybe America really *does* love to hear Darrell Waltrip shouting "Boogity, boogity, boogity!" just as much as he thinks it does.

One last thought on the subject: From the day it was founded, NASCAR's core mission was to promote its brand of automobile racing. At this it has succeeded beyond Bill France Sr.'s wildest imaginings. Make no mistake, despite NASCAR's rural southern origins and its corporate appearance of country boy simplicity, it is one of the savviest marketing entities in the country—in any field. It is far smarter about how to promote its product than any other major-league sport. It also wields the kind of politburo control over its sport that other sports executives, dealing with all those fractious, self-interested athletes and teams and cities, can only dream of. It's a nonunion shop. And for all its huckleberry modesty, it is a relentless self-promoter.

Maybe the reason that NASCAR seems so spectacularly successful is that NASCAR keeps telling you it is.

Summer

We snake down out of the Sierra and run flat out to the track just north of San Francisco Bay. It was announced this morning that it will no longer be known as the Sears Point Raceway, but will now and forever (or until the naming-rights contract expires) be called Infineon Raceway.

It is a road course set into the satin gathers of the golden hills halfway between Napa and Sonoma. By far the most beautiful ring on the circuit, it is one of only two stops that requires the drivers to turn left *and* right. The stock cars lumber and hurry around it like angry fat men as the Pacific wind carries their terrible noise across the valley.

On Saturday after practice we play hooky, hitch a ride into town for sandwiches and wine, walk the Napa streets, and visit another ghost house, Jack London's old place, a burned-out shell sitting high and silent in the dripping redwoods.

On Sunday, Ricky Rudd falls into the win when Jerry Nadeau's car breaks in front of him on the last lap. Only fair, really, given Rudd's recent luck. Jeff Gordon, born not 20 miles from here, leads from the start and looks unbeatable, but breaks a rear-end gear early in the day and can't get back in it. Sterling Marlin is still your points leader.

Now we're off to Colorado for another high-altitude holiday. This is the last down week of the season. Then it's 20 races with no rest or relief until the Monday after Miami. In November.

Having offered one example of NASCAR's deft handling of the numbers that bear on the public's perception of its success, I'll offer one more before we hide out in the mountains.

Bad Math 2

It is canonical out here that NASCAR is now America's number two sport. If pressed to explain how so, the opiner of same, usually someone in the NASCAR public relations office, but just as often a reporter, will add the feeble disclaimer, "on TV." The NFL is the clear leader in that field, by far the most popular sport on TV, and has been for years.

Forget about the Super Bowl, with its huge event viewership. Week in and week out, the NFL pulls an average 15 million viewers for each of its network broadcasts.

NASCAR bases its assertion of its Number Twoness on the ratings performance of other sports: basketball, baseball, hockey, and so on. It makes the comparison in what might at first appear to be a fair manner. It compares the rating of its national broadcast to the ratings of a national broadcast in these other sports. Our best example for the comparison in question might be baseball, the national pastime which NASCAR seems to have overtaken in the hearts and Nielsen boxes of America.

NASCAR's ratings for event races, like Daytona or the Brickyard, can generate some spectacular numbers. Up to 25 million people in this country might watch at least some of the Daytona 500. But let's make our comparison using something nearer the norm. Let's say the spring race at Talladega, a very popular event, gets a 6 rating and a 14 share, a typical number for that race over the last couple of years. That means that more than 6 million households were watching the race, and that they represented 14 percent of the households watching television at the time. NASCAR then compares that number to baseball's network game of the week, which might have gotten a rating of only 3 or 3.5. Clearly NASCAR has kicked baseball's flabby old ass.

The comparison seems fair. You can compare the numbers for a single weekend, or compare the average numbers across an entire season. More people, substantially more people, are watching network NASCAR every week than are watching network baseball. By this method NASCAR is the number two sport in America (on TV). Ask a few simple questions, though, and the comparison gets tangled.

Aren't there a lot more major-league baseball games on television during the week than there are Cup races? Aren't there a lot more major-league baseball teams? Playing a lot more games across the arc of a season?

Baseball's weekly television audience is hard to isolate because all 30 teams in the league have their own local or regional cable or broadcast deals. They play 162 games a season. Depending on which television market you inhabit, and how many major-league baseball teams call it home, there might be as many as a dozen games a week from which to choose just locally. And that doesn't include nationally televised cable games or satellite baseball packages. Baseball's audience is atomized across a huge number of games and a multiplicity of outlets.

NASCAR has one Cup race on Sunday on one network outlet 36 weeks a year.

Given those qualifiers, then, and in the spirit of the attendance experiment we performed 25,000 miles ago, wouldn't it be even fairer to compare the number of people who choose to watch Cup racing on TV each week to the number of people who choose to watch baseball on TV?

Based on figures compiled by the gnomic numbers crunchers at Major League Baseball, here are the averages for any given week in the baseball season.

> Local team coverage: 20,022,744
> National cable coverage: 10,415,000
> Network coverage: 3,600,000
> Average weekly number of viewers: 34,037,744

Even allowing for some inflationary wishful thinking on the part of MLB's statistician brain trust, that 6 rating for spring Talladega doesn't look quite so unassailably number two. On TV.

Still, the television crews have the run of the track, and the Beep and I are forever being yelled at and elbowed and banged out of the way as they hustle past on their way to do the next live crew chief interview. And why not? They bought it. They own it. It's their show now.

NINE

It begins and ends in winter, but it carries summer with it. Forget the date; its only true season anywhere and everywhere is high summer, hot and rank and cruel. Eternal, unrelieved, suffocating summer; the seconds and the minutes and the hours spinning fast across the asphalt, the pilgrims staggering toward blackout, until the sunset flares at last over the rim of the grandstands and ignites the sky. You look up. It's like the whole world has burst into flames.

Fittingly, second Daytona is humid hell, worst heat of the jungle season and a hot rain pissing down over everything. When the civilians aren't keeling over from the dead air and the Jaegermeister, they're getting hit by lightning when the thunderstorms rage through—eight fans flattened, if only temporarily, yesterday out front by the sponsor tents.

Those unblownup by nature detonate themselves with the recreational explosives they've smuggled in. We're shoehorned into the packed infield here for the Fourth of July weekend and the running of the Pepsi 400. We come out of the motorhome door in a crouch at all times, dodging the wobbling holiday daddies and their murderous bottle rockets.

Practice and qualifying are scheduled, scratched, rescheduled, and scratched again. The drivers hide in their climate-controlled motorhomes. To be made to drive one of those cars in this funk is a punishment. In fact, that infamous heat's the kicker to every argument you hear when asking whether drivers are really athletes or not.

"Well, consider that they have to operate a complex system competitively, at high speed and at great risk, while formulating race strategy and performing demanding physical tasks. And that *heat!*"

On race day the point is well taken. The race begins in early evening, but even the crewmen are passing out. You see the EMTs, ready to collapse themselves, hurrying along the pit walk to tend them. The tire guys and gas men who remain standing pour coolers full of ice water into their firesuits.

Dale Jr. and Michael Waltrip in their aeroslick DEI Chevy plateracers are expected to do well, and the race unfolds according to the tip sheets, Waltrip leading most of the way while the field seesaws behind him. Jeff Gordon goes a lap down when a 25-cent bumper brace breaks, and he wastes nearly a minute in the pits. The evening steams away as the grandstands fitfully doze and cry out their night terrors. The inevitable Big One comes on lap 135 and sends most of the peloton sideways through the first turns, the Hooters car burning festively on the backstretch apron. Many of the most likely challengers are gathered up, leaving Waltrip and Junior to duel for the win. With less than five laps to go, Junior pulls out of line to pass, and instead loses the draft, can't get back into line, and finishes sixth. Over the radio he laments to his crew, "I feel like a fuckin' asshole at y'all's expense." Everybody on the other end's pissed. "Keep it off the radio," comes the crew chief's stern reply. The race finished under yellow, never a fan favorite, when Ryan Newman pinballed off the wall, and now the chicken bones and beer cans and seat cushions rain down onto the track. To the surprise of no one, Sterling Marlin is still the points leader.

Picking our way through the empties and ducking the incoming, the Beep and I return to the Homer around midnight. We have no power. Lightning strike? Hillbilly missile? While I squint at the wiring diagram, the Beep ascends the roof to look for clues. She returns in just seconds, her eyes wide. Apparently the bottle-rocket daddies prefer live targets. "What is *wrong* with people?"

We fall asleep hours later, fanless and breathless, on sodden sheets, the M-80 explosions still echoing from the infield bathrooms. Yeehaw!

In a hurry to get to Chicago, we run up the white flag. We surrender. I find the hidden mystery circuit breaker at dawn and we're gone.

Our earbones ground to a fine powder by the cars, the fans, the incoming, and the repeated play of Sheryl Crow's trackside anthem "Steve McQueen," we're off to Joliet, Illinois.

The Chicagoland Speedway opened in 2001 and looks it. The squeaky clean mile-and-a-half tri-oval is virtually indistinguishable from others of its size and recent minting, but represents an important new market conquest for NASCAR.

Three items of interest this weekend, not one of them the race.

The track is beset by Japanese beetles. They are everywhere—crunching underfoot, bouncing off your face, flying down your collar. They're beautiful to look at, iridescent green and gold, best paint scheme of the week. It's likewise fun to watch them ricochet off the local television sports reporters while they try to do their stand-ups.

The track is also beset by Muppets. The big furries wander the stands and the infield and the pit apron, bending to shake children's hands and generally bringing age-appropriate joy to all who encounter them. Until, that is, they're banned from the track. Apparently there's a sponsor conflict with a competing line of animated NASCAR-licensed thingamajigs and the solution, courtesy of the in-house brain trust, is a lockout. Under the sympathetic umbrella of extensive television coverage, the Muppets spend the weekend out front, carrying picket signs at the gates.

Also of note was Jeff Gordon's high-fashion photo shoot. Trailing only eight assistants and two golf carts of equipment, famous-shooter-of-the-famous Peggy Sirota arrives in the drivers' compound to record Gordon's steely gaze for the glossy pages of *GQ*.

Clad in his firesuit, Gordon emerges from his motorhome with a faceful of bronzer and his hair all roostered up.

"Who the hell's that?" inquire the neighbors. "Get a real job!" they shout. It's the Alltel crew eating lunch at the Newmans' next door.

Gordon's gaze, if possible, becomes steelier.

"Ohhhhh. I like your *eyes*," Sirota says softly, bringing her giant camera 6 inches from Gordon's face. *"I want your eyes."*

Gordon, all steel and number 22 Egyptian pancake, obliges.

After a wild spin across the track apron in the opening laps on a hot, clear, midwestern Sunday, Kevin Harvick, last year's winner here, worked his way steadily up through the field. He had the strongest car and he is your winner. Sterling Marlin, whether you like it or not, is your points leader.

A thousand miles east, up past the capital and the L. L. Bean Outlet Center and that huge, counterintuitive rest-area liquor store right on the interstate, is the New Hampshire International Speedway. It's a quirky oval, flat, fast, and slick, slightly more than a mile around, with an infield veined by red water sump creeks, as if the place was mined, quarried out, and then paved. It holds 91,000 yahooing New Englanders.

Off the clock, the teams run down to Boston to go karting, or hold lobster boils at their motorhomes. Between practice runs, Jimmie Johnson and Jeff Gordon sit in Gordon's hauler watching *World's Greatest Police Chases*.

On Sunday all the drivers are hauled from the garages to the start/finish line in one of those minibuses done up to look like a vintage trolley. At 2 miles an hour, looking like a garden club on their way to the mallwalk, the drivers blush with shame. "Losers!" shout their snickering crews.

As predicted, Ricky Craven's introduction is greeted with a Juniorine roar. Twenty minutes later, after only a lap or two, as the fans entertain themselves doing the Wave and dropping their r's, the newly surfaced track begins to come apart. The cars tear up strips and bits and blocks of pavement in every turn, until the course is littered from curb to curb with debris. The cars skitter sideways, pigs on skates, into the wall. Those that don't crash outright shred their tires and then crash. There are many lead changes and many yellow flags. Fourteen, in fact.

A random sweep of the radio scanner we picked up at Michigan reveals the drivers' feelings regarding these developments.

"Well, I've got gravel, absolute goddamn gravel, coming up the fender wells now. Jesus."

"NASCAR needs to black-flag this thing. This is a mess, somebody's gonna get hurt out here."

"What a fuckup."

Proceeding on tiptoe, the field circles the track. The leaders crash and the cars behind them move gingerly up to take their place. They crash as well, and so on, in sequence, throughout the afternoon. Ward Burton wins by attrition, the checkered flag finally falling before he has the chance to crash. Again.

Sterling Marlin orbits the quarry with enough success to remain the points leader.

Most Sundays after a race, sun going down and the noise just gone, fans streaming out of the seats, everyone rushing to get home, there is a gathering of poets. Reporters run to interview the drivers. The rotors are already turning on the helicopters. The jets need to be wheels-up in 18 minutes, the G-3s and Falcons headed back to Charlotte. But tomorrow's newspaper can't be empty. Tonight's sports update needs footage. Reporters and producers and videographers scramble through the garages to get comments from the drivers. Radio, print, TV, a hundred interviews at once, everywhere you look, all around you, in five minutes. Cameras flashing, microphones everywhere, pens tipped to paper, they bend urgently to each other, the haiku masters of Talladega.

Q: How was it out there?
   You looked real good all day—
   A third-place finish.
A: The car ran real good
   And this team is just awesome—
   We were fast all day.

Q: You were slow right off
   Then started to run real good—
   What did you guys do?
A: We was tight at first
   But took out a spring rubber
   And after that run good.

Q: You were running good
   Until Jimmy tagged you—
   How did it happen?
A: He gets inside me
   Then rises up, not looking—
   I'm in the wall.
Q: You won again here
   And you ran real good all day—
   How did you do it?
A: The Number Eight crew
   Had the Budweiser Chevy
   Running good today.

You could be interviewing ol' Basho hisself. After a month you don't even hear it.

Compared to all that star power and all that effortful corporate buzz and all that resonant, unfocused voltage from the fans, the grandstands arcing and crackling all weekend long, the whole human turbine spinning a blur, nobody in the press box had any power at all. At least not among the writers.

What little nervous energy we had up there, or down in the media center, ran off a charge borrowed from the brilliant, billion-watt juice flowing past us. On our own, we generated no more than static electricity—a bright spark sometimes, certainly, surprising or even annoying, but always perfectly safe to the touch.

•   •   •

Depending on your own brand of insanity, you thought of it as either the best assignment in the world or the worst, the plum sports news job in America or a punishment gig, the kind of stoop work they'd hand you if you were on probation for trying to jump an editorial assistant at the publisher's Christmas party. A few punched the clock, in and out, pretending it was 9 to 5, just bookkeeping, until the clock started punching back, the endless weekends grinding on and those dark bags swelling beneath their eyes. Everybody took it differently and fought it however they could.

There were a few hardy ancients, bearers of the old knowledge, men like Chris Economaki, priests left over from the tail-fin days, wandering in and out some southern weekends.

In that old Daytona smokehouse press center, I had watched Economaki one afternoon, 50 years a race writer and announcer, the oboe voice of the sport a thousand years ago, slowly typing his weekly newspaper copy on a manual portable. Biggest race of the year, everybody bitching about bandwidth and throughput, and he's sitting there hunched over his manual portable in a cardigan sweater, editing his stuff with a penknife and Scotch tape and I loved him for it.

You'd never see the college of cardinals farther west than Talladega, or farther north than Richmond, the travel kept them home, but at the Stonehenge tracks, the original temples, they'd be there in small numbers. In their sixties and seventies, semiretired, they were newspapermen, on vague assignment from a regional features editor with a weakness for the leather-helmet era. They'd arrive in their 50-50 cotton/poly golf shirts and take the handshakes and murmured greetings of the few who still knew them, maybe introduce themselves around a little to get a feel for their old beat. Most were modest, a rare thing among writers, and didn't search your eyes when they met you, expecting you to remember their long-forgotten bylines.

For the first few hours of a Friday or Saturday you'd see them making the rounds: garages, haulers, press conferences. Notebooks out, they did what they had always done, looked for stories, but storytelling wasn't part of the dance anymore, just information management, and by the time they'd been spun off the fourth or fifth team publicist or corporate-brand strategist, they began to look as if they'd just walked out of the mall and couldn't remember where they'd parked the car.

In the afternoon, winded and overwhelmed by what they'd helped make, you'd see them huddled in the deadline room with the third generation of men and women who'd replaced them, sitting and smoking and gesturing, their fingers hooked and stiff, yellow as feed corn with the nicotine stains, telling the old stories and making it all seem human again.

"Who was it tried to return his rental car into the motel pool? Weatherly, right? Wanted to drive his rental car into the motel pool, at Daytona, I think."

"No, it was up in Columbia. I thought it was Turner, Curtis Turner."

"Drunk as a lord, 'course."

"The motels were crazy then, we'd all stay at the same places when they sent us out, drivers and reporters and crews, officials and everybody in the same couple places, sometimes the same rooms because we didn't most of us get travel expenses then, and, God, all those girls, and what went on was . . . well, I suppose that part of it isn't much different now."

"But it was smaller and everybody knew everybody else and we knew what we couldn't write, which was most of it, because half the time we were right in the middle of it, too."

"Walk into the wrong room back then and you could ruin two marriages."

"Three, maybe, counting your own."

"I have never once been so drunk as since then."

"You know, back then an awful lot of those men getting into those cars were hungover on Sunday morning. If one of 'em looked bad enough at the drivers' meeting, the others might suggest him not to run."

"You could stand right there and tell who was laid low and who wasn't. Plus you knew from the night before where everybody'd been and who with. Now you have to call to schedule an appointment to get five minutes in the back of the trailer with a driver nobody ever heard of."

"I don't know how you all put up with it."

And on into the late day, all the backstory and history the sport no longer has time for, until the younger ones had to stop listening and get back on the treadmill for their deadline.

On race day the elders would take an honored place in the press box (as long as nobody needed the seat to make a deadline), where they were doted on by the track PR department, and they'd write out a few spidery lines of notes. Or they'd walk along the pit road, hands knotted behind their backs, notebooks in their pockets and no radio headphones on, listening for anything familiar in all that sound.

As for the rest of us, the traveling press, we were every kind of nasty sarcast or ironclad true believer, oracular gasbag or nitwit savant, dumbstruck eager beaver or pompom-shaking cheerleader, warmed-over burnout or blinkered, hardworking pro.

I never earned my way even close to the center of it, a process of years based on tenure and expertise. Having neither, and not being a daily deadline filer, I was at the distant fringe of things. By the end of the year I knew all the regulars, the beat reporters and photographers and producers and publicists, well enough to recognize and greet, but had made only a small handful of friends. Part of that was purposeful, I tell myself, an honest effort to keep an outsider's neutral perspective on all that channeled madness, but equal parts of it were ignorance and fear and diffidence, too.

I had access, but didn't always know what to do with it, and I had time, but didn't always know how to spend it. The only thing I was ever certain of was the routine.

For print reporters and photographers, most Cup weekends (practice/qualifying on Friday, practice/Busch race Saturday, Cup race Sunday at noon or 1 P.M.) really begin on Thursday. Many of the reporters and shooters fly in or drive down to the track on that afternoon or evening. Pick up the rental car, check in to the hotel, maybe drive out to the track and look around, see who's where or try to grab an early seat at the media center if you haven't been assigned one.

The heavyweights all have assigned seats with working phone jacks. These include the writers from the wire services and the writers from *USA Today* and the beat writers from the big newspapers around the country. They also include newspaper writers from what were once thought of as smaller southern markets, too, Winston-Salem, say, or Gastonia, because they're writing for NASCAR's expert core readership and the participants themselves, and because those markets aren't so small anymore. The heaviest of the heavyweights, the truly elephantine, have a separate room of their own at some tracks, the deadline room, which further isolates and elevates them. At Miami, glass-walled and pristine, it looks like the sportswriter diorama at the Museum of Natural History.

The rooms were so crowded that you had to work with your elbows tucked in, so whenever you got up, quite naturally whoever was next to you would take the opportunity to exhale and then shift their desktop around to make a little more room. When you returned you reshifted it. Borders were drawn and redrawn with obsessive self-interest. The League of Nations spent less time remapping the Balkans. A series of low grunts were then exchanged to make sure no one's feelings were hurt. Work gets done, especially around 6 P.M., when deadlines are near enough that you can hear them pacing the hall outside in their sensible shoes, but there are more hours spent fiddling with the place settings than anyone wants to admit.

The first thing you see when you walk into a Winston Cup press room is the Sumerian ziggurat of free cigarettes. As in prison, the shadow economy here runs on them.

But what if you don't smoke? Then grab the Oreos off the desk in front of you, along with all the other snacks of a thousand other brands, endlessly restocked there for you by the publicists from Nabisco or Nestlé or Planter's or General Mills. An unsubtle reminder of corporate goodness and we're-all-in-this-togetherness and the insatiable appetite of the elephant press.

Having filled your fanny pack with free stuff to placate your oral fixations, what now? If you write for a newspaper, you filed your Friday story Thursday night, so you take a minute to open the paper or go online to see how it ran, to make sure the editors didn't ruin it— or worse yet make it better. It's your race weekend overview, usually, your take on what's at stake for whom in the upcoming race. Unless there's been a big story playing out all week long ("Busch and Spencer War of Words" or "Embattled Tony Stewart Fined for Photo Fracas"), it's nothing more than a recap of the stats and the points race and a few facts about the next track ("Win at Indy Could Change Everything," or "36° Banking at Bristol Makes for Great Race").

Thus does Friday begin, with weak coffee, a weak mind, and no idea what to do. Even if you're empty-headed, your skull no more than a maraca after too much time on tour and last night's expense-account dinner of California chardonnay and fried mozzarella sticks from room service, sit long enough in your hard-won seat and ideas will come to you ready-made.

You've been receiving e-mail releases all week, of course, at least one from every team, sometimes two or three, and have deleted them without ever reading them. Most merely recap what happened the weekend before ("Racer X Battles to Valiant 38th-Place Finish at Richmond!"), i.e., things which you already knew and didn't care about; or predict things you don't care about and can't believe ("Racer X Expects Great Run at New Hampshire!"). The remainder of these e-releases notify you of upcoming free meals and ribbon-cuttings ("Rubbermaid to Unveil New Paint Scheme at Friday Press Luncheon").

Beginning Friday morning you will receive some of these press releases again, and many other new ones, as the publicists orbit the media center handing out hard copies.

By 11 A.M. you'll have 43 teams trying to catch your attention, trying to get their sponsor's name or their driver's name somewhere in a story, any story. What starts as a flurry of paper will soon enough become a blizzard, and for those writers desperate enough to shovel through the drifts looking for ideas, the press releases may gradually start to sound better and better. Maybe as part of a catch-all, race weekend piece? Hmmm. Does Racer X *really* expect to do well? That might be interesting. What about that luncheon? You can write the lead in your pounding head as you sit there! You don't even have to walk next door for the actual announcement or the steam-table chicken dijonnaise. "Rubbermaid announced today. . . ." etc. Wait! You don't even have to do that! It's already written right there on the press release! "Rubbermaid announced today. . . ." etc. You can just retype it!

Second Pocono is tropical rain and slate-gray sky. Junior gets into the back of Steve Park on the very first lap, and the ensuing spectacular crash holds the race up for over an hour. They bring the field back to the pit grid. Sitting along the pit wall waiting, some of the other drivers watch Park's television interview on the big screen when he walks out of the track medical center. Park, his speech still slurred from last year's wreck at Darlington, thanks God he wasn't hurt. After missing that shift on the very first lap, his competitors grumble that he shouldn't even be driving. "He's been cleared, sure, but what hasn't he hit since he came back?" NASCAR can't keep him out of the car, either. Park's a private contractor, and barring him might open up a restraint-of-trade suit. "Fine, but *what hasn't he hit since he came back?* It was good the way Junior ran after him, though. Tough kid."

The drivers sit along the wall for a long time, waiting to get back in their cars. The fans stare down at them, strangely quiet. Walking, you pick up bits and pieces.

"Man, she called my *house.* Shit . . ."

"Good thing you had your usual awful start, otherwise you'd've been caught up in that thing, too. . . ."

"I heard he cut it when he fell on a pool deck at a skinny-dip party with the Hooters girls. They put dish liquid in the pool to make bubbles and he slipped on the suds. Didn't wanna let go of his drink. Sounds like him, anyway . . ."

"What's a redneck say right before he dies? 'Hey, watch this!' "

"I am flat bad in traffic . . ."

"How long is this gonna take? I'd as soon wait in the trailer . . ."

"That 44 car's had more drivers in it this year than Miss Winston."

They get the catchfence welded up, run a handful of laps, and it rains. Lap 23 of 200. This time the drivers wait it out in their haulers.

Best fan sentence overheard during the rain delay: "We need to raise our kids in a polka environment."

The drivers are back in the cars for a late-afternoon restart. If they could, I think most would jump the track and drive straight home. The sun's out just enough now to superheat the humidity. The fans timed their drinking for a 1 P.M. start, so half the grandstand's napping. Without the wreck and the rain, the race would have been over by now.

Driving with an urgency born of misery, the racers lurch and hurtle around the awkward angles of the Pocono Triangle until, mercifully, the sun begins to set. Clouds roll back in. At least the track has no lights. The race is shortened due to darkness and irritability. Bill Elliott takes the checkered flag and the crowd heaves a sigh of sweet relief. Sterling Marlin remains, well, you know.

As the crews roll the cars back onto the haulers their complaints are operatic.

"Tell me anything about that that didn't suck ass."

"The twenty-four fucking hours of Pocono."

"Push that car, Hoss, push that car! C'mon!"

"At least at Indy there's a goddamn front straightaway."

"Fuck me but I *stink*."

On to citadel Indy, where the new pagoda dances in the furnace heat. Above it a plane tows a banner for the Classy Chassy Go-Go Club across the limitless Indiana sky. This is the Brickyard 400 at the Indianapolis Motor Speedway, 160 laps around the most famous racetrack in the world, in front of more than 250,000 fans.

Cup's only been running here since 1994, but thanks to Indy's century-old cradle-of-racing street cred, its historic mystique, and its carefully tended mythology, this race already rates second only to the Daytona 500 in stocker prestige. NASCAR now basks in Indy's holy golden glow—a kind of gilt by association. To win here is a very big deal.

On Sunday the teams push their cars out of Gasoline Alley, out of the garages and onto to the long straightaway starting grid, into a canyon of humanity. The grandstands here line both sides of the frontstretch, 3,500 feet of fans stacked five stories high, 100,000 faces stretching away into the shimmer. Their noise is a tunnel of sound.

The #24 car crew, J-Bird and Stickboy and Stabber and Tony and Lupo and Stevie, walk Jeff Gordon's car out. Gordon is an Indiana transplant, and the cheers for his car are an avalanche.

"Jesus," says Stickboy with unabashed awe.

"I know," says J-Bird, sweat pouring from his shaved skull, "ain't it *cool*?"

Tony slows for a second, his hand light on the flank of the car. "It can't get any better than this, Hoss," he says. "It just can't."

The track's a griddle. The heat index at race time is over 100 degrees. Flags hang motionless and the marching bands waver in the radiance and the corrugated tin roof of the grandstands buckles and creaks in the sun. Fans slump in their seats or drop dehydrated in their tracks. EMTs run to water them.

"Be sure to drink plenty today" is the instruction in every pit.

On what may just be the worst weekend of his life, Tony Stewart leads briefly from the pole. As the race wears on, the lead passes from one marquee warhorse to the next, from Elliott to Martin to Jarrett to Wallace back to Elliott.

On lap 35 Jimmy Spencer avenges his honor and hammers Kurt Busch into the wall. Busch climbs from the car and waits for Spencer to circle the track. Busch, 24 years old as of today, spanks his ass hard with one hand on national television to indicate that Spencer should be moved to the rear of the field for what he's done. Spencer, chuckling, drives on.

It is Jeff Gordon's birthday too, but not his day to win. He'll finish sixth after a long afternoon in a balky racecar that the crew works to adjust on every pit stop.

At the end it's the venerables, Rusty Wallace and Bill Elliott, running the last 15 laps in front with the field dropping away behind them. Elliott's red car is the faster and he eases ahead of Wallace for the victory. Sterling Marlin, implacable, leads in championship points.

As Bill Elliott kneels at the start/finish line to kiss that strip of famous bricks, in Gasoline Alley Stickboy and J-Bird roll their car back onto the hauler.

"I gotta piss."

"That's good news, Stick."

"I haven't pissed since *Thursday*."

·   ·   ·

Let's face it, 40 weeks is a long time to do anything. The NASCAR season just goes on and on and on. And in a season where the championship points leader has held that lead for weeks on end, a certain inertia can overwhelm even the most ardent NASCAR scribe. Some seasons, thanks to the math, the points standings don't so much as budge from race to race, for a month or more, two!, three!, no matter who finishes where. Even the individual races themselves can get pretty dull in periods like this, with the cup and the kiss and the cash going to the racer with the best fuel mileage or the canniest tire management strategy. No more drama to it than a road trip with your maiden aunt.

And the second half of the season, 20 straight weeks, runs week in and week out without a break. In that setting, with an unmoving leader board and lackluster action, the big traveling medicine show can become mighty tiresome, even to the principals. Crews, drivers, owners, officials, publicists—everybody's tired, everybody's bored. Who won? Who cares. You can hear the resignation even in the radio announcers' voices, their usual Hindenburg at Lakehurst, five-exclamation-point delivery muted to something more like simple human excitement. Imagine, then, the spiritual exhaustion, the existential ennui, creeping over some of the more jaded members of the press corps.

It is during these slack times, though, that some of their most creative work is done. These are the dog days when the elders and big thinkers of the press box haul out their Serious Ideas for Reforming the Sport. Thick manila folders full of them. Entire laptop hard drives swollen to bursting with thoughts large and small on how NASCAR can make itself more reliably exciting. How can these mind-numbing lulls be prevented? Revise the scoring system. Revise, revise, revise— revise and conquer.

Another overcooked thematic chestnut often reheated when writers have too much time on their hands is the question of what to do about the Big One and bad racing at Daytona and Talladega, the restrictor-plate super-duper speedways.

The plates don't make the drivers any safer, but they make the fans safer, which is NASCAR's goal. The racing mostly sucks. So when idle time abounds, the columnists and editorial boards pull out the plate issue and run it through their fingers like a set of holy beads. Speed or safety seem to be the only two choices.

Buddha knows there's always a third way, though, even in questions of such immense metaphysical breadth, and the following example is another fine illustration of what a few Red Bulls and a couple of slow evenings in the middle of a long season can bring about. This idea was originally conceived by an EMT working the pits at Talladega, so send him the million dollars when you make out the check. I'm just in it for the finder's fee.

First thing you do is empty the grandstands. Make both races at Talladega (and both of the dates at Daytona, too, if you like) pay-per-view events on television. No live spectators allowed when there are cars on the track. End of safety issue. Then tell the race teams to build whatever sort of monstrous, hydrogen-turbine, nuclear-powered, antigravity Mach 2 supercar they have the ingenuity and guts and money to build. Anything goes. If they can find a driver crazy enough to race it, they're in. As a colleague of mine said when presented with the notion, "Gentlemen, enable your reactors!" Charge $49.95 per household, worldwide, to watch the show. Do that twice a year, four times a year, and NASCAR's only liability issue would be the repetitive-stress class-action lawsuit filed on behalf of the bank tellers disabled while trying to count the France family's incoming cash.

This only solves the problem at a couple of tracks, on a couple of dates. What about the rest of the season, when the Sunday doldrums set in and even the lunatic fans can't handle the boredom?

The answer came to some of us at Second Pocono. Rain delays, dull practices, a drab points race—one minute you're talking and sitting, staring at a handful of woeful fans and the next thing you know, ka-ching, another million-dollar idea.

"Worst headline to date?

"'Elliott Still Most Popular'?"

"Bingo. 'Franco Still Dead.'"

"Franco Still Popular."

"*Bingo* Still Popular."

"But not the *Most* Popular. That's Elliott's lifetime title. And yet . . ."

". . . not all that likable."

"But who'd believe us?"

"No one."

The sun faded behind another cloud.

"Do we really have to watch this whole thing on Sunday? Again?"

"Yes."

"Giving due credit to crashes and pit strategy and so forth, it's still very, very dull."

"Suggestions for improvement? And no fair revising the points system."

A moment passed.

"Blindfolds for the drivers?"

"The races would be shorter, I'll give you that."

"Blindfolds for the fans?"

"Sponsors wouldn't go for it."

"Ramp-to-ramp jumps?"

"Hot Wheels could pay for the whole series."

We could hear the track dryers working the far side of the triangle.

"I was reading the other day where one of the Flock brothers used to race with a monkey in his car. Tim, I think. Ran a couple of races with an actual monkey in his car."

(This is true. Back in the early 1950s Tim Flock made a few laps with a monkey in the cockpit. The monkey got agitated. The monkey's name was Jocko Flocko.)

"Monkey or chimp?"

"It said monkey, but who knows? Put an intern on it."

"Monkey in every car?"

"That'd liven things up."

"An *angry* monkey."

"Helmets?"

"For monkey safety? Sure, but I think you lose some of the visual. You have to be able to see their angry monkey faces as they claw at the drivers and fling feces, I think."

"Monkey safety should always be job one, though."

"Okay, little helmets, but open-face. No diapers."

"And they have to be really angry."

"I'm not sure how you guarantee that."

"You could pinch them."

"*You* could pinch them."

"Have Miss Winston do it, she's never busy."

"Honorary monkey pinchers some weeks. LeeAnn Rimes. Kid Rock. They're always here anyway."

"Done. Same monkey every week in every car? A team monkey, in other words?"

"Bud Monkey, DuPont Monkey? The monkey could be in their commercials. Spokesmonkey."

"The team might develop a relationship with the monkey, though. Or they might drug their monkey. Monkey-doping scandals. These monkeys have to be angry *and* impartial."

"What about a monkey lottery, like qualifying?"

"Or an Internet vote from the fans?"

"Gordon'd get the angriest monkey every week. I like the lottery, same time they pick their qualifying slot."

The day sagged on.

"What time is it?"

"Nearly three."

"I have to file something. See you guys."

"We'll walk back with you. Aero push? Jack Roush? Rain delay?"

"Something."

We started to walk back to the press center. One of the smart young Charlotte guys piped up.

"Hey, look at this," he said, and held up his reporter's notebook. In it he had written the words "Jack Roush" and "Aero Push." He had crossed out several of the letters in each word. "Did you know that 'Aero Push' is an anagram for 'Roush Ape'? It's a sign."

"Perfect."

"We're on the right track."

"So to speak."

"Gentlemen, angry up your monkeys!"

And we all walked back to the media center to write about something else.

Watkins Glen, hidden in the wine country at the base of New York's Finger Lakes, is another picturesque, snaky track most Cup drivers aren't much fond of. Not because they aren't up to its demands necessarily, but because the cars aren't. The cars are too heavy. The drivers wrestle them as best they can, but for these teams the weekend here has the feeling of something to be endured rather than enjoyed.

It feels that way for us, too. It took us more than an hour to level off on our infield campsite while our neighbors shouted helpful Euclidean tips on the many puzzlements of applied geometry. The whole weekend was a couple of bubbles off plumb, in fact, the lead singer from "Saliva" hacking away at the national anthem and then a 20-minute wait to start the race thanks to a grass fire touched off by the fireworks that followed. The flyover arrived five minutes late—so the fighters circled and flew over us twice.

There's no room in the Dust Bowl control tower press box to watch the race on TV, so I walk the pits. You see even less of the track at a road course, so the race is lost to me. Robby Gordon seemed to lead for quite a while, but then no longer did so.

I notice, however, that Junior is now dating a *Sports Illustrated* swimsuit model, because I see her sitting on the toolbox in his pit for the afternoon. Thus do I obtain my one solid NASCAR statistic for the day. Number of times crewmen walked into a nearby stack of racing tires while staring at her: 4.

Sterling Marlin will leave for second Michigan with a chokehold on the points lead.

Drained by the hours in his suffocating car, by his emotions, and by the weight of the baggage he drags behind him around every track, the race winner, Tony Stewart, climbs out of his car in Victory Lane, sags, and sits next to it with his elbows on his knees. He looks at the hundreds of people surrounding him. For a long time he doesn't say a word.

TEN

Imagine this sad world as it ought to be, not as it is. Imagine our dark, imperfect world, so harrowing now and sour and draped with shadow, brightening in your mind. Imagine the world you deserve. It should be easy enough, all this imagining—because everything will be the same. You will be the same person. It will be the same day in the same year. It will be the same orange car running low and loud and strong on the same long track past the same carnival crowd—with just one small difference. That's how Tony Stewart imagines his perfect world.

On that burning Friday before the weekend at Indianapolis when it all went wrong, Tony idled smiling around the drivers' compound on a monster hawg, a custom double fatbob streamliner twin raked and flaked in trick flame purple and merciless chrome. He wore a T-shirt that read: "YOU HAVE THE RIGHT TO REMAIN SILENT—anything you say will be misquoted and used against you."

He is rich, he is famous, he is a hero, and for reasons even he doesn't understand, he will spend his career poised to throw it all away.

In the sweeter world spinning away inside Stewart's helmet, he is the same man. He wrestles the same racecars around the same racetracks. The howling crowds are the same, and the noise and the heat and the infernal stink are the same, and the great, groaning haystacks of prize money are the same, and at the end of every busy, fantastic day, the same beautiful, unthinking moon floats above him as he sleeps.

But no one is there to write about it.

More importantly, no one is there to write about *him*, nor is there anyone skulking in the shrubbery to photograph or digitally capture him. That's the difference. No one analyzes, criticizes, or mythologizes him. No one shoves the swollen foam bulb of a microphone at him before he's even shut the damned car off, when he's still stump-deaf from a long run and the blood is still fizzing in his veins and every tortured, spidery neuron is still popping and sizzling in his brainpan to ask him how he *feels*. No one shows him a needy little smile and waves a battered tape recorder at him from the door of the garage hoping for a few minutes, please, Tony, just a few minutes, okay, to get some of your thoughts today on the weather, the track, the tires, your suspension, your sponsor, your valve springs, your haircut, your hobbies, your hopes and dreams and wants and needs, and your darkest appetites and your very deepest feelings about the sacred nature of the mysterious, holy combat between good and not quite good enough, and one last thing if you have another minute, Tony, please, tell my readers about the terrifying dread that you must surely sometimes feel, winding and uncoiling in your heart, yellow-eyed and thick with poison, when you get behind the wheel of this magnificent death machine, okay?

Or maybe the questions just sound like that struggling up through all the engine noise. In any case, there are no reporters in Tony Stewart's imagined world to yammer questions about the condition of his innermosts, because he believes the one thing keeping every other thing from being pretty near perfect in his real world is Fame. Not Fame, exactly, so much as it is Fame's bulimic handmaiden, the Media.

It's more complicated than that, of course. Since his Cup debut in 1999 Stewart's become one of the most popular, visible, and marketable personalities in the center ring of the V-8 bigtop. He is outrageously gifted and competitive, and the results over three and a half seasons prove it. Mostly, though, you have seen his name in your local headlines preceded by the words "troubled" and "embattled," in large part because the only machine on earth that Tony Stewart can't drive the wheels off, or even control, is the Star-Making Machine—the machine NASCAR built long ago to make him rich and famous.

Tony Stewart was born in Indiana in 1971. He grew up in Columbus, about an hour south of the scoring pylon at Indianapolis Motor

Speedway. For a lead-foot kid with spooky hand-eye coordination and a father willing to bankroll a go-kart, that's like growing up an ardent Shiite hajji an hour south of Mecca—you know to a passionate certainty where your whole life's leading. He started racing those nasty-fast little rolling chain saws at the age of 8. By the time he was 10 he was pulling G's like an F-18 pilot and running a quick, uncanny line around every track they raced. By the time he was 15 the kibitzers and touts at a nearby track were calling him the Rushville Rocket, and he knew that winning filled you up with everything you'd ever need to live and that losing left a hole in your chest like you'd been shot. At night, as his head took the cool off the pillow and his thoughts swam into sleep, his future as a professional racecar driver would unspool: the rush of a last-lap, last-gasp pass low in turn 4 for the checkered flag at Indy, the slow-motion roll onto Victory Lane, the awkward, hurried climb out of the car, the fans everywhere and clamoring for him, men and women and, Oh God, the girls, of course! all those smiling hundreds and thousands of freckled, bright-eyed midwestern girls! And the last thing he'd hear as they reached out their pale hands to him was the ovation rolling down from the grandstands.

By the time he was 18 he'd won every karting championship in the big wide open of the midwest and beyond, and had hauled home enough gaudy ceremonial hardware to shame a Caesar. And on the long, midnight drives home after yet another win, past the hidden fields of corn or sorghum or wheat, the giant trophy lying across the backseat of the truck, he and his friends and his dad might pull in at the Waffle House to eat a plate of eggs and laugh and talk some more about what it meant to go fast. Simple. By his own account he was a happy kid back then, not given to bouts of melancholy or rage.

In 1989 he moved up into the bigger, faster cars, the midgets and sprints and modifieds, brutal, butt-ugly open-wheel roadsters notorious for their lethal power-to-weight ratio. They could fire you down a straightaway as though you'd been launched from a carrier, or kick you around sideways until you were tumbling end over end and tearing up a hundred yards of catchfence on your way to the hospital and the highlight reel on *SportsCenter*. In these cars he acquired the nickname "Smoke," for his habit of lighting up the tires. By 1995 he'd won everything there was to win.

The next year he moved up to the Indy Racing League, driving the cars he'd so often dreamed about. In 1996 he was the series' Rookie of the Year. In 1997 he won the series' championship. For many decades the mastery of Indy cars was the American gold standard for a Professional Racecar Driver. For handling, for horsepower, and for sheer swagger, they are almost unmatched. The only thing an Indy car can't do these days is make you famous.

That's because by the late 1980s stock-car racing had overtaken open-wheel racing in this country as the prime mover of money and mythology in the field of automotive entertainment. Bickering between the two big-ticket open-wheel sanctioning bodies, indifferent competition, hit-or-miss television contracts, and a growing appetite on the part of the public for the Old Testament verities of NASCAR's brand of stardom thus made it possible for Tony Stewart to have achieved a many great things in motor sports without ever making himself famous.

That all changed in 1998 when he signed a contract to wrangle stock cars for NFL coach Joe Gibbs. Wanting to challenge himself against the drivers and machines he considered the most competitive anywhere, Stewart ran 22 preparatory races in NASCAR's triple-A division that year. As with most rotations through the minors, though, where they teach you how to play the game but not how to *play the game*, he came away with useful facts by the galvanized bucketful but nary a silver thimbleful of useful truth.

And the truth was that Stewart, a household name only along the nodding sunflower belts of southern Indiana and largely ignorant of the baffling etiquette of Fame, was now hardwired into the superconductor of NASCAR's high-voltage, high-tension celebrity power grid.

When he moved into Cup racing, the majors, in 1999, when he won three races and had 12 top-five finishes and folded more than $2.5 million in prize money into his wallet and won the Rookie of the Year award and wound up the year fourth in championship points for the best finish by a rookie since LBJ was president, what shocked him was not his great success, for he was a professional racecar driver after all, and a good one, but his sudden fame. Because now he was a *famous* racecar driver too, thanks to the dark arts of NASCAR marketing.

It is the smallest, most brightly lighted stage in sports. You drive a car bearing the logo of your corporate sponsor every week on television and you are the public face of that company no less than any actor or supermodel. You get more television time most weekends than the episode where Lucy and Ethel take work in the candy factory. In exchange, when you win a race, the first thing you must mention now is not your joy or your strategy or your devoted family watching back home or even the generous offices of the Kingdom of Heaven, but the name of the cereal millers who paid for your ride. Your name, face, car number, and color scheme will be bootlegged onto everything from children's lunch boxes to barbecue tools.

You are one of 43. Of these, a mere half-dozen become the superstar objects of public fixation.

And Stewart, almost from the moment he arrived in NASCAR racing and started winning, and through an imprecise formula known only to the alchemists of American celebrity, became one of these.

So that in addition to driving the car and trying to win every week and not die in a cataclysmic fireball, he became the automatic love object for however many crazed millions of autograph-hungry NASCAR fans, as well as a corporate spokesmodel for a national chain of home improvement stores (his primary sponsor), and fragrances and beverages and power tools, etc. (his associate sponsors), while also becoming the man whose job it is each weekend, upon leaving the captive majesty of the chain-link motorhome compound where the drivers are segregated in what amounts to a medium-security trailer park for millionaires, to circulate in the skyboxes and hospitality tents at every track glad-handing the preening regional sales reps (drywall or aftershave or cola syrup) and their wives and their kiddies, making inspiring predictions about how well the #20 car might run, barring cataclysmic fireball, thanks to their selfless help in the service of Speed and Free Enterprise. Then there's the photo session for the magazine layout, the prerace television and radio interviews, the luncheon to announce the latest partnership with the new associate sponsor and the meet-and-greet with the local Explorer Scout troop. All of this on top of the racing, the practice, the qualifying, the testing, the relentless travel, the meetings with the crew and the crew chief and the fabricators and the suspension tuners and the engine builders to figure out how to make the car go faster, and then the Make-A-Wish kids are coming down for 15 minutes, and there's that live appearance at the bass-fishing tournament and the autograph session two towns over, and then an hour on QVC to sell your newest collectible jackets, caps, and afghans, and then don't forget the dinner with those guys from corporate communications.

All at once his calendar for an entire year was parsed out in five-minute increments and he was expected to become a salesman and a matinee idol and a motivational speaker and a casino greeter and a role model and a stand-up comic and a humble, right-thinking crusader for the American Way. And that was the easy part. The hard part is doing and being, or at least *seeming* to do and be, all these things with modesty and an aw-shucks grace while under the microscopic scrutiny of NASCAR's ravening press corps.

A keen eye and a heavy foot aren't enough.

He mastered the cars and the tracks and the competition, certainly, over his next two seasons, winning six races in 2000 and finishing a dozen times in the top five. He banked over $3 million in winnings and ended that year sixth in championship points. In 2001 he won three times, made 15 top-five finishes and $3.5 million in prize money, and finished second only to Jeff Gordon in overall points. In fact the only numbers comparable to those of Stewart's first three seasons were Gordon's own, so the Media took him up with great enthusiasm.

It was a disaster.

Now most folks in the NASCAR garage—mechanics, officials, drivers—will tell you that Tony Stewart is a decent guy. But he can also be stubborn and contrary, too, they'll say, or broody or hotheaded. He runs a little tight, like a car that won't turn and wants to run up into the wall.

The very things that make a good driver—the necessary sense of infallibility, the lightning reactions, the boundless, bulletproof arrogance, and the bone-deep unwillingness to concede an inch, even conversationally—worked against him. He was either unwilling or unable to come up with the pleasant, empty line of patter most other drivers use to protect themselves.

So in the numberless press conferences on which the sport thrives, his certainty often sounded like superiority, or worse, condescension. For all that Stewart could make a racecar do anything he wanted, he flat stunk when it came to making a good impression with the press. They reciprocated by making an equally rank impression on him, mostly by asking what he rightly thought were vapid questions and then misquoting his answers or printing them as near non sequiturs in a different context.

But he still made good copy for the press, and within a year he had become the tour's necessary Bad Boy, the popular, exciting, and temperamental winner in the black hat whose refusal to ladle up the warmed-over corn in which most celebrity athletes specialize, and on which beat writers routinely binge and purge, served both Stewart and the Media well.

In his second season and for most of his third that symbiosis was kept in balance, although both parties were showing the strain. Even Stewart's advocates among the press were losing patience with his sometimes boorish and patronizing attitude, and Stewart was tired of being interrogated and photographed every time he walked to the bathroom. Claustrophobic by his own public admission, Stewart was further stressed by the growing number of fans allowed access to the pit areas and garages, so that he was swarmed and set upon for autographs the second he walked out of his trailer.

The tipping point came after a race in July 2001 when Stewart, angered by what he thought was an unfair ruling by NASCAR officials, swatted the tape recorder out of a reporter's hand when approached for comment. He then kicked the recorder, and what was left of his tenuous relationship with the press, under a truck. He was fined $10,000 and put on probation for the balance of the season by NASCAR.

The year 2002 got off to an inauspicious start for Stewart and his team when they blew that engine on the second lap of the 500. And they finished forty-third. Stewart was so upset that, rather than fly home with the team, he drove back home to Charlotte in the middle of the night by himself in a pickup truck. He stopped at a Waffle House on the way and pushed some eggs around a plate. He sat there for a long time among the truckers and the drunks and, because there was no trophy in the backseat to remind him, tried hard to remember what had ever been fun about any of this. Since then he and the team have been a small boat on an angry ocean of ink.

The low point of his season, it was thought, was Stewart's homecoming race at Indianapolis in early August. On the four weekends leading up to the Brickyard 400, Stewart and his team had finished thirty-ninth, third, thirty-ninth, and seventh. Despite the inconsistency they were still seventh overall in championship points. He had never won there before, but a win at mystical Indy, at once a historic cathedral and his backyard track, in front of hundreds of thousands of fans, and in front of his friends and family, could have righted Stewart's entire season. Instead he spent the long, hot weekend trying to shoot himself in the foot. He barely got it out of his mouth long enough to do so.

On Saturday morning at Indy, having won the pole position for the big race on Sunday, Stewart is interviewed at the brief press conference that is held every week for pole winners. He is asked how winning the pole makes him feel. He is supposed to say, as drivers do, that winning the pole makes him feel *good*. Perhaps *real good*. Instead he says that it doesn't mean all that much, he's won poles before, that he'd rather win the race on Sunday and that at the moment that's what he's thinking about. The Media, persistent in the call-and-response nature of these weekly catechisms, reframes the question. Deviously, he is asked if maybe winning the pole didn't make him make feel, say, *good*. Ignoring the prompt, and the chance at a clean getaway, Stewart stands by his original, more complicated answer. Then calamity. Trying to communicate his low esteem for the pole perhaps, Stewart suggests, but in a manner not so humorous as to actually be funny, that the men and women of the gathered world media could take whatever poles might come to hand and insert them, bodily one imagines, wherever and however the men and women of the gathered world media might find it convenient and agreeable to do so. The press conference draws to a very quiet conclusion not long after.

A few hours later, in the last stages of Saturday's made-for-television International Race of Champions, Stewart throws the Media another hanging curveball. The IROC series puts drivers from different racing series into equally prepared cars and sets them against each other. Stewart, having decided his car isn't very equal, pulls off the track long before the checkered flag falls, coasts to a stop in the garage area, and walks away. When asked about this a few moments later, live, by the Media, he says simply that the car was not only not equal, but that it was, in fact, a real shitbox. Perhaps this is an homage to A. J. Foyt, his idol and friend, who once, when asked to describe the throttle response of a certain car, said that stomping on the accelerator was like easing your foot into a bucket of warm horseshit. Perhaps not.

Still, the sun rises on Sunday morning.

And the day is incredibly hot. By noon the heat index shimmers near 100 degrees and the fans, all 250,000 of them, are red-faced and glassy-eyed and sweating in their seats or packed 20 deep around the fences and galleries and garages. Some of them faint, still clutching their autograph books. EMTs treat hundreds of them for heat exhaustion.

Stewart runs fast and well all afternoon, contending, but in the last 10 laps he mysteriously falls out of the lead pack and drops from third to finish twelfth. Maybe the car's setup—the arcane equation balancing tires, trackbar, shocks, and springs—went wrong somehow. No one is sure, because Stewart, usually voluble, even chatty on his car radio, isn't saying anything to his pit crew. He's embarrassed, or frustrated, or angry. Into the fraught silence of the 140-degree cockpit the crew radios him to pull around to the garage area. NASCAR, as it sometimes does, has asked for a random engine inspection.

He rolls the car slow across the concrete apron between the garages and he toggles off the ignition and the utter silence of the dead engine is more abrupt and shocking somehow than its noise. No one clamors for him, no one reaches out a pale hand. He is the first one back here and for an instant, before the other cars come yelping and drawling off the track behind him, there is a deep stillness. Clouds drape a flat sky, cicadas lathe the trees, and the sun drums a tired light through the dust. At the end of a race he hasn't won he usually unbinds himself from the car at the transporter tailgate; past his crew and into the privacy of the truck's small lounge, safe in the nonjudgmental hum of that air-conditioning, before the reporters and photographers and autograph hunters can run him down.

But this time, today of all days, NASCAR wants to wind his car up to full scream on the dyno. The tech officials want to test this car and a handful of others to find out who's got what under the hood, find out who's making what kind of horsepower and what kind of hot parts they're maybe running to do it. So he's got to park 500 yards away from the safety of his hauler and, today of all days, abandon the car he inhabits like a cocoon to the officials with their clipboards and their computers and their suspicions.

The moment of Pleistocene quiet is long gone. Now the postrace mob is surging back into the garage. Stewart is running ahead of them, away from them, and away from the recorders and notebooks and cameras they brandish like so many torches and pitchforks, across that hallowed concrete toward his hauler, only a few hundred feet to safety now, his face as white as hotel soap except for the dark smudges of exhaustion under each dark eye. Keeping step with him is a heavy man with a still camera to his eye. Maybe he's crowding Stewart or maybe he's said something to him. Stewart, still running, suddenly veers toward the man, lunging, and reaches out his right hand to claw the camera down from the photographer's face. But the arm holding the camera is already coming down, the threat already seen swimming orange and angry in the viewfinder, and Stewart rakes the air and misses the arm and the man and the camera entirely. His momentum carries him forward another step and he pushes the photographer hard with the flat of his hand—catches him just where the meat of his chest tapers into his shoulder joint and sends him staggering back. Then

Stewart balls the same busy hand into a fist and makes an awkward roundhouse swing and misses the photographer by the comic distance of a community theater stunt punch. Then, and this is what they'll laugh about and mimic all week down in the engine shops and paint booths and front offices of NASCAR-land—his truest punishment—he straight-legs the air with a perfectly ineffectual schoolgirl kick. Stewart's momentum is at last redirected toward his transporter by a representative of his corporate sponsor.

The consequences for Stewart were several and swift. Within days he was fined $10,000 by NASCAR and placed on probation again. He was also docked another $50,000 by his sponsor. He was alternately pilloried in print as an oafish bully who should have been pulled from the car but got off too easy or defended at length by those who thought the Media were ill-mannered and invasive and had at last got their comeuppance. A few others—I among them—muttered from the off-the-record safety of the press box buffet that what Tony Stewart needed was simply to have his ass kicked. And further, following a couple of hellfire-and-brimstone prayer meetings with the NASCAR elders and the corporate deacons, Stewart agreed to start seeing an anger management specialist.

Remarkably, he won the next race. Watkins Glen.

Or maybe it's not remarkable at all. Maybe Tony Stewart thrives on the constant swirl of agitations he seems to create for himself. I'll find out in two weeks at Bristol. He's agreed to an interview. In the meantime, Michigan.

At the second Pepsi 400, I ask one of the vice presidents from NASCAR what "probation" means.

"It means 'We've got our eye on you, bub.'"

I wonder if the word "bub" actually appears in the rule book.

The Michigan infield still seethes, but there's plenty of laid-off autoworker ingenuity on display. There's a schoolbus conversion here with a spiral staircase at the rear. It runs up to the roof right next to the stone chimney. A few doors down is another schoolbus with a balcony and a cabana awning and a lanai, where they've set up the grill and the outdoor pool table.

Kid Rock is in attendance, too, perhaps with current girlfriend Pamela Anderson, although I haven't seen her yet. He is head-to-toe Harley gear and looks very tough— perhaps because his bodyguard is the size of a vending machine.

Two T-shirts seen today and noted for their similarity and their humbling assertion of epistemological futility:

"It's a Bubba thing: you wouldn't understand."

and

"It's a southern thang: y'all wouldn't understand."

The latter bearing a Confederate flag.

At the beginning of the race Stewart is relaxed, clowning with his crew on the radio: "I don't know about you guys, but I'm having fun today." Jeff Gordon is not. "This thing is so damn loose right now it's fuckin' horrible." Dale Jarrett spins through the infield grass on lap 11 and gets shuffled to the back of the field. He begins working his way doggedly through the pack. "We'll get it," he says, and 188 laps later, smooth and fast beneath a postcard Michigan sun, Jarrett and Tony Stewart are neck and neck for the lead, Stewart working him high and low for the pass, but not getting by. Jarrett wins. Sterling Marlin's lead has dwindled to only 43 points over Mark Martin.

Up the Tennessee Ernie Ford Parkway for the night race at Bristol. Coming into the track there's a sign on the side of the road: "In the race of life let Jesus be your crew chief."

Saturday billows up early thunderheads and an angry rain. While the track steams, the touts in the press box handicap the night's main event, "I can't wait for the Jimmy Spencer–Kurt Busch battle royal, in which Jimmy Spencer throws one punch and Kurt Busch is instantaneously killed."

Bristol brings out the beast in everyone, it seems, and the race is no different. Cumulous clouds loom above Thunder Valley, the night is holocaust, and the fans couldn't be happier. The Busch-Spencer feud is only one of several bouts on the card tonight, and there's a little something for everyone.

As the exhaust and the tire smoke rises up into the lights, Junior looks set to run away from the field early, but there's no running away here, only running out front until you get shuffled back into traffic, which Junior soon is. Jeff Gordon leads for a time while the field behind him trades punches. The radios are quiet here, the drivers too busy to talk. Busch and Spencer jab at one another, but draw no blood. Cars batter their way around the track sideways. Cars hit the wall. Cars hit each other. Cars burst into flame. Junior retakes the lead at the halfway point. Gordon retakes it 50 laps later. By the time the race arrives at lap 377, there have been 14 caution flags. Robbie Gordon gets into Jimmie Johnson and spins him into the wall. Jimmie Johnson climbs out of his car, stands on the wall, and flips Robbie Gordon the bird. The fans remain standing. Twelve laps later Junior gets into Ward Burton and spins him into the wall. Ward Burton climbs out of his car, waits in the turn, and flings the tiny heat shields from his shoes at Junior's head. "I wish I'd had something I coulda shot through his window," Burton says on TV a few seconds later, making a small-caliber finger gun for the camera. Fifteen laps after that, Tony Stewart gets into the back of Jerry Nadeau and punctures his own oil line. "He missed the restart. We should go down there and slap the shit out of Nadeau when it's over," says Stewart on the radio. Maybe the anger management sessions haven't started yet. Fifteen laps after that Matt Kenseth takes the lead. Another 10 laps and Kevin Harvick takes the lead. With 40 laps to go, Jeff Gordon is fourth. With 20 laps to go, Rusty Wallace takes the lead and Jeff Gordon is third. With 18 laps to go, Gordon is second. The fans are on their feet, and most of us in the press box are, too.

With two laps to go, coming out of turn 4, Gordon noses the right front bumper of his car up under the left rear quarter panel of Wallace's. He bumps him up the track and runs by him for the win. Wallace is second, Junior Earnhardt third.

Gordon ends a modest 31-race losing streak. The burnout he performs on the frontstretch sends fired rubber up into the lights that will hang there for an hour. In Victory Lane he clings to the enormous trophy like a man holding on to a tree in a flood. The Roman candles go off, and the confetti cannons fire and the champagne showers down all around him, cheap and sweet, and there's a fine sheen of sweat and a cloying stink on everyone, even Miss Winston, and everyone is hugging and the shutters and flashes are clacking and firing and the crew blinks in the lights, hooting and hollering in their "Refuse to Lose" T-shirts and Gordon's not letting go of that trophy, but he squints and he swivels his head and he takes it all in. "What an awesome weekend," he says.

Sterling Marlin leads the points race. At 2 A.M. there are still fans at the gates, waiting patiently for whatever else they might see.

If you had visited Tony Stewart in his motorhome a few hours before the race at Bristol it would have been hard to tell if his recent experience had made him anything but tired.

He had won at Watkins Glen. He'd finished second at Michigan. During those two weeks he had also been busy seeking public absolution by suffering the Television Stations of the Cross, the process wherein you scourge yourself on television as often as you're asked to, by (a) admitting you have a problem, (b) apologizing for the problem, and (c) announcing you've sought help for the problem.

So by the time he rolled into Bristol he looked spent. Tired eyes and a small, dry voice. Again, he looks like he's two days past his last shave. He is hanging out a few hours before the night race with his stunning and stunningly quiet girlfriend and some of the guys from his team. He doesn't much want to talk about Indianapolis, but he makes a genuine effort to answer what you ask him otherwise.

Are you a happy person?

"I would say probably not. Am I going to be? Yes. You know when you get your first NASCAR license and you get your hard card the first year, they don't give you a pamphlet or an instructional video—there's nothing that tells you what's going to happen to your life, how your life's going to change. I love driving the racecars, I love being with the team, I'll love seeing a hundred forty thousand fans in the seats tonight. There's a lot of things that I don't like—some of them will change and some of them won't—it's just learning how to deal with it. I think once we learn how to do that we'll be extremely happy."

Were you a happy kid?

"Sure. Absolutely. I thoroughly enjoyed what I was doing."

So you're not a character out of Dostoyevsky?

"No, not at all. In fact, just the opposite: I'm very carefree, normally."

Have you been happy with the arc of your career?

"I've already done more in my life than I ever thought at the age of eighteen I'd ever accomplish. To me I'm on extended play on a video game. If my career ended today, I'd say I've had a successful career. Are there still things I want to do? Sure."

How is your relationship with the sporting press?

"I would say a disaster in all reality. (*Laughs*) For the most part. There's . . . You've seen what goes on. There's some people here that care about writing accurately what they see, and there's some people that aren't creative enough to come up with an idea for a story, so anything that's controversial, they'll feed off of that, like a leech, and so, you know, three and a half years into my Cup career I've learned that there's a very small group of people I trust in the media. The thing about the media, especially print media, is that they get the last word.

"I'll be honest, when I go to the media center, I'm nervous. Even if I've won a race; if I win the race tonight, when I go up to the media center I'm nervous—about who is going to be there and what is going to get asked. And then how it's going to come out in print the next day."

Do you need to be a less interesting interview?

"It's getting that way. I think it's cheating the race fans out of knowing who we are as real people, which I think is important. So what you learn as a driver is to say the most generic, shortest answers you can give to take away opportunities for the media to use it against you. That's all we worry about, the negatives, don't make it a negative. Emotion gets in *my* way of taking a step back and saying this is what I should say, to keep myself from worrying about it turning into a negative."

Which is the harder battle—to become blander or to say what's in your head and in your heart when you get out of the car?

"The harder of the two battles is to say what's on your mind. The easier of the two battles is just be bland, it keeps everybody happy. Being honest . . . You know, your parents teach you all your life that honesty is the best policy and always speak your mind. That's not true. Not in Cup racing."

Would you be happier if you could race at the same level of competition, but in a vacuum, without the press and the cameras and the distractions?

"Sure. I'd be much happier if I didn't have to deal with that. I'd be happier if there were two hundred forty thousand [fans] in the stands every week. But take away the cameras . . . not necessarily take away the cameras . . . but show it for what it is. Forty-three guys in forty-three cars racing and let it be at that."

A few hours later the night race at Bristol begins. The track has been compared to everything from a bullring to a bidet, but perhaps it more closely resembles the world's largest roulette wheel. It was a bad night for Stewart and his number didn't come up. He finished twenty-fourth.

Jeff Gordon wins again the next week at Darlington. "What'd we tell you? If he can win one, he can take 'em in bunches," Lupo and Stickboy tell me on their way to Victory Lane. Sterling Marlin hangs on to the points lead, but Gordon has moved up to second, right behind him.

It was not a raucous Southern 500. There was a knock on the motorhome door as soon as we pulled in. There were two evangelical Christians standing out there in a hard rain. Even their pamphlets were soaked. The shorter one said, "Good afternoon. Have you found Jesus Christ yet, sir?"

I stepped outside with them. I didn't know what to say.

"What was he wearing when you last saw him?"

Jeff Gordon's brief lucky streak ends at Richmond when he's thrown out of a golf cart by a giant rabbit. It's a Warner Brothers cross-promotional weekend, and many of the cars are carrying special paint schemes to honor WB's animated characters. As part of the orgy of brand strategy, there's a golf cart race scheduled for Saturday morning between your favorite Cup drivers, with your favorite cartoon characters riding along. A publicity stunt, as it were.

There's a short course laid out with orange cones on some asphalt adjacent to the three-quarter-mile track, and the furries, Tweety, Daffy, Bugs Bunny, et al., are going to help the drivers turn a few laps for the cameras. Someone, a publicist's assistant perhaps, has gone to the trouble of buffing and brightening the golf carts to a high, slippery shine. Including the seats. With some sort of oil-based vinyl protectant.

Gordon, riding with Bugs, gets the holeshot and is off to a strong start. At the apex of the first turn, however, he slides off the seat and into the air like he's been shot from a cannon. The last thing he sees as he's flung from the cart is a huge, white, four-fingered glove reaching for the wheel in a panic. Gordon bounces, but is uninjured.

He is clearly shaken, though, because not long after, he spins and wads up his primary car in practice, the one with the superexpensive cross-promotional Bugs Bunny / Warner Brothers / DuPont / NASCAR paint scheme.

"Bugs is fucked," J-Bird informs me.

It seems incongruous that this is the weekend NASCAR has chosen for the cartoon promotion, since it's also the first anniversary of the September 11 killings. The crews hold up lists of the victims' names along the pit road during the solemn prerace ceremonies. Peeking out at the crowd from behind them are your favorite Warner Brothers cartoon characters. The order to start engines comes via satellite from soldiers in Afghanistan.

Sterling Marlin crashes out on lap 8. It's a solid opportunity for Gordon to take over the points lead, but his backup car begins to slow on lap 54. He rolls into the garage. The engine let go.

Stewart runs as high as third, but then his car lets go, too. Matt Kenseth eventually wins. Despite the crash, Sterling Marlin is still the points leader. Ricky Rudd is attacked after the race by one of his engine builders, who sucker-punches him for having made some snarky comments about the recent low quality of their equipment.

Rudd sensibly responds by bouncing a bottle off the guy's head. Weirdest weekend yet.

A week after finishing eighth at Darlington, Tony Stewart traveled like the rest of us to Richmond, where on Friday a story broke on the wires that Stewart was being investigated on a possible charge of misdemeanor assault by the Sullivan County, Tennessee, sheriff's office. A woman identified as 30-year-old Amy Shaffer of West Virginia claims that after the night race at Bristol, Tony Stewart shoved her while moving through the pit area. It is said that the incident was witnessed by a deputy. Investigators travel to Richmond to interview Stewart and his crew and other potential witnesses.

That Saturday there were a couple of press conferences in which Joe Gibbs and NASCAR both asked that no one jump to any conclusions and said that they supported Tony Stewart and that they would facilitate the investigation in any way they could. Gibbs stated publicly that they had assigned handlers to Stewart after Indianapolis, and that the handlers saw nothing "out of the ordinary" at Bristol. Stewart issued a statement which read in part, "I am confident that once the investigation is complete, I will be cleared of any and all accusations. I will say, however, that I did not assault anyone. In fact, I am shocked and truly at a loss as to why someone would make such an allegation."

And while Sullivan County sheriff Wayne Anderson stated that the woman pursuing the complaint was "very credible," others close to the story maintained that it was the kind of incidental contact that occurs every time a NASCAR driver walks through a crowd of fans in the infield. For its part NASCAR again promised to look at the problem of overcrowding. Unintentionally, Stewart may have at last given them the excuse they needed to choke off fan access to the pits and the garages.

At the prerace drivers' meeting at Richmond that night, Dale Jarrett rose and said, "I've talked to a lot of these guys in this room, Tony, and you're a big reason for why all these fans are filling the stands every week. You've got all our support, and we'll do everything we can to help keep you in this sport. Keep your head up." Stewart finished thirtieth.

·   ·   ·

Ryan Newman wins the rain-shortened second go-round at the *re*-resurfaced New Hampshire, his first victory. After 26 weeks, more than two-thirds of the entire 2002 season, Tennessee weeps as Sterling Marlin gives up the lead for the championship. Mark Martin takes over. And looks as if he's just been handed a solid gold horseshoe.

Before that race at Loudon, a local paper printed a story in which a New Hampshire International Speedway EMT claimed to have been punched by Tony Stewart. The incident was said to have occurred during the July race at the track, when the EMT was helping Stewart from his wrecked car. But the television networks turned up video footage which clearly showed that Stewart had done nothing more than bat the man's hand away as he crowded in on him trying, perhaps a little too hard, to help. The piling on had begun. And true to the wild swings of his season so far, Tony Stewart finished the NHIS race third. On his way to Delaware for the next date he was fourth in the championship standings, only 59 points behind the leader in the tightest race in decades. He thought he had a good chance to win it all.

"I'm really excited about the rest of the season. Typically this is when we run the best. If we can stay on that pace like we have historically I think we've got a good chance at the championship."

Whether or not Tony Stewart wins the championship, or learns to manage his anger, or grows beyond simple gestures of enforced contrition into the genuine accountability of manhood, or ever makes peace with himself and with the schizophrenic central contradictions of his sport's raucous, two-fisted history and its genteel corporate futurism is up to him. Forty-two other drivers seem to do it most weekends. And whether he loves Fame or hates it, whether he thrives on it or is driven out of racing by it, "it is," as Stewart's crew chief Greg Zipadelli says, "what he signed up for."

In another month all the assault charges will be dropped.

In the world that Tony Stewart now wakes to every day, no explanation seems sufficient. In the world he imagines for himself, no explanation seems necessary.

Imagine the world he deserves.

ELEVEN

At the Dover track this week you can buy a shirt that reads, "Tony, Please Don't Hit Me!"

The dust blows and the dime slots grudgingly pay out and 150,000 American miniflags are distributed as Director of Homeland Security Mr. Tom Ridge delivers brief remarks about the troubling elusiveness of homeland security to open the MBNA All-American Heroes 400.

The "Let's Roll" car, a special paint scheme for the day, blows an engine on lap 115. It rolls, slowly, to the garage.

Earlier this season a young Navy lieutenant had used the same phrase when performing as the honorary starter for one of the Busch races. "When I say 'Gentlemen, start your engines,'" she said over the PA, "what I mean is, 'Let's roll.'"

That phrase "let's roll" chews at me. One of our great acts of actual heroism, an example of sublime selflessness and true courage, somehow reduced to a line of dialogue from an episode of *Starsky and Hutch* or *Rat Patrol*. On September 11, though, when most of us could only compare what they were seeing to another movie, I suppose it was all too apt. Now we use it to invoke the faux-heroism of the Sunday show. Another walk down the endless American hall of mirrors, the whole culture choking, swallowing its own tail. I've never much cared for the phrase "Homeland Security," either. Sounds too much like the Yellow Pages listing of an ambitious Wichita locksmith.

Jimmie Johnson, who seems to have broken the Dover code, whatever it may be, wins here for the second time in his rookie season. He leads the last 79 laps and takes it pulling away. "Mark Martin Leads Points Battle," read the Monday headlines.

Two young men, Chevrolet fans by their T-shirts and caps, are out walking. This is August.

"Wait a second, man, hold up. Wasn't that Gordon?"

"Where?"

"On that golf cart just went by . . ."

"What? On a golf cart? What the hell would Gordon be doin' out here on a golf cart?"

"No, seriously, dude, it was him. Look!"

"Like he'd ever come out here. No fuckin' way. Never happen. Gordon'd *never* come out here. Think about it. How drunk are you, anyhow?"

Long pause.

"Pretty fuckin' drunk, but it was still him."

One hundred yards away now, moving in the opposite direction, cresting a hill in the last of the sunset and trailing a cloud of dust and a wake of rubbernecking argument and beer-impaired finger pointing, it *is* Jeff Gordon, the four-time NASCAR Winston Cup Champion who, depending which fan you ask and which finger they're pointing, is either This Nation's Mightiest Hero, the Unyielding Defender of True-Blue Decency and the Blessed Four-Barrel Redeemer of the Pushrod V-8 Faith; or the Citified, Dandified, Sissified, Goody Too-Good-to-Be-True Shoes Destroyer of All That Was Once Holy and Noble in the Manly Art of Stock-Car Racing.

Gordon, in khaki pants and a blue knit golf shirt, is draped neatly across the backseat of a golf cart driven by NASCAR star Elliott Sadler and copiloted by rookie sensation Jimmie Johnson, and the night before the big Cup race they're joyriding the infield of the road course at Watkins Glen, New York. The three of them are barely disguised by their street clothes and slender sunglasses and unmarked baseball caps, and they are only imperfectly camouflaged by their speed, so that as they weave in and out of the wandering Saturday-evening crowds people half recognize them, people stop and turn and stare.

Eyes widen and blaze white from the shadows. There are thousands and thousands and thousands of ardent race fans camped out here, and what protects Jeff Gordon from being mobbed for autographs, overwhelmed, overrun, what defends him against being crushed to death by the sheer tonnage of their love, or just as likely torn to a scattering of hair and bone by their loathing, is the utterly incalculable un-likelihood of what he's doing. *Gordon'd never come out here! Think about it!* So Sadler keeps that golf cart moving, the gasps of recognition always 20 or 30 safe yards behind them, keeps it gliding up and down the snaking ranks and rows of candy-apple aqua motorhomes, through the stinging greenwood smoke from all those tribal bonfires, keeps it moving past the hundred homemade shrines to martyred Earnhardt—"Gone to Race in a Better Place," the eternal flame flick-ering atop the eternal tiki torch—past bright flags snapping in the fal-tering twilight for Martin and Wallace and Jarrett, Gordon and Johnson, Ford and Dodge, Viagra and Coke and the Confederate States of America, past the tight-ass white-wine garden parties and the ringing cornball horseshoe pits and the lard-and-skillet tent camps, past the 4-H Frisbee kids and the old-coot dog walkers and the rippling exhibitionist in-line bikini skaters, past the 40,000-watt Molly Hatchett air guitarists and the screaming Yankee drunks and the vague Rebel stoners, past the packs of giggling belly-shirt dollies surrounded by their sullen JV boyfriends, past the "Free Mammogram with Every Margarita Family Karaoke Stage," and the bad-vibe, date-rape keg-gers, past the lonesome cowboy DUIs and the angry redneck ADWs and the naked, gleaming flesh of a hundred Heart of Darkness barbe-cues, until at last they pass a sign made of empty Coors Light cans laid flat across the hillside grass and they're committed now, there's no going back, "Homo Gordon Sucks," it reads in the firelight and this is the end of the line, this is why they came.

Just beyond the sign there's a home-built school bus–camper con-version parked in a grove of trees, and it is shakily hand-lettered on every surface with hootin', hollerin', homophobic anti-Gordon slo-gans and slurs. In the destination window above the windshield a sign reads "Gordon Swallows." This is the kind of rib-tickler NASCAR's Internet cognoscenti are hoping for when they enter things like Fans Against Gordon into their search engines.

To question a driver's hetero manstuff, to mock his gender creds, his bravery, his backbone, his very *butch,* for crying out loud!, is an insult of the most cutting kind out here. Gordon has been attacked this way since the day he arrived on the tour in 1992. It is, of course, a challenge to honor of serious consequence, a muy macho th'owdown that demands a swift and terrible satisfaction.

There is no evidence anywhere that this guy roots for another driver—he simply hates Gordon. Makes his whole weekend out of it. Right now he's standing heavily in front of the bus, a blunt, profane middle-ager with a novelty-shop bullhorn and an empty dinner plate of a face, and every 10 seconds or so, between pulls on another Coors Light, he announces to the passing crowds, "Gordon's a fag!" or "Gordon sucks!" or "Brooke! Call me!"—a reference to Jeff Gordon's soon-to-be-ex wife—and a phrase that recurs on the man's T-shirt, a bestseller this season that reads "Brooke Call Me!" across the chest and then "Dial 1-800-I'm-Not-Gay," the punchline stretched tight across his belly.

A few feet away, in case the slow-witted have missed his point, is an easel holding a giant collage of doctored images of Gordon, Web downloads mostly, printed up and taped to a large white poster board: a Gordon *TV Guide* cover overdrawn with a mustache and horns and glasses; Gordon in pink tutu as ballerina; Gordon's head montaged onto bodies not his own—glistening, muscle-bound bodies knotted in Greco-Roman *flagrante.* The sign is under the supervision of another bleary, beefy unit in his mid-forties. Maybe he's the one who lettered the title, "What Has Jeffy Boy Been Up to in His Spare Time?"

This is where the golf cart stops.

The three drivers pile out and run around to the front of the sign. They pull off their hats and sunglasses, and the guy with the bullhorn to his lips is struck dumb. His shit-eating grin congeals. *Gordon'd never come out here! Think about it!* Oops.

Gordon looks at him squarely, expressionless, is clearly recognized, then turns to face the other guy. This one has a look in his eyes like a plowhorse trapped in a burning barn. Gordon and Sadler and Johnson converge on him.

Listed optimistically at 5 feet, 7 inches and 150 pounds, Gordon isn't very threatening physically, but the psychological violence of his arrival is stunning. Johnson's taller, heftier build is plainly neutralized by his Hardy Boy good looks. The unshaven Sadler, though, looks plenty nasty at 6-feet-plus and a muscular 200 pounds, so when he reaches fast down to his waistband and fills his hand with something solid and black, the plowhorse flinches a little and steps back. The dark grove, already charged with menace, crackles now with new electricity, and you wonder what the hell might happen and how far a thing has to go before it's gone too far, and then the rest of it unspools so quickly it takes an effort to sort it out.

Sadler, a big-time hunter off-season, raises his hand, and while he does so Gordon and Johnson lunge for the sign, brushing past the wild-eyed guy who's trying now, out of respect or resentment or simple panic, to wave them away, and whatever Sadler has in his hand is at eye level and aimed out in front of him and Gordon and Johnson duck down low and smile evil little smiles of their own and there's a blinding flash—as Sadler takes their picture.

Then Gordon and Johnson start howling with laughter, it's all a goof, a half-assed snapshot panty raid Jimmie's father helped set up, and as Sadler puts the camera away, Gordon jogs back to the golf cart. "Thanks, you guys," he calls over his shoulder, no irony in his voice. "Have a good weekend." And he and his posse are back on the golf cart, headed to the drivers' compound before a crowd can gather, and they're 30 yards away before Easel-Weasel croaks out a confused "Thank *you*." And it's a full minute before I hear behind me in the dark, from the trees, as deep and reverberant as four C cells can make a human voice, "You *still* suck!"

Point won, Gordon is long gone.

· · ·

While hardly an item for the police blotter, and certainly nothing that would knock Courtney Love or Michael Jackson off the celebrity-descent-into-the-snakepit page of your hometown paper, this sort of low-voltage prank, this awkward snapping of a damp figurative towel, was, for Jeff Gordon, a man once described as "the nicest robot you'd ever want to meet," a walk along the very brink of madness.

Sure he's one of this continent's red-hot racecar drivers and thus, at least as far as marketing strategies and household mythology go, a fire-breathing, death-eating meta-daredevil sex machine. In truth, in life, sorry, he's so normal he's nearly dull. He's a regular guy imprisoned in a sexy cliché. Not by his own imagination, but by the public's.

Gordon's won so many races that he's managed to take the wow out of it for us, to make the deadly extraordinary look routine. If you really consider it, even his public image, his working corporate persona, compared to other drivers', has always been a strangely dull concoction—1 part hot-rod bravado to 9 parts dutiful consumer. You see that Ace Racer face lasering right-angle rectitude back at you from a box of Frosted Mini-Wheats or a can of Pepsi or the pages of DuPont's annual report, that earnest deadpan of handsome capitalism, and you're not buying excitement, you're buying his soothing reassurance—and not just about sales or soda or cereal, either, but about yourself, about America, about the world. His very face guarantees there won't be any unpleasant surprises. Zany, he ain't. Pulling his cap around backwards is about as wild as he gets in public.

In private? Ditto. On top of which Gordon has always guarded his off-track life, maybe more vigorously than is strictly necessary, because the motoring press never really challenged his privacy, never dug very deep or even seemed very interested—not beyond the most perfunctory sort of fan-club "favorite flavor" Q & A anyway, figuring perhaps that once Gordon uttered the word "vanilla," everything that needed saying had been said, literally and metaphorically, to ensure the stability of the sport.

·　　　·　　　·

He will say to you, with a straight face, "For some reason, no matter what happens in my life, I always seem to have a piece of my heart that says everything is going to be okay."

Think, then, how Jeff Gordon—your Platonic Ideal of the Heroic American Christian Square; the buttoned-down, laced-up, blue-eyed, strong-jawed paragon of devotion to purpose and an insatiable, ambitious seeker of achievement; the best stock-car driver of his generation, completely private and perfectly happy, perfectly married, perfectly perfect—must have felt when his storybook marriage blew a tire and went straight into the wall! When he found himself literally homeless! When his multimillion-dollar divorce, suit and countersuit, was splashed across the supermarket tabs! When his racecars broke down and his luck dried up and his losing streak stretched on and on and on! When he was flung from a moving golf cart by a giant cartoon character! And don't forget the rumored "surveillance tapes"! And those gossip columns citing "marital misconduct"! And supermodels "frolicking topless"! Bunnies falling out of the sky! Then there was the goatee! Bad weirdness! Foul language! Pranking and spanking the fans! Hobnobbing with Regis and Kelly! Kid Rock and Pamela! Bob Dole and Britney and Carrot Top! Oh, the humanity! For Jeffrey Michael Gordon, 2002 was the best and worst of times, the long morning of his great awakening, the year when tragedy and comedy and every exclamation point he'd ever swerved to avoid at last gathered him up and it was madness, I tell you, madness!

As the 2001 series champion, Gordon entered the 2002 season answering the usual champeen questions. How do you feel? How's the team? How's the car? Can you repeat? Of such gray stuff are weekend features knitted. Somehow the one question that never got asked was the one boiling away in everybody's subconscious, the one steaming in all those gearhead stewpots up in the grandstands and out in the garage and over in the media center, blistering every brain in NASCAR, including Gordon's, and it was the only question worth asking and of course it was the only one you could never answer or even ask. Jeff Gordon is the All-Time Money Winner. Jeff Gordon changed stock-car racing forever. Dale Earnhardt is gone; 2001, the Season of Mourning, is over. Is Jeff Gordon, at last, The Man?

Jeff Gordon was born August 4, 1971, in Vallejo, California. A northern exurb of the San Francisco metroplex, Vallejo slopes down into the eastern reach of San Pablo Bay. It is home to the Mare Island Naval Shipyard and solidly middle class, neither as pretty nor as self-consciously precious as its more famous neighbors, Napa and Sonoma.

When he was just over a year old, Gordon's mother, Carol, was divorced from his biological father, Bill. In May 1973 she remarried a man she'd met at work named John Bickford. When Gordon says "Dad," this is who he's talking about.

Like Tiger Woods, or Pinocchio, Jeff Gordon was turned on the lathe of a father's ambitions. Bickford, who made his living engineering and building modified vehicle controls for the handicapped, had himself been a motorcycle racer as a young man and loved it—but it hadn't much loved him back. So maybe an old, unrequited passion made Bickford see what he wanted to see in a child so young. Even at two or three, John Bickford says now, Gordon had possessed "phenomenal hand-eye coordination." If Bickford had played in the high school marching band, Gordon might have gone to Juilliard.

Like so many California kids in those years, though, as soon as he could ride a bike, Gordon had started fooling around with BMX racing. He was a tiny natural, four years old and fast, but Carol worried from the first moment she went to the local track. "They were hauling the older kids away in an ambulance. With broken arms, broken legs, cracked ribs—that's what I envisioned happening to him. I knew that one thing would lead to another, like motorcycles, so I complained, probably pretty heavily, to John. 'Isn't there something we can do that's a little bit safer than this?' A week later, well, that's when he came home with the two cars. I thought, This is crazy!"

Bickford had shown up in the driveway with two quarter-midget racers, one for Jeff and one for his older sister, Kim. John explained to Carol that these were much safer than bikes or 'cycles because of the roll cages and the bodywork. Standing on the lawn, looking at the small roadsters, one black, one pink, "It made sense, somehow," Carol says, laughing now while she tells it. "John has that ability, to make everything make sense."

Within a few weeks Gordon was lapping a vacant lot against a stopwatch. Kim, however, was immune. "I didn't bring the cars home to push the kids into racing," says Bickford. "I just wanted to give Jeff a chance to see if he liked it." By the time he was five he was racing. By the time he was five and a half he was racing every weekend. By the time he was six he was winning.

Gordon was a small, shy kid but he wore the car like a second skin. He had the knack, even then, of feeling what the car was doing under him, though he couldn't necessarily articulate it. And racing, even at that level, is a sport of mechanical increments and adjustments. The driver has to be able to tell the mechanic what the car's doing when it's on the track. Gordon couldn't yet, not in sentences, anyhow, so his mechanic, John Bickford, worked out a kind of trial-and-error dialogue for them to use every time they practiced. Gordon would run a lap against the stopwatch and come in. Based on how he was running, Bickford would say to him, "Let's try X," and X would be a stiffer suspension setting. Gordon runs a lap. Comes in. Like an optometrist, Bickford asks, "Was it better/worse/the same?" And Gordon would give his answer, "Worse." Then Bickford would show him the stopwatch. "No, Jeff, you were eleven one-hundredths faster," or, "You're right, you're slower, let's try Y." On and on through long afternoons like this, X, Y, Z, better/worse/the same, Gordon parsing time and distance into ever smaller pieces, until the stopwatch itself became the opponent, the object of fixation. "He'd never really get mad at me," Bickford says now, "but he'd sure get mad at that stopwatch." The stopwatch was their common enemy.

As Gordon got more deeply involved, so did the rest of the family. Carol would run practice laps with him in another midget, weaving in front of him, slowing him down, passing him, tailing him, cutting him off so he could hone his skills. She and Kim were at the races, too, and their family time, driving to the track or eating sandwiches at the track or driving home from the track, was still family time.

The year he turned 7 Gordon won 35 main events in northern California. The next year he began to race more widely and won the Grand National Championship in Denver. He won 52 other events that year. They slept in their car. They slept in their truck. They bought a used motorhome. For the next several years, in quarter-midgets or go-karts, from California to Illinois, he won almost every time he showed up. By the age of 12 he had won hundreds of races. He signed autographs for packs of fans, and his family sold Jeff Gordon T-shirts off the back of the trailer. He was a star. He was also completely burned out—on the travel, on the stopwatch, even on the winning. He took up water-skiing. Within months he'd become so good that he briefly considered a career as a professional.

Instead he wound up doing the sensible thing and racing sprint cars. Imagine a lawn tractor with a 700-horsepower engine bolted into it and you'll have a good idea what a sprint car looks like. And how it handles. They are horrifying, primitive machines, all neck-snapping straight-line acceleration and Ben-Hur terror in the turns. When it got around that Bickford was looking for a sprint car for his 13-year-old son, the phrase "child abuse" was spoken, loud and often and without sarcasm. Gordon responded with public statements that he wanted more than anything to drive one of these monsters, that he was qualified and knew the risks, and that given half a chance he'd win. Eventually Bickford, the most single-minded, methodical, and obdurate person you're ever likely to meet, wore down the sanctioning bodies, the insurance companies, the car builders, and the other drivers. And Gordon, too short to see out of the racer without a booster chair, got his chance at sprint cars.

He didn't win immediately, but he did eventually, and while most guys his age were busy trying to figure out the narrative arc of *The Red Badge of Courage*, or the molecular composition of bong water, or how to finesse a copy of *Playboy* onto the school bus, he was meeting with potential sponsors and risking his hide racing weekends against men two or three times his age trying to earn their rent money. He was good at what he did, as good as they were, and he beat and slid and pounded those unforgiving tracks without complaint. When the opportunity arose to fly halfway around the world to race a sprint series in Australia, he jumped at it. Then he got busy trying to finesse a copy of *Playboy* onto the airplane.

That was the year, when he turned 14, that the whole family moved to Pittsboro, Indiana, the heart of the heart of sprint-car country. Kim was headed off to college in any case, and by then John and Carol were so deeply invested in Gordon's life as a racer that it made sense, at least to them, to do it. And they weren't rich. They sold John's business and kept a close eye on their diminishing savings account as they raced away the principal.

Gordon started high school while racing in several different series. He kept winning. By 1989 he was becoming a fixture on ESPN's *Thursday Night Thunder* broadcasts from places like Indianapolis Raceway Park and Imperial Speedway, and his name was on the short list of talented comers who might rate a tryout on a big-money circuit.

What Gordon chose was NASCAR. He'd looked into Indy-style cars and off-road trucks, but after he went to the Buck Baker Driving School at Darlington in 1990, he knew what he wanted to do. Even today, when Gordon describes his first couple of laps in a stock car, he makes a noise like a feral mall rat, "It was like, wwhoooooooaaaaaaa! This is for me."

That was also the year Gordon met Ray Evernham. "The very first time I saw Jeff was when he walked up to me. He looked about fourteen or fifteen years old. His mother was with him, and he had a briefcase in one hand. He called me 'Mr. Evernham.' He was trying to grow a mustache at the time, and when he opened his briefcase, he had a video game, a cell phone, and a racing magazine in it. I asked myself, What am I getting myself into?"

When Gordon began racing full-time in the Budweiser Late Model Sportsman series (the forerunner of the Busch series), last stop on the way to The Show, in 1991, Evernham became his crew chief, in charge of X/Y/Z and better/worse/the same. By then Bickford had assumed the managerial role in his son's career.

He started 30 races that year, soaking it all up, the cars, the tracks, the strategy, like a sponge. He was the Rookie of the Year that season, winning over $100,000 in prize money.

In 1992 he won three times in 31 starts and banked $412,000 to lead the series in earnings. He finished fourth overall in the season standings. That fall he also made his one-race Winston Cup debut, center ring under the big canvas, at the track in Atlanta. The afternoon of his first race was the afternoon of Richard Petty's last, but only the keenest fans, the most devoted, felt anything new on the wind.

In 1993 he raced his first full Winston Cup season. He won a 125 qualifier at Daytona, but no points races, and finished 11 times in the Top 10. He won over $750,000 in prize money and finished fourteenth in the overall standings. He was named Rookie of the Year. By the end of that season, a great many fans had taken him up with sensational enthusiasm. He was their boy! Ten times that many hated him.

For both his seasons in the Late Model series he had driven a Ford for Bill Davis Racing. In the off-season he and Evernham had been wooed away by team owner Rick Hendrick to drive a Cup car sponsored by DuPont. It was, and remains, a Chevrolet. This struck many hard-core NASCAR fans, for whom the Ford-versus-Chevy question is not merely conversational but a form of ecclesiastical debate, as the worst kind of disloyalty and opportunism, and many never forgave him.

It was around this time that Gordon was picked up by the mainstream press. His picture was now being published more widely and his story more often told. He was being interviewed on radio and television. What those hard-core fans heard and saw was even more disturbing to them than a Ford left crying at the altar. To them he was just a scrawny geek northerner with a ringing Indiana twang in his voice and a bad, a very bad, mustache. Worse still, rather than the required instep-kicking modesty, he often expressed his on-track abilities and ambitions with unbecoming candor. Worst of all, he had been born in California, the very rumpus room of evil on Earth. The southerners who were the sport's core constituency cheered for men like Earnhardt or Waltrip, rugged, homegrown men in the tradition of the outlaws and strivers who grew the sport from the root, who seemed to have earned their stature through dogged determination and guile and sacrifice and in whom the fans saw a brighter, better reflection of themselves. In Gordon they saw nothing of their experience. He had been programmed his whole life to race and only race, and had been privileged, spoiled, enough to do so. He represented change and change was bad. To them Gordon was only a dangerous stranger.

Then he started winning.

He won his first Cup race in 1994, his first Cup championship in 1995. At 24, he was the youngest driver of the Modern Era to do so. It was around this time that Dale Earnhardt, the seven-time champion with the really fine mustache, coined Gordon's derisive nickname, "Wonderboy." Gordon couldn't have cared less; all he could see was that damned stopwatch. He was bringing new fans into the sport by the hundreds of thousands, broadening NASCAR's appeal north, east, and west, and creating a counterweight to the legions of Gordon haters. He still looked like the kid who bags your groceries. He won two more championships with Evernham in '97 and '98, and now when he was introduced, he was cheered as loudly as he was booed.

Ask John Bickford to describe Jeff Gordon in one word and he'll pause a moment before saying, very slowly and clearly, "Relentless." I wonder how he got that way.

The first time I met Mr. Bickford, exchanging phone numbers and schedules, he asked me, "You're twenty-four-seven, right?" I didn't have the heart to tell him that I'm 10 to 2 M/W/F. A few weeks later we met again at his home to talk. The whole time I was there he was sweating and straining and heaving these huge, interlocking concrete landscaping blocks around. I offered to help, but he wouldn't let me. It was like interviewing Sisyphus.

In Gordon's first five seasons he won 42 races and earned nearly $25 million in prize money. With all the success came all the trappings of success: the houses, the boats, the planes, the businesses, the charity foundation. He owned the requisite garageful of fantastic cars even though he spent all his time being driven around in a motorcade-quality Suburban with tinted windows. Corporations clamored for his endorsement as he fashioned a generic, middle-American public personality for himself. He'd pull himself sweating from the car after yet another victory and, waiting until the TV microphones got to him, carefully thank "the crew of the awesome #24 Dupont Chevrolet Monte Carlo" and a neat succession of associate sponsors.

In 1994 he had married Brooke Sealey, a former Miss Winston he'd met the year before in Victory Lane after winning that 125-mile qualifier at Daytona. They seemed perfectly suited to each other. Brooke, a model, a stone hottie, and a devout Christian, would tape scripture to his dashboard before every race. She taught him how to dress and talked him out of that mustache. By then Gordon had embraced a vigorous Christianity as well, and the two of them went everywhere together and prayed together at the side of the car before each race and they were profiled by Christian magazines and sports magazines and Christian sports magazines and they were trim and rich and pious and beautiful and it was all the more reason to hate him. Or love him.

If you wanted to hate him, you could point to the fact that he'd stepped out of one controlling relationship right into another: the year he got married he fired his own father. If you wanted to love him, you could note that he'd eased Bickford out because, as Gordon says, he was anxious to take control of his own life, pull his own strings. If you wanted to hate him, you could say that the only reason he won was because Rick Hendrick threw outrageous money into his racing operation, money he earned from a huge network of successful car dealerships. If you wanted to love him, you could look to the future and see that this was the way the sport was heading. If you wanted to hate him, you could point to the fact that Hendrick had pled guilty to that indictment on charges of mail fraud in the mid-1990s. If you wanted to love him, you'd see only that Gordon raised millions of dollars for leukemia research, the disease with which Hendrick had been stricken at the same time. If you wanted to hate him, you'd make note of the fact that the original rainbow paint scheme of the #24 car was reminiscent of a gay rights bumper sticker. If you want to love him, you had a hard time arguing that one.

Love him. Hate him. Gordon receded into the background of his own life while the fans fought over who he really was.

In 1999 he finished the season sixth overall. Ray Evernham, the shambling mad scientist of the X, Y, and Z, and the real brains, some said, behind all those wins, left to orchestrate Dodge's return to NASCAR. Gordon and Hendrick hired Robbie Loomis, a 35-year-old Floridian who'd once been the crew chief for The King himself, Richard Petty, to run the team for the 2000 season. With Loomis, a quiet, thoughtful man with a personality halfway between Sheriff Andy Taylor and Gautama Buddha, running things they finished the year ninth. In 2001 they won another championship, Gordon's fourth. By the time the 2002 season began, Gordon and company had won 58 career races, banked over $45 million in prize money, and rewritten the record book. Jeff Gordon was 30.

His 2002 season started reasonably enough. The big difference for the year was going to be Gordon's new role as co-owner, along with Rick Hendrick, of the #48 car driven by Jimmie Johnson. Gordon ran ninth at the opener at Daytona on February 17 and for the next three weeks everything went as it always had. At Atlanta, though, the weekend of March 10, rumors began to circulate that Gordon and his wife had separated. The next week, at Darlington, it was announced that Brooke had filed for divorce. Gordon issued a press release: "Being a personal matter, I hope everybody will respect our privacy as we work through this difficult time. I also hope everybody will understand that it would be improper for me to discuss or comment on this matter publicly. I appreciate the support I've received from my family, friends and those in the racing community." Meeting with the press at the tailgate of his transporter that weekend, he declined comment when asked if the situation was hurting his performance. "You can talk to me about sitting on the outside front row. I'd love to talk about that because we've got a really good car, we're runnin' good." You didn't know whether to hug him or slap him.

Marriages collapse for a hundred reasons or no reason at all. The law requires a reason, though, and the one cited on Brooke's petition for divorce was that "The marriage between the parties is irretrievably broken as a result of the Husband's marital misconduct." You can explain to people all you want that in legalese this phrase is as broad and soft as a blanket, that like "irreconcilable differences," it could mean burning the meatloaf or rooting for the Red Wings or failing to put the seat down. But it can also mean the very worst things you might imagine in a marriage, and once the petition hit the Internet, the supermarket papers and the gossip columns had a track meet.

She was asking for temporary and permanent alimony, the house, the Porsche and the Mercedes 600, use of the boats and the plane, and the salaries to pay the chef, the maids, the groundskeeper. He could keep the maroon Suburban. A month later, just as the tabs were running out of things to write about the original petition, Gordon filed his counterpetition with the Palm Beach County Court. In it he agreed that the marriage was "irretrievably broken," but denied any marital misconduct. What kept the presses rolling was his assertion that, thanks to his "extraordinary contributions to the acquisition of funds as a result of his hazardous, life-threatening occupation," he wasn't willing to split the marital assets 50-50. He had, however, moved out of their baronial home in Highland Beach, Florida, and was flopping, at least on the nights he wasn't camped at the track in his baronial motorhome, un-champeenlike, on a friend's couch in Charlotte, North Carolina.

From race to race things went on as before, at least in the garage. The 100-hour work week for the crew didn't change, nor did the hundreds of items on the race-day checklists they taped to the car. For Loomis and J-Bird and Lupo, Rooster and Stabber and Stickboy, Tony and Stevie and CeeCee and Champ and Penske and Opie, and all the others who tweaked or torqued or sweated over that car, who went over the wall in the pits or bent themselves into the engine bay, the banter went on as before and the work went on endlessly, and the weirdness swirled around them but never much took hold. By the end of May they'd lost 20 in a row going back to the Kansas race the year before—a long dry spell for no one but Gordon. "We've been through worse," they'd say to you before you even asked a question. "We'll get it."

"Yeah, there's no 'I can't' in motor sports."

"Well, sure there is. Just not for us."

They're all wearing their "Refuse to Lose" T-shirts.

"'Can't' is not part of our vocabulary . . ."

"You have to *want* it . . ."

"Right."

"Wait." J-Bird runs a hand over his gleaming skull. "I'm pretty sure I *can't* grow hair . . ."

"But only because you don't *want* it enough, J-Bird . . ."

"That's true. It's really a failure of ambition."

They hammer at the car and bang and twist and polish. Stickboy stands at the rear deck, squinting out into the sunlight, watching the crowds surging past the garage.

"Look at this, look at this, look at this!"

Out on the apron a redheaded lizard skitters past their door, hurrying and bouncing spectacularly on 4-inch heels.

"Hey! Slow down!

"Slow down!"

"Hey!"

"Hell, no, miss! Keep runnin'!" J-Bird is unfailingly polite.

Gordon, too, was loosening up. For him. During that off-week in early May before the races in Charlotte, he grew that goatee. He wore it for one afternoon at the track. "I don't know, it's just somethin' to do." They wrote about it for weeks.

A few days before the Dover, Delaware, race in June, Gordon visits DuPont headquarters in nearby Wilmington for their annual NASCAR Day. It's also DuPont's 200th anniversary, so the global conglomerate wacky-maker has been dialed up to about 17. Banners line the streets, there's music in the air, and the early over/under on another supergiant corporate anniversary cake is 1,000 pounds.

DuPont has been Gordon's primary sponsor since he landed a ride in The Show, and the relationship has been of great mutual benefit. Sponsors are routinely tight-lipped about return-on-investment figures when it comes to NASCAR, in some cases because they have no sure way of tracking that there is one. Companies as shrewd and successful as DuPont, though, aren't going to spend upwards of $15 million a year if they don't know to a fine certainty that someone, somewhere, is buying DuPont's widgets because they saw Jeff Gordon driving that car. Published reports put DuPont's return at about $5 for every $1 they spend on their racing program.

Gordon's car was originally sponsored by the automotive finishes division, but in the wake of his success, some of the other divisions have gotten a nod, too, on the rear deck lid or hood. Today's event begins at the Tyvek Building, for example. Tyvek is, and here I'll quote the corporate handout, "tough, durable sheeting used for packaging, envelopes, banners and building insulation."

Ah, the glamour of racing. Sex! Death! Vapor barriers!

But the folks gathered here are darned proud of what they make and of Jeff Gordon, too. There's a banner hung above the front door of the building—printed on Tyvek, one assumes—welcoming Gordon and Loomis to "Tyvek Town." Below it the townspeople themselves circulate, taking an hour or two off, waiting for their driver to appear. Bits of conversation are carried by the morning breeze around the parking lot.

"I'm from Indianapolis, so I'm a real race fan."

"I wish I'd brought my camera."

"I hear we're really downsizing."

"I think they airbrushed his wedding ring off."

Which is true. The semi-life-size cardboard cutout of Gordon positioned near the temporary stage has a newly naked ring finger.

Around 10 A.M. that finger arrives and is greeted by a polite round of applause. Gordon takes the little stage by the front door and makes a brief address as to the awesome job the folks over here are doing. There are maybe 50 employees gathered, but every one of them gets a look straight in the eye from Jeff Gordon as he explains how important a tough, high-quality house wrap is, not just in general, but to him personally. To illustrate the value of toughness, he tells the short version of a story about losing his power steering at Martinsville back in April. It's a nice story he tells on himself, in which Loomis has to coax and cajole and shame a weakening Gordon into staying in the car. Without power steering, driving a Cup car on a short track is like holding a bowling ball at arm's length in each hand for three hours, so in Gordon's story he's near tears and on the brink of quitting for most of the race. Buddha Loomis murmurs encouragement while Gordon pleads into the radio that he's only human. He finishes twenty-third and returns to the garage. The punchline of the story is what he says to Loomis when he gets there. "If I could lift my arms, I'd wring your neck."

Then he spends a few minutes politely answering their questions. The questions Gordon is asked in situations like these don't vary much: "How do you think you'll do this year?" or "How did you feel when you won at (track name)?" or "How did you feel when you crashed at (track name)?" The correct answers to these questions are as follows: "good," "good," and "bad." But unlike a lot of other drivers, or athletes, or humans, Gordon makes an effort to listen to each question and then answer it as though it's the first time he's heard it.

This year he's getting a lot of questions about what it's like to be a car owner. The answer is, most often, "I'm really enjoying it. I'm learning a lot from Jimmie."

And that's true. Not only does Gordon study Johnson's setups keenly with an eye toward making his own car faster, he spends huge amounts of time just hanging out with Johnson because they get along so well and have so much in common.

But Johnson isn't on the guest list today, so Gordon will be spending most of his time with Loomis, who does his best to bluff the role of superstar crew chief on days like this, but ends up looking as awkward as Aunt Bee at a wet T-shirt contest. There are a few more questions, the last of which sets Gordon up for a good laugh. A fellow down front in the crowd asks, "Did you know that there are going to be 1,525 DuPont employees sitting in turn 1 for the Sunday race at Dover?" To which Gordon responds, "No, I didn't. Note to self: Don't hit the wall in turn 1." And like any savvy performer he uses the laugh to cover his exit. While they're still laughing he says, "Thanks for everything you do," and hops off the stage awash in their applause.

Then the motorcycle escort forms up for the parade into the center of town. Gordon and Loomis each get behind the wheel of an actual team racecar, fire the engines, and take off out of the parking lot, heading for the city streets, snarling like Cerberus, at about 4 miles an hour.

The press follows in a town car. During the brief ride downtown, the driver is asked what there is to do here. He hems and haws about last week's Greek festival and the Italian festival the week before that and finally says with a sigh worthy of Sartre, "Really? Nothing. There's nothing to do here. *Nothing.*"

When Gordon and Loomis arrive at Rodney Square Park, the hub of urban Wilmington, they both look the worse for having idled 750-horsepower stock cars through the city streets. In addition to the broiling engine heat, and the near-instantaneous deafness, the exhausts on these things empty almost directly into the driver's compartment, so if you're not going 180 miles an hour to vent them, you'll asphyxiate yourself in a matter of minutes. How many minutes is something the DuPont scientists probably worked out pretty precisely when they planned the parade route, because neither Gordon nor Loomis seems to have blacked out or suffered permanent impairment. They just look red and sweaty.

But then so do the 5,000 local citizens who've gathered here today to help the city's largest employer celebrate 200 years of employing local citizens. It's nearly noon now, and hot, and the park is very crowded. There are free giveaways and contests and food, and once Gordon arrives there are the cars to look at, too. The crowd circulates while a couple of local burghers make nasal oratory on the subject of full employment for local citizens. Then Gordon and Loomis are introduced and take the stage along with late-arriving team owner Rick Hendrick. The applause is so loud you can almost hear it over the lite rock still pouring out of the PA like water from the sluices at the Glen Canyon Dam.

Gordon and company are seated on a portable stage on one side of the park. Farthest from the stage are the crack addicts and the toothless confused for whom the park is home and to whom all this wholesome argle-bargle is an upsetting intrusion. In front of them are the construction workers and lunch-hour bystanders drawn by the noise and the smell of free food. In front of them are the casual fans, DuPont employees mostly, and another group for whom the whole thing seems a terrible inconvenience, the reporters and television news crews. Beyond them, pressed hard to the foot of the stage, are the diehards, the true believers and dress-alikes, who understand Gordon not just as a racer, and not just as a matinee idol, but as a bringer of good news, a messenger of salvation. What message he brings, what radiant grace is his to dispense, seems a mystery. Once again, if you don't get it, no explanation is possible. A goodly portion of his fan base feels this way, and it is at once alarming and comical and heartbreaking to see.

One woman has brought her son to the lip of the stage. He is swaddled from head to toe in Gordon's team colors. "If I can just get Jeff to see him," she says, trailing off. It is hot and clear and the boy is reddening with sunburn. "I just want Jeff to see him," she explains to herself. The boy's twin sister is here, too. Jostled by the pressing throng, she holds the boy high above her head for Gordon to see. Her eyes never leave Gordon. Gordon is answering audience questions. "Good." "Good." "Bad." The boy is the size of a $6 eggplant. The boy is an eight-week-old preemie. Gordon won't remember seeing him.

Not only is there going to be big cake today, there is going to be cake big enough to require its own tent. The crowd begins to wander in that direction when they hear phrases like, "Well, summarizing the last nine years . . ." coming from the stage. Those who leave too early, though, miss hearing the day's second telling of the Martinsville power-steering failure. It is the unabridged version this time, longer in the telling. The cake tent has its own air-conditioning system and "If I could lift my arms I'd wring your neck" is almost lost in the compressor noise. But the laugh follows and the dignitaries clear the stage to go see the big cake.

The sides of the tent are rolled up to reveal a cake the size of a car. In fact the cake *is* the car, a near-life-size version of #24 blah, blah, blah decked out in the orange yada-yada 200th-anniversary paint scheme. The tent has its own A/C to protect the 540 pounds of buttercream frosting, which, like the guests, is now beginning to sag just a little in the heat.

Gordon excels at moments like this, though, and wins the grudging affection of local television crews by saying, and then repeating when they miss it the first time, "We're going to need a much bigger knife." Once that pump is primed, you can't stop him and he MCs the next five minutes of cake mayhem. "Two hundred years deserves a cake this size," he says, and "Let's give them all a hand," referring to the exhausted bakers standing next to it. He's cutting pieces for the crowd the whole time and passing them down the cake-brigade line until everyone within 20 feet of him has orange frosting smeared around their cakeholes. As in Daytona, Gordon never actually tries any. Delicious gross weight of big cake? 3,160 pounds.

He is then whisked across the street by a phalanx of cops for a luncheon with Wilmington notables. An hour and a half later he's back at the DuPont campus, this time to sign autographs outside the Performance Finishes Building. Their parking lot setup is substantially more elaborate than Tyvek Town's and passionate interdivisional jealousies are probably still sparking hard words in the company lunchroom. There are race simulators and pit-stop demonstrators and lots of cars here, but the focus of the afternoon is the gauzy awning beneath which Gordon and Loomis, flanked by two state troopers, will sit to sign autographs for 200 lucky employees. First, though, there are the introductions to be got through. And the audience questions. And, "If I could lift my arms I'd wring your neck." Truer words were never spoken.

If Gordon didn't have to interact with anyone, speak to anyone, he could probably sign 500 autographs an hour. As it is, though, he chats pleasantly with everyone coming through the autograph line. "How are you?" he'll ask to start, or "What's your name?" and then 10 or 15 or 30 seconds later, after they tell him stories about people he'll never meet or events he doesn't recall or places he'll never go, he'll politely conclude with "Thank you very much. Have a good day." He signs hats, posters, model cars, and shirts. Soda cans and quarter-scale car hoods and bandannas and bumper stickers and stolen pit-lane gas cans. He signs so many pictures of himself that you wonder what he sees when he looks down at that face. He is right-handed and efficiently moves everything from left to right as he signs, the pen held very lightly in his hand. His hands are small and well proportioned, no rings, wedding or otherwise, and no watch, which is unusual in the racing community, where even the Hooters girls wear immense chronographs.

He rises and comes around in front of the table to meet people in wheelchairs. He has a snapshot with nearly everyone, too, and smiles the same smile for them all and helps pose and arrange the baffled children that people hand him so they can have their picture taken with the stranger their father gets so excited about. "He gave up a field trip to be here, Jeff," one says. "I appreciate it," says Gordon, and the man looks as if Gordon has just given the boy a kidney. "Thank you, Jeff, thank you. Good luck, Jeff."

While they wait in line people ask each other what they're going to say to him. Once they've seen him they clump together and ask each other what he said to them. It's getting late and in a few minutes they'll take him inside for a special photo session with more employees' children. He won't leave here until he's signed or posed or talked to everyone who wants signing or posing or talking. It'll be a nine-hour DuPont day and Gordon won't roll his eyes or stamp his feet. "It's a big part of my job. And for the most part I really enjoy it."

Toward the end of the autograph signing a woman approaches the table. She is in her thirties, pale and freckled, red-haired with pretty green eyes, well dressed, and as soon as Gordon says, "Hi, how are you?" she begins crying. She is instantly wracked with sobs and shaking uncontrollably and smiling at the same time and can't get even her name out of her mouth. Gordon signs an 8-by-10 of himself for her. She stands before him, beaming and weeping inconsolably. Her face flushes red as a valentine. She remains there for several seconds, until someone steps up from behind and gently guides her away, from left to right. She is literally choking on the words, "Thank you."

At Gordon's shoulder the older state trooper turns to the younger. "She does that every year."

A week later at a small-town fire station, he attends a meeting of the Jeff Gordon Fan Club. This is the day before the Cup race at Pocono.

The multipurpose room of the Penn Forest Township fire hall has been taken over by 200 lucky fan club members. Lucky because they had to win a lottery to get here. Ten thousand people submitted applications to attend, but the Penn Forest Township fire hall multipurpose room, while nicely paneled, is only so big.

Everybody here already knows him. They know he likes scuba diving and bowling and pizza, movies and video games and motorcycling. They know that his favorite TV show is *Friends*, and that his favorite hymn is "Awesome God." That if he couldn't drive a racecar he'd like to be an astronaut (or maybe anything else that puts you a couple hundred thousand miles away from the nearest autograph seeker). Ask these folks, the truckers and teachers and school bus drivers, the steelworkers and nurses and linoleum salesmen, why they've come and they're slow to speak. Not because that question's hard to answer but because it's so easy. For every one of them the answer is different, but it's always completely obvious. Often, before they say anything, they smile. Because they feel sorry for you. Because to even ask the question is an admission that you don't get it.

"He's touched so many hearts."

"He's so good for the kids that don't have."

"He's what I think, what I *believe*, America used to be, should be."

"I just love him, is all."

And in their eyes is the iron certainty of faith. "Isn't he something?" a woman sighs as he walks out the door.

Back at Daytona a month later, 100 people stand ankle-deep in rainwater during a violent lightning storm to watch him give an outdoor radio interview. You don't know whether to hug them or slap them.

Winning percentage is a statistic that NASCAR doesn't much use. People are too conditioned by baseball and the high standard of the .300 hitter. It's an apples-and-oranges thing, but the best drivers in history look anemic compared to even the lightest-hitting middle infielder. The highest lifetime average, for example, belongs to Tim Flock, back when he was driving for those disproportionately dominant Carl Kiekhaefer teams. Flock won 40 races in a very brief career, only 189 starts, for a winning percentage of .212.

In the Modern Era, with 84 wins in 809 starts, three-time champion Darrell Waltrip's lifetime average was .104; with 76 wins in 676 starts, the late Dale Earnhardt's lifetime average was .112; Richard Petty, 200 wins in 1,177 starts, had a lifetime average of .170. David

Pearson, with 105 wins in 574 races over 26 years, had an outrageous .183 average lifetime. Gordon's average through the beginning of the 2002 season, 58 wins in 293 starts, was .198.

Before 2002, Gordon won every fifth race he entered.

To put that in some sort of perspective, consider again Michael Waltrip, the hunky 15-year veteran who has earned millions of dollars in prize money and endorsements. At the beginning of the 2002 season, he'd won once in 498 starts. For a lifetime winning percentage of .002.

Perhaps this is why Gordon's 2002 "losing streak" was of such endless interest to the press. Or maybe it was simple hillbilly schadenfreude, joy in the failure of Jeff Gordon.

Through the middle third of the season, despite all the distractions brought on by the divorce, Gordon and the team hovered near the Top 5 in the point standings. The distractions included rumors of "surveillance tapes" that got started when Gordon's lawyers asked, as a matter of routine, to see whatever materials Brooke's lawyers might have gathered. There was also the presence—at every track every week, it seemed—of celebrities wanting to exploit NASCAR's new popularity for their own promotional needs. And of course they all wanted to meet Jeff Gordon. So in and out of the garage they came, clapping their hands over their ears whenever J-Bird revved the engine, looking lost and a little frightened, the professional wrestlers and the senators and the singers and the supermodels and the actors and the comics. Most of them lasted an afternoon, then got as far from the track as they could.

Gordon's lowest moment probably came at Sears Point, the road course in northern California 25 miles from where he was born. He always runs fast there. He was leading, running away from the field, when he fragged the rear-end gear. He finished thirty-seventh.

A few weeks later he finished second at Chicago, but then fell to twenty-ninth the week after that at New Hampshire. He and the team were all over the place. At the second Pocono race of the year they started twenty-eighth and finished twelfth and the crew was angry when they rolled the car back onto the hauler. "We got our ass handed to us today, man."

At Indy they snap a drive shaft in practice and tear up the bottom of the car. The crew has to reinstall everything from the oil lines to the axles, and the work is frantic, but they're not. "If we dig deep for Jeff, he'll dig deep for us."

On his birthday at Indianapolis, another home track, he finishes sixth. He's fourth in points even though he hasn't won a race and he's in a good mood. He radios the crew, "Great job, guys, that was fast, smart racing."

The next week, at Watkins Glen, despite all the infield hijinks ("That sign was the funniest thing I think I've ever seen. I mean, those guys don't know me at all, so I can't really hold it against them."), he finishes twenty-second. Then nineteenth at Michigan. The season is two-thirds over and he hasn't won yet. The losing streak stands at 31, the longest since his rookie season.

The next week at Bristol, Gordon wins the pole and tells the press, "As much as you guys like to write about me losing, I'd like to win one." And he does, contending all night, then punting Rusty Wallace out of his way with two laps to go. "What are they gonna write about now?" he shouts into his radio as he heads for Victory Lane. "Man, we needed that bad!"

Walking into the press box around midnight for the postrace interviews he says to the writers, "Nice to see you folks again."

Walking out an hour later, surrounded by dozens of reporters and team executives and publicists, he walks past the night cleaning crew. A stout woman in her forties, her eyes rimmed red with fatigue, is emptying trash from one of the suites. She watches him go by. She turns to her coworker and says, "He's just little. Did you see that? He's just *little*."

He wins again at Darlington the week after that. "He can win 'em in bunches, man, bunches," the crew guys had said to the press, "so look out."

But at Richmond the next weekend they're punished for their

hubris. Not only does Gordon crash the primary car, but he's flung to the ground by that bunny.

Worse still, they finish the race fortieth after the backup engine blows.

"This was not our best weekend," Gordon says.

The chance to win it all probably slipped away from them four or five months earlier. It's been the year of the young'uns, the successful, raced-from-the-cradle twenty-somethings for whom Gordon paved the way. Jimmie Johnson, Kurt Busch, Ryan Newman, and Matt Kenseth are all doing well. Strangely, those new guys don't get booed. All that fear and loathing remain Gordon's to absorb. And despite all the dire hand-wringing and the newsprint forests of "Whither Gordon?" pieces and the divorce and the losing streak, he seems happy.

In fact the whole year, good day or bad, high finish or low, at the car or in the garage or on the grid, racing go-karts against his crew or meeting the press or the Make-A-Wish kids or pranking the haters, people say he's been looser and goofier than they've ever seen him. They all want to say he's changed, that he's a different man. Is he? Robbie Loomis has perhaps the smartest answer: "I hear that a lot. I haven't really noticed a difference in him. I think the Jeff Gordon that was there we only got to see a little bit. Now everybody in the garage—the officials, the teams, the other drivers—they see a lot more of the Gordon that always *was* there. He's the same Jeff Gordon, you just get to spend more time with him."

Per Gordon? "I don't feel like I've changed. I'm just more myself."

I asked Ray Evernham the other day to clarify a quote of his that's been making the rounds. "I never said there were only two great drivers in the world," Evernham explains, "What I said, at the risk of making some people mad, was, 'There are only two *drivers* in the world, Michael Schumacher and Jeff Gordon.'"

At the beginning of the season, sitting in the blond maple and stainless steel majesty of his motorhome, I asked Gordon what he felt he'd traded away to win all those races over all those years, to win all those hearts and minds, to make all those deadly enemies. To be loved and hated by so many strangers. What was the price for something like that?

"As successful as I've been on the racetrack the last couple of years, I feel like a lot of things have passed me by." Then he paused. His cell phone rang in the other room. "Maybe that'll change."

Maybe not The Man, not yet, maybe never, but a man at least in full. Or just Pinocchio grown, a real boy, out on his own at last.

TWELVE

There's a woman up in Michigan with a NASCAR garden. Her website says she created it to honor the NASCAR Winston Cup Series, the memory of Dale Earnhardt, and five very important children's charities. In the flowerbeds in front of her house she has made 23 little concrete racetracks, just like the ones on the tour. According to the website, "Each track is 1:1100th scale and is pointing true north." She also painted her front porch black-and-white, "to look like the checkered flag."

The website suggests donations be made to the charities and explains every step of the material procurement and construction process for the garden. Like a winning driver, she mentions the brand names of all her sponsors—Home Depot, Lowe's, Sears. These are the places she went to buy the concrete and paint and wood chips she used. "They don't even know I'm doing this," it says on the site. Still, she's grateful to them for being there. In addition to the flowers, each track has a little sign with a company logo stuck in it. "All the logos are protected in 3M photo laminating sheets, purchased at Target. The logos for each racetrack and the charities are attached to glowsticks I think I got at Dollar General."

The Daytona and New Hampshire tracks are planted with bleeding hearts, the website says, "for obvious reasons." The whole project took five months.

The site strikes me the way a lot of NASCAR fan pages do, the homemade paeans to favorite drivers and preferred paint schemes. They seem to me not just an expression of devotion or self-involvement or obsession, but rather as gestures toward community—of a longing for contact and commonality. They are correspondence of a kind, dispatches sent out across the ocean of the world, bearing as much lonely hope as a message in a bottle.

Not quite so fraught with hidden longing is another website, slugged gaytona.com, where the only message to be gleaned from an empty bottle is that someone needs to order more champagne. All of its longing is right out there in the open.

Devised, written, and presided over by the bawdy Ms. Betty Jack DeVine, the site is a funny, lusty, technically savvy weekly weblog of driver profiles, race recaps, and garage gossip. Most of the postings chronicle Betty Jack's madcap brunch bunch as they gather to watch the big Sunday show, drink quite a few too many mimosas, and argue the various benefits of performing the bump and run. Emboldened by cocktails, they're also apt to comment on which driver they'd most like to perform it with.

From pictures posted on the website, one might construe Ms. DeVine to be a daft, insatiable maiden aunt in the southern gothic style—witty, tipsy, and profane—a former Miss Firecracker, circa 1973, trailing a comet's tail of relieved and heartbroken beaux behind her. Her astute use of the first-person plural possessive only bolsters the impression of genteel entitlement and humid corruption. She's kind of a riot. Dame Edna by way of Blanche DuBois by way of Jayne Mansfield by way of Scarlett O'Hara. Fabulous. Her real name is David Goldman. Ms. Betty Jack DeVine is a drag queen from Atlanta.

And while that attribute alone might make the site noteworthy on the unbending straightaway of the NASCAR blogosphere, it is rather the blog's avidity and generosity of spirit that distinguish it.

Gay NASCAR fans, do you find it difficult to hook up with like-minded guys or/and dolls? Do you want to talk track with some pals who really get how hot these speed jocks are? Well darlings, Betty Jack DeVine is here to lead all you gay NASCAR fans from the gloom of the closet out to the glory of the speedway!

The website's voice is one of high southern camp, or at least one of high Southern Comfort, and Ms. DeVine's insights into the runnin' and tunin' nuances of the sport are rivaled only by her warm encomiums to her favorite drivers, who are collected in a group she calls the DeVine 9½.

And why "9½"? Oh honey, why NOT?

On Michael Waltrip:

Mikey was another of our first favorites when we got into NASCAR. He always seems like he's having fun, even when he's not winning. And what can you say about that voice? With that "country-boy in cosmetology school" accent, Mikey should be a source of pride for every kid who ever got taken for his mama when he answered the phone.

On Mark Martin:

We love it that his racecar caused millions of parents to have to explain to their children why erections are important.

Not long ago gaytona.com became the number one result if you Googled "Gay NASCAR." Not that long ago thinking about Googling "Gay Nascar" would have seemed insane.

The site's an affirmation of something fundamentally good, I think, although just what I'm not sure. Tolerance? Progress? The sovereignty of comedy in the face of bigotry? The inevitability of inclusion, leading us all inexorably toward some distant point in human history where everyone can enjoy everything everywhere without injury or insult to anyone?

Or perhaps I just get a kick out of the idea of men sitting around laughing and drinking, in toreador pants and really big slingbacks, watching the Pepsi 400. Tolerance has to start somewhere.

Fall

We have been called off the Kansas Cup race by *Sports Illustrated*. The Beep and I are directed to return to Indianapolis for the U. S. Grand Prix. We are to witness Formula One.

Indy has been transformed by the arrival of the F1 show, and there's no way to compare it to what we saw at the Brickyard 400. Whole areas of the infield have been cordoned off behind temporary crowd-control screens. Security is remarkable, everyone clocking in and out from area to area with electronic key cards. In the catering tents, people are dressed as if for the opening night of the London Symphony. Face-painted fans wearing liederhosen and carrying Ferrari flags stagger past, singing what I can only assume to be the overture from *The Student Prince*.

A couple of other sportswriters and I have been told that we will be talking to Michael Schumacher when he finishes practice. In the meantime we are offered espresso and biscotti by the Ferrari publicists. They are pleasant and vague in about seven languages. "We are not so sure of his time to speak yet. But maybe." We wait

Six hours later, one of the Euro flacks returns. "Sadly, the car has crashed," she says. It wasn't even Schumacher's car. It was his teammate's, Rubens Barrichello. The car got loose in practice, swapped ends, and slid into the wall. Barrichello wasn't hurt, but now the interviews with Schumacher are off.

"The car has crashed," she says again. Then she purses her lips and shrugs.

"What happened to Barrichello?" asks the Associated Press.

"Steve Park got into the back of him," answers *USA Today*.

"The car has crashed and the time has, pfffft." She blows a petite Euro raspberry indicting the evanescent delicacy of time itself. Hyper-caffeinated, we skitter away to our hotels and motels and motorhomes like hummingbirds.

•   •   •

On the last lap of Sunday's race Schumacher, having led all day and leading now by a great many car lengths, slows down very precisely and lets Barrichello race past him for the win. Schumacher finishes second, only a few hundredths behind. This he does to repay his teammate for having done the same last year at the Austrian Grand Prix, which guaranteed Ferrari the 2001 drivers' and constructors' championships. Team orders. Even other Formula One teams decried these moves and said they'd made the sport a "laughingstock."

Most Americans don't much cotton to Formula One, for a variety of reasons: our casual xenophobia, the current absence of competitive 'Murcan drivers, our big-block V-8 distaste for these fragile, effete cars.

I think, too, that F1 suffers here because on the track it seems canned, somehow. Too much information management, not enough daredevil highballin'. Not fixed, strictly, because it isn't. But after watching the bump-and-grind of NASCAR, F1 strikes an American eye as too orderly, too neat. No *action*. No damn fun.

Or, as I heard one American fan say as we walked out of the gate and headed for Homer, "Well, *that* was a load of bullshit."

The same day, at the new mile-and-a-half cookie cutter at Kansas City, Kansas, Jeff Gordon bounces back from the Bugs Bunny Curse and wins. Mark Martin surrenders his brief points lead to freshman superhero Jimmie Johnson.

Rolled in to the best party on tour again, Talladega, Club Jed, for another go-round at the big ring and some étouffe. Or maybe another platter of that fine fish fry up at the Gateway Diner by the highway.

There's a legend you're likely to hear when you come to 'Dega, and it might just give you the jimjams when you walk the grounds at night. The track is haunted, ghosts everywhere, built atop an ancient Indian burial ground. The track was laid down over an old airfield, but beneath them both lies the last rest of the native people who played among these homeland pines so long ago. In the flicker of all this trackside firelight it feels more than probably true, and the thought can prey until you're in a state of high heebie-jeebies indeed.

That's what it did to Bobby Isaac back in the early '70s. Bobby was a hard runner from North Carolina, a champion and nobody's fool, but as he circled the track here one humid afternoon he heard voices in his head. "Get out of that car," they said, "get out of that car." And, according to the legend, he did what he was told—pulled off and hustled away from that car like it was a burning hearse. Touched by that madness, some say, he was never the same. Spooky.

The Coors Light team announced this week that Sterling Marlin was going to have to get out of his car, too, although for nothing so otherworldly as buried American voices. He had hit hard at Kansas and then at Richmond, and the two impacts had cracked a cervical vertebra. His neck was "near broke" and another crash might leave him paralyzed or worse. Wearing a giraffe brace and a pained smile, he handed the keys of the #40 car over to Busch racer Jamie McMurray, not even yet a rookie on the Cup tour. Marlin's monotonous best season ever was behind him.

But then the misery index was high all the way around this weekend, hot and humid as gumbo, and Alabama losing to Georgia in the big Saturday game. On Sunday six cars with Hendrick engines blew up in that mothering funk, and both Jimmie Johnson and Jeff Gordon dropped a few spots in the points race. All six engines had been running radical new valve springs, chasing more horsepower in an attempt to catch the DEI plateracers, but the X-parts vaporized, leaving the Junior juggernaut to do as it wished.

Which was win, and Junior did so. Another fan millionaire was made, too, through Big Tobacco's bonus payout, a woman named Debra, who "just came off disability" and in whose '87 Firebird "the motor's starting to go." So the news wasn't all bad.

Loose-cannon Tony Stewart takes the points lead, which is being played in the papers as the tightest in history.

Home again for Second Charlotte. I saw another cryptic T-shirt today: "Everything else is just a game." Race fans understand the allusion immediately, of course, to the candy-ass nature of all other athletic endeavors. The full quote from which it's derived is routinely attributed to Ernest Hemingway or Bill France One or Two, but I think you could trace its variants back into history as far as you cared to go. "There are only three real sports," it avers, "boxing, bullfighting, and racing. Everything else is just a game."

But games and sports aren't the big sellers out here, of course. More like sex and death. One's never farther than a few feet from the other when there's a crowd in the house and cars on the track. Every stop on the DisasterLand tour burns a sexual inferno. All that nasty heat and deadly risk and, er, hrrrrmph, *sensation,* everyone poised all weekend on the slender blade of something thrilling, ready to tip themselves this way or that into the flames. The Pit Lizards and semipro skanks circulating in their pneumatic profusion, a willing source of Sirenic temptation to all those crewmen and drivers not bound tight to whatever masts are handy. Then again, these are all men who might at any moment be snatched up by the Big Kaboom, too, so every race offers a plausible excuse for some desperate, life-affirming sport fucking.

That kind of delirious groping byplay thrives among the superstar husbands and splendid wives out here as well, just as it does in any small town or at any suburban key party, although it gets no public mention—the appearance of solid Christian rectitude and missionary fidelity being one of NASCAR's greatest come-ons to the buying public. It's sold as a Family Sport, after all, despite its horny origins and priapic conceits and Maximum Dad's "Show us your tits!" exuberance.

The whole sex deal might be better and more profitably played by NASCAR as a series of blind items fed to the papers, the way they do it out in Hollywood. Which married hotshoe maintains a second motorhome as his at-track love nest? Which long-wed roundy-rounder is hiding his new girlfriend in another man's pit stall, hoping no one will notice her there? Which driver spent last week's prize money on a diamond ring the size of a number 10 Mepps spinner to lure his wife back from the rockin' trailer of another married front-runner? Etc.

I've watched pit crews while away an entire race checking out the grandstand talent with a borrowed telephoto lens; or humping stacks of Goodyear Eagles when a particularly awesome Christian lizard, her sterling silver cross warming in her swelling décolleté, materializes on the NASCARvision big screen.

It may or may not be the intimate proximity of all that calamity making the stolen sex so hot, but Death's a fickle pimp out here and sometimes all you get's the fire.

Here at Charlotte, out on the backstretch, occurred one of the worst in history. Early in the spring race in 1964, Edward Glenn Roberts, one of the sport's best racers, long nicknamed "Fireball," got tangled up with a couple of other cars and turned around and went hard into the wall. His fuel tank ruptured. Roberts was allergic to the flame retardant used in the firesuits, so he wore untreated, tailored coveralls. He burned. Ned Jarrett and Junior Johnson pulled him from the car, but they couldn't save him. Roberts lingered until July, shivering in a shroud of gauze, then died.

The next year, Firestone introduced a new fuel cell, a foam-core contraption inside a puncture-resistant bladder inside a steel box, a Chinese puzzle that greatly reduced the risk of fire after even the hardest collisions.

And that's the way it's mostly been done out here. Something bad happens and then a countermeasure is devised to deal with it. After Dale Earnhardt died, and Adam Petty and Kenny Irwin, head and neck restraints for the drivers were finally, slowly made mandatory. They had existed before these deaths, were in wide use in other racing series, but had never been ruled a requirement in Cup racing. Even then, Sterling Marlin's neck was nearly broken. So NASCAR began installing "soft walls" at some tracks, too, a foam-and-steel energy-absorption system that diminishes the impact of a 3,400-pound car hitting concrete at 200 miles an hour. Because: "It's not the speed," as they say, "it's the stop that kills you."

Safety has always played a role in NASCAR's institutional thinking, but historically they've been reactive rather than creative. Earnhardt's death changed that. NASCAR just opened a new research and development facility up the road for the design and testing of new safety measures, hoping to get out front of the carnage for a change, but there are still plenty of complaints from drivers about the general state of readiness.

A good illustration of which may be Dale Jarrett walking back to the pits in frustration after he wrecked at second Daytona back in July. It took so long for the safety crew and the ambulance to reach him that he took off walking in a fury and refused a ride when they finally showed up.

NASCAR uses local safety workers and area doctors whenever it visits a track. Other major racing series, like Formula One, travel with their own crews of professional rescue workers and doctors. While you can never engineer crashing out of the cars, the drivers argue, you can certainly improve the training and response time of the people hired to peel you out of the debris. It's mighty expensive, though.

"Our way works for us," responds NASCAR president Mike Helton.

Race day comes around with rain and the feeling of a picnic spoiled. It is another long afternoon of track drying and delays. So into the night they race, the lead changing like clockwork among the usual suspects, Gordon and Stewart and company, until a crash in the midpack on lap 230 sends a third of the cars spinning across the infield grass directly at the pits. Yeehaw! No one is hurt, but the pack's reshuffled and the track's wide open and the rest of the night they'll be flatfootin' it all the way around. Out front with about 100 laps to go is the #40 car, the Coors Light Silver Bullet that Marlin bequeathed to McMurray at Talladega. No one expects him to stay out front, though; he's just a kid after all, 26, a subbing scrub, and this is only his second race in the big leagues. He'll fade.

And yet, he does not. As the race winds down, 80 laps to go, 50, now 40, Gordon and Stewart and Bobby Labonte run at the boy, high and low, right side and left, into the turns and out of them, but cannot catch him.

With 25 or so laps left, the crowd begins to realize what might happen and a roar goes up and stays up. The greats chase him, fast and furious in their lust, etc., but he is smooth and untouchable. With 10 to go everyone in the stands is on their feet. Five. Labonte and Stewart and Gordon are arrayed behind him, a flying wedge of frustration. Four. Three. Two. They reach but they cannot grasp, he's too fast. Coming out of the final turn you can hear the crowd, as one, pause to draw breath. As Jamie McMurray hits the finish line, winning in only his second start ever, the crowd sets loose their cheer. The only thing louder is McMurray's burnout. It is the *Aida* of burnouts, the Chicago Fire, the Tunguska Blast. Best burnout of the year.

Second start ever. A great race. A triumph for youth, if not inexperience. In Victory Lane he urges live television viewers everywhere to crack open a beer on his behalf. Beguilingly, he is actually excited at having won. "Everyone's asking if I'm nervous. I promise you guys I'm really frickin' nervous!"

He's the V-8 Ruby Keeler, a shooting star! Driving for a team that led in points for most of the season!

Which, among the grumpier elephants, stamping out happiness wherever they tread, raises a question. Is it the car or the driver? Is he any good or did they just hand him a really hot car? NASCAR's Gargantuan Unanswerable.

Is it hard to drive a racecar? Yes. By now I've seen the error of my early ways and have learned enough to know how very hard it is. Harder still to do it well. I am ready to say not only that the drivers are athletes, but they are good ones, too, and that the skills they possess are singular. Beyond which original gifts, the very best of them excel in ways that even their colleagues don't quite understand.

But car or driver? That's a different question. Deus or Machina? Is a good driver in a bad car better than a bad driver in a good car? Do the really good drivers always get rides in the really good cars? Or are there genius drivers out here trapped in really bad cars? The questions can force you cross-eyed, because there's no answer. And there's no one to ask in any case, because there's no driver living who doesn't think he could win it all if he just had the right ride under him.

Despite all the teleological horseplay, Jamie McMurray will be a great story for at least a week. He won. He's good-looking and personable. This season's kissable Miss Winston gave up her sash to date him. What's not to love? Everything else is just a game. Tony Stewart leads the points race.

We linger and loaf in Dirty 'Mo, hoping for a glimpse of Junior Earnhardt in a red Corvette on his way to the Whataburger, where the air-conditioning is set to "stun" and the jokes taped to the cash register read thus: "The best mathematical equation I have ever seen is 1 cross + 3 nails = 4given." We revisit DEI. We do our hot whites and warmwash colors at the Sherwood Park Coin Laundry. We watch old men in straw hats with vents at the crown rocking on their porches. We lurk late-night in the tidy aisles at WallyWorld to watch the shoppers swoon. We haunt the Lucky 13 Tattoo Parlor next to the North Carolina Department of Corrections Office ("Parking in front for gov't vehicles only—probationers must park in gravel lot") and the Sea Shell Pet Shop and the Gibson brothers furniture store, with its display of hand-carved stock-car étagères. He is nowhere to be found. There are 30 Earnhardts in that local phone book with Dale Earnhardt on the cover. We resist the impulse to call them all. How the mourners and the seekers and the stalkers must exhaust them.

We go to Vinnie's, a restaurant and bar out on the lake. This is where the drivers and the crews hang out, especially on Wednesday nights. Pit Lizards and popcorn shrimp. Junior doesn't show, but we meet a racer with a great racer name, Jimmy Kitchens. He has an open, emphatic face and is as earnest as a good handshake. He's up from Alabama, and he was the stuff 10 or 15 years ago on the tracks near Birmingham, but has struggled ever since. He lives in a small, nearly empty apartment not far from here. Into his forties now, he drives or crews for the fringe teams in Busch and Truck. Couple hundred bucks a weekend. He has, by his own accounting, nothing. "Every year I tell myself to hang on one more year," he says, "So I do. I'll get there."

We drive past the brand-new NASCAR Training Institute, a school for mechanics and future crewmen gouged out of the woods not far from Lancaster's BBQ. We drive through the empty "lifestyle mall" down the highway, where folks can buy a condo above the Williams-Sonoma or the Banana Republic, and live in a merchandising diorama in the middle of a cornfield, the latest reinvention of the citizen-consumer. We see Ryan Newman on his way into the AmStar-14 theater one night (*8 Mile*? *I Spy*? *Red Dragon*?), and scores of crewmen at the coffee shop, but Junior eludes us.

We visit the Levine Museum of the New South down in Charlotte, across the street from the Comedy Zone. The New South is now 137 years old.

We drive through Kannapolis, a town built by Cannon Mills a hundred years ago. Those mills have gone dark and quiet now after a series of crippling bankruptcies. It was once part of the New South, too. Over at the ballpark, the name of the local minor-league team is "The Intimidators."

We drive over to the Petty operation and museum in Level Cross, North Carolina. On a 7-mile stretch of state Route 62 headed east you'll pass the Friendship Baptist Church and the Cornerstone Baptist Church and the Sure Foundation Baptist Church and the Not Ashamed Baptist Church. The crosses hereabouts are small, and Jesus is no King Kong. He is the skinny scarecrow Jesus or the hot Tom Cruise Jesus.

The Petty shop has been at their family home for four generations. Behind a run of white fence like a horse farm, the house where Richard Petty was born isn't 50 feet from the low, white sheds where the teams bang together the cars. The museum is a long wood-paneled room, and if you walk all the way to the back, past the curling pictures and the yellowed clippings and the trophies gone to tarnish, there's a display of Adam Petty's few mementoes. It makes you angry and sad at the same time. On the way out you can make a donation to the sick kids camp the Pettys want to open in his name.

Coming into Martinsville, five races left in the season, the points race shakes out like this:

Tony Stewart	4,128
Jimmie Johnson	4,031
Mark Martin	4,006
Ryan Newman	3,963
Rusty Wallace	3,946
Jeff Gordon	3,917
Matt Kenseth	3,823
Bill Elliott	3,787
Kurt Busch	3,766
Ricky Rudd	3,758

You can swing 50 or 60 points up or down pretty easily in a single race. Dale Earnhardt Jr. is thirteenth in points, and probably won't win the championship this year, but over the course of the season he has undeniably become the sport's biggest, most salable star. There are seven championships among the drivers in front of him on the list. His marketability has eclipsed them all.

Racing at Martinsville is all bumpers and brakes and the day is a 12-caution mayhem. But everyone's still in it until lap 400, when new arrival Hideo Fukuyama spins untouched and hammers the World Berries car into the wall. "Banzai!" yell the press boxers. Fukuyama, a racer from Japan, arrived out here two-thirds of the way through the season to drive a few short-track races. Brought a sponsor with him, too. He doesn't speak a word of English, but he's got a smile on him like the pope of Pepsodent, and he's obviously having the time of his life. "It is an honor just to be here," he says, beaming, through his translator. The elephants refer to him jokingly as "that good ol' Japanese boy."

But the elephants grow angry when they spot a Dale Earnhardt impersonator circulating below them in section HH of the grandstands. The guy's name is Danny, he's down from Lynchburg, and people tell him "all the time" that he "looks more like Dale than Dale." He's wearing the full Goodwrench drag too, and the Gargoyle sunglasses. He takes photos with the fans for fun and they seem to like it. The pachyderms are not amused. "That's not right," they say. "That's *way* worse than an Elvis impersonator."

Kurt Busch keeps his battered car intact long enough to win. Tony Stewart maintains his points lead.

Mike and Dean. Those aren't their real names, but they were real enough and they were parked next to us out in the holler past the railroad tracks that run parallel to the Martinsville backstretch. You have to wait for the coal train to pass to walk into the track.

The weather for the weekend is good enough, but the ground is soaked from rain. People sit and watch the new arrivals pull in, watch the family motorhomes getting stuck in the mud.

"That motherfucker's sunk."

That's the first I heard from Mike and Dean. They had eased in to the space next to us Thursday afternoon, and before they even began to unpack, they were dogging the ignorant and unfortunate, the ones who didn't get out of their rigs to check the soft ground before they tried to park. Just then they were right—some old booger in a 40-foot periwinkle blue Executive Dream had bogged himself hub deep in the mud. Nobody much walked over to help, just stood and stared, because you couldn't push something that big out with just a strong back and your good intentions; they'd have to wait for a tow truck or somebody with a 4-by-4 and a winch, which was nearly everybody, to come around and horse them out.

Mike and Dean didn't have much unpacking to do. They were doing the whole weekend in the back of a pickup truck with a canvas tent set over it. Once they got the tent up and the flaps rolled back it looked like a covered wagon, the chuck rig on a cattle drive. They had a couple of cots and sleeping bags up in there, too, and a folding propane stove set on the tailgate. They would toilet up at the shower house. Mostly.

They had six cases of Miller Lite stacked neatly by the left rear wheel, and two more chilling in coolers, which were 8 or 10 feet from our door, so they would be our neighbors on that side. From what I could tell they had nothing to eat but potato chips and canned chili.

They were both bruisers in their late thirties, Mike the taller of the two at about 6 foot 3 and Dean an inch or two short of that. Couple hundred pounds each. They were both broad through the chest and belly, muscular, with thick forearms and chapped, freckled hands. Jeans and T-shirts on both, Carhartt jackets, work boots. Dean wore his sandy hair cropped high and tight to his skull and had a drooping brush mustache; Mike had brown hair, longer, combed straight back and hadn't shaved for a couple of days.

I was in and out that day, back and forth to the track to work. On the first trip past them I introduced myself. After that I made a point of saying hello to them as I came and went, or maybe I just waved or ducked my head in a nod. They always waved or nodded back, the etiquette of the NASCAR campsite ritually observed: Everyone's a good neighbor until they prove themselves otherwise.

They weren't loud, in fact they were quieter than most, but there was something unsettling about them, some alpha tough-guy vibe they both gave off that went way beyond the norm.

The tough-guy pose was everywhere out here all the time, of course, a thing young men and boys put on right before they came to the track, like a Home Depot T-shirt or a Budweiser cap. It was part of the uniform of the American adolescent male: the feigned scowl, the gunfighter squint, trying to look hard and indecipherable and sexy. A strategy for attracting the dollies without having to say too much.

Mike and Dean, though, weren't high school boys; nor were the hard eyes a fashion item. Every time you got near them the horizon tipped a little toward something you weren't sure you wanted to see.

Friday evening on my way back from the press center I stopped by their tailgate for a while to get their stories. Mike and Dean were unemployed machinists down from Michigan. They'd stopped over in Pennsylvania looking for tool-and-die work on the way south to Martinsville.

"Lookin' for work sucks, but it's nice to be on the road," Mike said.

"Yeah, and we're both getting divorced, too, so it's nice to get away from all *that* bullshit for a while," Dean said.

"You guys are getting divorced at the same time?" I asked.

"Just the way it worked out," Mike said; "we managed to get fed the fuck up at the same time, is all."

It was getting colder at night now, and the ground mist was heavy and starting to settle on the fields. They were both wearing hooded sweatshirts under their jackets. "You guys going to be warm enough tonight?"

"Hell, yeah, we're fine."

"It was good last night, the sleeping bags and stuff, real good, I thought. Kinda cold when you walk out to piss is all."

"Maybe you didn't drink so much beer, you wouldn't have to piss so much."

"Look who's talkin'. Jesus, but this man was drunk last night."

"Not like you I wasn't."

"We were both pretty hammered. Part of the fun of comin' to the races is the parties. Sort of lock ourselves in here and nothin' bad can really happen to you, right? I mean, there aren't many cops around and you're walkin' everywhere, so you can do what you want without gettin' hassled for it."

"Hey, watch this," and Mike pointed off into the darkness, where another late-comer was trying to squeeze a 35-footer into a 24-foot space and about to get stuck front and rear in the mud doing it. "Dumb fuck," Dean said. We listened to the engine race for a minute, up and down, that turbo-diesel scream, whoever it was trying to spin themselves out of trouble but only getting in deeper. After a time it went quiet again. You could see people gathering in the headlights, pointing down at the wheels. I asked how long they'd been fans.

"What," Dean said, "maybe twenty years, I guess."

"Maybe that for me, too, more than fifteen. I don't know. Seems like a long time."

Who did they root for?

"We pull for Rusty Wallace, both of us, more me than him, but Rusty, yeah," said Dean. I asked why.

"Man, I don't know. I've just always liked him. Real old-school, I guess."

"He was comin' up the same time we came into it, and I guess I hitched onto him then. But I follow Junior, now, too."

It was dinnertime, so I got ready to walk the 10 feet home. I asked what they were going to do for their big Friday night.

"Just walk around," Dean said, "find some trouble."

"Or let her find us," Mike added.

Saturday night I saw them outside heating their chili. "You guys have any fun last night?" I asked.

"Guess it depends on what you mean by fun," said Mike, unsmiling, drinking a beer and stirring chili.

"We had some fun, I think, what I can remember of it," Dean said. They were halfway between hungover and drunk again. They were wearing the same clothes they'd worn the day before and the day before that. They looked like the last two men out of a mine collapse. They were down to their last three cases of beer. "Didn't feel too good when we got up, but we're comin' around again. Do you want some chili or something? We're gonna eat then go up grab a shower."

"No, thanks, we're going to eat in a couple of minutes ourselves. What'd you guys wind up doing?"

"We just walked around for a while," said Mike, "and then we stayed at a party for a while over there," and he gestured with his beer out to the farther campgrounds, "and then we came back."

"Biiiiig party," said Dean. "Must have been a hundred people there. Smoked a couple bowls, drank some beers. And we had a great time 'til my boy here got into it with some local."

Mike didn't say anything.

"What happened?" I asked

"Wasn't much," Dean said, "Mike just got into it with a guy about some girl and we came home."

Mike took a pull of beer and said, "This guy wanted to hook me up with a friend of his, but I told him I couldn't go with her 'cause I was on probation is all. Then he wouldn't let go of it."

"She was young, I guess," Dean offered.

"Damn right she was young. Too young, and so I said, 'Man, I appreciate it, but I'm on probation right now in the first place and I can't go near her.'"

"But the guy keeps after him on the probation, right?" Dean says, and they're both telling it while the chili sputters and pops.

"Yeah, he's all curious about it and what for and like that and I don't wanna talk about it, but he won't shut up."

"Would not shut up," Dean adds, "So you finally say to him . . ."

"And I finally say to him, 'Dude, just please shut the fuck up,' but he won't."

"So Mike tags him."

"Just the once, but he had it comin'."

"He had it comin'."

"And then we came back here. It was late anyhow."

Turns out Mike's on probation for a DUI back in Michigan. "That was all a big fuckup is all that was," he says, "it wasn't ever serious. If we could've got the car outta the swamp before the fucking cops got there, we'd of been fine." And a misdemeanor resisting. He shouldn't be anywhere south of Ann Arbor.

"You know it's just the whole fucking thing sometimes," Mike says, taking the chili off the grill and banging spoonfuls onto a couple of plastic plates, then sitting on the tailgate and lighting a cigarette. He smoked for a minute or two while Dean began eating. "It's the whole fucked-up, fucking thing. I do not ask for this when I go out, I do not, but there it is. Christ, I even get it at home, and I *know* I'm not asking for it there." He didn't sound angry, just tired. I asked him what he meant.

"I don't know, just that, you know, there's so much bullshit to wade through sometimes."

Dean nodded. It sounded like something they'd talked about before.

"You know, like work. We can't find any work. Tonks took all the jobs. Can't find anything for skilled work anywhere."

"Tonks?"

"You know, Tonks. Smokes. 'Tonk' is the sound the billy club makes when you hit a nigger on the head with it. But you can't say that anymore, so now we call 'em Tonks."

Dean nodded again.

"So, you know, you got no job and no, what, outlook, for another one, and your wife throws you out of your own fucking house and then you come down here to have some fun and wind up trapped in somebody else's crazy bullshit again." Mike crushed the cigarette out with his boot and began eating.

"I'll let you guys eat in peace," I said. "Have fun tonight. I'll probably see you at the track tomorrow."

"Sure," Dean said, "you too."

I missed them in the grandstands on Sunday, but I saw them that evening after the race. They were sitting on the coolers. All the beer was gone. They looked sunburned and dehydrated, spent. Before I went inside I stopped to ask if they needed anything. Mike couldn't even hold his head up.

"No," Dean said, "we're fine. We just maybe partied a little too hard last night is all, and then we were out at the track all day, you know, in the sun. That's what you get, right? I mean, we had it comin'."

When we left the next morning they were still asleep.

Like Charlotte, Atlanta wrestles with its Old South–New South issues: what to keep of the one and what to abandon of the other. Up in Charlotte the result's an insistent neutrality, a downtown so quick to dismiss its own history that it's been left without an identity. It feels like it could be anywhere, or everywhere—a place to change planes.

Atlanta takes the opposite approach, and rolls everything left of its history right out front where folks can keep an eye on it. E.g., we pass part of the week at a campground in the Atlanta suburbs, beneath Stone Mountain, the world's largest mass of exposed granite says the brochure, where the heroic figures of Robert E. Lee and Stonewall Jackson and Jefferson Davis are chiseled into the rock many hundreds of feet high. At night there's a laser show.

A day later, downtown, we visit Dr. Martin Luther King's memorial and the Ebenezer Baptist Church on Auburn Avenue. There is no laser show of which I'm aware.

And while I know what the Lincoln scholars and the Sons of Dixie will say, that the War Between the States was never about race but about states' rights and macroeconomy and the needs of union, what to make of a place that can hold these two opposing thoughts in its big Buckhead at once?

Baffled, we hasten to the track.

A quick disquisition on race in racing. This year there is one African American driver running in any of the top three NASCAR circuits. That's 1 in about 150. His name is Bill Lester. He has a ride in the Craftsman truck series and runs high in the midpack consistently, about where the quality of his equipment should have him. He is not the only man or woman of color out here, there are African American crewmen and officials and fans after all, but the sport remains, on the track and in the grandstands, overwhelmingly, blindingly white.

I feel sorry for Bill Lester when I see him on local TV, responding resolutely to interviewers' questions about race in racing. Every track he visits it's the same. I'm pretty sure he just wants to drive the race-car, not bear the weight of the nation's racial baggage every time he climbs from the car. "I'm living the dream," he'll say sometimes, and the reporter nods gravely, as if something's been resolved.

NASCAR may or may not have good intentions when it comes to enlivening the sport's palette, but its record on the matter of color is abysmal. Every year, it seems, there's a new initiative on diversity, and serial press conferences announcing its corporate rededication to minorities. But the initiatives and the announcements and the press releases come and go and nothing seems to change. For a while they even paid Jesse Jackson and PUSH to consult for them, but stopped signing the checks when the fans rose up and cried extortion.

Paradoxically, just as the northern African American middle class is returning to Atlanta and the New South in great numbers, a Great Migration in reverse, NASCAR is busy exporting the traditional comforts of its Old South medicine show north and east and west. Welcome to NASCAR! Please reset your watches to 1957.

The race today was a rain-shortened, rain-delayed 200-mile-an-hour drowse, Kurt Busch running out front whenever he chose to in a very fast #97 car. Kurt Busch is your winner. Tony Stewart leads the points.

It was wet in Atlanta, and the jet driers were roaring on the track and you couldn't hear a word. The rain had stopped and so had the wind, but now the clouds weren't moving and mist sagged cold out of a low gray sky, and the air was heavy with humidity and gloom.

They wore matching short-sleeved CAT shirts. CAT being short for Caterpillar, a maker and renter and financer of heavy equipment, and the sponsor of Ward Burton's #22 Dodge. CAT's famous color scheme is black and bulldozer yellow with royal red trim. The pastor, a pale man, wore a dark charcoal suit and a checkered-flag tie. Against the gray scale of the asphalt and the stands and the pastor and the sky, then, the bride and groom were as festive as trout lilies wrapped in newspaper.

They were getting married in Victory Lane. Couples get married at tracks all around the circuit all the time. Sometimes a dozen at a crack. Sometimes it looks like fun.

This was Friday at 1 P.M. on race weekend in October. The groom wore his CAT colors and a precisely blocked black bull-rider cowboy hat and black jeans. Incongruously, he was wearing puffy white sneakers, as if on his way to Jazzercise class. He was in his forties, heavyset, and with a gray goatee. Tattooed on his right forearm was the name Crystal. He seemed nervous.

The bride wore the same black jeans and swollen white sneakers with her backhoe/skid loader/bucket-shovel shirt, but had no hat. She was a few years younger than the groom but of like size, both of them built to the same heavy-duty earth-moving specifications as the sponsor's equipment. Her dark brown hair was feather-cut in the roller boogie style of the late 1970s and she carried no flowers.

At 1:07 Ward Burton himself arrived. In addition to standing witness at the wedding of strangers, it was his forty-first birthday, as specified in the press release. After the wedding there would be a multipurpose cake. For the occasion he was wearing his CAT driver's suit, also bright yellow and black, with cherry-red fire rising on the legs and the sleeves, the flames licking at his hands and feet. He is a small, tidy man, and as he walked toward the pastor and the bride and groom he picked his way around the puddles with his tiny studded driver's shoes. His wife walked beside him holding up an umbrella. He took his place as best man and wore the expression of someone with a sharp seed stuck between his teeth.

There were five or ten of us there watching from the Victory Lane fence—drawn by boredom and the rain delay and the press release—and a bare handful of people up in the stands. A pair of photographers splashed around taking pictures of the couple and taking pictures of each other taking pictures of the couple. The publicists who'd arranged this late-season photo-op stood off to one side talking, cupping their hands over each other's ear to do so.

At 1:10 the bride and groom joined hands and the pastor's lips began moving, but you couldn't hear anything because race officials had to dry the track for practice and the jet driers, which move very slowly, were right there on the frontstretch for the entire ceremony. It was like a wedding on the outbound flight line at Atlanta International.

The pastor's lips kept moving and he swiveled his head from one to the other and he spoke, I'm sure, of the holy nature of this solemn union and the need for love and trust and respect in marriage, and of the permanence and transcendence of the human spirit intertwined, and about the necessary work of understanding between husband and wife, and of patience and of passion, and how valuable a thing is courage, as well as honesty and fortitude, and how in good times and bad it always helps to have a sense of humor, and of the responsibility and honor that fell now from heaven to them both. He looked likely to say those things, but I'll never really know because all I could hear was the scream and blast from those jet engines.

At 1:13 Ward Burton handed the groom a ring and he slipped it on the bride's finger. At 1:14 the four of them bowed their heads in prayer. At 1:15 the couple kissed and the pastor smiled and raised his hand and presented the newlyweds to the world and a polite round of silent applause, every face changed now except Burton's, the whole thing mimed in the deafening air-strike roar from that fleet of captive turbines. Passing at last, they blew a gale and the mist flew and swirled and everyone hurried inside for cake.

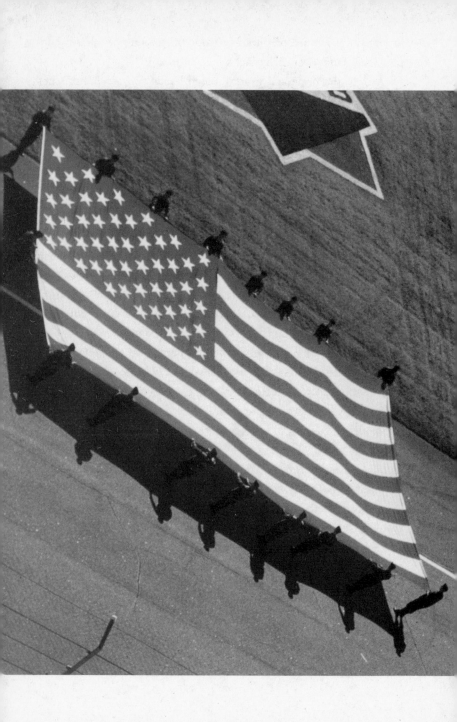

THIRTEEN

Back to modest Rockingham and boil p-nut country.

On Saturday, Jimmy Kitchens works the Busch race pits for the #44 car, to be driven by Mike Harmon. It is a shoestring team with a bad car and an improvised crew, everybody too young or too old and wearing mismatched helmets and coveralls. They don't have enough tires. The matte black car carries a one-race sponsorship from Elizabeth Dole, currently running for the U.S. Senate as a native daughter of North Carolina. The crew's radio goes out almost immediately, so every time Harmon pits, it's a surprise to his crew. Unlike the Cup teams, with their gymnastic, tightly choreographed 15-second stops, the service here is at once frantic and slow, the car sometimes idling anxiously for nearly a minute to take on fuel and another set of lightly used tires begged from other teams. They end the day 16 laps down, in thirty-sixth.

Jimmy finds a way to sound upbeat. "We finished, at least," and he high-fives the rest of the pickup crew and walks back to the hauler to help put away the tired racecar. The half-empty grandstands got a look at the sponsor's name for a few hours, which is the point, after all. Not that the crowd needs much reminding to vote Republican. The NASCAR fan base, in addition to its arctic whiteness, is also very conservative. Asked to point out a Democrat or two, Richard Petty chuckles. "You'd have a tough time finding any out here."

Over in the Cup garage, the topic is mathematics, not politics. With three races to go, Martin and Johnson still have a solid chance to unseat Stewart for the season points championship.

•   •   •

The rest of Saturday afternoon is occupied by the World Championship Pit Crew competition. There are no teams here from Norway or Argentina, but most of the Cup front-runners take a turn. Four tires and fuel, fast as you can—the usual. The teams take this contest very seriously, there's prize money on the line, and bragging rights, and the late day snarls with cars in and out for 18 seconds at a time. Matt Kenseth's crew wins for the second straight year: 16.823 seconds. Their catchcan man dropped the fuel overflow bucket as the car screamed away, a clear violation, but was docked no time. One expects controversy, argument, appeal, but strangely no one says a word. In fact, the prevailing vibe around the pits and the motorhome compound and the garages and the grandstands these days is one of perfect fatigue and resignation and let's get it over with. The NASCAR schedule, as the flacks never tire of telling you, is "the longest season in professional sports!" With three weeks to go you feel every day of it.

Sunday is bright sunshine and easy summer. It is the third day of November and the stands are about two-thirds full.

At the halfway point, 200 laps along, Tony Stewart is thirty-second, two laps down with a terrible car. Martin is running second, behind his teammate Kurt Busch. If they stopped it right now, there'd be a huge points swing. Of course they don't stop it and the afternoon grinds on. The sky goes gray at about three-thirty. Martin is still running near the front, Stewart near the rear. With 30 laps to go, Johnny Benson in the Valvoline car eases into the lead. Martin is second, Busch third. Stewart is nineteenth. Johnny Benson, with no victories in over 200 starts, holds up and is your surprise winner today. He is showered with popcorn in Victory Lane, this being the Pop Secret 400. Benson is ecstatic and his wife cries and everyone feels good for them both. Martin finishes second, Busch third. Tony Stewart is fourteenth. Jimmie Johnson, who burned up a hub on lap 379, 16 short of the checkered flag, finishes thirty-seventh. Stewart's running bad. Martin's running good. And Martin, after 20 years, ever the bridesmaid, is within 112 points of his first championship. For a day.

On the Monday following the race, it is announced that Martin's team is being docked 25 points for running an illegal front spring. The suspension piece in question may or may not have improved his performance; it may, in fact, have hurt it. Whether it was inadvertently installed or constitutes a cunning cheat is immaterial. Despite the sport's well-advertised Christian underpinnings, everybody cheats all the time out here, *everybody*. But it was an unapproved part and NASCAR chose to bust them on it. NASCAR also invokes section 12-4-A, actions detrimental to stock-car racing, its catchall, when it hands down the ruling.

And that heavy metaphorical horseshoe lands squarely on Martin's foot.

This was the second time in his career that a late-season penalty had forced Martin back in the standings with a championship within reach, and the press, off the record, knows it's over. "He's done," I hear one say. "I mean, it's Mark Martin, right?"

He'll appeal the ruling, of course, and the points race will get plenty of excited play in the headlines and on television, and the mathematical combinations and permutations of the next two events will be explained and explored and recalculated again and again, but there's a weird sense of futility and insincerity to the entire exercise, because up in the press box nobody's really buying it. Barring cataclysmic fireball, the championship will belong to Tony Stewart.

Seeing these crowds week in and week out you could imagine the web of intimacies and enmities that bound every individual to the next. Through those grandstands ran all the synaptic wiring for the battered American nervous system, sparking with every human impulse, firing lightning down every row of seats. And radiating up from it all the heat and energy of the entire angry hive, the whole restless collective.

"These are the people who fight our wars" is the way it had always been put out here, the highest compliment imaginable from a beaming track owner or NASCAR executive, sweeping his arm across the seething grandstands whenever some visiting Ivy Leaguer on anthro-safari asked about the race-day fan base. Now, though, in a world newly shadowed with darkness and loss, The Show was more than theater.

Every Cup event everywhere was being staged in a daze of jingoistic hyperpatriotism; starched flags snapping in the breeze, with music and prayers heavy on the war drums and that Old Testament kung fu, 100,000 fans rampant, sending up a fearsome shout-out to sweet two-fisted Jesus.

In the weekly prerace ritual you could feel the whole frightened country tightening like a fist. Call it what it was: the drumbeat of payback's-a-bitch, retribution music, a rhythm pounding sore and steady as an abscess, and we rode it, month after month, the entire season.

You could see the next war in it even then, hear it coming, a year before we pulled the trigger. You couldn't miss it, even if you didn't know which way to look or which war we'd fight, there it was, all around you in the honor guards and the booming flyovers, the bellicose benedictions and the defiant music and the thundering fireworks, hat over your heart for the anthem and standing razor-straight no matter how drunk you were, or how cynical or disaffected, you were swept along by it, swept up in it, unquestioning, it was like seeing the American flag for the first time some weekends, and a hundred thousand throats tightening with pride or sadness or Mother Love, love of country and love of freedom and love of horsepower and of Wal-Mart and Junior and Tony and little Mark Martin and every other thing and before you knew it your eyes were wet with patriotism and your heart bent to every loss and went out to every 9-11 widow and sank for every corrupted American body on every battlefield since first Manassas, and sweet Christ, the firefighters and the cops, too, gone! the heroes of every Boomer's second-grade reader, gone in the endless instant playing over and over on the national video loop, that fire blooming again and again and the black smoke flowering, and the buildings and all those people falling, you couldn't get any of it out of your head even if you wanted to. Those people were still falling and so were you, you could feel the floor dropping out from under all of us, the rush of bad velocity in the pit of your stomach, you couldn't stop feeling it, and the networks and NASCAR and the White House and the Pentagon wouldn't let you if you tried, we were all still falling, the whole country, all you had to do was look around at the Osama Fucks His Mama bumper stickers or the bootleg NYFD T-shirts or the Never Again 9-11 Twin Towers murals airbrushed on some of the motorhomes, hellfire and kerosene smoke and shame mushrooming into a Tiffany-blue American sky, to know that laying waste to an already wasted Afghanistan would satisfy no one and that rounding up and dry-shaving a few thousand Taliban goatherds wasn't ever going to be enough. We were hurt and we were scared and somehow someone somewhere was going to be made to pay for it.

I'm down along the walkway behind the pits. Hundreds of people: cops, crewmen, firemen, fans. It's a whirlpool of color, smell, noise, commotion, confusion, flesh, heat, light. I hear the lull of the benediction over the loudspeakers. "God the Father, we are your children . . ." The amplified prayer sounds digitized and inhuman, shot through with electrons, "hmmmmm, we ask your blessings hmmmm. . . ," like it's echoing down into the bowl from another planet, "hmmmm-mmm, and grace for their safety . . . hmmmmmm, Ah-men." Here comes the anthem. Everyone looks around, locks on the flag.

Even the drunken daddies on top of the campers in the infield put down their MGD Lights, clap hands over their shirtless hearts, and stand straight as they can. Every hat comes off.

An opera singer delivers the anthem straight-up and funkless, with a workmanlike application of Juilliard elbow grease. It's the kind of singing you rarely hear anymore, beautiful and square, nearly chaste, a great voice drawing right angles around the sort of unsexed musical arrangement you hear only at Christian beauty pageants and Marine Band benefit concerts in these voluptuous and filigreed times.

Two-thirds of the way through the song, the eagles are set loose.

They fly up and up on a slow pulse of muscle and music and symbolism, weightless and grave, unblinking, banking silent above the crowd, above our squalid human foolishness, borne aloft by the force of unspoken hope. They glide gracefully home, fold themselves seamlessly back onto the arm of the handlers, returned to the hood and the cage and the luxuries of their confinement.

What chokes me up as the birds rise and fly isn't just patriotism. It's the sudden awareness of the breadth of my own crippling skepticism in relation to my patriotism. I love my country very much and I very much wish that loving it were as simple as cheering when they set loose that pair of captive eagles.

Somewhere the fireworks start blasting. Smoke bombs and flash pots thumping, the place as loud as you can imagine anyplace anywhere to be, you feel a rumble under your shoes. It's not the crowd noise. It's not the artillery report of the black-powder charges, either. Those you feel like the hard pressure of deep water. It's not even the cars. This is a rumble. Tectonic. Subaudible.

All at once that rumble bursts up out of the ground and explodes a thunderclap out of a clear sky. It's the flyover, four matte-gray F-16s in close formation with the burners lit, 200 feet off the deck at 400 miles an hour pouring out jet exhaust and screaming deafness across the breadth of Volusia County. The wind in the faraway palms shrieks like a steelmill furnace.

In the wake of the turbine howl from the vanishing jets, I can hear and feel the serial concussions from the last salvo of fireworks. People all around me are flinching, ducking, cringing. It's like being strafed. The smell of cordite billows across the infield.

They haven't even started the race yet and the afternoon's already bursting through that grandstand nervous system, those hundreds of thousands of faces out of Bosch or Brueghel all shuddering with the tension and spasm and sweet release of tantric patriotism.

I turn to a guy standing a few feet away from me on the other side of the pit lane chain-link. He's still looking up, following the flight of the planes as they make for the horizon. He's a tough-looking mother in his late forties, 6-foot-3 or -4, a gut-sprung 225, worn leather biker gear top to bottom and a salt-and-pepper beard on him like ZZ Rasputin. Got his Oakleys pushed back on his head and his meaty right hand is still fanned out over his heart. I look up at the planes too, tip my chin that way, and shout, "Our tax dollars at work, huh?"

He turns to me. Looks down through the beard, spent, emptied, blue-eyed and red-faced in the heat. "Damn straight," he says, "damn straight," as the tears course down his cheeks.

"Gentlemen, start . . . your . . . engines!" A second later they fire the cars.

I should have known better than to joke. In America it wasn't funny and never really had been, in any variation, because to get the joke you had to acknowledge that you, that all of us, are the butt of it. "Our tax dollars at work." Even if the knowing throwaway was delivered by Stone Age headliners like Twain or Mencken or Rogers, Hope or Benny, you could never really laugh at it, you could only wince when the punchline boomeranged and hit you in the face, because to get the gag at all was to understand that we were doomed forever to be our own worst enemies.

And here we all were, caught on the wrong end of a 900-year-old blood feud. After the shock of what had happened the year before, could it be anything but a comfort and a balm to see those planes? Week in and out, the whole dark arsenal flew past, everything in the inventory: F-14s, F-15s, F-16s, F-18s, B-1s, B-2s, B-52s, and C-130s and the tankers and the transports and the attack helicopters. Here was America, painted matte gray, flying low and sure and fast in front of heartbroken Americans. And the question all season long, at every track, in every campground, in every state we found ourselves, was the same. "Why do they hate us?"

I learned to keep my mouth shut about the flyovers.

Homeland, Motherland, Fatherland, the expressions on our faces said everything. Anger. Resolve. Eye for an eye. That was the message we sent up the chain, all of us, all the way to the threat rooms and the war rooms and the blast bunkers under Washington. Lead us. Let's roll. *Git some.* Our faces and our voices and our fear authorized and sanctified everything that might follow. Those five minutes before each race were an object lesson in earnestness hard-earned, in willingness and love and sadness. The run-up to the green flag wasn't just hackneyed pregame sports pro forma anymore. The moment had become instead, at last, a national sacrament.

Flung west one last time by NASCAR's tortured calendar, past the J's and the Jesus, we've rolled into the awkward, asymmetrical 1-mile oval at Phoenix. A strange track, slow for its size and half-flat in the turns, it's an important stop on the tour because it serves the ever-expanding Sunbelt. The racing isn't very good here, but Phoenix and the desert Southwest are fantastically important growth markets for NASCAR. That the mushrooming population is made up almost entirely of displaced persons, including lots of folks who fled the rotting economy of the New South, makes NASCAR's job a little easier. Stock-car racing's a natural sell. It's nice to see some Hispanic and Native American faces around the garages for a change, too.

Managed at last to answer a deep, season-long mystery in the press center today when I went online. Announcer Darrell Waltrip's skull-splitting catchphrase, the words "boogity, boogity, boogity," comes from the lyrics of the early sixties hit, "Who Put the Bomp (in the Bomp, Bomp, Bomp)?" by Barry Mann, who later wrote "You've Lost that Lovin' Feeling." Go figure.

With Ryan Newman on the pole, the field sets off and plods away for the next 2 hours, 44 minutes, and 25 seconds. Newman and Junior Earnhardt dominate the first 100 laps, trading the lead between them. Junior runs out of gas on lap 118, an unforgivable lapse in pit savvy and track math by him and his crew. Up in the NBC booth, color man Benny Parsons is incredulous. "This can't be happening!" And yet it is, and it is the only interesting moment to that point in a race distinguished only by its rhythmic deliberation.

Kenseth and Gordon lead briefly, then Kurt Busch, who leads the middle third of the race unchallenged. Martin and Johnson struggle to the front. Tony Stewart orbits just outside the Top 10. The wives and girlfriends watch from the top of the toolboxes, Katie Kenseth keeping lap times using a pen with a plastic daisy at its top, Pattie Petty, stylish and barefoot as always, watching Kyle cycle through the afternoon. Kurt Busch's girlfriend, his high school sweetheart, is wearing sandals with heels like daggers.

The crowd reawakens briefly when McMurray crashes out on lap 253, then rolls over and closes its eyes. As they snore and twitch, Matt Kenseth inherits the lead from Johnny Benson. With 50 laps to go he keeps it and wins. Rusty Wallace is second, Jeff Gordon third. Mark Martin finishes fourth, but to no avail. Tony Stewart has come in eighth, and only a very complex set of circumstances, like Stewart being abducted by aliens, can bring Martin the championship now.

She was beautiful. Was she 16 or 17? Twenty-five? Thirty? Is it even possible in the NASCAR/Britney Nation to have a sense of such things? This was at Phoenix, the desert track set against the base of that small mountain along the Gila River and the bunchgrass and the cactus and the sagebrush shimmering in every direction for miles in that clean, dry heat under a high, electric sun and a sky as simple and emphatic as a cornflower petal.

She was standing in the infield—this must have been Saturday afternoon, the Busch race echoing off the hills—and the crowds seemed to bend around her like water. And even though the young woman's features were outlined in sharp relief by the bright slant of the desert sun, and even though there were hundreds and hundreds of people there, if you watched her for a few minutes the crowds flowing past her blurred and were softened somehow, everyone becoming vague and losing their light and their faces and their specificity to hers, until the effect was that of a young actress alone under a spotlight on a darkened stage. She seemed not to notice this.

She was alone, and must have been waiting for someone, because every so often she would turn very slowly and scan that featureless crowd as it surged past her. There was no impatience in her face.

She was smoking, and she would bring the cigarette to her mouth with long, straight fingers. Her nails were not manicured, but they were well kept. She wore several silver rings on each hand. Thin silver bracelets on both wrists..

She was of medium height and stunningly made, 5 foot 6 or 7 and maybe 125 pounds. She had hair that fell in fat cascades of auburn and brown and gold to her shoulders. Her face was a smooth, flawless oval. Huge dark eyes. High, pale forehead and a blush in her cheeks. Her lips were fine and uncomplicated and she wore a soft coral lip gloss.

She wore black sandals with heels. She wore a single toe ring on the ring toe of each foot. She wore an orange belly shirt and low-rise acid-washed jeans that rose only barely to the swell of her hips. She had a pierced navel and wore an elaborate, dangling belly ring.

She was phenomenally attractive, and every man in the crowd turned to her as they passed. Some of them wore clear expressions of want and others tried to catch her eye and others slowed or stopped for a few seconds, just staring, until the crowd swept them along. She smoked and waited.

Her face was a perfect mask, every mystery of youth and ancient power hidden behind it. Here was the new American Sphinx. You saw them everywhere at the races, the silent daughters of Madison Avenue and Ventura Boulevard, ultrasexualized, at once omnipotent and clueless, a construct out of magazines and movies and music videos, the Gap and Old Navy; the knowing innocent, the porn queen/prom queen, the virgin slut, latest creation and casualty of mass culture. She was someone's daughter, someone's sister, she was loved by someone somewhere for who she was, not what she wore, had consciousness and perhaps a vibrant mind and heart; but to the men who stared as they passed, she was only the flawless unattainable, the transcendent salvation fuck they'd longed for since high school. Her thoughts, her dreams and fears were unknown to them, and immaterial. Love her, cherish her, use her, abandon her, she was the root and solution to every one of their problems and the cause and consequence of every prayer they'd ever spoken. She was the first love and the last gasp, absolution and dissolution.

Did she know what she was doing? What *was* she doing? Anything? Nothing? Just standing in the sun. But she was somehow the model product of her age, an object of sublime immodesty, mute and inscrutable. She seemed an object nonetheless. Or perhaps she really was an innocent, a victim of free enterprise, citizen in a nation run by 50-year-old men with their hand on the babysitter's knee. Another madonna squandered.

I wondered for a long time standing there if any of us understood the cultural or economic forces at work on her, or copped to our own culpability in it, all that national appetite lapping up the soft-core marketing savvy pouring out of those corner offices in Burbank and Manhattan, where it was just good business to sell jailbait sex back to all of us disguised as everything from the career of Christina Aguilera to the latest fashion for juniors and young misses. I wondered if she'd had any choice as to who she was, or if she'd been molded into this version of herself by the fantastic heat and pressure of this American world. I wondered if I felt these things out of sadness for her or resentment or pity or fear of her incredible, possibly mindless, power. I wondered what could ever become of her.

As I wondered, the only man there who dared keep her waiting arrived. He was in his late twenties, I suppose, and dressed in a kind of hip-hop mourning: baggy black denim pants, black jacket, black T-shirt, black work boots, black #3 ballcap, visor aft. How hot that gear must have been here in the desert. He had his hair pulled into a ponytailed mullet and wore wraparound sunglasses. He was about 6 feet tall, slim, and had to bend just a little to kiss her. She stretched to him. That's when I saw it.

There, below the belly ring, half-hidden where the waistband of her jeans had been cut away to allow them to ride even lower, arced a tattoo.

The lettering was done in vibrant green and yellow, in a kind of antique playbill type, elaborate and Victorian, the sort of thing you'd have seen a hundred years ago on the sign above the door of a Broadway nickelodeon or on the window of a North Point saloon. It wasn't small, but it took a moment or two to figure out. It read:

Lucky You

Back swift across the South on the I-10, all the way to Miami, back to Florida bobbing witless and limp in the tub of the Caribbean: 45,648 miles so far.

The math's been done and in this last race of the season Tony Stewart needs to finish twenty-second or better to take the crown. There are other variations, too complex to mention, in which Mark Martin could win—the aforementioned interplanetary kidnapping or long-shot parade lap fireball and so forth—but race day in the garages, despite the public hype, has the feeling of a done deal. Martin, like the rest of us, has little control of his destiny. No other drivers are within reach.

If not for that Rockingham penalty, Mark Martin, 89 points behind, would still be right in it. On Saturday he and Jack Roush make their appeal to NASCAR. It is denied.

The Miami track is actually in Homestead, southwest of the beaches and the nightclubs, set in the swampy vastness of what looks to be a palm plantation. All the trees for miles in the emptiness are starter-sized and carry little tags.

The grandstands are painted in the mid-1980s palette you expect, no surprises here, aqua and ocher and medium blue, the hippodrome itself ringed with merchandise sellers and Bloody Mary huts and palm trees. This is the track where they shoot all those sexy commercials for beers and cars.

It is a strange, rushing weekend, everyone hungry for home and worn to the bones by the grind. In the deadline room the elephants snort and trumpet and kvetch. The drivers bitch about the track and the fans. The racers' kids over in the Motor Racing Outreach playground sound frazzled, hyper and tired and ready to put this all behind them. Publicists scream into their subminiature phones. Even the shirts are too loud here.

On Saturday, the best line of the season. It was worth waiting for. Those semifamous blonde *Playboy* triplets arrived with their corporate skank wrangler, who led them from garage to garage to garage, there to be measured and eyeballed by the drivers and the crews and the television cameras. They wore body-hugging matching white leather jumpsuits. Having looped the apron at least twice, they were at last led away.

The line has been attributed to Ward Burton, but I believe it was actually spoken by one of his crewmen.

"Did you see those twins? Man, there were *three* of 'em."

So the weekend and the season descend into moral and physical exhaustion, decadence and turpitude. Thunderstorms blow in that night, raging like Lear, to wash us all clean again.

On Sunday the pack comes down out of the fourth turn to the green flag two by two and the colors stream past and I wonder why NASCAR hasn't crossed over with the Grateful Dead crowd, all this music in the noise and the prism breaking rainbows right in front of you for four hours at a time.

Stewart goes off in sixth position and drops like an anchor through the field. Martin, ever his own worst enemy, has qualified poorly and over the slow tropical afternoon must haul himself and his Viagra car up from thirty-fourth on the grid. To his credit, this he does. Stewart, on the other hand, is all triage and trauma whenever he pits, the crew desperately trying to figure what's wrong with the car. That Britney Spears herself is visiting in his pits makes the treatment no easier.

"What the fuck is wrong with this car?" comes the question from the cockpit. "We'll get it, buddy, don't worry," comes the soothing reply from crew chief Zippadelli on the toolbox.

One of Bobby Labonte's crewmen is badly burned when there's fire in the pit. Then Jimmy Spencer backs up into the wall in the third turn, and the fuel line bursts and a fireball explodes up past the catch-fence. A photographer, our friend Bobby, is standing right there, and he's burned, too, on his hands and his face. He makes it back to the media center swathed in ointment and gauze, his camera blackened, his eyes shocky and unfocused. We try to find him a ride to his hotel, but he wanders back outside to keep shooting.

Jarrett and Gordon and Busch work the front of the field while Martin and Stewart seesaw behind them. Stewart is midpack and struggling, the car never coming around, getting caught up behind even slower cars. When Spencer crashes, Stewart's trapped in the pit and goes a lap down. Out front it's Busch and Wallace and Gordon.

With 34 laps to go John Andretti detonates an engine and oils the track for the trailing racers, and Stewart has to swing to the apron to avoid being gathered up and ruined. Martin has made his way to fourth, Busch leads, Stewart, flailing, is running far behind. Could the elephants and experts have been wrong? Could Mark Martin actually win the championship? Only if he hadn't taken the penalty. When the final flag falls on the season Kurt Busch has won yet again. Mark Martin is fourth. Tony Stewart is eighteenth and wins the Cup championship.

Kurt Busch is celebrating his win a few hundred feet away in Victory Lane. The championship ceremony is down the track on a flatbed set, the whole thing miked for televison, so you can't hear any of it standing there. The fans cheer and the confetti falls, but whatever Tony's saying is known only to him and several million TV viewers.

Stewart stands with his trophy, bathed in the light of fame, as the sun goes down.

There was a young umbilical couple standing out along the pit wall, way up near turn 4, during the race. They had two sets of headphones connected to a single race radio, so they were never more than 2 or 3 feet from each other.

I was standing in the same pit stall. As we stood there, the husband gestured to me. The cars were streaming past in that maniac parade not 50 feet away, so we could only talk by shouting into one another's ear. It is a strange intimacy of the racetrack, but you find yourself bending close to people this way whenever you need to speak.

He wondered if I would take a picture of them as the cars poured out of the turn.

For a couple of laps I took two or three frames with his digital camera every time the lead pack blurred past behind them. I gestured that I was done, and he stepped to me to take back the camera. His wife was 2 feet behind him, looking back at the track, at that hypnotic cascade of cars rushing out of the turn. He leaned to me. Would I like him to take a picture of me standing there? He could e-mail it to me.

I put my lips to his ear and yelled, "Why?"

The cars were still coming down hard off the turn and the noise was everywhere inside us and outside us both, so it came to me like a whisper,

"To prove you were here."

On Monday morning they are already testing the cars for next season. The Beep says, "Can we go home now?"

The season officially ends in New York City. The drivers are all tucked in with their families at the Waldorf-Astoria and the sidewalks along Park Avenue are quiet with snow. Fans and their cameras click and whisper in the lobbies.

The awards ceremony is held at a theater up the street. The night feels near enough like the death of the good ol' boy racer to think that maybe, in a way, Bill France killed this whole deal the day he organized it. It's a television series now. The drivers accept huge checks from the points fund and give speeches in which they methodically thank every sponsor. Tony Stewart pulls a camera of his own from beneath the podium and fires a frame at the photographers down front. Everybody has a good laugh.

Cut loose at last from the cannonballing circus train, driving down America from the Wal-Mart to the Waldorf, the Beep and I head north, and home, into that snow. Anyone who tells you that you have to get off the interstate to really *see* America doesn't know anything about either. America *is* the interstate.

Six weeks after the awards banquet Jeff Gordon, fourth overall for the season, is back in New York to host *Saturday Night Live.* He strides on-stage at the top of the show in black pants and a black leather jacket and a purple shirt, entirely fly and too handsome by about half. He is still the Heroic American Christian Square, of course, the buttoned-down redeemer/destroyer, the unironic daredevil avenger and the square-jawed seller of stopwatches and corporate reassurance. But he is also willing to risk his dignity, it seems, or at least muss his hair, to have a little fun. Or maybe he's only there because NBC airs NASCAR and needs some late-night cross-pollination. In any case he doesn't suck—he's no worse than De Niro was. "Man, they had me doing things on TV I wouldn't do at home in front of my mirror."

That same week a gossip column in the *Daily News* ran a squib under the headline "Wrong Turn" that said, in part, "NASCAR star Jeff Gordon moves fast—on and off the track . . . The brunette beauty who was frolicking topless with him last week on St. Jean Beach was model Amanda Church . . ."

Madness! The kind of thing you'd expect from Dale Earnhardt Jr.!

His divorce settlement rings in at $15.3 million.

NASCAR's success may be the story of how far we've all spun past the deep old identifiers, about how millions of us all over the rolling belly of America are looking for something to do with our Sundays, trying to find grace and sensation at the racetrack, not distraction but defini-tion, then transcendence, in the cars and the drivers and the carnal carnival divine, those long, strange racing weekends at once as fixed and unchanging as the Tridentine mass and as hopped-up with improvised jitterbug mysticism as a Pentecostal prayer meeting, a quarter of a million people all speaking at once in tongues.

NASCAR distills to an essence America's obsession with speed and sex and death. In it beats the heart of our national experience as citizen-consumers and hell-bent rebel yellers. In it, we fire and forge our next generation of disposable American heroes. In it we rediscover our restless frontier habits, our deep rural need to move fast across the land, fleeing the oppression of boredom, pursuing a different sun gone down on a new horizon, and finding at the end of that day peace or satisfaction or, perhaps, only ever, always, ourselves.

When I was just a little squirt I clipped pictures of racecars from magazines and taped them to my bedroom walls. From floor to ceiling and wall to wall ran the elegant and delicate Formula One machines of the mid-'60s, like the Lotus and the BRM, fragile and complicated as insects. Next to them were the exotic 24-hour GT-prototypes from Sebring and Le Mans, the blunt Porsches and the swooping Jaguars and the perfect Ford GT 40s. Among them ran the muscle-bound and slab-sided family sedans from Plymouth and Chevy, big-block Detroit iron, their V-8 pistons fat as feedbuckets, thundering around the southern stock-car circuit. Beside these were the last of the bulging, broad-shouldered front-engine Indy cars, poky and old-fashioned as stagecoaches even then.

I scissored out pictures of the drivers, too, and around the room grinned the heroic faces of Hill and Clark and Stewart, the Unsers and the Pettys, Foyt, Andretti, Yarborough and Lorenzen, even the great Fangio. I dreamed of being one of them.

At night, in the desolate freedom of those dreams, I moved across a shadow landscape at terrifying speeds, goggled and tattooed with grime, rakish and death defying, trailing behind me the noise of a distant crowd. Speed was everything then, and forty years later it remains so.

At that speed the wall is liquid. At that speed you are deaf to everything but the greedy furnace blast of the engine, blind to anything but the tunnel you drill through the glare. At that speed time itself thins and your future, that impossible mirage of fame and adulation beyond fantasy, of privilege beyond measure, of houses and cars and those hillbilly millions uncountable, shimmers out there in that demon heat 6 inches ahead of you, and your past, that earthbound and dismal history, is nothing but a greasy breeze feathering into the stands 600 yards and a lifetime behind you. Drive fast enough and you hit life's escape velocity: dead or famous, and you're better off either way.

At that speed you are bared to the marrow, stripped of everything human except ambition and want—you become a pure, hard consciousness without love or regret or identity. You are speed itself, simple acceleration, a rushing vector of possibility. You are fast, out of all proportion to sense or physics or the slow and tortured turning of the Earth. You are fast, centrifugal, orbital, as vast and ancient and celestial as something flung down from heaven to wreak a black and unblinking havoc on a thousand thousand generations of sinners.

But no matter how fast I go, I finish back where I began.

On October 14, another fine, big day in America, they unveiled a statue of Dale Earnhardt in a small memorial park on South Main Street in Kannapolis, just around the corner from the Dress Barn and the Yankee Candle Shop and the Southern Charm Christmas Shop.

We're late getting there and the chairs from the dedication ceremony are already being packed away into the Party Time rental truck. The mobile stage is being struck. Two Charlotte television crews are still parked at the curb, microwave antennas up, preparing for live shots on the local news. That's a couple of hours away, though, so the engineers and the shooters are just standing around, talking and smoking. Their reporters are both walking in circles in the street, talking on cell phones. It's 3:15. The rest of the media left an hour ago. Thirty or forty regular people, civilians, are walking around the little park. Across Main Street is a parking lot, beyond it the railroad tracks.

The park isn't finished. The brickwork on the low perimeter walls is incomplete and the walkways aren't done and the rest of it is bare earth and wood chips, still damp from the morning rain. Someone thought to set out potted plants for the ceremony. There is a terrible smell coming up from the wet bark mulch, though, something sharp and septic, rank as infection, an old, open wound.

The park is a rectangle with an oval promenade inside. At the center of the oval is the statue. Compared to the statue at Daytona, this Earnhardt is immense, nearly 9 feet high. The statue is photorealistic, as if Earnhardt had allowed himself to be enlarged somehow, dipped in hot bronze, and then polished.

He is wearing Wrangler jeans, of course, boot-cut, and on his giant size 20 feet are pointed cowboy boots in some rare and complicated hide. His legs seem very long, subtly and attractively lengthened, like those of a Vargas girl. Above his wide, simple belt he is wearing a button-down short-sleeved shirt. Folded in his breast pocket are the trademark Gargoyle sunglasses. Even in death, the sponsors get their nod.

He is standing with his arms crossed over his chest. His forearms are massive, the size of Yule logs, thick-veined and striped with muscle. His wedding ring is clearly visible on his bronze ring finger. His neck looks immensely strong, that of a draft animal, and above it the familiar face is creased with a smile. The brush mustache is perfect. The head seems small in proportion to the colossal body.

The bronze eyes seem to gaze ahead into the heroic middle distance, into the future he'll always see but never reach. In fact, he's looking out of the park and slightly up, across West B Street, into the second-floor windows of the Cannon Village Office Suites, where only two of the fourteen available offices are occupied.

Thirty feet from the statue there is a black, polished granite memorial stone sent by some fans from up north. It is carved with their regrets and their love and was sponsored by a radio station, a trucking company, and an importer of granite memorials. It reads, in part,

IN OUR HEARTS YOU WILL BE
THEN—NOW—AND FOR ETERNITY
OUR 7-TIME WINSTON CUP CHAMPION
A LEGEND INDEED

It looks like a headstone.

"Daddy, is that where he's buried?" a little girl asks in a loud voice. She and her father are standing in front of the big black stone. They are both wearing black T-shirts with the #3 car pictured. He strokes her hair and shakes his head but doesn't say anything. He is crying.

Everyone here has a camera and they walk back and forth to the statue to have their picture taken in front of it. A blonde woman in her forties wearing a white leather Goodwrench jacket sits at the foot of the statue sobbing. People wait for her to compose herself so they can step forward for their photos. No one seems impatient.

Some folks sit on the low walls, looking on quietly. "He's bigger than life. Get it?" says a middle-aged man to his wife, nodding toward the statue, irritated, as though she'd missed the point of a movie they'd just seen.

A few minutes before we leave an old man arrives. He is 75 or 80 years old. He walks with small, precise steps, as if pacing off an important measurement. With two hands he holds the elbow of the younger man who walks with him, his grandson perhaps.

The old man is white-haired and parchment-skinned, his pale blue eyes clouded, with a pink bulb of a nose and wild white eyebrows. He's wearing a white western dress shirt, mother-of-pearl buttons snapped all the way to his skinny throat, and blue Dickies denim overalls, brand new and stiff as sails. His sneakers look new. He and the young man shuffle slowly to the foot of the statue.

They stand there. Still holding onto his grandson with his right hand, the old man reaches into his back pocket with his left hand and pulls out a large red handkerchief. He mops his rheumy eyes and his nose with it and then, the kerchief still bunched in his fist, gestures emphatically up at the face of Dale Earnhardt with it and says, "That's racin'!" His voice is thin and strident and he says it again and again, waving his fist up into the statue's face, "That's racin'!" He says it like he's trying to make the young man understand something. He clutches the young man's elbow. Shakes it. He lifts his left foot and puts it down. Lifts it again and puts it down. Looks up into the young man's face, lifts his left foot and puts it down. "That's racin'!" he yells. Even the television reporters turn to look. I can still hear him as we walk to the parking lot. He has a voice like a rusted tobacco knife. "That's racin'!"

EPILOGUE
2003 AND BEYOND

The Beep and I left the South and sold the motorhome.

The country went to war.

NASCAR rolled on into its gleaming future without the slightest pause for either.

Matt Kenseth, a really nice young man from Wisconsin, won the 2003 NASCAR Winston Cup championship. This he did by lulling his competition into a fugue state of existential dread with his metronomic consistency. Thus hypnotized, they could do nothing. He won only one race but led the points standings for almost the entire season. As a racing performance it was exemplary, exactly what the championship was supposed to be about: solid finishes week after week after week across the interminable grind of a 10-month campaign. It brought Jack Roush his very first owner's championship. The season was a model of engineering ingenuity and driver talent and team solidarity, hard work and endurance and sportsmanship.

As theater it sucked. In fact, the Quiet Assassin's dogged run for the championship was thought to have been so powerfully monotonous, so utterly absent of any (marketable) *drama*, that the scoring structure of the sport itself was at last revised for the 2004 season.

It wasn't all Kenseth's fault. NASCAR had been eyeballing changes in the points mechanism for years, but hadn't mustered sufficient interest from anyone except sportswriters and math buff shut-ins to actually remake things. The fact that Ryan Newman won eight races and finished sixth in points, along with the catatonia and lackluster television ratings into which the 2003 season sank, was incentive enough to rejigger the sport's arithmetic.

Against howls of protest from fans and drivers alike, a new system was made public on January 20, 2004. Called the "Chase for the Championship," it specified a split season, in which the first 26 races set the stage for the last 10. Only the Top 10 points leaders, and those within 400 points of the leader, would be in the running to win the championship. A playoff, stock-car style, and the first major overhaul of the points system since 1975. That it took so long to come up with so little left nearly everyone scratching their heads. The hollow language of the announcement left little doubt as to who would actually benefit by the revision.

"The 'Chase for the Championship' will provide a better opportunity for more drivers to win the championship," said Mike Helton, "creating excitement and drama throughout the entire season. In addition, the 'Chase for the Championship' will showcase our drivers' talent, increasing the value for all teams and their sponsors."

Isn't that what fans clamor for—added sponsor value? And won't *fewer* drivers, by definition, be in the running for the championship?

Perhaps Chase Bank can underwrite the thing.

Kenseth was the last Winston Cup champion ever, of course, as a surprising announcement in the spring of 2003 brought the news that the R. J. Reynolds folks were giving up their sponsorship of the sport at the start of the 2004 season or whenever a replacement could be found. Even with a few years remaining on its contract, RJR decided to let NASCAR know that it was time to start courting another partner. And while the public expressions of sadness at having lost their longtime bedmate were warm and sincere and tinged with genuine regret at the passing of their common history, NASCAR swiftly and privately sought younger, more attractive companionship. There is no ex-lover so compelling as to prevent a vigorous middle-aged partner from moving—swiftly, gleefully—toward a hotter, more elastic, more robust replacement. Especially one without the leathery skin and that chronic smoker's hack.

With a tidal wave of tobacco-related lawsuits cresting and poised to break over Winston-Salem with breathtakingly expensive results, Winston Cup racing, as successful an affiliation as there had ever been in sports business, was simply getting too costly to keep on the books. RJR needed to build a war chest, not visibility or even goodwill, and every loose dime in the company was being pulled from the sofa cushions and set aside to cover the costs of someday paying off all those pale, litigious widows and orphans.

For its part, NASCAR managed to appear publicly solemn about the separation, while madly thumbing through its little black book of eligible corporate hotties in private.

American companies of every kind have been queuing up for years for a chance to hop in the sack with NASCAR, and there must have been a real stampede when the news got around that RJR had packed its bags and moved home to live with mother. Coca-Cola, McDonald's, Target, Pepsi, AT&T, Time Warner, and a hundred others all had preexisting deals of one kind or another when the split was announced. If you could fund a race team, or underwrite the official french fry or sports beverage or motor oil of NASCAR, why not finance the complete kit and caboodle? What business wouldn't want its name drilled into the captive, endlessly receptive skulls of a putative 75 million citizen-consumers?

Every blue-chip in the Dow was floated as a hot prospect, but when word came at last that a suitable match had been found, the response from press and public was less a "Wow" than a "Who?"

Nextel, a wireless telephone company, was announced as the new sponsor of NASCAR's premier racing series in June 2003. In a cluttered field of national telcos, their only claim to fame, other than 8 percent of the national wireless market, had so far been as early purveyors of the push-to-talk function on their cellular phones. This, they explained, made them the blue-collar wireless company for the working man, a favorite of builders on the job site, farmers, truckers, emergency workers, and so forth. (That their television commercials all seemed to highlight actors talking to their agents wasn't mentioned.) This proletarian theme was of course echoed many times by the Kremlin NASCAR politburo during the announcement.

Apparently that walkie-talkie feature had been quite remunerative for Nextel. Because even though they're a relatively small wireless service, and even though they hadn't shown an actual profit, as I understand the word, according to their own annual reports, until the year 2002, they were growing fast and were thus able to strike a 10-year sponsorship deal with NASCAR for something just north of $700 million. When that figure was made public, they got their "Wow" after all.

It makes all sorts of sense for NASCAR, at this point in its history, to align itself with a fast-lane company in a shiny, high-tech, noncarcinogenic growth sector like data or electronics or wireless communications. It guarantees instant access to all those 'tween and teen demographics, since those are the age groups most naturally passionate about those technologies. It ensures a symphony of cross-promotional synergy, too. In Nextel's case, that means everything from network television campaigns to driver-themed faceplates for the phones to realtime wireless race telemetry for the fans. The Pa-Kettle-on-the-north-40 push-to-talk ethos is the key to this deal, though, because it gets NASCAR all the benefits of a tech-sector sponsorship without immediately alienating the sport's lower-middle-class core constituency. All this, and fewer malignant tumors, too, which means you aren't killing off your own fan base as fast as you used to be.

What Nextel paid for was an all-access pass to the American consumer's hungering subconscious, and it would have been cheap at 10 times the price.

* * *

The year 2003 was a good one for Brian France: September 13 he was named chairman and CEO of the family business. At 41, he had been working as an executive vice president for NASCAR, in charge of marketing. His father, Bill France Jr., stepped aside, demoting himself to vice chairman of the board, but hung around for the balance of the season to offer advice and guidance. As he will, of course, until the day he dies. The year 2004 was Brian's first full season as the field general of the March on the North, and he will have opportunities in front of him of which his father and grandfather never even dreamed.

But he's going to face a lot of unrest among the fans, too, because 2004 turned out to be the year when everything changed.

Not only did RJR jump ship, but the official fuel supplier to NASCAR, ConocoPhillips/76, pulled out as well. All those familiar bright orange Union 76 balls were pulled down at every venue. They were replaced by the red Sunoco arrow at the beginning of 2004. Winston signs were all hauled down over the winter, too. Some were auctioned off, some were kept, museum pieces now, and others—most—just thrown away. Nextel signage was up everywhere by the time they ran the first Daytona of 2004.

So fans will find themselves in new and uncertain surroundings when they get back to the track; if, in fact, their track still has a race date. "Realignment 2004 and Beyond" was breezy NASCAR double-speak for the long-term plan to further prune the sport at the root. With the robust growth of crowds (and television audiences) for the tracks in Fontana and Chicago and Kansas City, those empty seats at places like Rockingham and Darlington began to look a whole lot like lost money.

And while the first cut may not be the deepest, it's a sure bet to be the one that shocks and hurts the most. Such was the case when NASCAR announced its initial reshuffling of race dates. Rockingham lost a date, Darlington gave up the time-honored Labor Day Southern 500, and the track at Fontana got a second race, to be held that holiday weekend, traditionally the marquee weekend of the season's latter half. Core fans expressed their dissatisfaction with the new calendar long and loud, but NASCAR had a point. With Darlington and Charlotte and Rockingham so close to one another geographically, it had become harder and harder to fill the seats for two races at each track every year. Even the diehard fans weren't showing up in numbers enough to justify the old schedule.

A further, and longer-term, concern to NASCAR is how to grow the sport into new markets with a fixed number of races on the schedule. There isn't a driver or a crew member or a team owner out there crazy enough to want another week's work, no matter how attractive the setting or the financial incentives. For NASCAR to add dates in its dream markets, then, like the Pacific Northwest or New York City, means that dates have to be trimmed from other, older tracks. This is part of what NASCAR calls its "Historical Problem."

With a zero-sum schedule, to expand it must simultaneously contract. That means another kick in the ass to history and the abandonment of some of the oldest and most revered tabernacles. That NASCAR's already fiddled with Darlington shows its willingness to buck public sentiment in service of expansion, and that trend can only be expected to continue. Bristol seems safe, since it draws huge numbers on television and sells out for every race. In fact, look for Bristol to become a model for another track that might be constructed over the next decade somewhere, because of its astonishing seating capacity and relatively small footprint. It might be the only model for a major metropolitan area, really, given its compact size and explosive bang-to-buck ratio.

But as indispensable as Bristol seems, it might be in play one day for a race date. Certainly little Martinsville, charming as it is, will lose a date in the very near future, and Richmond, perhaps, too. New Hampshire is on the bubble as well, but may be spared for several years since that's the only track available to service the rabid New England audience. Watkins Glen might be allowed to die, having already been allowed to wither, and why they still have two races a year at Pocono is something known only to God and the France family. Proximity to New York is the best guess anyone can make.

Vegas wanted a second date and so did Texas; and there are nifty tracks now in Kentucky and Tennessee and even Colorado. Where does that leave the old-line stalwarts like Michigan and Atlanta and Dover in five years' time?

I don't think even the five-year planners at Kremlin NASCAR know, because some of this is going to depend on things unforeseen, like the national economy and projected corporate growth rates and land becoming available for tracks to be built and the breadth and depth of the next television contract.

What Cup racing one day becomes also hinges on the volatile détente between ISC and SMI. A fixed number of dates and a reshuffling of tracks can only lead to conflict between the two major speedway companies. Whether it's fought as a series of small insurgencies or open war remains to be seen. ISC had the initial advantage, as a de facto division of NASCAR, but SMI had the doomsday weapon in an antitrust lawsuit, which, had it successfully detonated in 2004, would have left France, if not in ruins, at least in disarray.

Instead, in late spring, there came a brokered cease-fire in which Rockingham lost everything and Texas got another date for 2005. Phoenix, too. NASCAR/ISC, which is where all the money winds up eventually anyway, saved itself the expense and exposure of a trial in open court, and SMI got what it had wanted all along. Some fight. The only true casualties were southern fans.

And on a hundred other fronts Brian France will have to defend NASCAR for, from, and to its fans. Even on commonsense issues as simple as public safety—getting people out of the way of speeding cars, for example—battle lines will be drawn. NASCAR started limiting garage passes in 2003, requiring a special "hot" pass anytime there were cars on the track, and will further limit fan access in the years ahead. This is a change the drivers have been pleading for, in the spirit not only of safety but of productivity, because with all those fans wandering everywhere nobody could get any work done. The press lobbied for it, too, because the drivers were hiding in their haulers rather than risk the autograph riot to which they had become accustomed. It wasn't that long ago that journalists got most of their best material from the stars by trailing them around the garages. By the end of 2002 the drivers were barely willing to peek out the hauler door.

NASCAR eventually had to go along too, because the risk of liability, of some lizard or day tripper or halfwit getting flattened, scalded, skinned, scalped, drilled, decapitated, blown up, laid out, or run down grew with every pass they issued. One old geezer with his bolo tie caught in that fan belt or a baton twirler crushed under a rolling toolbox was all it might take to bankrupt the entire tent show. And all those newbies, never knowing which way to jump! Sure, there were disclaimers on the back of the tickets, but these are just people after all, human, clueless, and there are as many ways to die as there are parts on a car. The reality of those millionfold risks, and the oblivious fun-lovers bending closer to get a better look at them, finally caught up with NASCAR's actuaries.

To the true believers, though, it was another small outrage, another cold shoulder, another inch lost in the tug-of-war with NASCAR, which to them seems intent on nothing less than ruining the sport.

Aren't we the ones who came year in, year out when no one else cared? they ask. Aren't we the ones who made you rich and famous? Aren't we the ones who sat out here 40 years ago in the blinding Florida sun and ate egg-salad sandwiches from the scotch cooler on the tailgate of our station wagon? Aren't we the ones who sat dazed in the Alabama heat watching Bobby Isaac try to outrun those howling injun ghosts when you opened that Talladega track in the pine forest middle-of-nowhere? Aren't we the ones who lifted Lee and Richard and David and Dale and Junior and Joe and Fireball and all those others up on our shoulders? Up on our shoulders and out of that red-clay dust and out of that impoverished obscurity and impoverishing cliché and into something fine and heroic and almost holy? Money didn't do that, sponsorship didn't do that, Tom Wolfe and NBC and Fox and Mr. Jeffrey Goddamn Gordon didn't do that. We did that.

And now you want $100 for a one-day ticket and 35 goddamn dollars American for a goddamn souvenir hat? Brian France has got a lot of explaining to do.

The truth is that the longtime fans have a point. The sport has been taken away from them, irrevocably, by the passage of time. It will never again be as it was on those white-sand afternoons on the beach track at Daytona, never be what it was when the anarchic noise of a hot-rodded V-8 rose up out of a clearing in the lonesome Georgia woods, or threaded its way between the dusty rows of struggling lettuce plants on the flats outside of Bakersfield. It can never again be what it was when it was strictly an us-versus-them proposition; the sweetest secret that the old New South ever kept from the North, the roaring delinquent passion at the far margin of polite society, the promise of pure gearhead transcendence for the lucky outlaw few, the sensational sacred thrill hidden at the dark edge of town. Stock-car racing caught on, and now everybody in America wants some.

But the hard-core fans get it wrong, too, mistaking for a culture what has long been a business. Stock-car racing, especially southern stock-car racing, is a culture. NASCAR is a business that sells stock-car racing.

It's an entertainment business fighting for face time in the busiest, most competitive arena in America. NASCAR isn't competing with ARCA or USAC or the IRL anymore, it's battling for shelf space with the NFL and MLB and CNN and AOL and Disney and Microsoft. If you're at the track, you're not at the Xbox; if you're at the movies, you're not watching Speed Channel; if you're reading *Driver #8*, you're not reading *People*. In a nation of wall-to-wall-to-wall 3-D interactive holographic distraction, NASCAR has to wage war on a 360-degree front to attract the attention and hold the interest of an atomized and incredibly volatile audience.

NASCAR is still shaking off the hayseed clichés of its heritage. If it can't selectively abandon parts of its arch-cracker past, if it can't remake itself in the utterly neutral, endlessly "diverse" style of other major-league sports and entertainments, it's never going to achieve the sort of market penetration those sports enjoy. Baseball and football transcend regionalism, parochialism, elitism. Not the individual franchises, of course, but the *idea* of football, the idea of baseball. Football qua football, as the eggheads say. The idea of these sports exists as part of the national wallpaper, a given, as things so fixed and generic in our consciousness that we never give them a second thought. Baseball, football, cheeseburger, car, job, home—concepts so fundamental and deeply wired in the American motherboard that further explanation is at once unnecessary and impossible. Stock-car racing isn't quite there yet.

The strategies that NASCAR's been borrowing from the megasport mainstream to broaden its appeal beyond the suburban DMZ—the luxury skyboxes at the track, season-ending playoffs, cross-cultural outreach programs—are the very things most alienating to the core fans. As important as it may be in the short term to hang on to the diehards, NASCAR clearly understands that they have to be abandoned, albeit gently, quietly, for the sport, or at least for the economic model of the sport, to grow. Whether or not anyone feels true sadness about this at the highest levels of NASCAR management is an open question. I believe some of them do, the Rebel elders at least, but it's an interview question to which I've never been given anything but a tactical nonanswer.

A better, clearer answer can always be found in what NASCAR actually does. In 2004, for example, for the first time, a foreign manufacturer was allowed into one of the top-tier series. Japanese colossus Toyota entered the Craftsman Truck Series. Core fans were stunned.

One of the bedrock verities of NASCAR, at least to most fans, has always been an all-American field of cars. Detroit iron was and always had been the only standard for the sport. It was the abiding first principle at the founding.

The entry of a foreign competitor into one of NASCAR's premier series is cause for great alarm on the part of purists. That Toyota meets all the eligibility requirements is of no comfort. The truck, called the Tundra, has been made in Princeton, Indiana, since 1998. That the vehicle be made in America is the stipulation in the rule book. That the profits flow back to Japan is the insult to the true believer's spirit.

The benefits to Toyota in piggybacking on NASCAR's momentum, in terms of visibility, marketing, promotion, and potentially increased sales, are pretty easy to see.

Less apparent is why NASCAR ever let them in. NASCAR could have made plenty of terrific promotional mileage with its most devoted fans, in fact, by fighting, tenaciously, patriotically, publicly, to keep Toyota out. It could even have forced Toyota to sue its way in. A court battle. Something showy, something with a lot of swell rhetoric on the courthouse steps, something that left the whiff of cordite on the air, the noble aftermath of the good fight fought. That didn't happen.

NASCAR's easy welcome to Toyota is a window into how NASCAR now thinks of itself: as a global entertainment company operating on a worldwide scale. Its strategy is no longer simply to cultivate its franchise on this continent, but to dream of the 10 years ahead when it might be a missionary presence in new countries and new markets. There's no reason for NASCAR management not to at least imagine themselves as another Formula One, another international traveling show.

I think driver Jimmy Spencer spoke for many fans, however, when he welcomed Toyota to NASCAR at a press conference in Texas, "Them sons of bitches bombed Pearl Harbor, don't forget. I hope Chevy,

Ford, and Dodge kick their ass." They took second place in their first race ever.

At a time in history when globalization is seen by many Americans as a plague, the expansion of NASCAR onto the world stage is a risky move.

"Buy American" is an instruction seen on as many bumpers today as it was 25 years ago, even though what "American" means is up for grabs. If you buy a bath towel sold by an American company, and that towel was knit in Guatemala or Guadalajara or Guangzhou, are you still buying American? Was that pillowcase you bought last week the one that took Pillowtex under? Who among us, citizen-consumers all, has the time, the energy, the conviction to stand in the heaven-bright aisles at the SuperCenter trying to work our way back through the global flowchart of runaway production? To sort out those knots of possible consequence? That's why the American car was so important for so long in NASCAR. The car was traceable, knowable, fixed. You knew, or at least you thought you knew, where you were both from.

To NASCAR fans of recent minting, the whole question probably doesn't matter as much as it might have all those years ago. Ford? Chevy? Toyota? WWJD? Whatever.

But to the hard-case lifers, fans who've lived through the happy Dark Ages of $10 seats and ankle-deep chicken bones to see the dawning of NASCAR's first Gilded Age, the entry of Toyota into the sport might be the next to last straw in a continuum of hurts and turnabouts and small treasons that they fully understand but can't continually forgive. (That broadcasters Larry McReynolds and Darrell Waltrip, native sons of the boiled peanut, both have ownership stakes in new Toyota CTS teams is perhaps the unkindest cut of all. To the diehards it feels like collaboration. To the rest of us it just feels like a conflict of interest.)

Brian France, reaching out with one hand for the future as he opens his other hand to let slowly go of the past, has his work cut out for him.

How were we to know that 2002 would be the last days of the old NASCAR? The Beep and I watched the 2003 season on television nearly every week. It looked the same, but slicker, a beta upgrade, as it will most every year for the rest of its history.

We saw Newman's shuttle launch at Daytona and Sadler's flight at 'Dega; saw Busch and Craven finish the closest race in history at Darlington, fender to fender, sparks flying, smoke billowing—a rebuke, a sharp reminder from the Old Lady in Black that she's still red-hot.

The Beep and I heard about Jimmy sucker-punching Kurt ("We never forget," indeed), and saw Kurt's subdued win at Bristol. (How much do people have to dislike you to boo you for getting your ass kicked?)

We saw that the anomalous Year of the Young Gun has become instead the model for the mainstream, and in 2003 and 2004 a lot of older drivers were being pushed out, pushed aside, their Cup rides shuffled to younger (perhaps less expensive) drivers. Look for a lot of formerly familiar Cup runners to fetch up in the Truck series, or Busch, if they're lucky. John Andretti, Johnny Benson, Dave Blaney, Brett and Todd Bodine, Jeff Burton, Derrike Cope, Christian Fittipaldi, Jerry Nadeau, Steve Park, Mike Skinner, Jack Sprague, and Kenny Wallace all lost their seats or their sponsors or both. Even Jimmy Spencer (or perhaps especially Jimmy Spencer) was hunting some money to run.

Losing your ride's part of the business and always has been, but all these veterans queuing up at the CTS soup kitchen points toward a much more serious problem. The worm in NASCAR's big apple these days is the fact that team sponsors are leaving faster than they're being replaced. That Jack Roush, coming off his first championship season, couldn't find a full-time 2004 sponsor for veteran ace Jeff Burton was the early harbinger of trouble to come.

It doesn't get talked about much, especially on the cheerleading television broadcasts, but racing's become so expensive that a $20 million-a-year deal with your primary sponsor may not put a very competitive car on the track. It's going to cost that much just to roll off the truck before long, and no company wants to sink their $20 million into a thirty-seventh-place finish. So in a rotten economy teams are struggling to hold sponsors and cut costs. One of the quickest corners to cut is your veteran midpack driver. You can pay the young'un less and expect, these days at least, about the same results at the track. He also, not to put too fine a point on it, might be a little more camera-ready than the man you're letting go. Sponsors want to win, and they need to look good doing it.

The cautionary model for NASCAR's money worries is Formula One, where the end of every season brings another team bankruptcy, another team reorganization, another team in default. And more and more, once those teams are gone, they're gone; no one's in the wings waiting to replace them. So the F1 race grid continues to shrink. How small a show might NASCAR have to run one day—40 cars? 35? 25? Can NASCAR downsize? Is it recession-proof? Will they design a one-model-fits-all racecar to curb the current arms race? Has Cup run its course? Will the money bubble burst? Or will NASCAR just grow and grow and grow, like Wal-Mart, until it envelops every one of us? The final triumph of the machines!

By 2004 the Beep and I had fallen out of synch with the tour and everyone on it and had lost the habit of the Sunday shows. I offer fragments then, bits and pieces, trims and ends.

The "Young Guns" have been reified as a commercial enterprise by the folks at Gillette. No longer just a sports-page cliché, the YG were using their downy chins to shill $15 razors. The sudden success of so many young racers also raised another uncomfortable question for the turkey-leg and home-perm fans. If you can come into the sport at the age of 18 or 19 or 20 and run *good*—not just hold your own, but really succeed—how hard can it be? Another blow to the verities.

A track worker at Daytona was hit by a racecar and killed the week before the 500. OSHA later fined the speedway $11,175 for safety violations. The *Charlotte Observer* has reported that the total number of fatalities in U.S. automobile racing since 1990, including fans, is no fewer than 330.

Dale Jr. won the 2004 Daytona 500. And that year became the first human, other than Colonel Sanders himself, to have his face rendered on a bucket of KFC chicken.

NASCAR Dad came and went, as if seen from the window of a fast-moving car. He was a fiction, a hypothetical, a statistical mean. He was the median reach of some imagined bell curve, a jingle, a brand name, a catchphrase. He was a Sunday morning staple of the Numinous Absolute, a two-column thumb-sucker on the weekend op-ed page. He was the anthropomorphized mascot of the destabilized center, the patriot angel and the hillbilly boob, a strategic abstraction in the shadowbox of American politics. He was a scarecrow flapping on a stick.

But for a time at least, like the political holy ghost, he was everywhere and he was nowhere. Whatever happened to him?

The Petty family's "Victory Junction Gang" camp opened to children in June of 2004.

That same month NASCAR issued three separate public apologies for bad scoring and officiating, and folks began to wonder again if an actual printed NASCAR rule book had ever existed anywhere at any time in the whole long history of the world.

Magic Johnson was brought in to consult on NASCAR's diversity effort.

The 2004 Pulitzer Prize for criticism went to Dan Neil of the *Los Angeles Times*. He writes a car column.

The Pontiac brand left Cup racing, and its most successful team owner over the last dozen years left, too. Joe Gibbs announced his return to the Washington Redskins and the NFL. Perhaps Tony finally wore him out.

Kerry Earnhardt is still looking for a regular ride, and Jimmy Kitchens is in and out, up and down, earning points and a couple of bucks and still fighting to catch on.

Phrases like "non-NASCAR tendencies" and "NASCAR-type manliness" began not just to appear, but to recur, in the pages of the *New York Times*.

A Busch Series race was announced for Mexico City in 2005.

On October 24, 2004, a Hendrick Motor Sports Beech 200 crashed on Bull Mountain, 7 miles west of the Martinsville airport. Among the 10 dead were Rick Hendrick's brother John and John's twin daughters. Rick Hendrick's own son Ricky, a former Busch driver, also died in the crash.

Weapons of Mass Destruction were found, and the dangerous process of destroying them began. Thousands of gallons of the deadly nerve agent sarin are being destroyed in the chemical-weapons incinerator at the Anniston Army Depot in a project expected to last nearly seven years. The sarin is from the aging U.S. Army inventory of WMD. The base is located 20 miles northeast of the track at Talladega, Alabama. The Army shuts off the incinerators on race weekends.

NASCAR began fining drivers for knocking products from sponsors other than their own off the roof of their cars in Victory Lane.

Race name of the year: "The Gould Pumps/ITT Industries Salute to the Troops 250, Presented by Dodge."

The owner of a rival driving school accused the Petty Experience of fudging the "top speeds" of its students upward by more than 10 percent. Following a story in the *Charlotte Observer*, the Petty school undertook a new method of reporting Maximum Dad's top speed.

NASCAR started floating trial balloons over the Manhattan skyline in the spring of 2004, making it known that it was scouting for a substantial, track-sized land deal on Staten Island. It may come to nothing, but now is the time to begin preparing yourself for the "The Trump 250," and "The What the Fuck Are *You* Looking At? 500."

Kurt Busch is your 2004 Nextel Cup champion. The week of the awards ceremony in Manhattan, he drove the #97 car straight down Broadway, and the blast of that engine was everywhere, roaring, overwhelming for a moment even the noise of that thundering city.

Acknowledgments

My gratitude goes out, bound with every book, to these people, all of whom I hope the reader might one day meet.

Thanks first in ample, equal portion to my editor David Hirshey and to my agent Heather Schroder, for their gentle patience and their endless encouragement and for knowing when not to call. Special thanks to Nick Trautwein, and to Chrissie and Margot for calmly staffing the crisis center phone bank when I needed to call *them*, to "reschedule" another "deadline."

My heartfelt thanks as well to Bob Roe and Rob Fleder and Terry McDonnell at *Sports Illustrated* for their help and support and friendship, and for everything they've taught me.

I thank Ed Meyer, too, for his teachings and his strength and his love, and for the repeated use of his Florida washer-dryer. And Polly Gordon, who appears nowhere in this book but inhabits every page, for teaching me forgiveness. My parents.

Thanks, of course, to Eugene and Tatiana Evanitsky, my in-laws, who subvert cliché by being people I not only love but genuinely like and admire. Without them there'd have been no mail, no money, no light in the window leading us home.

Thanks also to the rah-rah sisterhood, Roxanne and Alysia, for their love and help. And thanks to brother Steve and sister Karen for theirs.

Thanks to the family on both sides of the aisle.

Thanks, as well, to Mimi Pizzi, spirit sister, for her love and support and the keys to Penthouse B. To Art Kimbro, best man/brother man, and his family, for love and support of the California kind, and for always being there when it mattered most.

To P. J., Erik, and Katie, our Colorado clan, love and thanks and hugs all around. And to Carole and Horseshoe Gordon, likewise. We all miss you, Frank.

To Joel and Kathy and Cole and Ellen and Spencer, in the Nebraska family mansion, love and thanks.

To Gloria and David, Erin and Raul, thanks and love for the dinners and the driveways and the sunsets over the mountains of New Mexico.

To Jill and Jeremy of the Connecticut delegation, I send love in great measure, and thanks, for reinventing me.

Thanks and love to Will and Deb and baby Hazel, storybook princess of Indiana.

Love and awestruck thanks to Bill Heinz, king of Vermont, and maybe the best who ever lived.

Thanks to Mike for that long walk in the redwoods.

Thanks and love to Kitt and Brett and Brian for moving us out of New York without ever letting go of us.

Thanks to the Whitneys of Illinois, for feeding us and loving us.

Loving thanks to Mike and Joanne Barrier back in Mooresville, North Carolina, for keeping an eye on us at our home away from home.

And boundless love and special thanks to Bob and Janice for their amazing generosity and inspiration, and for the use of the magical house that became our home away from home away from home.

To Russell and Heather our love, and to Susan and Nancy and Kathy, George, and Ev and Verna, and everyone else who offered a meal, a shoulder, a hand, while we were set loose on the land, I say thank you.

Thanks go out as well to the op-ed offices of the *New York Times* and to the abandoned hallways of *Maximum Golf* and to the writing programs at Yale and Ohio State. To Katy and Tobey and Mary and Sam, to MJC, to Don F. and Lee K., and to anyone and everyone who ever took me half as seriously as I took myself, I say thank you.

Especial thanks to the incredibly helpful cast and crew of the Great American Speed Circus, too many to name, and too various in their hundredfold generosities to describe. Much gratitude to my colleagues in those smoky deadline rooms as well, whose names I withhold only to keep y'all out of the big, formerly red, truck. Many thanks to NASCAR, too, and its fans, for the access and the assistance and the incredible experience.

Our thanks to the folks at Lazy Daze for building the mighty, mighty motorHomer the way all of us wish everything were built. Thanks to Wal-Mart, who, busy as it was with its battle for global conquest, still kept a light on for us, and to the Flying J, for perfecting the $5, All-You-Can-Eat shower.

To the folks along the way who may have been stuck behind us, sorry, we were driving as fast as we could. And to the 200 million Americans who managed not to hit us with their cars, we thank you.

A final thank you to the one person I can never adequately thank, though I'll spend the rest of this life and all others trying. To Olya—wife, photographer, Beep made real—I say this: Without you in the world there is only darkness.

Now, about that trip around the world in some sort of small boat?

About the author

2 Meet Jeff MacGregor

About the book

4 *Sunday Money:* The Limited-Edition
Unrated Director's Cut

Insights,
Interviews
& More . . .

Read on

15 Have You Read?

Meet Jeff MacGregor

© Olya Evanitsky

JEFF MACGREGOR was born in Evanston, Illinois, and grew up all over the place. An only child, his earliest ideas about America were formulated from the window of a moving car. America is a colorful blur to him—and a cooler full of his mother's egg salad sandwiches.

His patchwork education includes undergraduate and graduate programs at the University of Minnesota, Ohio State University, and Yale University. He is two credits away—generally in dance or the history of theater—from every advanced degree he ever sought. He has taught both fiction and nonfiction writing at Yale University. Go figure.

MacGregor has lived and worked everywhere from New York to Los Angeles, and has done a great many things—the particulars of which are largely a matter of intense personal privacy and/or profound personal forgetfulness. He has earned his

66 MacGregor has done a great many things—the particulars of which are largely a matter of intense personal privacy and/or profound personal forgetfulness. 99

living as a writer since 1993, "and that," he says, "is really why we're all here, isn't it?"

Yes it is. Here, then, are the professional details: MacGregor is a special contributor to *Sports Illustrated* magazine. He has written regularly for the *New York Times,* wherein his work has appeared under such irregular headlines as "Foul Enough to Be Funny," "And the Road Runner Fosters Disrespect for Speed Limits," and "Don't You Sass Me, Mr. Micro-Smartypants!" A six-time National Magazine Award nominee, he has written for the *New Yorker, Esquire, Men's Journal,* and *Details.* His nonfiction appears in many collections and anthologies, among them *Best American Sports Writing* and *Sports Illustrated: Fifty Years of Great Writing.* His fiction, meanwhile, has appeared in *Story, Esquire,* and *Land-Grant College Review.*

His acknowledged influences include Michael Herr, A. J. Liebling, W. C. Heinz, Robert Benchley, S. J. Perelman, Salman Rushdie, Martin Amis, Tom Wolfe, Hunter S. Thompson, and Lorrie Moore. "I've been lucky enough," he says, "to study at the feet of some real rabbis too—like Robert Stone and Roger Angell and Bill Kennedy and Lee K. Abbott." ❧

Sunday Money
The Limited-Edition Unrated Director's Cut

Sunday Money **Paperback Bonus Material,
the Limited-Edition Unrated
Director's Cut,
Including Commentary, Errata, Outtakes,
Insights, Updates, Downloads,
Ruminations, and the Last Few Sentences
I'll Ever Write Anywhere, for Any Reason,
About Automobile Racing**

I'D FIRST LIKE TO THANK sharp-eyed readers who pointed out several typographical and editing errors I made in the hardcover edition. Those mistakes have—to the best of my ability—been corrected. Most were just mechanical errors or transpositions on the order of getting Robbie Loomis and Robby Gordon tangled up in the copyedit so that one or the other had (or needed to have) an "ie" instead of a "y" and/or vice versa. I send a fond shout-out to them both.

Also to Thomas Kinkade, millionaire dean of the Lollipop Cottage School of Decorative Painting, who takes a second "k" in his name instead of the "c" I undeservedly gave him.

That Mr. Kinkade's painting—like NASCAR racing—is a retreat into an oversimplified, antihistorical past in a fairy-tale world that never existed explains (I think) the popularity of both in these dark and dire times.

I'll resist the impulse here to update the state of the sport. For NASCAR, 2005 (in big-picture, big-business terms) was very much the same as 2004.

Of note, though, are a few small things. First, Major League Baseball finally roused itself in the autumn of 2005 to publicly dispute NASCAR's television ratings claims. Having made the same point I won't repeat myself. But it's nice to see baseball defend itself against NASCAR's self-serving promotional arithmetic—especially in light of the ongoing steroids scandal. Of course, if NASCAR ever begins a random testing program for performance enhancers like sour mash whiskey or midnight skinny-dips with the Hooters girls, they're in trouble too.

In that same vein, I'll answer a question I've been asked frequently by readers and interviewers since *Sunday Money* was first published. No, I don't believe for a moment that there are seventy-five million NASCAR *fans* in this country.

It all hinges on your definition of the word "fan." I think there are probably *more* than seventy-five million Americans who've *heard* of NASCAR and are aware of it now, but that's a different thing entirely. Perhaps NASCAR counts anyone who ever heard of Richard Petty—or who has ever owned an American car—as a fan.

Since NASCAR's doing the polling I have little hard evidence to support this contention, but base my sense of the overestimation on two things. First, if there were that many real, rabid fans the television ratings would be higher than they are. ▶

> " If NASCAR ever begins a random testing program for performance enhancers like sour mash whiskey or midnight skinny-dips with the Hooters girls, they're in trouble too. "

Second, the number itself comes from the Kremlin NASCAR data bunker and is duly transmitted by a complicit and complacent sporting press. So until proved otherwise the number has to be taken for what it is—a marketing tool with which to lure sponsors.

Many sponsors are entering the sport on a very limited basis—one race, two races. These rolling sponsorships are NASCAR's short-term answer to the problem of mounting costs. Having six or seven primary sponsors in sequence throughout the season may be the owners' solution to unloading a reasonably competitive car from the hauler, but what does it do to brand loyalty—and to the kind of driver/product identification that made the sport such a smart ad buy in the first place? Dale Earnhardt = Mr. Goodwrench, Jeff Gordon = DuPont, Mark Martin = Viagra, etc. Quick, who sponsored Carl Edwards this week? NASCAR's money troubles will continue—unremarked upon in public—despite its many successes.

Responses to other questions that arose on the first book tour allow me to present some material that we trimmed from the hardcover edition in the interest of space-saving. For example this perennial favorite (most often asked by devoted RVers): What do I have against a motor home upholstered entirely in electric teal? I gave my answer in an early version of Chapter One.

The English language is a magical and wonderful thing. It is adaptable, fluid, powerful, and manifold. Somewhere in the Unabridged Edition of the Oxford English Dictionary there is an apt word for every idea and every thing known in Heaven and earth and every emotion felt in the hearts of men and women. Except for this shade of blue. And how it made us feel.

It wasn't really teal. But it wasn't quite turquoise. We didn't hate it. But we didn't quite not hate it either. It appeared in subtly varying shades, too, from the carpet to the sofas to the valances. And in several patterns—everywhere you looked—each more tealicious than the last. It was like stepping into a gay time machine and arriving in the lobby of a Miami hotel circa 1959. Maybe that was it: South Beach teal. South Beach transvestite in a '59 T-Bird teal. Or perhaps it was more of a loud, hot rod aqua—like a dentist's chair at a bankruptcy auction. Antacid tablets. Hospital gowns. Hello Kitty pencil boxes. If motion sickness had a signature color, this was it. Teal. Turquoise. Aqua. Aquoise? Turqueal? Tealoise?

Sometimes even language fails.

I have been asked about what lasting effects our tour of NASCAR America may have produced. Spiritually and emotionally our love for the kaleidoscopic beauty of this country, for its unending variety and limitless horizons (actual and imagined), and for the serial generosity and crackpot genius of its citizens has only deepened. Physical effects? Here's a trim that came out of the first Daytona Sketchbook that proved sadly prescient.

First formal press conference I attend has a moral to it—a warning— and it comes right at the top. Dave Marcis is announcing his retirement. He's going to run one last Daytona 500 and call it quits. He's been racing out here since 1968—farther back into the hardscrabble days than all but the oldest owners, officials, or fans can remember. Farther back than live television. Farther back into the darkness than even Winston's sponsorship—back into the long gone days of the Grand National circuit. He's made 881 starts and won (according to the media guide) five times. Still, he's earned over 7 million dollars in that span—plenty of it when there was no money in the sport to speak of. And for most of those many seasons he's been listed as his own team owner, so you know he's as tough and canny as they come out here. He's also three times the age of some of the guys he's racing against. He'll be 61 years old in two weeks and wants at last to get out of the car.

Dave Marcis is an affable dinosaur, a nice guy from Wisconsin known most famously for racing in a pair of black wingtip dress shoes. "They've worked real well for me. I never really thought about making a change." Drivers these days have special shoes, of course—ultra-tech, heatproof, flame-resistant high-tops. They have shoe deals with Puma and Nike. A closet full of shoes that are color coordinated with the firesuits. I think Marcis buys Florsheims. ▶

Sunday Money: **The Limited-Edition Unrated Director's Cut**
(*continued*)

He's old school and decent and the last of his age, so NASCAR and the media want to make note of his impending departure. A press conference is set up.

Opening question comes from the back of the hall. It's a longish, convoluted run-up to a valedictory—all the changes you've seen, what do you remember most, where's the sport headed, etc. It's actually about seven questions. And Dave Marcis's answer is cautionary. I take it as such.

"Didn't get that. I don't have my hearing aids in so you gotta holler."

Note: buy better earplugs.

Despite this warning—and our devotion to auditory protection of the most elaborate kind—my wife and I both suffered perhaps a 15 percent hearing loss that year. We are both pretty well restaurant-deaf now, for instance, which means that (like your parents) if you take us to a nice dinner someplace crowded we'll only catch every third word you're saying. Sorry.

People mostly see what they want to see. It is therefore possible (at least hypothetically) to go to a NASCAR race somewhere and not see anyone overdrinking. If you go to the track just for the day, for instance—being sure to avoid the infield and the campgrounds entirely. Park your car very close to the entrance and walk very fast straight to your seats in the single, tiny alcohol-free section of the grandstand—looking neither left nor right, nor up nor down—and you have at least a theoretical chance of making it up to seats A and B in Row 32 without being accosted by a very hairy heavyset man in orange nylon Daisy Dukes with a funnel in one hand, a pony of Icehouse in the other, and a test-tube bandolier full of Jell-O shots. (He will offer you a free ride on the Vomit Comet. Shun him.)

I have been asked whether I selectively overstated the kind of drinking that goes on at a NASCAR event. I did not. It is quite epic. Nay, titanic. It makes the bleachers at Wrigley Field seem like an afternoon in Carrie Nation's parlor. In fact, I took out several scenes involving the demon hootch and its effect on human cerebration. This excision from the first draft offers further proof.

Quick story. We're parked at Martinsville just outside the track. Guy in the camper next to us (other side from Mike and Dean) starts his day at 6 A.M. with a beer. Scrambles his eggs with beer. This is Friday. He's been drinking every waking moment since Thursday afternoon when I saw him roll in. Plans to go through at least a case of beer every day by 6 P.M. Has said as much. Has calculated for himself a four-day, 96-hour binge. He's got five more cases stacked next to the grill. He is never less than utterly baked. His eyes spin like cherries in a dog track slot machine. Can't form sentences. Just before dinner he pulls out a quart jar of homemade. Pours a thimbleful into the jar lid and sets it alight for us to see and there it burns in the twilight with a flame as clean and blue and holy as the Sistine ceiling. Between six and eight he drains most of the quart. Never touches his dinner. By 8:30 he's so drunk he can only bark. Finally, he staggers past the grill and pulls a fingerful of lukewarm pork shoulder off the charred hock and tries to get it to his mouth. Greases his cheek with it a couple times, then manages to poke it into his gob. Still chewing, he opens the screen door on his little camper, totters past the silent wife and noisy kiddies and falls—straight-legged and neat as Buster Keaton—face down on their tiny bed. He does not move.

Saturday morning at seven he's pouring Keystone Light into his scrambled eggs again. I'm walking out the door to go to the press box. Bright eyed and rosy cheeked, he's got a smile on him like Carmen Miranda's head shot. "Man, that meat made me sleepy," he says.

A lot of good folks have asked about the many allusions to ghosts and patriotism and religion that occur in the book. This deleted sequence from the first draft of Chapter One was an attempt to explain our frame of mind as we embarked on the project.

I got the idea for a series of stock car racing articles in the spring of 2001, when I saw all that public heartbreak cut loose over Dale Earnhardt's death. Not discounting the loss of John Lennon (or of poor, fated Di), no entertainer's or sportsman's death had really hit the country like this since Elvis or maybe Valentino—candlelight vigils, prayer services, fans racked in a national spasm of genuine grief.

But then the story changed before it ever got started. In September ▶

2001 the Towers came down and all the stories changed for everyone. We were living up on East 89th Street then and the Beep was working down on Wall Street. She was in a building a few blocks from the World Trade Center that day. We were on the phone together talking about the first plane when she felt the second plane hit. She said, "I have to go." She put the phone back hard in the cradle and ran down 48 flights of stairs and then 120 blocks home. On television I watched the buildings burn and fall. The explosive boil of that gray dust seemed to me like something volcanic set loose from the center of the earth—the last moments of Pompeii.

Whenever they turned the news cameras on the people streaming up from the Financial District I searched for my frightened wife in that river of faces. For a long time I didn't know where she was. We had been married for seventy-four days, and until she walked through our door a few hours later I had no idea what the word "married" meant.

We sat for a long time after that—dazed. The smell, that sharp smell no one dared name, pressed itself to the window glass the rest of that day and night and for the rest of that marginless week. We breathed it in, stared at the TV coverage, and saw the smoke billowing up to us out of the shadows from the tip of the island. It was like watching an ocean liner go down slow by the bow.

The smoke and shadows rose and fell over the rest of the country too that week—and the weird quiet and fear and sense of jittery imminence. Whatever had happened and whatever else was about to happen—you couldn't hide from it anywhere. Whatever flyweight pop-cult sports story I'd half imagined had become something altogether different.

For the next couple of weeks we wrestled with the question of stay or go. Everything felt too fluid—life loose on its hinges and all the signposts down. Walk out of the apartment for groceries and stand instead for half an hour on the corner where the flyers fluttered and curled on the streetlamps. Snapshots taken before the world lurched, they all asked, "Have You Seen?" More wishful ceremony. More prayers. Frightened and sad, we didn't want to leave the city we both love when it most needed what small help we might give.

NASCAR started up again on the weekend of September 23—the races at Dover, Delaware. After that I watched some of them on television, looking for answers in all that color and noise. The races felt impossibly important/unimportant—a failed reach for what had been normal a month before in an America that no longer existed. But so did everything else that didn't come straight off the high-definition headline ticker. It all ground forward and felt wrong. "Don't let the terrorists win," was the mantra we all chanted, but they already had and the cast of *Everybody Loves Raymond* couldn't change that. The new normal, the next normal, comes around in its own time—in a matter of years, not days—and with all the pain of the past hidden up both sleeves.

The races themselves were as they had long seemed before we joined NASCAR's traveling show—two-hundred-mile-an-hour billboards circling the asphalt, boredom interrupted only by panic or free enterprise, by crashes or commercials, the afternoon wearing away like the tires, and the announcers drawling on about drafting and pit strategy and fuel windows.

But there were NASCAR drivers coming in and out of the city that autumn too—guys like Jeff Gordon visiting the heartbroken neighborhood firehouses and being taken down to Ground Zero. Public relations, certainly, but genuine too—seeing on the local news the faces of the firemen he met and for whom he signed autographs it was clear that even heroes need heroes (real or imaginary). It ran both ways, and these drivers weren't just characters in some showboat melodrama, but players on a much brighter stage.

That wasn't an original thought, certainly. But after the 11th, when everything we knew about anything was in doubt, it meant that the whole project had to be driven across the strange new landscape—at once threatening and reassuring—of a newly wounded America.

Favorite story I had to cut for space? This one—regarding an actual, everything-but-the-pith-helmet anthropologist conducting a season-long study of NASCAR mores/folkways/culture the same year we were ▶

*out there. Working on it for his doctoral dissertation. Nice guy. And he
did it in a motor home! Kindred spirit? Crazy person? You decide.*

He is on the go most weekends, out of sight over in the campgrounds
with his digital video recorder and his questions about racing and race
and class and religion—drinking with the folks and eating potato salad
and corn dogs and forever in danger of going entirely native. He looks
very tired when we see him.

He's become something of a rock star out here with his picture and a
profile in the local papers almost every Thursday or Friday. It's a sidebar
to the upcoming races and a nod to NASCAR's unstoppable popularity—
look, they've got their own social scientist! Like all fame, these stories
bring him attention both good and bad. Good because—as a circuit
celebrity—he gets lots of access at the track. Bad because when people at
the track see him coming they're now apt to keep their mouths shut for
fear of being culturally deconstructed.

There are other liabilities to fame of course, and he encountered one
the night before we saw him. A local woman who'd spotted his handsome
two-column picture in the paper came knocking on his trailer door. A
very tall, very blond woman—a perfect Valkyrie (if Wagner wrote runway
grind for strippers)—she was the bodacious ex-wife of a professional
wrestler and brought to that door two bottles of expensive vodka and a
screenplay. She was interested in his assistance in rendering the vivid
world of professional wrestling into movie form, she said, and thought—
given his expertise at codifying the aberrant behaviors of sporting
monocultures—that he might lend her a hand. He agreed to look at the
work. And while their meeting on that topic was inconclusive, after a
couple of buckets of martinis it became apparent that aberrant behaviors
were about to be explored more fully. Would he perhaps be interested in
less cerebral pursuits? Something naked, perhaps? Best two falls out of
three right there in his motorcoach? With a girlfriend back home he
demurred, but found himself wrestling out of his weight class anyhow.
It took a long time to maneuver her back out the door. "She was a big
woman," he says with an exhausted sigh. "A very big, determined woman.
And she knew so many *holds.*"

Last Add/Full Disclosure:

While I was writing the book I consulted on a 3-D IMAX NASCAR movie that made the rounds of those headache-making theaters beginning in the winter of 2004. "Consulted" means I read the narration script on several occasions and made comments and suggestions—none of which were very helpful, I'm sure. Another writer from *Sports Illustrated* did the real writing and the expository heavy lifting and deserves all praise for same. He shall remain nameless—in deference to our friendship and to whatever colorful stories he intends to concoct to win the grudging respect of his as-yet-unborn children.

It was a corporate orgy of a project, everyone in bed together cross-branding like rabbits until you couldn't tell the communications arm of one from the promotional arm of another. Warner Brothers and NASCAR were, I think, behind getting the movie made in the first place. Warner Brothers is a division of TimeWarner, which also owns TimeLife, which in turn owns *Sports Illustrated*—which in turn accounts for how we wound up involved. Don't hold me too strictly to this hierarchy though, because down here at the bottom of the food chain it's hard to know who's doing what to whom among the higher life-forms. That AOL is also a part of TimeWarner and sponsors a Cup car accounts for the terrible AOL punchline and plug on page six of the script. You'll know it when you hear it/see it. We fought to cut it, but we were only two little men against a boardroom of corporate giants. Or a bedroom of corporate rabbits. Either way, we were powerless.

The film is really a fifty-minute primer on NASCAR and its history—enlivened by spectacular pictures and mind-liquefying audio. What most interested me about the process of making it was what it revealed about the blithe revisionism of NASCAR and its reflexive hypersensitivity to any version of events other than its own—or which don't serve its current promotional needs. I offer a few examples:

- We were asked not to use the word "moonshiners."
- We were asked to reduce the number of shots in which Ryan Newman's ▶

#12 Alltel car appeared. (NASCAR had just signed Nextel as the series sponsor.)

- We were asked not to use the phrase "traveling carnival" when describing Cup weekends, but rather to substitute "community," "population," or "city."
- We were asked to remove any reference to Dale Earnhardt's death having increased national awareness of stock car racing—because NASCAR maintains that this isn't true.
- We were asked not to refer to Teresa Earnhardt as a "widow."
- We were asked to remind the audience that NASCAR is "the number two sport in America . . . on TV."
- We we were asked to remove a shot that included a Confederate flag.
- We we were asked to remove a shot of shirtless fans. This was accompanied by the note "Let's find some KIDS!!!!" Several shots later we found one—a boy about seven years old—but were asked to remove him because he was wearing a red T-shirt that read "BUD."

Which raises this question: If you don't want to encourage beer drinking in seven-year-olds, why do beer logo shirts come in children's sizes?

As NASCAR says, "Our way works for us." ⌒

Have You Read?

Cheating: An Inside Look at the Bad Things Good NASCAR Nextel Cup Drivers Do in Pursuit of Speed, **by Tom Jensen**
This is a nuts-and-bolts look at all the things you might do with your nuts and bolts to gain an advantage on the track.

The World's Number One, Flat-Out, All-Time Great Stock Car Racing Book, **by Jerry Bledsoe**
Now thirty years old, this book remains the best of its age and one of the few worth reading on the subject.

The Kandy-Kolored Tangerine-Flake Streamline Baby, **Tom Wolfe**
For those interested in reading the Tom Wolfe piece to which I occasionally refer in these pages, *The Last American Hero* can be found in this collection of Mr. Wolfe's seminal magazine work from the 1960s.

On two other fronts, two further recommendations:

The Sweet Science, **by A. J. Liebling**
Now back in print (North Point Press) after a long absence, this book bears between its covers perhaps the best long-form sports writing ever done. For its elegance and humor and ambition, for its style and devotion to history, and for its understanding that sports are only one of many strands in the grand ▶

tapestry of human enterprise, it should be required reading for every writer everywhere.

Dispatches, by Michael Herr

While this is a book about war, not sports, these two things are near enough each other in the American mind that we use the language of one to describe the other. Thus I mention it here. For its unflinching honesty, for the music of its language, for its madness and empathy, and for its perfect rendering of the hallucinatory quality of being deeply embedded in the absurd consequences of America's love and the workings of our hate, it is a work of genius.

66 This book bears between its covers perhaps the best long-form sports writing ever done. 99

Don't miss the next book by your favorite author. Sign up now for AuthorTracker by visiting www.AuthorTracker.com.